D0849124

Natural Law
and the
Theory of Property

Natural Law
and the
Theory of Property

Grotius to Hume

STEPHEN BUCKLE

CLARENDON PRESS · OXFORD
1991

Oxford University Press, Walton Street, Oxford OX2 6DP
Oxford New York Toronto
Delhi Bombay Calcutta Madras Karachi
Petaling Jaya Singapore Hong Kong Tokyo
Nairobi Dar es Salaam Cape Town
Melbourne Auckland
and associated companies in
Berlin Ibadan

Oxford is a trade mark of Oxford University Press

Published in the United States
by Oxford University Press, New York

British Library Cataloguing in Publication Data
Buckle, Stephen
Natural law and the theory of property: Grotius to Hume.
1. Natural law. Theories
I. Title
171.2
ISBN 0-19-824239-5

Library of Congress Cataloging in Publication Data
Buckle, Stephen.
Natural law and the theory of property: Grotius to Hume /
p. cm.
Includes bibliographical references and index.
1. Natural law—History. 2. Natural law—Psychological aspects—
History. 3. Property—History. 4. Ethics—History. I. Title.
K455.B83 1991 340'.112—dc20 90-46342
ISBN 0-19-824239-5

Typeset by Hope Services (Abingdon) Ltd
Printed and bound in
Great Britain by Biddles Ltd,
Guildford & King's Lynn

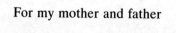

For my mother and father

Preface

This study seeks to bring out important underlying continuities in the development of early modern political thought. It does so by tracing some major themes in the theory of property, and of the account of the foundations of social order and moral action on which it relies, from the seventeenth-century natural law theories of Hugo Grotius and Samuel Pufendorf to David Hume's theory of the origins of social order. It is argued that the continuities revealed are sufficient to allow classifying Hume's theory as itself a natural law theory. Part of the justification of this view lies in the account given of the moral sense moral theory Hume inherited from Hutcheson and Shaftesbury: it is argued that moral sense theory is taken up by Hutcheson and Hume not as an alternative to natural law (as Shaftesbury had envisaged it), but in order to resolve some problems in natural law theory, and, no less importantly, to flesh out its account of human nature.

To help show how this conclusion is possible, it will be helpful to provide at the outset a brief sketch of the main lines of the argument. In the opening two chapters, the two main variants of modern natural law theory, those of Grotius and Pufendorf, are explained in some detail. Their understanding of natural law, as a science of morals grounded in human nature, is spelled out, and it is shown how this results in an understanding of property relations as a natural response to the changes in human circumstances wrought by increasing sophistication in human social life. It is a *natural* response because it reflects the requirements of human nature, such reflection being shown by the fact that it arises necessarily, through peaceful processes, from the recognition of the elemental moral realm of what is 'one's own'.

The notion of 'one's own' is a central feature of both Grotius's and Pufendorf's theories, specifying as it does not only a morally inviolable realm which it is the purpose of political society to protect, but also the place of the individual within the social order. A distinctive feature of this study is the account it offers of

Pufendorf's view on these matters. Rather than assimilating his position to Grotius's, it is shown how his revisions of the Grotian view, motivated by the need to debar Hobbesian conclusions, are more than merely cosmetic. In the end, he provides an account of social life in which individual rights are derived from fundamental duties of sociableness. It is then indicated that the resulting picture of the place of the individual in the social order, the influence of which is discernible in the subsequent views of John Locke and the eighteenth-century Scots, debars 'possessive individualist' interpretations of those theories.

However, there is no doubt that the role of the market, as a force for social good, plays an important role in the same theories. This can be traced in the treatment of the problem of slavery. The question of the justifiability of slavery, given the existence of a right of necessity, is an awkward problem for Grotius in particular. But Pufendorf recognizes that the problem can be reduced if the principal incentive to voluntary enslavement, material necessity, can itself be overcome. In this way the problem of slavery can have an *economic* solution. Locke affirms this insight, but provides an even stronger argument against slavery by examining the implications of the basic notion of 'one's own', which, following English practice, he calls property in one's person. He concludes both that slavery is always unacceptable in political society and that the origin of property in no way depends on consent. Rather, property is shown to be the inevitable consequence of human self-preserving action in a world given to us by God. Neither does material necessity provide a reason for enslavement: on the one hand, the right of charity of the poor against the surplus of the wealthy makes enslavement an avoidable option for the individual; and on the other, the productive power of improving labour is so great that, where a system of private property is established which secures the fruits of their industry to the industrious, necessity (and thereby slavery also) becomes avoidable for a whole society, by making even the worst off wealthier than the richest in a primitive economy.

Thus the question of property undergoes a significant shift. The concern of Locke's successors with political economy, and the manner in which this concern modifies their interest in slavery and necessity as serious problems for society, shows the extent to which Locke's conclusions win the day. The question of what it is to have a social theory which is grounded in human nature becomes very pressing, however, because of difficulties perceived to be generated by Lockian (and, more generally, all 'self-love') theories of human motivation. Such theories appear to compromise the natural law stress on the naturalness of human social life. The issue hinges on the nature of *obligation*. Hutcheson (and, following him, Hume) defends an account of human motivation which allocates a central role to impartial benevolence, and which thereby offers an understanding of moral obligation independent of theological commitments. Hutcheson's programme runs into difficulties in its account of property, however, stressing the necessity of strict rule-following while at the same time providing general principles which threaten it. Hume's account of the source of our obligation to respect the rules of property (the cornerstone of justice) is explained as an attempt to overcome this tension, by adapting some Pufendorfian distinctions to account for different types of moral obligation, grounded in different aspects of human sociability. In this endeavour he also is not entirely successful. Nevertheless, the understanding of his programme which emerges shows that, despite established assumptions to the contrary, Hume can be recognized to be an important contributor to the natural law tradition. The study concludes by briefly summarizing Hume's relationship to his predecessors.

    At this point, it remains only to acknowledge the most salient of the many debts incurred in the conceiving and writing of this work. My principal debts are to Knud Haakonssen and Thomas Mautner, who helped to set the general shape of the work and provided valuable comments along the way. For much stimulating (and often very sceptical) discussion about the issues covered, I owe a good deal to Jerry Gaus and the late Stanley Benn. I received very helpful comments on the whole manuscript from John McCloskey and James Tully in particular, and regret that I have not been able to incorporate more of their suggestions. Finally, I would particularly like to thank John Kleinig, Peter Singer, and Chin Liew Ten for their valuable support and advice at different times, and also David Bennett and Nona Bennett for their expert management of a difficult word-processing program.

S.B.

Melbourne
January 1990

Contents

Abbreviations

De Officio	Samuel Pufendorf, *De Officio Hominis et Civis Juxta Legem Naturalem Libri Duo* (1673), trans. F. G. Moore (New York: Oxford University Press, 1927)
DJBP	Hugo Grotius, *De Jure Belli ac Pacis Libri Tres* (1625), trans. F. W. Kelsey (New York: Oceana Publications, 1964)
DJNG	Samuel Pufendorf, *De Jure Naturae et Gentium Libri Octo* (1672), trans. C. H. and W. A. Oldfather (New York: Oceana Publications, 1964)
DJPC	Hugo Grotius, *De Jure Praedae Commentarius* (1604), trans. G. L. Williams, with W. H. Zeydel (Oxford: Clarendon Press, 1950)
ELN	John Locke, *Essays on the Law of Nature*, ed. Wolfgang von Leyden (Oxford: Clarendon Press, 1954)
Enquiries	David Hume, *Enquiries concerning Human Understanding and concerning the Principles of Morals*, 3rd edn., ed. L. A. Selby-Bigge, rev. P. H. Nidditch (Oxford: Clarendon Press, 1975)
Essay	John Locke, *An Essay concerning Human Understanding* (1690), ed. P. H. Nidditch (Oxford: Clarendon Press, 1975)
Essays	David Hume, *Essays Moral, Political and Literary*, ed. T. H. Green and T. H. Grose, 2 vols. (London, 1882; repr. Aalen: Scientia Verlag, 1964)
Illustrations	Francis Hutcheson, *Illustrations on the Moral Sense*, in *An Essay on the Nature and Conduct of the Passions and Affections,*

	with Illustrations on the Moral Sense (1728), reprinted in *Collected Works*, 7 vols. (Hildesheim: Olms, 1969)
Inquiry	Francis Hutcheson, *An Inquiry concerning Beauty and Virtue* (2nd edn., 1726) (New York: Garland Publishing, 1971)
ML	Hugo Grotius, *Grotius on the Freedom of the Seas* (*Mare Liberum*, 1609), trans. R. V. D. Magoffin (New York: Oxford University Press, 1916)
Passions and Affections	Francis Hutcheson, *An Essay on the Nature and Conduct of the Passions and Affections*, in *An Essay on the Nature and Conduct of the Passions and Affections, with Illustrations on the Moral Sense* (1728), reprinted in *Collected Works* (Hildesheim: Olms, 1969)
Short Introduction	Francis Hutcheson, *A Short Introduction to Moral Philosophy* (1747), reprinted in *Collected Works* (Hildesheim: Olms, 1969)
System	Francis Hutcheson, *A System of Moral Philosophy* (1755), reprinted in *Collected Works* (Hildesheim: Olms, 1969)
Treatise	David Hume, *A Treatise of Human Nature* (1739–40), 2nd edn., ed. L. A. Selby-Bigge, rev. P. H. Nidditch (Oxford: Clarendon Press, 1978)
Two Treatises	John Locke, *Two Treatises of Government* (1690), critical edn. with introd. and notes by P. Laslett (Cambridge: Cambridge University Press, 2nd edn., 1967)

History, experience, reason sufficiently instruct us in this natural progress of human sentiments, and in the gradual enlargements of our regards to justice, in proportion as we become acquainted with the extensive utility of that virtue.

David Hume,
Enquiry concerning the Principles of Morals, iii. 1

1

Hugo Grotius

1. HUME'S FOOTNOTE

Towards the end of the *Enquiry concerning the Principles of Morals*, in the appendix on justice, Hume remarks that 'This theory concerning the origin of property, and consequently of justice is, in the main, the same with that hinted at and adopted by Grotius.'[1] With this remark, Hume probably intends to link himself with other self-consciously modern theories of justice, because the fame of the Dutch lawyer Hugo Grotius (1583–1645) rested on the widespread belief that in his major work, *De Jure Belli ac Pacis* (1625), Grotius had instituted a distinctive new approach to questions of justice, particularly international justice. However, Hume intends more than merely to point up his modernity. He indicates also a debt to the content of Grotius's theory by including a short quotation from *De Jure Belli ac Pacis*, a quotation meant to show the link between the two theories. However, the link is not immediately apparent.

The passage in question runs as follows:

From these sources we learn what was the cause on account of which the primitive common ownership, first of movable objects, later also of immovable property, was abandoned. The reason was that men were not content to feed on the spontaneous products of the earth, to dwell in caves, to have the body either naked or clothed with the bark of trees or skins of wild animals, but chose a more refined mode of life; this gave rise to industry, which some applied to one thing, others to another.

Moreover, the gathering of the products of the soil into a common store was hindered first by the remoteness of the places to which men had made their way, then by the lack of justice and kindness; in consequence of such a lack the proper fairness in making division was not observed, either in respect to labour or in the consumption of the fruits.

---

[1] D. Hume, *Enquiries concerning Human Understanding and concerning the Principles of Morals* (3rd edn.), ed. L. A. Selby-Bigge, rev. P. H. Nidditch (Oxford: Clarendon Press, 1975), 307 n.

At the same time we learn how things became subject to private ownership. This happened not by a mere act of will, for one could not know what things another wished to have, in order to abstain from them—and besides several might desire the same thing—but rather by a kind of agreement, either expressed, as by a division, or implied, as by occupation.[2]

As it stands, this extract reveals little about the connection between Hume's and Grotius's theories. It seems to be no more than a potted history of the origin and development of private property from primitive communistic beginnings. So how is the connection to be understood? The question is more difficult to answer than may at first appear, because of the already mentioned fact that Grotius was widely recognized as a fountainhead from which flowed a modern tradition of theories of natural law. So, in order properly to understand Hume's remark, we need to know whether he means to place himself with Grotius and the whole tradition he spawned, or with Grotius rather than with his successors. For both these reasons, it would be inadequate to seek to resolve this matter simply by comparing Humean with Grotian doctrines. The main outlines of the intellectual tradition stretching from Grotius to Hume also need to be understood. The first task of this book is therefore to sketch in the major elements of that tradition, in so far as it is germane to the theory of property; and then to bring to light some of the deeper connections between Hume and his predecessors. Another (if not uncontentious) way of putting the point is that this study will be concerned to elucidate the main features of the modern theory of natural law, and to chart the continuities and discontinuities within the natural law tradition, especially as it was taken up in England and Scotland.

It is important to point out, however, that by tracing the development of the theory of property in the natural law theories stemming from Grotius, the focus here will be both broader and narrower than may be expected. In the first place, the theory of property is not, for natural law, a matter which can be settled independently of other issues of moral and social philosophy. Rather, property is the first and most essential element of justice;

---

[2] H. Grotius, *De Jure Belli ac Pacis Libri Tres* (1625) trans. F. W. Kelsey, Carnegie Endowment for International Peace (New York: Oceana Publications, 1964), Bk. II, Ch. 2, sect. ii. 4–5. (Subsequent references to this work will be abbreviated; e.g. *DJBP* II. 2. ii. 4–5.)

justice is the pillar on which society rests; and society, in its turn, is necessitated by the essential features of human nature. The theory of property is thus inextricably linked with conceptions of human nature and society, of psychology and history, of action and obligation. As the later chapters will show, increasing concern with these wider issues, especially with questions of moral psychological notions of motivation and obligation, have a profound effect on shaping the moral and political theories of eighteenth-century Scotland—and so also tend to mask the extent to which those theories are dependent on seventeenth-century natural law.

In the second place, the focus on property will have a narrowing effect by separating out those philosophers who, despite their dependence on the Grotian tradition (to whatever degree), nevertheless have no place for a theory of property. Hobbes is the most notable member of this camp, the existence of which, according to Richard Tuck, reflects the fact that *De Jure Belli ac Pacis* 'is Janus-faced, and its two mouths speak the language of both absolutism and liberty'.[3] Tuck's claim has its limitations: it will be suggested below that Grotius's *magnum opus* is rather less two-faced than Tuck believes, and his contrast between absolutism and liberty ignores the fact that sometimes absolutism was seen as a key to liberty, by controlling the ravages of the nobility. However, his remark does neatly capture the fact that different aspects of Grotius's work produced political theories of markedly different kinds. The absolutist version produced no theory of property because absolutism needs no such theory: property is, on such views, just what the absolute ruler decrees. In this study we will therefore be concerned only with the anti-absolutist strand of natural law theories.

As Tuck notes, there are two aspects of Grotius's thought where the anti-absolutist strain is most explicit: these concern the right of property and the right of resistance, those rights characteristically associated with the political thought of John Locke. Both these rights are recognized, however, by all the writers on the anti-absolutist side of the Grotian tradition. We will not be concerned with the right of resistance, but it is worth remembering that the various theories of property to be considered are in each case part of a larger political theory which includes a right of resistance, and

[3] R. Tuck, *Natural Rights Theories: Their Origin and Development* (Cambridge: Cambridge University Press, 1979), 79.

which is formulated in self-conscious opposition to absolutism—
whether of a Hobbesian or of an older form (as, for example, with
Filmer). The theory of property is part of a political theory of a
fundamentally anti-absolutist stamp.

2. NATURAL LAW AND HISTORY

In opposition to some widespread assumptions, it will be shown that
the theories of property to be considered are evolutionary theories in
an important respect. They are, in fact, characteristically part of a
wider conception of the evolution of human society. The evolutionary
character of society and of social laws is increasingly stressed by the
later writers in this tradition, but it is important to recognize that
this is more a matter of an increased level of self-consciousness
(especially of methodological self-consciousness) than a new
departure. For the earlier writers, principally Grotius's seventeenth-
century descendants, the evolution of society and of social laws—
including relations of property—is a genuine but not a self-
conscious feature of their social theory. This is accurately caught
in Duncan Forbes's remark, in his important book *Hume's
Philosophical Politics*, that

for none of these thinkers is the idea of social evolution at the centre of
attention; nowhere is it dwelt on or elaborated for its own sake. However it
is not a forced or distorted interpretation which points out how, for the
natural law writers, as for Hume, government or 'civil society' is a purely
human expedient which emerges with the development of society to meet
human needs.[4]

It is important to recognize this fact not least because it is so
frequently denied. Natural law within the Grotian tradition is
commonly understood as an essentially ahistorical enterprise.[5]

A notable example of this view is provided by Paul Foriers and
Chaim Perelman in a dictionary article on natural law. They claim
that 'Grotius' method opened the door to the construction of a
rational law no longer verified by experience but deduced

---

[4] D. Forbes, *Hume's Philosophical Politics* (Cambridge: Cambridge University
Press, 1975), 28.
[5] For a recent ex. of this view, see P. Bowles, 'The Origin of Property and the
Development of Scottish Historical Science', in *Journal of the History of Ideas*, 46
(Apr. 1985), 197–209.

abstractly, without considering "any particular fact", taking as initially given only the nature of man'.[6] Perhaps it is true that some of Grotius's methodological remarks were used to 'open the door to' an anti-empirical form of natural law, but this tells us rather little of value, couched as it is in such vague terms—after all, what we can be said to 'open the door to' need not be part of either our intentions or our practices. It is not either part for Grotius. This will be shown in more detail in the following sections, but, to give an idea of Grotius's method, it is sufficient to consider one of his more important methodological remarks. There are, he says, two ways of establishing that something is 'according to the law of nature':

Proof *a priori* consists in demonstrating the necessary agreement or disagreement of anything with a rational and social nature; proof *a posteriori*, in concluding, if not with absolute assurance, at least with every probability, that that is according to the law of nature which is believed to be such among all nations, or among all those that are more advanced in civilization. For an effect that is universal demands a universal cause; and the cause of such an opinion can hardly be anything else than the feeling which is called the common sense of mankind.[7]

Of these two ways of establishing the law of nature, it was the *latter* which most distinguished Grotius's approach. As Forbes notes, the a posteriori approach 'was the approach which Grotius seems to have been usually regarded as having made peculiarly his own', and for which he was stoutly criticized: his heavy reliance on authorities was seen as a major weakness.[8] (Whether fairly or not will not be considered here, although it should be noted that Grotius was not naïve in his use of authorities.)[9]

If Grotius's characteristic method was seen as the a posteriori method, then it is difficult indeed to see how he could have opened the door to 'rational law no longer verified by experience'. The fact that he allows also the a priori method does not establish the

[6] P. Foriers and C. Perelman, 'Natural Law and Natural Rights', in P. Wiener (ed.), *Dictionary of the History of Ideas* (New York: Charles Scribner's Sons, 1973), iii. 20.

[7] *DJBP* I. I. xii. I (cf. the intriguingly different formulation at *DJBP*, Prolegomena, 40).

[8] Forbes, *Hume's Philosophical Politics*, 18.

[9] Cf. *DJBP*, Prol., 40: 'Not that confidence is to be reposed in them without discrimination; for they were accustomed to serve the interests of their sect, their subject, or their cause. But when many at different times, and in different places, affirm the same thing as certain, that ought to be referred to a universal cause . . .'

conclusion drawn by Foriers and Perelman. Even more importantly,
however, Grotius's practice of what he calls his a priori method
shows it to be not an 'abstract deduction . . . taking as initially given
only the nature of man'. Rather, for Grotius and his successors, an
essential role is played by their assumptions about history. Their
method consists in showing that the acknowledged facts of human
history are not arbitrary or accidental, but necessary. The a priori
method attempts to show the logic of history. This is not to say that
it is devoted to elaborating laws of historical development, if such
there are, but with elucidating what has been called the 'logic of
situations'.[10] Grotius's a priori method characteristically proceeds
by showing how the facts of human nature, concretely realized in
specific social situations (commonly drawn from ancient, especially
'sacred', history), so drastically constrain possible solutions to given
problems that the particular outcome or outcomes can be seen to be
inevitable. He could be said to hold the view that human history
reveals the logic of the distinctively human situation.[11] Recognizing
this is the key to understanding why it is that—especially in his
earlier published work, *Mare Liberum* (1609)[12]—Grotius treats the
law of nature as both innate and historical.

[10] Cf. K. Popper, *The Poverty of Historicism* (London: Routledge & Kegan Paul,
1957), 149: 'There is room for a more detailed analysis of the *logic of situations*. The
best historians have often made use, more or less unconsciously, of this conception:
Tolstoy, for example, when he describes how it was not decision but "necessity"
which made the Russian army yield Moscow without a fight and withdraw to places
where it could find food.'

[11] To post-Kantian eyes, this sort of connection between logic and history looks
like either fudging or the thin end of a Hegelian (or 'historicist') wedge. It was not
always perceived thus, as is illustrated by the remarkable statement of W. Duncan in
his *Elements of Logick* (1748) that 'Logic may be justly stiled the history of the
human mind in as much as it traces the progress of our knowledge from our first and
simple perceptions' (quoted by Forbes, *Hume's Philosophical Politics*, 15 n.) Of
course, everything here depends on what is to count as logic, but the sense employed
by Duncan is consistent with that implicit in the notion of a logic of situations.

[12] *Mare Liberum* was published in 1609, but the discovery of the unpublished
treatise *De Jure Praedae Commentarius* in 1864 showed the former work to be, in all
essentials, Ch. 12 of the latter. This study is limited almost exclusively to the
originally published piece, since what is at stake is Grotius's influence on subsequent
natural law writers. At times it will be useful, however, to take advantage of the 2
readily available trans. of *Mare Liberum*, the 2nd of which is part of the trans. of *De
Jure Praedae*. The 2 sources are: *Grotius on the Freedom of the Seas*, trans. R. V. D.
Magoffin, Carnegie Endowment for International Peace (New York: Oxford
University Press, 1916) (hereafter cited as *ML*); and *De Jure Praedae Commentarius*,
trans. G. L. Williams, with W. H. Zeydel, Carnegie Endowment for International
Peace (Oxford: Clarendon Press, 1950) (hereafter cited as *DJPC*).

The following section will examine some aspects of his earlier account of the law of nature, and will then go on to show how this account is implicit in the accompanying discussion of the origin and limits of property. There are two advantages to be gained from an investigation of the earlier work before turning to the more extensive account in *De Jure Belli ac Pacis*. Firstly, it will show Grotius's implicit commitment to a form of historical understanding as the manner of understanding appropriate to social phenomena such as property—a commitment which, although preserved in the later work, is less explicit. Secondly, it will show his explicit acknowledgement that the concept of property has itself evolved *pari passu* with this history. So, as long as due limits are observed, Grotius's account can be described as evolutionary in character. Recognizing this is the first step in coming to see that the historical science of society developed most notably in eighteenth-century Scotland, a science to which Hume is such an important contributor, is a natural development of the Grotian natural law tradition, not a decisive break from it.

3. *Mare Liberum*: THE LAW OF NATURE AND THE HISTORY OF PROPERTY

In *Mare Liberum*, Grotius's principal concern is to criticize the Portuguese, the public opponents of the principle of the freedom of the seas. The specific causes of this dispute are well documented, and so will not be repeated here.[13] For our purposes, the important feature of the work is the role played by the law of nature. Grotius appeals to it as the highest tribunal, because it spells out the principles of natural justice, principles which are not arbitrary because founded in nature. Defenders of the natural law are thus necessarily in opposition to those powerful men 'who persuade themselves, or as I rather believe, try to persuade themselves, that justice and injustice are distinguished the one from the other not by their own nature, but in some fashion merely by the opinion and the custom of mankind'.[14] In fact, not only is the law of nature not arbitrary, it is so firmly grounded in nature that it cannot be ignored or denied, not even by the most powerful of authorities. Grotius

---

[13] See e.g. J. Brown Scott's introd. to *ML*, pp. v–x.   [14] *ML* I.

points out, for example, that 'It is also a fact universally recognized that the Pope has no authority to commit acts repugnant to the law of nature.'[15] The importance of the law of nature is thus beyond dispute. But in what way is it to be understood?

It is, first of all, a divine creation: 'the law of nature arises out of Divine Providence.'[16] It is not, however, merely a divine command, the command of an arbitrary divine ruler, because the divine providence is shown in the internal constitution of our nature: 'He has drawn up certain laws not graven on tablets of bronze or stone but written in the minds and on the hearts of every individual, where even the unwilling and the refractory must read them.'[17] The model for the law of nature is thus not positive law of any kind, not even the tablets of stone of the Decalogue. Rather, the law is a set of innate ideas. Its innateness guarantees its immutability, as another passage makes clear: 'The law by which our case must be decided is not difficult to find, seeing that it is the same among all nations; and it is easy to understand, seeing that it is innate in every individual and implanted in his mind.'[18] By consulting this innate law, human beings have created systems of positive justice. Of course, not all systems of positive law can be characterized as just (men of great wealth and power in particular are able to construct legal systems which ignore this innate law, observes Grotius),[19] and hence attributable to providence. Nevertheless, Grotius must hold that providence will prevail, and so he concludes that positive law springs from the law of nature: 'those very laws themselves of each and every nation and city flow from that Divine source, and from that source receive their sanctity and their majesty.'[20]

To say this, however, appears to create a problem: how is it that positive law, which is mutable, can flow from the immutable natural law written on our hearts? How is the mutable a product of the immutable? In one passage Grotius even appears to deny that it is. He says: 'since the law of nature arises out of Divine Providence, it is immutable; but a part of this natural law is the primary or primitive law of nations, differing from the secondary or positive

---

[15] Ibid. 46. This is not mere Protestant ideology. Grotius's claim that the limit to the Pope's authority is 'universally recognized' is clearly meant to remind Catholics of their *own* position. *Mare Liberum* is, at least in intention, an attempt to persuade the learned world, Protestant and Catholic alike, of the insupportability of the Portuguese position.

[16] Ibid. 53.   [17] Ibid. 2.   [18] Ibid. 5.   [19] Ibid. 1.
[20] Ibid. 2.

law of nations, which is mutable.'[21] This passage separates the
positive, mutable laws of nations from natural law, which goes no
further than the 'primitive' law of nations. But the preceding
passage states that the laws 'of each and every nation and city',
which cannot be anything but positive laws, all 'flow from that
Divine source'. So the secondary, or positive, laws of nations, even
if not identical to natural law, must nevertheless 'flow from' that
law. How is this possible?

The complete explanation of this problem will not be available
until Grotius's account of the development of positive laws of
property has been considered. In general outline, however, the
answer can be obtained by considering what at first looks like a
further complication: Grotius's acceptance of the ancient notion,
shared by Latins and Greeks, that the law of nature was the
historically original law, the law of the 'Golden Age' before any
positive laws existed. He speaks, for example, of 'the primitive law
of nations, which is sometimes called Natural Law, and which the
poets sometimes portray as having existed in a Golden Age, and
sometimes in the reign of Saturn or of Justice'.[22] The implication
here is not that in the Golden Age only the law of nature existed,
because there was as yet no positive law, but that the rule of the law
of nature was limited to that bygone age, and has now (in some
sense) been replaced by the rule of positive law. Clearly this can be
so only if the original natural law has somehow been incorporated
into the subsequent positive law, or, as Grotius himself puts it, if
positive law can be seen to 'flow from' natural law. Grotius's
remarks here are not, then, merely metaphorical, but to be taken as
they stand: positive law can be seen as flowing from natural law if
there is a procedure which is itself sanctioned by natural law. His
remarks concerning the development of positive property laws bear
out this interpretation. Despite the fact that 'in the eyes of nature no
distinctions of ownership were discernible'[23] (i.e. there was no
ownership in the Golden Age), the development of positive laws of
property was not contrary to nature because 'The present-day
concept of distinctions in ownership was the result, not of any
sudden transition, but of a gradual process whose initial steps were
taken under the guidance of nature herself.'[24] These initial steps

---

[21] Ibid. 53.   [22] Ibid. 23.   [23] *DJPC* 227.
[24] Ibid. 228. Cf. *ML* 24: 'the transition to the present distinction of ownerships did
not come violently, but gradually, nature herself pointing out the way.'

involved both the recognition that 'a certain form of ownership was inseparable from use',[25] and also the requirement that the law of property which thus arises must in some way reflect this inseparability. The second of these requirements will be examined below. First it must be recognized that positive law arises in response to natural promptings, and (in so far as it is just) reflects these promptings: 'The recognition of the existence of private property led to the establishment of a law on the matter, and this law was patterned after nature's plan.'[26]

It is of course possible to have a variety of laws which could be plausibly regarded as 'patterned after nature's plan'. Equally clearly, however, not any positive law could plausibly be so regarded. So, if positive laws are not to be contrary to nature, they can allow of a measure of variation, if not of boundless diversity. Mutable positive law can thus be part of immutable natural law as long as it is recognized that the mutability of the former is not unlimited, and that the immutability of the latter does not imply a set of hard and fast rules, but a starting-point attended with procedural constraints. Positive law is part of natural law as long as it is 'patterned after nature's plan'.[27] Grotius shows what is involved in following nature's plan in his account of the development of property law in *Mare Liberum*. Elements of this account have so far been alluded to, but it is now time to consider it in detail.

If we are to understand how property has arisen, Grotius points out, we must first recognize that the concept of property has itself undergone development. The story of the origin of property is not a story of the spontaneous generation of the modern concept of property, arriving fully-fledged in an underprepared world. Rather,

it must be understood that, during the earliest epoch of man's history, ownership [*dominium*] and common possession [*communio*] were concepts whose significance differed from that now ascribed to them. For in the present age, the term 'ownership' connotes possession of something peculiarly one's own, that is to say, something belonging to a given party in

---

[25] *DJPC* 228.

[26] Ibid. 229. Cf. *ML* 25: 'When property or ownership was invented, the law of property was established to imitate nature.'

[27] Grotius goes even further, repeating 'the accepted precept and rule that all things are supposed to be permitted which are not found expressly forbidden' (*ML* 55). His account of the development of property, however, implies a narrower, more directed rule. Nature does not simply allow what is not forbidden, but points out the general direction in which laws are to develop if they are not to violate nature.

such a way that it cannot be similarly possessed by any other party; whereas the expression 'common property' is applied to that which has been assigned to several parties, to be possessed by them in partnership (so to speak) and in mutual concord, to the exclusion of other parties. Owing to the poverty of human speech, however, it has become necessary to employ identical terms for concepts that are not identical. Consequently, because of a certain degree of similitude and by analogy, the above-mentioned expressions descriptive of our modern customs are applied to another right, which existed in early times. Thus with reference to that early age, the term 'common' is nothing more nor less than the simple antonym of 'private' [*proprium*]; and the word 'ownership' denotes the power to make use rightfully of common [i.e. public] property.[28]

Grotius's point can be summarized as follows: the Latin term *dominium* (commonly translated as 'ownership' or 'property'), which now is taken to mean private or exclusive property, did not always have this meaning. Instead, it originally meant the power to make use of what was not privately possessed. It identified a use-right. So, when we ask about the origin of ownership, or the origin of property, we need to understand whether we mean property in the developed modern legal sense (exclusive property), or property in its original sense of a use-right. There are then two separate questions we can ask: What is the origin of the use-right, and, How was the concept of a use-right transformed into the modern concept of exclusive property?

Grotius's answer to the first question is only alluded to in *Mare Liberum*, but is not the less important for that. Rather, his view that the natural world exists 'for the use of mankind'[29] is not considered there in any detail because he takes it for granted—as also does his audience. That the world exists for the use of human beings, in so far as that use is necessary for their preservation, is a commonplace of natural law theories. As we shall see, Grotius gives a more explicit acknowledgement of the principle in *De Jure Belli ac Pacis*, but the long pedigree of the principle is best displayed by considering an authoritative medieval source. In the *Summa Theologica*, Thomas Aquinas points out that

the order of the precepts of the natural law is according to the order of natural inclinations. Because in man there is first of all an inclination to good in accordance with the nature which he has in common with all substances, inasmuch as every substance seeks the preservation of its own

[28] *DJPC* 226–7.   [29] *ML* 2.

being, according to its nature; and by reason of this inclination, whatever is a means of preserving human life and of warding off its obstacles belongs to the natural law.[30]

With this principle in hand, it is only necessary to recognize that 'man is helped by industry in his necessities, for instance, in food and clothing'[31] in order to see that an original right to use at least parts of the natural world is a necessary part of natural law. Grotius's comparative silence on the matter is no more than a reflection of the extent to which this principle lies beyond dispute. He is quite happy to apply what he will later call the a posteriori method. He approvingly quotes Seneca: in the earliest ages,

> To all the way was open;
> the *use* of all things was a *common* right.[32]

Turning now to the second question, How does the original use-right develop into modern private property? Grotius gives a brief but revealing sketch of this process. In the Golden Age there was a universal use-right. Anything could be freely used by anyone for the purposes of their preservation. But some things, once used, cannot be re-used, or at least cannot be used without a diminution of their value. To some degree, using may amount to using up. To the extent that this is so, the initial user excludes the possibility of subsequent users. Where use amounts to using up, then, the exercise of the original use-right is in practice the exercise of an exclusive right. Where using does not amount to using up, but does result in a diminution of the possibility or extent of re-use, exercising the use-right approximates more or less closely to the exercise of an exclusive right. Some cases of exercising the original universal use-right can thus be regarded as the creation of *de facto* private property:

[30] T. Aquinas, *Summa Theologica*, I–II, Q. 94, A. 2; in *The Political Ideas of St. Thomas Aquinas*, trans English Dominican Fathers, ed. D. Bigongiari (New York: Hafner Press, 1953), 45–6.

[31] *Summa Theologica*, I–II, Q. 95, A. 2; ibid 56.

[32] Seneca, *Octavia*, u. 402 ff., in *Seneca's Tragedies*, trans. F. J. Miller (London, Heinemann, 1917), ii. 439 f.; *DJPC* 228. Although, in *Mare Liberum*, Grotius does not describe his reliance on authorities as the a posteriori method, as he does in *De Jure Belli ac Pacis*, he is nevertheless already quite self-consciously adopting it *as* a method. He says: 'Moreover, we ought not to be censured if, in our explanation of a right derived from nature, we avail ourselves of the authority and express statements of persons generally regarded as pre-eminent in natural powers of judgment' (*DJPC* 226).

there are some things which are consumed by use, either in the sense that they are converted into the very substance of the user and therefore admit of no further use, or else in the sense that they are rendered less fit for additional service by the fact that they have once been made to serve. Accordingly, it very soon became apparent, in regard to articles of the first class (for example, food and drink), that a certain form of private ownership was inseparable from use. For the essential characteristic of private property is the fact that it belongs to a given individual in such a way as to be incapable of belonging to another individual.[33]

The very practice of exercising the original universal use-right thus gives rise to a form of natural private property. The creation of a positive law to recognize such forms of natural property will thus mirror nature itself, or 'imitate nature':[34]

The recognition of the existence of private property led to the establishment of a law on the matter, and this law was patterned after nature's plan. For just as the right to use the goods in question was originally acquired through a physical act of attachment, the very source (as we have observed) of the institution of private property, so it was deemed desirable that each individual's private possessions should be acquired, as such, through similar acts of attachment. This is the process known as 'occupation' [*occupatio*], a particularly appropriate term in connexion with those goods which were formerly at the disposal of the community.[35]

To illustrate the naturalness of the legal principle of occupation, Grotius refers to a famous example of Seneca's: 'the equestrian rows of seats belong to *all* the Roman knights; yet the place that I have *occupied* in those rows becomes my *own*.'[36] In this way, in the imitation of nature, the first principle of private property arises through the recognition of the consequences of exercising the original universal use-right. Once the implications of occupation have been recognized in a human community, an elementary form

---

[33] Ibid. 228. A somewhat similar argument, which likewise stresses the inseparability of using an object from consuming the object itself, was employed by Aquinas in criticizing usury. Aquinas says (*Summa Theologica*, ii–ii, Q. 78, A. 1) that 'there are certain things the use of which consists in their consumption: thus we consume wine when we use it for drink, and we consume wheat when we use it for food. Wherefore in suchlike things the use of the thing must not be reckoned apart from the thing itself, and whoever is granted the use of the thing is granted the thing itself' (*Thomas Aquinas*, ed. Bigongiari, 148).

[34] *ML* 25.

[35] *DJPC* 229.

[36] Seneca, *De Beneficiis*, vii. xii, in Seneca, *Moral Essays*, trans. J. W. Basore (London: Heinemann, 1935), iii. 485–6; *DJPC* 229.

of private property has come into existence. The process which
leads to the development of modern forms of property is thus
underway.

Grotius's particular purposes in *Mare Liberum* lead him away
from considering the nature of this development in any detail. Since
all forms of property acquisition depend, either directly or
indirectly, on occupation,[37] and since his main aim in this work is to
show that neither the Portuguese, nor anyone else, can lay claim to
the open sea because, unlike the land, it cannot be occupied, his
concerns are both limited to the principle of occupation and
preoccupied with its starting-point. If, with respect to the sea, it is
not possible to begin a process of occupation which in any way
imitates nature, then clearly the law of nature does not allow that
the sea can be occupied. Given these aims, it is not surprising that
Grotius here limits himself to a few remarks on the manner in which
the initial form of occupation leads to other, more extensive, forms
of occupation. Nevertheless, what he does say is quite revealing.
After pointing out that, because in some cases using involves using
up, 'a certain form of private ownership is inseparable from use', he
goes on to show how this basic form of property is extended:

This basic concept was later extended by a logical process to include articles
of the second class, such as clothing and various other things capable of
being moved or of moving themselves. Because of these developments, it
was not even possible for all immovable things (fields, for instance) to
remain unapportioned, since the use of such things, while it does not consist
directly in their consumption, is nevertheless bound up [in some cases] with
purposes of consumption (as it is when arable lands and orchards are used
with a view to obtaining food, or pastures for [animals intended to provide]
clothing), and since there are not enough immovable goods to suffice for
indiscriminate use by all persons.[38]

Here we see, in brief, Grotius showing how the logic of historical
situations leads to the extension of the notion of property to include
new forms of occupation—in fact, to create a new, extended
concept of occupation itself, since occupation in these later cases no

---

[37] The nature of this dependence is an important feature of Adam Smith's
jurisprudence, in which the development of the different rules of property is tied
closely to the development of different stages of society. See A. Smith, *Lectures on
Jurisprudence*, ed. R. L. Meek, D. D. Raphael, and P. G. Stein (Oxford: Clarendon
Press, 1978), LJ(A) i. 27–35, 63–7; ii. 97–9; iv. 3–9; LJ(B) 149–51.

[38] *DJPC* 228. (Square brackets enclose additions by the trans.)

longer requires physical attachment. The original principle—the use-right sanctioned by the natural law of self-preservation—is adapted and interpreted to meet the exigencies of particular factors and situations (such as the limited re-usability of some things, and pressures caused by limited amounts of usable land) as they come to bear. The 'logical process' mentioned in the quotation is a process of reasoning[39] conducted from within a historical situation, about that situation: i.e. a process which produces principles relevant to that situation, principles which will stand in need of revision as new situations arise. Grotius is quite happy to idealize history[40]—a practice which, to some degree, no historical method can avoid—and this fact, together with the purposes of *Mare Liberum* referred to above, means that he provides no extensive historical investigations into the development of property. Nevertheless, human history is the stage on which the story of property unfolds.

Before turning to consider the account of property and i.s foundations in Grotius's mature work, it is worth noticing one factor which serves not only to encourage a historical approach to the elucidation of social relations such as property, but also to discourage extensive or detailed historical investigations of a modern kind. This factor is the role of providence. Providence is a historical notion, a reflection of the Judaeo-Christian idea of sacred history—the purposes of God are worked out, and thus shown in, the history of his people (whether Jews or Christians, but of course in characteristically different ways for Judaism and Christianity). For any social theory in which providence is to be accommodated, then, not only must history play an important role (thus encouraging the development or maintenance of historical social theories), but it must play a particular kind of role, a role which shows the providential logic of successive situations. The historical concerns of such theories will thus be idealized and thematic, showing the broad sweep of the providential hand, rather than

---

[39] *ML* 24 trans. the expression as 'the process of reasoning'.

[40] Ibid. 22: 'It will be most convenient . . . if we follow the practice of all the poets since Hesiod, of the philosophers and jurists of the past, and distinguish certain epochs, the divisions of which are marked off perhaps not so much by intervals of time as by obvious logic and essential character.' Cf. *DJPC* 226: Property 'will be very easily explained if . . . we draw a chronological distinction between things which are perhaps not differentiated from one another by any considerable interval of time, but which do indeed differ in certain underlying principles and by their very nature.' This strategy is—in fact, must be—adopted by all historical theories which aim to elicit stages of historical development.

highly detailed. Unlike much modern history, such theories will be concerned to show the forests rather than the trees. Keeping this in mind helps to explain why it is that even in *De Jure Belli ac Pacis* Grotius gives a historical account of human society, with sketches from history (where needed) to illustrate important principles, but without any great concern for examining historical detail. The contrast with later theories is quite marked: where providence is put aside, detailed histories become necessary to fill the breach. Having noted this, we can now turn to consider the more detailed foundation Grotius provides for natural law in *De Jure Belli ac Pacis*, and the nature of the account of property he builds upon it.

4. THE FOUNDATION OF NATURAL LAW

Grotius's ambitions in *Mare Liberum* have a markedly practical stamp. As a result, he devotes little space (and all of it in a preface) to explaining the foundations of natural law. As we have seen, he contrasts natural law with the doctrine of the abritrariness of moral distinctions. Natural law is denied by all those who hold 'that justice and injustice are distinguished the one from the other not by their own nature, but in some fashion merely by the opinion and the custom of mankind'.[41] In contrast, natural law holds that justice is distinguished by its own nature. In so far as there is an 'author' of nature, natural law can also be said to flow from this author. This is Grotius's view. God, being 'the founder and ruler of the universe', and especially being therefore 'the Father of all mankind', is the author of the natural law itself. The natural law is the law of our nature, and so Grotius provides a thumb-nail sketch of the main elements of our nature. God has, he says, given human beings 'the same origin, the same structural organism, the ability to look each other in the face, language too, and other means of communication, in order that they all might recognize their natural social bond and kinship'.[42] The point is not further elaborated in *Mare Liberum*, but its importance can be seen with the benefit of hindsight, since it

---

[41] *ML* I.
[42] Ibid. 2; cf. Seneca, Epistle xcv ('On the Usefulness of Basic Principles'), in Seneca, *Epistulae Morales*, trans. R. M. Gommare (London: Heinemann, 1925), iii. 58–103. (Pufendorf likewise relies on Seneca for his account of the elements of human nature, as we shall see in the next ch.)

provides an early indication of the important role to be attributed to human sociability in Grotius's later work.

In sharp contrast to the restricted polemical purposes of *Mare Liberum*, *De Jure Belli ac Pacis* aims at providing a 'comprehensive and systematic' treatment of 'the mutual relations among states or rulers of states'. It aims at providing the first complete treatise of this kind, the first to deal with 'the whole law of war and peace'. Such a treatise cannot be concerned solely with the foundations of the natural law, but must include consideration 'of treaties of alliance, conventions, and understandings of peoples, kings, and foreign nations'.[43] In short, it must be a study of the foundations of natural law, and an empirical study of human history, of the particular sets of circumstances in which positive laws are produced, and against which they must be judged.[44] The empirical study, as it relates to the institution of property, will be considered in the next section; here we will be concerned with Grotius's more detailed later account of the foundations of the natural law.

The first concern of *De Jure Belli ac Pacis* is, as it is for *Mare Liberum*, to show what natural law must deny. The opponents of natural law are all those who hold that there is no real or objective distinction between justice and injustice. To hold this is to be sceptical about morality itself. For all such moral sceptics, Grotius chooses Carneades as mouthpiece, 'in order that we may not be obliged to deal with a crowd of opponents'.[45] Or, it would be more accurate to say, he chooses Carneades as a paradigm of the sceptic but without allowing him the role of mouthpiece. Instead, he settles for quoting Horace's thumb-nail sketch, in the *Satires*, of the scepticism of the Academy. This is not too surprising, however, since there are no extant writings of Carneades (nor of the other principal sceptic of the later Academy, Arcesilaus). Grotius's choice of Carneades as the paradigm of the sceptic depends on two famous orations made by Carneades in Rome: in the first, praising

---

[43] *DJBP*, Prol. 1–2.

[44] Cf. ibid. 55: 'The French have tried . . . to introduce history into their study of laws. Among them Bodin and Hotman have gained a great name . . . their statements and lines of reasoning will frequently supply us with material in searching out the truth.' And cf. also ibid. 37–8, where Victoria and others are said to lack not only system, but also 'the illumination of history'.

[45] Ibid. 5. For a much more detailed consideration of the role played by Carneades at this point—the 'crowd of opponents' he is taken to represent—see R. Tuck, 'Grotius, Carneades and Hobbes', *Grotiana*, NS 4 (1983), 43–62.

justice, showing its foundations in natural law; in the second, praising injustice, while reducing justice to mere expediency.[46] Grotius thus describes him as having 'attained to so perfect a mastery of the peculiar tenet of his Academy that he was able to devote the power of his eloquence to the service of falsehood not less readily than to that of truth'.[47] To show the falsehood of Carneades' position, Grotius needs, firstly, to provide a natural foundation for justice, and, secondly, to show that this foundation is more than the purely expedient.

The first, or more general, of the sceptic's claims, summarized (for Grotius) by the poet Horace's line

And just from unjust Nature cannot know[48]

depends, according to Grotius's account of Carneades' main argument, on the claim that all human beings act solely from self-interest.[49] Justice is, on this view, either a cloak for self-interest, or an expedient adaptation to it. Grotius takes it for granted that self-interest is the motivation of animals (and that therefore—we may conclude—there is indeed no justice natural to animals). If the sceptical denial of natural justice is to be met, then, it must be met by showing that human nature differs crucially from animal nature. This is his response:

Man is, to be sure, an animal, but an animal of a superior kind, much farther removed from all other animals than the different kinds of animals are from one another; evidence on this point may be found in the many traits peculiar to the human species. But among the traits characteristic of

[46] P. P. Hallie, 'Carneades', in *The Encyclopedia of Philosophy*, ed.-in-chief P. Edwards (New York: Macmillan and The Free Press 1967), ii. 33.

[47] *DJBP*, Prol. 5.

[48] Horace, *Satires*, I. iii. 113. This is the trans. provided in *DJBP*. Cf. the trans. of H. Rushton Fairclough, in Horace, *Satires, Epistles and Ars Poetica* (London: Heinemann 1926) (Loeb Classical Library): 'Between right and wrong Nature can draw no such distinction as between things gainful and harmful, what is to be sought and what is to be shunned.' The view being presented here is that, unlike the natural difference which exists between the gainful and the harmful (X is gainful, Y harmful, precisely because of their natural characteristics), there is no such natural difference between right and wrong. Typically, two kinds of conclusion are generated from this position: justice is said to be mere convention, or, alternatively, it is said to be, as Thrasymachus put it, 'the interest of the stronger'.

[49] This is the main version. There is also a derivative version of the doctrine which holds that, because most people most of the time pursue only their self-interest, one ought to pursue one's own interest also, since to fail to do so will be, in such an environment, simply to do oneself harm. See *DJBP*, Prol. 5.

man is an impelling desire for society, that is, for the social life—not of any and every sort, but peaceful, and organized according to the measure of his intelligence, with those who are of his kind; this social trend the Stoics called 'sociableness'. Stated as a universal truth, therefore, the assertion that every animal is impelled by nature to seek only its own good cannot be conceded.[50]

Grotius does admit that some animals other than human beings can also be impelled by motivations other than self-interest. His explanation for this need not detain us, since the notion of sociableness he has in mind is more than having some sorts of altruistic motivations, and more than what we might now call 'sociability'—i.e. the enjoyment of the company of others. Rather, he has in mind a special capacity for *disinterestedness*, for the framing of a general understanding, and for acting from general motivations. The mature man (and also, to a lesser extent, children and some animals) has 'some disposition to do good to others', and this is indeed part of sociableness. But, in the relevant sense, sociableness is more than this:

The mature man in fact has . . . an impelling desire for society, for the gratification of which he alone among animals possesses a special instrument, speech. He has also been endowed with the faculty of knowing and of acting in accordance with general principles. Whatever accords with that faculty is not common to all animals, but peculiar to the nature of man.[51]

The 'impelling desire for society' here referred to is clearly more than an impelling desire for company. It is a desire for a social order, for being part of a culture: the mature man desires a society 'organized according to the measure of his intelligence, with those who are of his kind'. Sociableness in this sense is thus the foundation of human social organization, and the impelling desire for such organization is itself the source of law. Sociableness is therefore the natural foundation of law, the foundation of a law natural to human beings. The basic requirements of an organized social life are the basic principles of the natural law. Its main elements are as follows:

This maintenance of the social order . . . which is consonant with human intelligence, is the source of law properly so called. To this sphere of law

[50] Ibid. 6.   [51] Ibid. 7.

belong the abstaining from that which is another's, the restoration to another of anything of his which we may have, together with any gain which we may have received from it; the obligation to fulfil promises, the making good of a loss incurred through our fault, and the inflicting of penalties upon men according to their deserts.[52]

Examining all these elements is not to our purpose here, but this passage clearly indicates the important role played by the notion of 'what is another's', or, more generally, what can be said to be 'one's own'. The passage shows that, for Grotius, sociableness does not imply the absorption of separate individuals into an amorphous social whole, but requires instead the clear delineation of what is one's own and what is another's, of what is due to each. Since founded in sociableness, then, natural law must give an account of the nature of one's own, and how it can be modified. Explaining the nature and development of what is one's own is thus a major concern of this essay.

How does Grotius's account of sociableness answer the second, the more specific, of the sceptic's two claims: that justice is not natural because it is merely expedient? Once again his discussion of the issue begins with a quotation from Horace's *Satires*: 'Expediency is, as it were, the mother of what is just and fair.'[53] This view is, he

---

[52] *DJBP*, Prol. 8. Note that the final feature of the natural law listed here is the naturalness of *punishing*. Locke's 'strange Doctrine' (*Two Treatises of Government*, critical edn. with introd. and notes by P. Laslett (Cambridge: Cambridge University Press, 2nd edn., 1967) ii. 8–9) of the natural right to punish is certainly not a *new* doctrine.

[53] Horace, *Satires*, I. iii. 98; as trans. in *DJBP*, Prol. 16. As a statement of the sceptical position Grotius wishes to attack, this passage will undoubtedly serve. But his use of it is nevertheless rather odd. Expediency is one part of a larger sceptical position, in which a self-interested psychology of action is the cornerstone. This allows that, in a different context, expediency need not serve a sceptical purpose. Horace's context is one such case: he is making an Epicurean-style attack on the Stoic doctrine that all evils are all *equally* evil. Expediency is thus appealed to as a way of differentiating degrees of evil: 'Those whose creed is that all sins are much on a par are at a loss when they come to face facts. Feelings and customs rebel, and so does Expedience herself, the mother, we may say, of justice and right' (Horace, *Satires*, trans. Fairclough). The role played by expediencey here does not make it part of an attempt to *reduce* justice, but to show what is its *point*. Hume's different use of this passage—see Ch. 5—helps to underline this point. The misunderstandings he had to ward off also helps to show the risks implicit in invoking considerations of expediency: expediency is not always *mere* expediency. This is his point when he says in a frequently quoted letter to Francis Hutcheson (immediately after quoting this very passage from Horace), 'I have never called justice unnatural, but only artificial' (Hume to Hutcheson, 17 Sept. 1739: letter no. 13 in *The Letters of David Hume*, ed. J. Y. T. Greig (Oxford: Oxford University Press, 1932). For Hume the artificiality of

says, 'not true, if we wish to speak accurately'. It is not that it is
simply false, more that it is misleading. Expediency occupies an
important place, but the foundation of justice lies not in expediency
but in human nature: 'the very nature of man, which even if we had
no lack of anything would lead us into the mutual relations of
society, is the mother of the law of nature.'[54] As for the positive law
of specific human societies (which Grotius calls municipal law),[55] it
is a natural descendant of the law of nature, and hence is also
founded in 'the very nature of man', or nature itself: 'the mother of
municipal law is that obligation which arises from mutual consent;
and since this obligation derives its force from the law of nature,
nature may be considered, so to say, the great-grandmother of
municipal law.'[56] Thus the law of nature and its descendants arise
necessarily from 'the very nature of man'. Even if there were no
advantage to be gained therefrom, that is, 'even if we had no lack of
anything', society would still arise, and with it the law of nature and
positive municipal law.[57] However, human weakness implies that
society is advantageous. Natural law, although not founded in
expediency, therefore is expedient: 'The law of nature nevertheless
has the reinforcement of expediency; for the Author of nature
willed that as individuals we should be weak, and should lack many
things needed in order to live properly, to the end that we might be
the more constrained to cultivate the social life.'[58]

Not only is social life itself expedient, but political societies are
formed directly because of expediency. That is, they are formed
precisely because they are advantageous: 'expediency afforded an
opportunity also for municipal law, since that kind of association of

justice is not evidence for its unnaturalness because justice arises *necessarily*. See *A
Treatise of Human Nature* (1739–40), 2nd edn., ed. L. A. Selby-Bigge, rev. P. H.
Nidditch (Oxford: Clarendon Press, 1978), 484, cf. *Enquiries concerning Human
Understanding*, 3rd edn., ed. L. A. Selby-Bigge, rev. P. H. Nidditch (Oxford:
Clarendon Press, 1975), 307. Grotius's point is much the same: justice, although
expedient, is not *mere* expediency because it arises necessarily from human
sociableness.

[54] *DJBP*, Prol. 16.
[55] 'Municipal law is that which emanates from the civil power' (Ibid. 1. 1. xiv. 1).
[56] Ibid., Prol. 16.
[57] 'Even if no advantage were to be contemplated from the keeping of the law, it
would be a mark of wisdom, not of folly, to allow ourselves to be drawn towards that
to which we feel that our nature leads' (Ibid. 18).
[58] Ibid. 16. Cf. Hume's account of the natural disadvantages of human beings, and
of the consequent advantages of society (*Treatise*, 484–5).

which we have spoken, and subjection to authority, have their roots in expediency. From this it follows that those who prescribe laws for others in so doing are accustomed to have, or ought to have, some advantage in view.'[59] In this sense, positive municipal law has its roots in expediency. But both natural law and its grandchild, municipal law, are therefore expedient without being ultimately founded in expediency. Rather, the ultimate foundation of the law of nature, and thus of its descendants, lies in the natural sociableness of human beings.

Grotius's account of the relationship between natural law and expediency may appear to be something of a storm in a teacup, but it has some important consequences. Firstly, the positive side of his position—that natural law, even if not founded in expediency, 'nevertheless has the reinforcement of expediency'—implies that there is no conflict between his natural law theory and those later 'utilitarian' theories for which utility is a function of a determinate (sociable) human nature; a nature which, in its turn, requires an organized social life. Unlike Bentham's utilitarianism, the theory of David Hume is one such theory, self-consciously worked out by Hume as a development of some basic principles of natural law theory. To draw a stark contrast between natural law and all those theories which make an appeal to utility is thus simplistic. Secondly, the fact that natural law is not reducible to mere expediency means, most importantly, that laws are not suspended in that situation where they are often inexpedient, in war. Grotius sees the claim 'that war is irreconcilable with law' as one of the characteristic elements of the denial of natural law. He treats it as also similar to the more general view 'that for those whom fortune favours might makes right'; and both these are treated as 'of like implication' as the mere expediency thesis.[60] For Grotius, all such views are implicit denials of natural law, which, far from holding that all laws are suspended between combatants in times of war, holds instead that there are laws of war governing specific sorts of belligerent situations. To show what these laws are is a governing concern of *De Jure Belli ac Pacis*, and it is for his stance on this matter that Grotius earned his reputation as an irenicist, despite Rousseau's attack on him (as an apologist for the powerful) in *On the Social Contract*.[61]

---

[59] *DJBP*, Prol. 16.   [60] Ibid. Prol. 3–4.

[61] Grotius's reputation as a man of peace is well illustrated in Günter Grass's recreation of aspects of the intellectual climate at the end of the Thirty Years War (in

Grotius's irenic aims may also have contributed to what was, for his contemporary readers, the most provocative of the conclusions he drew from the basic doctrine that the foundation of natural law lay in human sociableness. It is stated in the famous *etiamsi daremus* passage: 'What we have been saying would have a degree of validity even if we should concede that which cannot be conceded without the utmost wickedness, that there is no God, or that the affairs of men are of no concern to Him.'[62] This brief remark, by affirming the possibility of at least a partially secularized political theory, exercised a powerful influence on subsequent political thought. In an age of intense political conflict arising from or reflected in religious differences, it also offered the prospect of peace despite continuing religious differences. However, its significance can be overrated, or misunderstood. It is certainly not the thin end of an atheistic wedge; it is, rather, a conclusion typical of the theological rationalism of the late sixteenth and early seventeenth centuries, a theory which met its most famous rejection in the philosophy of Descartes. Descartes developed his theological voluntarism in self-consciousness opposition to the *Metaphysical Disputations* of Francisco Suárez (1548–1617), one of the most famous of the rationalists. It is not surprising, then, to see that Suárez, in his work on natural law, grants the law of nature a degree of autonomy comparable to that provided by Grotius's account. In answer to the question, whether God can grant dispensation from natural law, Suárez argues in favour of the opinion that 'those commandments which involve an intrinsic principle of justice and obligation are not liable to dispensation'. The most notable of those commandments of which this is true are the Ten Commandments, so Suárez adopts the conclusion that 'none of the Commandments of the Decalogue

1647), the earlier periods of which form an important part of the political background of Grotius's major work. See G. Grass, *The Meeting at Telgte*, trans. R. Manheim (Harmondsworth: Penguin Books, 1983), 22–3, 87. For Rousseau's attack on Grotius, see esp. *On The Social Contract*, Bk. I, ch. 2: Grotius's 'most persistent mode of reasoning is always to establish right by fact. One could use a more rational method, but not one more favourable to tyrants', *On The Social Contract*, ed. R. D. Masters, trans. J. R. Masters (New York: St. Martin's Press, 1978), 47. Although not entirely accurate, Rousseau's objections are not empty. It is also worth noting that Locke's rather easy justification of killing in the state of war (see esp. ch. 3 of the *Second Treatise*), is not contrary to Grotius's defence of law in the state of war, since, for Grotius, 'by the law of nature it is permissible to kill in defence of property' (*DJBP* II. I. xi).

[62] *DJBP*, Prol. 11.

admits of dispensation, even by the absolute power of God'. Moreover, Suárez does not present this as a bold and innovative thesis: in its favour he several times cites Aquinas, who had, he says, declared that 'not even God is able to grant [such] a dispensation; for He cannot act contrary to His own justness'.[63]

If God cannot change the natural laws, it is because he cannot do so *justly*. But if the natural laws cannot be justly changed by God, but must be understood to be *necessarily* willed by him, since he cannot but be just, then it could be said, as Grotius does say, that the natural law would have 'a degree of validity, even if we should concede . . . that there is no God'. In so saying, Grotius stresses that he is not denying the natural law a divine source:

the law of nature of which we have spoken, comprising alike that which relates to the social life of man and that which is so called in a larger sense, proceeding as it does from the essential traits implanted in man, can nevertheless rightly be attributed to God, because of His having willed that such traits exist in us.[64]

The obligations imposed by the law of nature are 'in themselves' obligatory, because 'it is understood that necessarily they are enjoined or forbidden by God'.[65] But, we may ask, if God does not exist, would there still be an obligation to conform to the law of nature (since this law would be enjoined or forbidden by no author)? Grotius appears to accept that there would be, but in so doing he failed to satisfy Pufendorf and others, and thus helped to make the question of our obligation to obey the law central to the later natural law debates. Grotius himself seems rather untroubled on the matter—he is content to spell out, in very rationalistic terminology, the nature and foundation of natural law.

What is the law of nature? It is, says Grotius, 'a dictate of right reason, which points out that an act, according as it is or is not in conformity with rational nature, has in it a quality of moral baseness or moral necessity'.[66] To understand this passage, it is necessary to

[63] F. Suárez, *De Legibus ac Deo Legislatore*, in *Selections from Three Works*, trans. G. L. Williams, A. Brown, and J. Waldron (Oxford: Oxford University Press, 1944), 297–8.　　[64] *DJBP*, Prol. 12.

[65] *DJBP* I. I. x. 2. Cf. the position adopted in *DJPC*, where Grotius holds simply that 'a given thing is just because God wills it, rather than that God wills the thing because it is just' (p. 8). See R. Tuck, 'The "Modern" Theory of Natural Law', in A. Pagden (ed.), *The Languages of Political Theory in Early Modern Europe* (Cambridge: Cambridge University Press, 1987), 112.

[66] *DJBP* I. I. x. I.

determine what Grotius means by 'a dictate of right reason'.[67] Such dictates of reason are discerned by having 'a quality of moral baseness or moral necessity'. Exactly what such a quality would be he does not say, but an important clue is his remark that he has made it his concern 'to refer the proofs of things touching the law of nature to certain fundamental conceptions which are beyond question, so that no one can deny them without doing violence to himself'.[68] So it seems that the dictates of right reason are those principles we cannot deny without doing violence to ourselves, to our fundamental characteristic of sociableness in particular.

The notion of sociableness is acknowledged by Grotius to be of Stoic origin, and his elucidation of the relationship between the dictates of right reason and instinctive nature shows another element of affinity with Stoic (and other ancient) views. The law of nature has its beginnings in instinctive nature, but it is certainly not a mere cloak of rectitude over our instincts. Rather, reason is our highest characteristic good, and so the law of nature must in some way reflect our rational nature. He approvingly quotes Seneca to this effect: 'Just as in every case a nature, unless brought to its highest perfection, does not manifest its type of good, so the good of man is not found in man unless reason has been perfected in him.'[69] The law of nature is, then, the law of our nature, and thus of rational nature: it is not merely the transformation of instincts into laws.

Even so, it does not take our instinctive nature lightly. Grotius follows Cicero's account (which is, in fact, shared by the Stoics and other ancient writers) on the relation between reason and our instinctive nature. In general outline, the account is as follows. All animals are, from birth, impelled by the 'first principles of nature'. These principles imply that the animal 'has regard for itself and is impelled to preserve itself, to have zealous consideration for its own condition and for those things which tend to preserve it, and also shrinks from destruction and from things likely to cause destruction'.[70]

---

[67] Cf. Locke's remark that 'the Law of Nature . . . is the Law of Reason' (*Two Treatises*, i. 101).

[68] *DJBP*, Prol. 39.

[69] Seneca, Epistle cxxiv ('On the True Good as Attained by Reason'), in *Epistulae Morales*, iii. 447; quoted at *DJBP* 1. 2. i. 2 n. 1.

[70] Ibid. 1. Cf. Cicero: 'the first "appropriate act" . . . is to preserve oneself in one's natural constitution' (iii. vi. 20, spoken by Cato the Stoic); 'every natural organism aims at being its own preserver, so as to secure its safety and also its preservation true to its specific type' (iv. vii. 16, spoken by Cicero in an approving account of the doctrines of

This natural impulse of preservation gives rise to a 'duty to keep oneself in the condition which nature gave to him', and also to live 'in conformity with nature', and to reject what is 'contrary' to nature. This is, however, only one's 'first duty'. If such a 'first duty' was incorrigible, then the law of nature would amount to no more than a cloak of rectitude over the instinctive. But the quotation from Seneca suggests that the 'first duty' is to be regarded as a kind of initial approximation to the truth.

Grotius's position can be spelt out a little more fully as follows. As human beings grow and develop the use of their reason, their initial instinctive principles are re-examined and, where necessary, recast in the light of reason. This is appropriate because the mind is more worthy than the body (and, or because, it is more truly characteristic of the nature of human beings). To live in conformity with nature thus requires our living in conformity with reason, the most important element of our nature:

there follows a notion of the conformity of things with reason, which is superior to the body. Now this conformity, in which moral goodness becomes the paramount object, ought to be accounted of higher import than the things to which instinct alone first directed itself, because the first principles of nature commend us to right reason, and right reason ought to be more dear to us than those things through whose instrumentality we have been brought to it . . . in investigating the law of nature it is necessary first to see what is consistent with those fundamental principles of nature, and then to come to that which, though of later origin, is nevertheless more worthy—that which ought not only to be grasped, if it appear, but to be sought out by every effort.[71]

‘the ancients’). From *De Finibus Bonorum et Malorum*, trans. H. Rackham (Cambridge, Mass.: Harvard University Press, and London: Heinemann, 1914) (Loeb Classical Library).

[71] *DJBP* I. 2. i. 2–3. Cf. Cicero, *De Finibus*, IV. vii. 16–17: the ancients affirm that, to better achieve the aim of preservation, ‘man has called in the aid of the arts also to assist nature; and chief among them is counted the art of living, which helps him to guard the gifts that nature has bestowed and to obtain those that are lacking. They further divided the nature of man into soul and body. Each of these parts they pronounced to be desirable for its own sake, and consequently they said that the virtues also of each were desirable for their own sakes; at the same time they extolled the soul as infinitely surpassing the body in worth, and accordingly placed the virtues also of the mind above the goods of the body. But they held that wisdom is the guardian and protectress of the whole man, as being the comrade and helper of nature, and so they said that the function of wisdom, as protecting a being that consisted of a mind and a body, was to assist and preserve him in respect of both.’

This shift—from an original, but lower, principle to a higher, but later—would not particularly deserve attention if it were not for the fact that the two principles are not only different but recommend different ends. The point of establishing a hierarchy of principles is, obviously, to show which principle is to be followed in the case of a conflict. In stressing the superiority of reason over instinctive nature Grotius thus affirms, as did the ancients, that reason must triumph over mere passion.

There is a need to be careful here, however, and to recognize that this does not in any way imply a fundamental opposition of reason and passion. Neither, therefore, does it imply the most common version of this oppositional psychology, the Platonic political metaphor of reason as the ruler over the unruly, anarchistic, passions. The account of the superiority of mind over body given above would not, of course, make sense if, in cases of conflict, reason did not have sway over the passions; did not *direct* them. But the relationship between reason and passion is not to be understood as opposing tendencies. Rather the relationship is that between knowledge and ignorance, or between the sighted and the blind. Cicero speaks of 'wisdom' as being 'the guardian and protectress of the whole man . . . the comrade and helper of nature',[72] and, given his explicit approval of Cicero in this context, we can reasonably regard Grotius to be following a similar line. Reason is, on this view, the natural guide of instinctive nature, the guide of the passions.[73] The fundamental aims of instinctive nature—in particular

[72] Ibid. 17.

[73] Some instructive comparisons can be made with Hume's view. It is first necessary to recognize that his famous dictum, that 'Reason is, and ought only to be, the slave of the passions' (*Treatise*, 415) is a potentially misleading account of Hume's psychology of action. His view could be described in like manner to the Ciceronian view, as according to reason the role of guide of the passions, in that his theory also is concerned to show that the passions are blind and can only be directed by reason. However, this would not do justice to the differences between his account and the Ciceronian (and more common ancient) view, since the latter, although not fundamentally oppositional, allows the possibility of conflict between reason and passion—a possibility denied by the former. The similarities between the 2 views are genuine—they both firmly reject the oppositional psychology built into the political metaphor—but the difference can be caught by recognizing that, on the Humean view, the passions are not only blind, but know themselves to be so; they therefore seek the help of the sighted. (The model of the blind person led by a guide dog is apposite in this case.) On the ancient view, the passions are blind (or near-sighted) but do not recognize themselves to be so; reason points out their errors but frequently has trouble convincing them of the fact. Conflicts are inevitable but not constant.

the fundamental urge of self-preservation—are thus not denied by reason, but fulfilled. We act in conformity with our nature when we pursue our fundamental aims rationally instead of instinctively; with our eyes open to the relevant circumstances, rather than from blind internal imperatives. In this way we act more *successfully*; we successfully conform our actions to our natural ends. In this light it becomes clear why the law of nature, as a dictate of right reason, is nevertheless in accord with the fundamental aims of our instinctive nature. The law of nature is the guardian of our natural tendency to preservation, and also of those tendencies which flow from it, whether specific cases like self-defence,[74] or the more general tendency of sociableness already discussed.

The law of nature is also a dictate of right reason because it is founded on the essential human trait of sociableness. Sociableness is, for human beings, a specific aspect of the more general phenomenon of the necessity of preservation. Because the law of nature has this determinate character, it 'would have a degree of validity' even if there was no divine author of nature. Here we can usefully distinguish between the origin and the content of natural law. For Grotius, it can make no sense to speak of the origin of natural law without speaking of God, because God is its author. The content of natural law is, however, a different matter. God has made the world such that it has a determinate character, so we can discuss this character without discussing its author. The elaboration of the law of nature is thus independent of theology, in the sense that the dictates of the law of nature are discovered by examining what the essential trait of sociableness requires.

What exactly does sociableness require? Grotius spells this out most succinctly in a passage concerned with the justifiability of force (part of the larger question, 'Whether it is ever lawful to wage war'). After pointing out that 'the first principles of nature' (that is, instinctive nature) are not opposed to the use of force, he goes on to consider the higher implications of our rational nature:

Right reason, moreover, and the nature of society . . . do not prohibit all use of force, but only that use of force which is in conflict with society, that is which attempts to take away *the rights of another*. For society has in view this object, that through community of resource and effort each individual be safeguarded in the possession of *what belongs to him*.[75]

---

[74] For the justifiability of self-defence, see *DJBP* I. 2. iii; II. 1. iii.
[75] Ibid. I. 2. i. 5 (emphasis added).

We see here that the implication of sociableness is not to merge all individuals into an undifferentiated social whole, but precisely to preserve the original distinctness of persons. Grotius employs two expressions in this passage to express the distinctness of others from ourselves: he speaks of 'the rights of another' (a better translation would be 'the *right* of another'), and of 'what belongs to him'. These two expressions are not quite identical in meaning, but they are closely related. Explaining them will explain the distinctive character of the natural law tradition stemming from Grotius's work.

What belongs to a person is what is one's own—in Latin, *suum*. The notion of the *suum* is pre-legal (that is, prior to *positive* laws), as Grotius makes clear immediately following the above quotation. What belongs to a person is prior to private ownership according to positive law. Essentially it includes a person's life, limbs, and liberty: 'It is easy to understand,' he says, that society aims at preserving or protecting what belongs to a person 'even if private ownership (as we now call it) had not been introduced; for life, limbs, and liberty would in that case be the possessions belonging to each, and no attack could be made upon these by another without injustice'.[76] The *suum* is thus a set of essential possessions, understood by Grotius to be—at least—life, limbs, and liberty. It is what naturally belongs to a person because none of these things can be taken away without injustice. Reason and the nature of society thus dictate that the life, limbs, and liberty of individuals be protected. The law of nature is, in other words, ineluctably committed to the defence of the *suum*.

If the vitally important realm of the *suum* can be *extended*, then the law of nature is likewise extended. Grotius hints at this extension in the immediately following passage: where there is no private ownership, but only the original *suum*,

Under such conditions the first one taking possession would have the right to use things not claimed and to consume them up to the limit of his needs, and any one depriving him of that right would commit an unjust act. But now that private ownership has by law or usage assumed a definite form, the matter is much easier to understand.[77]

[76] Ibid. Note the reference to 'private ownership (*as we now call it*)' (emphasis added), which illustrates a continuation of the sensitivity to language already observed in *Mare Liberum*.
[77] Ibid.

This is a most important passage. It shows that the *suum* necessarily gives rise to a use-right, since the preservation of life requires the using of natural resources. Since the use-right arises precisely because of the person's needs, it extends no further than the satisfaction of those needs. But, as the *Mare Liberum* passage on the development of property points out, some kinds of use imply, or result in, using up. Thus the exercise of the use-right amounts, in important cases, to the operation of an exclusive right. The exercise of the use-right, which is no more than the satisfaction of needs, thereby gives rise to a form of property. The necessity of recognizing publicly this form of property begins the institution of private ownership, so through this process the satisfaction of our needs comes to require the institution of private ownership. The *suum* has thus been extended: it comes to include not only life, limbs, and liberty, but also other socially recognized private possessions. Private property (as we know it) is the set of extensions to the *suum*, and for this reason private property laws become an essential part of the system of natural justice.

Not every positive law of property is part of (extended) natural justice, of course. The positive law must be the product of a just process, and such a process is a reflection of the fact that we naturally possess a justified power to act to preserve the *suum*. These *moral* powers Grotius brings to the fore in reintroducing the notion of rights.[78] A right is the power to act rightfully, thus rights are the powers necessary for the just extension of the natural law. He introduces them as follows: 'There is another meaning of law viewed as a body of rights . . . which has reference to the person. In this sense a right becomes a moral quality of a person, making it possible to have or to do something lawfully.'[79] Since the *suum*, and the rule of law, can only be extended through lawful actions, it is thus through the exercise of rights that the realm of law is extended. It is also through the possession of rights that the obligations of natural (and thus positive) law are limited. Each of these aspects can be considered briefly.

The exercise of rights is essentially concerned with the protection and extension of the *suum*. There is, however, another class of moral quality which promotes social goods other than the protection of the *suum*. Grotius considers such goods 'fitting' (and

[78] For the earlier history of natural rights, see Tuck, *Natural Rights Theories*.
[79] *DJBP* I. I. iv.

thus good but not obligatory), and so he describes these moral qualities as *aptitudes*. The stronger, *suum*-protecting qualities he calls *faculties*. These latter moral qualities are the rights. Only moral faculties, or rights, give rise to legal rights, so they alone are the qualities which give rise to 'justice properly or strictly so called.' Moral faculties can therefore be called 'perfect', whereas the moral aptitudes are 'not perfect'.[80] The perfect moral qualities include the following:

power, now over oneself, which is called freedom, now over others, as that of the father and that of the master over slaves; ownership, either absolute, or less than absolute, as usufruct and the right of pledge; and contractual rights, to which on the other side contractual obligations correspond.[81]

The imperfect moral qualities, on the other hand, are 'associated with those virtues which have as their purpose to do good to others, as generosity, compassion, and foresight in matters of government'.[82] Since only the perfect moral qualities extend the obligations of the law of nature, there can be no legal obligation to generosity, compassion, or the like. So, in Grotius's hands, the law of nature does not stipulate a morally exacting, or even morally demanding, social order. Rather, 'it is not . . . contrary to the nature of society to look out for oneself and advance one's own interests, provided the rights of others are not infringed'.[83] Through his distinction between rights and imperfect moral qualities, Grotius thus limits

[80] Ibid. iv–viii.

[81] Ibid. v. Grotius thus places rights over slaves on an equal footing with rights to freedom. How he is able to do this (or, whether he is consistent in so doing) will not be considered here—but it is precisely remarks such as these which earned Rousseau's ire. For Locke, as for Rousseau, the natural liberty protected by the law of nature renders slavery unjustifiable. [82] Ibid. viii. 1.

[83] Ibid. 2. i. 6. The rights to which Grotius refers here must be perfect rights, since the exercise of the imperfect rights will necessarily involve each individual in practical regard for others, both as individuals and as members of a shared social order. There is no doubt that, thus understood, Grotius's position represents a clear rejection of ancient and Renaissance conceptions of the vital importance of the *polis*, the public sphere, to human life. It is also not unreasonable to attribute to him some measure of 'possessive individualism', in the sense made famous by C. B. Macpherson in *The Political Theory of Possessive Individualism: Hobbes to Locke* (Oxford: Clarendon Press, 1962). Macpherson's summary of the constitutive elements of possessive individualism (pp.263–4) shows that Grotius's view cannot, without considerable licence, be understood accurately in such terms, even though there are several features of the Grotian position which are thoroughly conformable to the possessive individualist picture. The idea that individuals are not indebted to their society, and can therefore legitimately live a life in which one can 'look out for oneself and advance one's own interests' is one such; and this conformity is emphasized by the

the law of nature to the protection of the *suum* of each individual
member of society, restraining it from requiring any positive acts of
general benevolence. In this light, it is not surprising that laws of
private ownership should be a central element in the natural laws
which govern human society. Neither, however, are these laws an
arbitrary matter. There is a rational process which governs the just
extension of the original right over one's own (the original *suum*,
comprising life, limbs, and liberty) and its accompanying use-right,
to the development of complex forms of private ownership.
Grotius's account of this process, the historical development of
property, will be examined in the next section.

  Before turning to that task, a brief remark on the nature of the
enterprise is in order. Since the history of the uses of a social
institution can readily amount to no more than a catalogue of
abuses, writing the history of property may seem a pointless task.
But for Grotius there is a rational history of property—the *natural*
history of property—which is the story of extensions to the *suum* by
just processes. This latter history is thus simultaneously a
justification of property. The important question then is, What is
the relationship between the two histories? Rousseau's attack on
Grotius in *On the Social Contract* shows that he thought Grotius
guilty of collapsing the latter history into the former, thereby
producing a mere apology for tyranny.[84] Many of Grotius's

proprietarian rationale which underlies much of Grotius's social theory. As Tuck
notes, Grotius's views were distinctive in part because of his willingness 'to explain
relationships in terms of the transfer of *dominium*, and to treat liberty as a piece of
property' (*Natural Rights Theories*, 60). Even so, the possessive individualist
interpretation should not be too readily embraced as an account of Grotius's
position, because it tends to underrate the influence of the distinctive early 17th-
cent. factors—most importantly, his ambition to lay the foundations for domestic
and international peace. Tuck correctly points out that, even in *De Jure Praedae*, he
had connected peace with a more limited conception of the concerns appropriate to a
human life: 'Grotius was . . . able to argue that the law of nature was in effect the
obligation men are under to preserve social peace, and that the principal condition
for a peaceful community is respect for one another's rights' (ibid. 73). It will be
shown in subsequent chs. that the notion of possessive individualism has rather little
interpretative value for those of Grotius's successors with whom this study is
concerned, because Pufendorf redefines both the relationship between rights and
duties and the requirements of human sociability.

  [84] See esp. his own footnote, quoting the Marquis d'Argenson: 'Learned research
on public right is often merely the history of ancient abuses, and people have gone to
a lot of trouble for nothing when they have bothered to study it too much.' This is,
Rousseau adds, 'exactly what Grotius has done' (*On The Social Contract* I. 2. 47).

successors are very conscious of the issue, and attempt to deal with it in different ways. Hutcheson, on the one hand, distances his political enquiries from history;[85] Adam Smith, on the other, employs his account of the distinctively moral standpoint to generate a critical history of social institutions, including property. Grotius's confidence in the manifest logic of history (that is, the degree to which the facts of human history are able to mirror natural history) is not a confidence entirely shared by his successors.[86]

This aspect of the critical reception of Grotius's thought, however, is of only limited relevance here, because his more contentious uses of history do not include his account of the origin of private ownership of *things*. His treatment of the origin of private ownership of human beings—i.e. of slavery—is another matter, and for this reason many of his successors are greatly concerned with the question whether the natural law account of property can allow slavery, or whether it renders it impossible. This question arises directly from Grotius's own concerns in his treatment of property. Although the historical character of the account of the origin of property has been stressed in the preceding sections, this is not of particular concern for Grotius himself: not because he lacked a historical story, but because he treated it as a matter of course. Both *Mare Liberum* and *De Jure Belli ac Pacis* offer only brief historical accounts of the origin of property simply because such an account could be taken for granted, and was not in any case the point of the account of property. It could be taken for granted because it is part and parcel of the classical accounts of the origin of human society, accounts on which he frequently and explicitly calls.[87] It is not the

---

[85] 'We are inquiring into the just and wise motives to enter into civil polity, and the ways it can be justly constituted; and not into points of history about facts', F. Hutcheson, *A System of Moral Philosophy* (1755) (Hildesheim: Olms, 1969), ii. 224–5.

[86] This distinction, between natural history and actual history, is treated most directly by Adam Smith in Bk. III of *The Wealth of Nations*. Smith contrasts the 'natural progress of opulence' with its actual progress from ancient times to modern commercial society. Such a distinction is necessary for the writing of a critical history of social institutions, which Smith attempts to carry out. See *An Inquiry into the Nature and Causes of the Wealth of Nations*, ed. R. H. Campbell, A. S. Skinner, and W. B. Todd (Oxford: Clarendon Press, 1976), Bk. III. ch. 1 (the natural progress of opulence), and chs. 2–4 (the actual progress of opulence in Europe).

[87] See e.g. the brief account of the development of society in Horace's *Satires* (I. iii. 99 ff.)—a passage which Grotius refers to a number of times in the Prolegomena to *DJBP*; and the detailed account of the history of society in Lucretius's *De Rerum*

point of his account of property because—especially in *Mare Liberum*—his aim is to show not just how property can be acquired, but also how it cannot (i.e. without injustice). His aim is to show the naturalness of appropriation, and also thereby its natural limits. In *De Jure Belli ac Pacis*, as in *Mare Liberum*, he denies the possibility of occupying the open sea. More importantly for our purposes, however, he also denies that the property of any person (understood as a set of extensions to the original *suum*) can ever be so extended as to invade the *suum* of another. This is because, in the world of developed property relations, the original use-right implied by the *suum* is not lost, but is retained in the form of a general right of necessity. It will be shown below that this particular right has far-reaching implications especially with respect to the possibility of slavery. These implications, not fully appreciated by Grotius, become the centre-piece of the political theory of Locke's *Two Treatises of Government*.[88]

Perhaps one reason for failing to see that Grotius provides a historical account of the development of property is that the historical sources on which he calls are no longer regarded as historical documents. This should not deter us, however: to offer a historical account of the development of any phenomenon is not to offer an *adequate* historical account. Our explanations can only ever be as good as our sources, so, if Grotius's sources are to be regarded as myths,[89] his historical explanations will not compel assent, and may perhaps seem bizarre. But the further question of historical adequacy should not blind us to the type of explanation being offered. An account based on modern historical researches is not a different kind of account, but a more sophisticated, more cautious explanation of the effects of changed circumstances. It is,

---

Natura (v. 925–1457). In *DJBP*, unlike *ML*, Grotius does not simply follow these classical sources, but blends them into an account based on the Book of Genesis.

[88] To put the matter a little more accurately: the problem for Grotius arises out of a tension in his doctrine of rights. The right of necessity, if it is to play any sort of role at all, needs to be understood as an *inalienable* right. But his general doctrine of rights—that they are moral powers possessed by individuals—allows them to be freely alienated as if they are just like the ordinary possessions of individuals. For a more detailed account of Grotius's conception of a right, see K. Olivecrona, *Law as Fact* (London: Stevens & Sons (2nd edn., 1971), app. 1 (pp. 275–96).

[89] The word 'myth' is used here in its anthropological sense. In this sense, a myth is not necessarily false, but is a belief which serves a special symbolic or religious purpose within a community. It *is* an outsider's (an observer's) term, but it is meant to be employed neutrally.

among other things, to upgrade the data.[90] As Grotius tells us, his
data in *De Jure Belli ac Pacis* come principally from 'sacred
history'—that is, the Book of Genesis—with supplementation from
the 'philosophers and poets' of the classical sources. He makes this
explicit when explaining one aspect of his account. Contrasting his
method there with that of *Mare Liberum*, he says: 'This is what we
are taught in sacred history; and it is quite in accord with what
philosophers and poets, whose testimony we have presented
elsewhere, have said concerning the first state of ownership in
common, and the distribution of property which afterward
followed.'[91] With this in mind, we can now turn to a direct
consideration of Grotius's account of 'the first state of ownership in
common' and the subsequent distribution of property.

5. PROPERTY: DEVELOPMENT AND LIMITS

Grotius begins his chapter on property by considering 'the division
of that which is our own'. This division, of the *suum*, reveals two
parts: 'some things belong to us by a right common to mankind,
others by our individual right.'[92] The story of the development of
private property is a story of the creation of an individual right out
of the 'right common to mankind'. To understand this transition it is
first of all necessary to determine the nature of the 'common' right.
In an important passage, Grotius describes it as follows:

Soon after the creation of the world, and a second time after the Flood, God
conferred upon the human race a general right over things of a lower
nature. 'All things', as Justin says, 'were the common and undivided
possession of all men, as if all possessed a common inheritance'. In
consequence, each man could at once take whatever he wished for his own
needs, and could consume whatever was capable of being consumed. The
enjoyment of this universal right then served the purpose of private

[90] This task is carried out in extensive detail by Adam Smith in his *Lectures on
Jurisprudence*, a work which explicitly acknowledges its debt to Grotius's form of
natural jurisprudence. The historical task built into modern natural law is
overlooked by Bowles, 'Origin of Property', as his simple contrast between natural
law and historical science serves to illustrate. Whether or not it did so successfully,
modern natural law aimed at producing historical science. For a more extensive
account of Smith's natural jurisprudence, see K. Haakonssen, *The Science of a
Legislator: The Natural Jurisprudence of David Hume and Adam Smith* (Cambridge:
Cambridge University Press, 1981).

[91] *DJBP*, II. 2. ii. 3.   [92] Ibid. i. 1.

ownership; for whatever each had thus taken for his own needs another could not take from him except by an unjust act.[93]

To illustrate this Grotius refers, as he did in *Mare Liberum*, to the example of the seats in the theatre, on this occasion giving the version employed by Cicero: 'Although the theatre is a public place, yet it is correct to say that the seat which a man has taken belongs to him.'[94] This passage shows that the original 'right common to mankind' is the same as the use-right implied by the *suum*, as described above. The right is common to mankind in the sense that everyone has it: it is not a right to a common possession (in the sense of joint ownership). A common right in the latter sense would give more than a simple use-right, it would also give rights to control or limit the activities of others. Grotius gives no hint that the right common to mankind gives anything more than the right to use things for the purpose of one's preservation (of satisfying basic needs), so he must mean only that this right is a right which everybody has.

The quotation from Justin must, therefore, be treated with care. All things can be 'the common and undivided possession of all men' only in a weak sense: only, in fact, in that sense Grotius refers to in *Mare Liberum* as the original meaning of 'common'—not private.[95] So all things were 'the common and undivided possession of all men' only in the sense that there was nothing which was a private possession. The 'common inheritance' of all humanity referred to by Justin thus refers to the same situation described by Seneca (and quoted in *Mare Liberum*) as

> To all the way was open;
> The *use* of all things was a *common* right.[96]

That all things were originally the 'common inheritance' of all humanity does not mean, then, that in the earliest ages of human history all human beings were to be regarded as joint owners of the earth: no such ownership then existed. Like all distinctive forms of ownership, joint ownership is the creation of a later historical age. The earth was originally a common inheritance only in the sense

[93] *DJBP* II. 2. ii. 1.
[94] Cicero, *De Finibus*, III. xx. 67. This is the trans. provided in *DJBP*, II. 2. ii. 1. In *Mare Liberum* Grotius had employed Seneca's version. (See the text to n. 36 above.)
[95] See *DJPC* 226–7 (text to n. 28 above).
[96] Ibid. 228. (Cf. n. 32 and text.)

that it could be used by all, and it is the 'poverty of human speech'[97] which sometimes obscures this from us. (Part of Pufendorf's acievement—as the next chapter will show—was to overcome this particular problem caused by the poverty of speech in his account of the origin of property.)

The original common inheritance of all humanity was the use-right implied by the *suum*. This use-right was the 'universal right' which 'served the purpose of private ownership'. However, the purpose of the original use-right was to satisfy human needs, to preserve the individual and the species, so the purpose of private ownership must have been the same. Grotius is thus committed to holding that at least the first purpose of private ownership was to protect the things or actions necessary to preservation—in other words, to satisfy needs. Private ownership and the original use-right both have the purpose of guaranteeing (as far as possible) that 'whatever each had thus taken for his own needs another could not take from him except by an unjust act'. Of course, this requirement does not preclude private ownership from serving additional ends as well, but it must at least serve this end. Grotius recognizes the point. His discussion of the rights of necessity, treated in some detail below, shows this quite clearly.

The more immediate question, however, is this: If the original use-right served the purpose of private ownership, why was the introduction of private ownership necessary? Why should human beings have abandoned this original condition in which their needs were satisfied? Grotius's answer is that 'This primitive state might have lasted if men had continued in great simplicity or had lived on terms of mutual affection such as rarely appears.'[98] He appears to be of the opinion that, since the 'terms of mutual affection' are so rare, they can be regarded as a historical accident. The norm is a rather limited degree of mutual affection, so it was the abandonment of the lifestyle of primitive simplicity which was the crucial factor in the development of private ownership. The abandonment of the simple life was the abandonment of the self-subsisting life: to satisfy the needs of all subsequently required the fair division of a heterogeneous and diversely produced product. But the normally limited degree of mutual affection, together with the logistical

---

[97] Ibid. 227.
[98] *DJBP* II. 2. ii. 1.

problems created by the spread of human population, made such a
fair division unlikely. This is the kernel of Grotius's account. If we
consider it in a little more detail we can see the use he makes of
history—that is, of sacred history and the classical authors.

For a modern example of the primitive simplicity of human life,
Grotius turns, as do so many of his contemporaries, to 'certain
tribes in America'; but he calls on Tacitus and other classical
authors to demonstrate that such simplicity was the original
condition of human society. Original simplicity displayed a kind of
moral purity, but a purity born of 'ignorance of vices rather than
knowledge of virtue'. For this reason the condition of original
simplicity was not stable: the original state of innocence, having no
knowledge of vice, could not resist it. So, although the state of
innocence had a somewhat idyllic character—'They lived easily on
the fruits which the earth brought forth of its own accord, without
toil'—it inevitably succumbed to a succession of different vices.[99]
Grotius's account of these vices is heavily dependent on the Genesis
account, again with supplementation from ancient authors, especially
Philo and Seneca. He identifies three main sources of corruption—
knowledge of good and evil, rivalry, and ambition. Each of these is
represented in passages from Genesis.

The first corruption, the knowledge of good and evil, is obviously
centred on the story of the Garden of Eden. The symbol for this
knowledge, says Grotius, 'was the tree of knowledge of good and
evil', and this knowledge was itself 'a knowledge of the things of
which it is possible to make at times a good use, at times a bad use'.
This would not appear to exclude much, but Grotius mainly has in
mind the pursuit of frivolous enjoyments. He quotes an ancient
source to this effect: 'to the man who came after the first the craft
and various inventions devised for the advantage of life proved not
to be very useful; for men devoted their talents not so much to the
cultivation of bravery and justice as to devising means of
enjoyment.'[100] The same indulgence in physical pleasures occurred
again 'after the world had been cleansed by the Deluge'. There was
on this occasion 'a passion for pleasure, to which wine ministered'.
This rather surprising remark becomes clear if we remember that,
after disembarking from the Ark with his family, Noah is shamed by

---

[99] All the quotations in this paragraph are from *DJBP* II. 2. ii. 1.
[100] Ibid. 2.

being seen naked after becoming drunk.[101] The wine comes from a vineyard planted by Noah after the Flood, so this event has a distinctively post-diluvian character. Grotius's reference to the 'passion for pleasure, to which wine ministered' is thus not an abstract speculation, but a reference to what is for him a specific event in sacred history.

Similarly, there are references to specific biblical narratives in the accounts of the other two sources of corruption. The second form of corruption is rivalry, which grows into violence. Such rivalry resulted from the division of labour, as is shown by the story of Cain and Abel: 'The most ancient arts, agriculture and grazing, were pursued by the first brothers, not without some interchange of commodities. From the difference in pursuits arose rivalry, and even murder.'[102] This gave rise to an age of violence, an age swept away by the Flood. The principal destroyer of the harmony necessary for maintaining the original state prior to private property, however, was the third form of corruption: 'Harmony . . . was destroyed chiefly by a less ignoble vice, ambition, of which the symbol was the tower of Babel.'[103] How did ambition destroy harmony? Ambition commonly causes rivalries, but Grotius has already dealt with rivalry. He must, therefore, have in mind a different factor. Since he immediately follows the above quotation with the remark that 'presently men divided off countries, and possessed them separately', he appears to be relying on the story of the Tower of Babel. The aim of that story is to explain the division of humanity into separate nations with separate tongues, which through loss of understanding makes the avoidance of conflict so much harder. The division into nations and tongues, since it is a source of conflict, is understood as a curse on the human condition, and the human ambition to achieve divinity is seen as the cause of divine punishment.[104] In this way ambition can be seen as a separate cause of loss of harmony through the divine creation of separate nations. In fact, it is only if Grotius is relying on the Babel story that there is reason for treating the separation of humanity into nations as the effect of ambition.

A final indication of the constant background presence of biblical narratives is provided by Grotius's remarks about the further

[101] See Gen. 9: 20 ff.
[103] Ibid. 3.
[102] *DJBP* ii. 2. ii. 2.
[104] Gen. 10: 11.

division of lands after the separation of nations. After the division into countries, he observes,

> there remained among neighbours a common ownership, not of flocks to be sure, but of pasture lands, because the extent of the land was so great, in proportion to the small number of men, that it sufficed without any inconvenience for the use of many . . . Finally, with increase in the number of men as well as of flocks, lands everywhere began to be divided, not as previously by peoples, but by families. Wells, furthermore—a resource particularly necessary in a dry region, one well not sufficing for many— were appropriated by those who had taken possession of them. This is what we are taught in sacred history . . . [105]

Not only do we have here the explicit reference to sacred history; we have also a significant reference to wells. Why should Grotius (writing long before archaeological discoveries in Mesopotamia and the Near East) connect the early history of human beings with arid regions of the world? The natural answer is that once again he has in mind the patriarchal narratives of Genesis. It even seems likely that the division of the land into the separate possessions of families, to which he refers above, is based on the story of Abram and Lot. Genesis tells us that, because their respective flocks had grown so large, there were numerous incidents of friction between their respective servants. Their solution was to divide the land of Canaan into separate western and eastern territories, with the two households restraining themselves within their respective territories. [106] Given the incidental clues (to wells, for example), and the other references to Genesis already discerned, it seems undeniable that Grotius's view, that 'increase in the number of men as well as of flocks' led to the first division of land by families, is based on the story of Abram and Lot. What appears at first sight to be vague or speculative remarks about the early history of human society must be understood to be indirect references to what is for Grotius a historical source—the Book of Genesis. So, when Grotius tells us that his account is 'what we are taught in sacred history', he can be taken at his word: he aims to provide, in outline, an account of those developments in human history which made the primitive system of common ownership impractical.

Grotius's summary of the causes of abandonment of common

---

[105] *DJBP* ii. 2. ii. 3.
[106] Gen. 13.

ownership is thus a summary of the significant events of sacred history (with gaps filled in by philosophers and poets):

From these sources we learn what was the cause on account of which the primitive common ownership, first of movable objects, later also of immovable property, was abandoned. The reason was that men were not content to feed on the spontaneous products of the earth, to dwell in caves, to have the body either naked or clothed with the bark of trees or skins of wild animals, but chose a more refined mode of life; this gave rise to industry, which some applied to one thing, others to another.

Moreover, the gathering of the products of the soil into a common store was hindered first by the remoteness of the places to which men made their way, then by the lack of justice and kindness; in consequence of such a lack the proper fairness in making division was not observed, either in respect to labour or in the consumption of the fruits.[107]

Obviously all the details of this potted history are not simply extracted from Genesis—for example, the problem of remoteness does not seem to be considered there at all—nor from any other single source. But it is important to recognize that Grotius is not making it up, nor saying what must have been. As already pointed out, the refined mode of life has numerous instances in Genesis; the division of labour is the story of Cain and Abel; and the lack of fairness in dividing pasture is the problem resolved in the story of Abram and Lot. He is simply reminding his audience of elements of their own established history of the beginnings of human society, as described in the sacred book devoted to that subject.

The end of common ownership, made necessary by the factors referred to in the above quotation, is not the beginning of private ownership. It is, rather, the beginning of a process which culminates in private ownership. Before private ownership is achieved, the originally undifferentiated use-right in the earth is, as we have seen, transformed by agreement or division into the territories of first, nations, and secondly, households. The development of private ownership is a further stage in a sequence of divisions or agreements. Thus the factors which lead to the abandonment of common ownership are the same general factors which lead to the establishment of private ownership (even though these are quite distinct events):

---

[107] *DJBP* II. 2. ii. 4.

At the same time we learn how things became subject to private ownership. This happened not by a mere act of will, for one could not know what things another wished to have, in order to abstain from them—and besides several might desire the same thing—but rather by a kind of agreement, either expressed, as by a division, or implied, as by occupation. In fact, as soon as community ownership was abandoned, and as yet no division had been made, it is to be supposed that all agreed, that whatever each one had taken possession of should be his property.[108]

The problems of sharing out a common stock ('the lack of justice and kindness') eventually make even the more restricted forms of common ownership—those which arise from the early divisions of the earth into the property of peoples or families—unmanageable. The simple abandonment of such sharing creates a form of private possession: every man now provides only for his own, principally by being left in possession of flocks or land which no longer produce common goods. If this original private possession is allowed to continue to exist (i.e. is not incorporated into a new collective possession), then it can only be regarded as a private *occupation*. To allow it to remain in private possession is to recognize, or tacitly to agree to, the legitimacy of such possession, and thus to recognize it as private property through occupation. This is why Grotius speaks of occupation as implied agreement, and why he says that 'as soon as community ownership was abandoned', but where no express division had been made, 'it is to be supposed that all agreed' that private possessions should be regarded as private property. In modern terms, Grotius's position is that, at least in cases of this sort, there is no morally relevant difference between acts and omissions. To fail to object to a situation is tacitly to accept it. The collapse of a system of sharing, actively or passively accepted by the concerned parties, is the beginning of private ownership. To establish private ownership as a socially recognized rule, an express agreement is perhaps the norm, but passive acceptance of a state of affairs is itself to be regarded (can only be regarded) as a public act of acceptance.

So for Grotius the fact or otherwise of an explicit original agreement or contract is of little importance. Private property arises in a series of steps, steps which may or may not involve explicit agreements. It is no doubt preferable to have explicit agreements wherever possible, since these more easily and more emphatically

---

[108] *DJBP* II. 2. ii. 5.

satisfy the requirement that a publicly recognized act has occurred; nevertheless omissions are to be regarded as acts of forbearing or abstaining, thus exhibiting the necessary public character, and thus showing the fact of agreement, even without an explicit act.

Grotius's unconcern about whether explicit agreements occurred reflects not only his treatment of omissions as effectively equivalent to actions, but two other factors as well. The first is perhaps the more theoretically significant: it is the fact that the *suum* implies an original use-right, and 'the enjoyment of this universal right then served the purpose of private ownership'. Or, to put it another way, private property stands in no *special* need of justification, since it is a social institution developed to serve the same purpose as the necessary purpose served by the universal original use-right. In the light of this perspective, *how* property comes about can be regarded as a matter of only moderate importance: what matters is just that it comes about as a natural response to circumstances generated when human beings abandoned their original life of primitive simplicity.

The second factor is his straightforward belief that the development of property was in fact a process involving a number of distinct events, some of which involved explicit agreements while others did not. The abandonment of primitive simplicity was, as we have seen, the simple seduction of human beings by tempting pleasures of a (not initially recognized) vicious character. The development of the division of labour, as indicated in the story of Cain and Abel, was, it seems, a matter of rivalry between the first brothers. The division and scattering of human beings into separate peoples was, as the story of the Tower of Babel shows, the consequence of excessive human ambition. All these are important elements in the story of the development of property, but none of them involves explicit agreements. They all indicate significant but not intended developments. The archetypal division of the land according to families rather than nations, however, is contained in the story of Abram's and Lot's division of the land of Canaan, and this is a specific agreement. So, for Grotius, the actual history of the development of property involves both explicit agreements and tacit acceptances of established fact. As already observed, he is inclined to identify natural history with actual history; and when the sources of his history are sacred books this tendency is certainly not discouraged. The combination of these two factors, then—the purpose of property and its actual history—leads him to regard the role of explicit agreements as an indifferent part of the natural history of property. The battles to be fought over this issue by subsequent philosophers are here not even imagined.

The important matter for Grotius in *De Jure Belli ac Pacis* is, as it was in *Mare Liberum*, that 'the transition to the present distinction of ownerships did not come violently, but gradually, nature herself pointing out the way'.[109] Whether this transition was principally or even crucially a matter of explicit agreements is rather beside the point. What matters is that property relations have developed over time because such changes as were accepted were so accepted (tacitly or explicitly) because they were recognized to be in accord with the purposes of the original use-right: to secure effectively the preservation of human beings. The fact of their acceptance is important principally, it seems, because such acceptance is necessary if the history of the development of property is to be a peaceful, not a violent, process.

It is also worth noting at this point what may be an important difference in doctrine between *Mare Liberum* and *De Jure Belli ac Pacis*. In the earlier work, nature points the way to private ownership in a stronger sense than that to which the later work is committed. The argument of *Mare Liberum* is that the exercise of the original use-right, by using up consumable goods and thereby effectively excluding others from likewise using them, implies that 'a certain form of private ownership was inseparable from use'.[110] On this account, the largest role that can be accorded an explicit original agreement concerning consumables is the mere rubber-stamping of a natural *fait accompli*. In the later work, however, Grotius says only that the original use-right and later private property serve the same purpose.[111] This allows a larger role for agreements: they must be constrained by the necessary purpose, but need not be a mere rubber-stamp. It is unclear, however, whether this represents a tension between the two works: it may be only that the later work is (innocently) silent on one feature of the original human state of primitive simplicity.

---

[109] *ML* 24; cf. *DJPC* 228: 'the present-day concept of distinctions in ownership was the result, not of any sudden transition, but of a gradual process whose initial steps were taken under the guidance of nature herself.'

[110] *DJPC* 228.

[111] *DJBP* ii. 2. ii. 1.

This completes the examination of Grotius's account of the rise of property. No treatment of his views on property would be complete, however, if it failed to show how the original use-right, which 'served the purpose of private ownership', and thus out of which the institution of property grew, also operates to constrain private ownership in particular circumstances. Private ownership, being a set of extensions to the *suum*, cannot justifiably conflict with the original use-right implied by the *suum*. By excluding all but the owner from free enjoyment of its product, however, systems of property will, if applied indiscriminately, exclude even those in dire necessity. The use-right to the fruits of the earth possessed by those in dire need would therefore be denied in such cases. This is to deny the natural purpose of private ownership (the preservation of human beings in sophisticated societies), so such a situation cannot be tolerated. The way of protecting the original use-right, and thereby the purpose of private ownership, is achieved in modern or developed societies through the recognition of a *right of necessity*.

For Grotius, the right of necessity takes two forms: 'the right to use things which have become the property of another';[112] and 'the right to such acts as human life requires'.[113] Of the two, the former is the more important, since, unlike the latter (which Grotius seems to understand as a right to trade in necessities), it is 'a question of what may be done against the will of an owner'.[114] So we shall turn first to consider this most important right of necessity.

Grotius introduces the problem by asking 'whether men in general possess any right over things which have already become the property of another'. He is well aware that this may seem an odd question to ask, but attributes its apparent oddity to a misunderstanding of the purpose which private property was intended to serve:

Some perchance may think it strange that this question should be raised, since the right of private ownership seems completely to have absorbed the right which had its origin in a state of community of property. Such, however, is not the case. We must, in fact, consider what the intention was of those who first introduced individual ownership; and we are forced to believe that it was their intention to depart as little as possible from natural equity. For as in this sense even written laws are to be interpreted, much

---

[112] Ibid. vi; discussed ibid. vi–xvii incl.
[113] Ibid. xviii.; discussed ibid. xviii–xxiv incl.
[114] Ibid. xviii.

more should such a point of view prevail in the interpretation of usages which are not held to exact statement by the limitations of a written form.[115]

As Richard Tuck observes, Grotius employs this appeal to the original intentions of the founding fathers on a number of occasions.[116] Nevertheless it is potentially misleading to describe the argument, as Tuck does, as an appeal to 'interpretive charity'.[117] It is better understood as a reminder—to recognize the problem which the introduction of property was designed to solve, and which therefore supplies the *natural limits* of the right of property.[118] It is not simply that we should *assume* that the founding fathers had the best or most appropriate intentions; rather we are *forced* to believe 'that it was their intention to depart as little as possible from natural equity'. And, because natural equity implies the original universal use-right, this right can never be denied. From understanding the point of first introducing private property, 'it follows . . . that in direst need the primitive right of user revives, as if community of ownership had remained, since in respect to all human laws—the law of ownership included—supreme necessity seems to have been excepted'.[119] After noting that this principle in favour of necessity is recognized 'even among the theologians'—most notably by Aquinas[120]—Grotius adds:

The reason . . . is not, as some allege, that the owner of a thing is bound by the rule of love to give to him who lacks; it is, rather, that all things seem to have been distributed to individual owners with a benign reservation in favour of the primitive right.[121]

He needs to stress this because, by allowing the right of necessity to use what belongs to another, he may seem to be requiring that there exists a general duty of charity; that the welfare of others is our

---

[115] *DJBP* II. 2. vi. 1.

[116] See Tuck, *Natural Rights Theories*, 79–80.

[117] The term is borrowed from Quine, as Tuck acknowledges, *Natural Rights Theories*, 80 n.

[118] It appears that Tuck is himself the first victim of the misleading potential of his own terminology. At least, this is so if we can apply his position here to a passage he treats 'similarly' to the one quoted. He says of that passage: 'In principle, Grotius was arguing, all our rights *could* be renounced; but interpretive charity requires that we assume that all were not *in fact* renounced' (ibid. 80). Rather, Grotius's view is that all our rights could not be renounced 'without injustice' (see *DJBP* I. 2. i. 5), or without doing violence to nature by ignoring the way she points out (see *ML* 24).

[119] *DJBP* II. 2. vi. 2.

[120] See *Summa Theologica*, II–II, Q. 66, A. 7; *Thomas Aquinas*, ed. Bigongiari, 138.

[121] *DJBP* II. 2. vi. 4.

necessary concern. But he has already denied just this: 'It is not . . . contrary to the nature of society to look out for oneself and advance one's own interests, provided the rights of others are not infringed.'[122]

The right of necessity to use things belonging to another is thus no more than a limit on the natural extent of property, since it captures those cases where the private owner's advancing of his own interests infringes the rights of another. It is not to impose on the property holder a general duty to secure the welfare of the less fortunate. Grotius thus rejects the traditional adage that 'property has its duties'; an adage which seems to capture the most humane elements of the medieval world. Grotius's adage, if we are to treat it so, would not be without humane effect, but it would indicate nevertheless a less interdependent social world: property has its *limits*. This is not to suggest that he errs in calling the limit to property 'a benign reservation'. It does guarantee that no one need be faced with the dilemma: if not starvation, then crime. Since it is a principle which operates only in situations of direst need, he stresses that it does not apply when the need is not genuinely serious; when, as he puts it, the necessity is avoidable.[123] Further, it does not entitle the needy to take from another in equal need, and it is to be treated as a debt to be repaid if possible—it is not the simple abolition of the property-holder's right.[124]

At this point Grotius also discusses another use-right which cannot be denied by the owner of property, even though it involves no necessity. This is the right of 'innocent use', and holds wherever using the property of another 'involves no detriment to the owner'.[125] It is a general right, and covers such important cases as

[122] Ibid. I. 2. i. 6.
[123] Ibid. II. 2. vii. This principle provides a clue to why the right of necessity is steadily eclipsed in subsequent theories which allocate a prominent position to an optimistic political economy. The process is clearly under way in the writings of both Pufendorf and Locke, but the eclipse is virtually complete in the work of Hume and Adam Smith, at least with respect to the question of physical survival. From the late 17th cent., not the least of the perceived virtues of commercial society was its capacity to put an end to economic necessity. On the other hand, Smith recognizes that it creates new kinds of spiritual necessity, and so he becomes a strong advocate of public education. For a discussion of these issues, see D. Winch, *Adam Smith's Politics* (Cambridge: Cambridge University Press, 1978), esp. 72–80, 113–20.
[124] *DJBP* II. 2. viii–ix.
[125] Ibid. xi. This right can be regarded as the converse of the rights of property which arise naturally wherever using results in using up. If there is no using up, then neither is there ground for exclusive use.

the right to use running water, and the right of passage over land and rivers.[126] Like the right of necessity, this right can also be regarded as 'a benign reservation in favour of the primitive right', since all such innocent uses are implied by the original use-right.

The second right of necessity is the right to such acts as human life requires. Grotius appears to mean by this a right to engage in trade for the purpose of satisfying needs. It concerns 'acts indispensable for the obtaining of the things without which life cannot be comfortably lived'. However, it does not require the same degree of necessity as the right to use things belonging to another, since in this case 'it is not . . . a question of what may be done against the will of an owner, but rather of the mode of acquiring things with the consent of those to whom they belong'. Nevertheless, necessity is not weakened too much, since it remains true that 'we are here dealing not with things which are superfluous and ministrant to pleasures only, but with things which life requires, as food, clothing, and medicines'.[127] Most conspicuously, this general right includes the right to buy necessary goods, and at a fair price.[128] Surprisingly, it 'does not oblige a man to sell what belongs to him', since 'every one is free to decide what he will or will not acquire'[129]—and, presumably, part with. The right to buy necessary goods cannot, however, oblige anyone to sell; it is 'not . . . a question of what may be done against the will of an owner'. Presumably, Grotius regards the profit to be gained from sale to be a sufficient consideration in these cases. The point of the right, then, seems to be simply to protect trade in necessities. It is directed against political authorities who try to restrict such trade, and is not directly an attempt to protect those in dire necessity. Nevertheless it is connected to necessity: it is not a right to free trade *per se*, only a right to free trade in necessary goods, and to pay a fair price for them. It is not a right to economic *laissez-faire*.

For our purposes, the right to acts that human life requires can be set aside. One important point, however, needs to be made about the principal right of necessity, the right to use things belonging to another where necessity requires: this right makes one important form of slavery, self-enslavement because of poverty, quite unnecessary. Grotius allows that rights are transferable, and this prevents him from disallowing self-enslavement out of hand; that is,

[126] *DJBP* II. 2. xii–xiii.
[127] Ibid. xviii.   [128] Ibid. xix.   [129] Ibid. xx.

it prevents him from treating self-enslavement as a necessarily unjust act, as Locke was later to do. This does not mean (*pace* Rousseau) that he does not care about slavery. He condemns self-enslavement as a base act: 'The basest form of voluntary subjection is that by which a man gives himself into complete slavery, as those among the Germans who staked their liberty on the last throw of the dice.'[130] Nevertheless, he is forced to regard it as an unfortunate, but not an impossible act. It is not an impossible act principally because, for him, it does not violate the fundamental right of self-preservation. In a rather sympathetic assessment of slavery, he says

That is complete slavery which owes lifelong service in return for nourishment and other necessaries of life; and if the condition is thus accepted within natural limits it contains no element of undue severity. For the lasting obligation to labour is repaid with *a lasting certainty of support*, which often those do not have who work for hire by day.[131]

Grotius's account is inadequate because it overlooks a crucial fact: although the slave has a lasting claim of support, he or she has absolutely no certainty that support will in fact be forthcoming. If the master chooses to ignore his side of the relation, the slave's dependent condition leaves no comeback. Grotius recognizes this fact in the section immediately following that quoted above, but without, apparently, seeing the problems it causes for his account of the slave's situation. To answer the question, 'To what extent the right of life and death may be said to exist in the right over slaves', he says:

Masters do not have the right of life and death (I am speaking of complete moral justice) over their slaves. No man can rightly kill a man unless the latter has committed a capital crime. But according to the laws of some peoples the master who has killed a slave for any reason whatsoever goes unpunished.[132]

The master, in other words, although not in possession of what is 'properly called a right', nevertheless has impunity in action. Here we can see clearly why, although Grotius does not 'establish right by fact' as Rousseau later claimed,[133] he nevertheless earned the latter's polemics. (If impunity in action can extend to power over the lives of others, what could possibly be gained by having a *right*?)

---

[130] Ibid. 5. xxvii. 1. [131] Ibid. xxvii. 2 (emphasis added).
[132] Ibid. xxviii. [133] Rousseau, *On The Social Contract*, 1. 2. 47.

The fact is that, because of the master's impunity in action, the slave not only has no 'certainty of support', but is in a situation in which self-preservation is constantly under threat. The master's impunity of action is a latent denial of the compatibility of the institution of slavery with the right of self-preservation.

Grotius accepts that the most powerful cause of acts of self-enslavement is the very necessity which he has recognized as founding a right to the use of things belonging to others. Considering the question whether enslaved parents are allowed to sell their children into slavery, he says:

Surely, if there were no other method of bringing up the children, the parents could adjudge to slavery, along with themselves, the offspring liable to be born to them, since under such conditions parents are allowed to sell children born free.

But since this right derives its origin from necessity only, without such necessity the parents do not have the right to enslave their children to any one.[134]

But if without such necessity the parents lack the right to enslave the children, while under conditions of necessity they have an escape-valve, since they then have the right of necessity to use things belonging to others, how can self-enslavement or the enslavement of one's children ever be other than an unnecessary and unjust act? The right of necessity makes such enslavement unnecessary or avoidable; the insecurity of the right of self-preservation under slavery makes enslavement a deliberate exposure to the possibility of injury. Although Grotius is not recklessly insensitive to the vulnerability of slaves—he does allow that, 'if the cruelty of the master is excessive, even those slaves who have voluntarily given themselves into slavery can take counsel for their welfare by flight'[135]—his concessions are clearly inadequate. No slave has protection against the arbitrary violence of the master, yet no enslavement through necessity is ever reasonable. In allowing enslavement through necessity he has emptied the right of necessity to use things belonging to others of its principal significance. Conversely, if the right of necessity to use things is treated seriously (and if the right to such acts as life requires is expanded to include the right to those actions which safeguard one's future), then the right of necessity will serve to bar any form of slavery. This insight

---

[134] *DJBP* II. 5. xxix. 1–2.   [135] Ibid. 2.

informs the position Locke comes to develop in the *Two Treatises of Government*.

This chapter has not attempted a complete account of the intellectual corpus Grotius bequeathed to posterity. The aim has been, rather, to identify some main themes which are taken up in various ways by his intellectual successors, and also to rebut a common misunderstanding of his method. The misunderstanding concerns the nature of his rationalism, and hence of the role of history in his thought. Although he describes the law of nature as 'a dictate of right reason', he does not take this to imply the freedom to determine the nature of human laws wholly by abstract deduction. Rather, reason is a tool human beings use in specific situations and thus is the guiding principle behind necessary (unavoidable) historical developments. Reason is a historical force, perceived historically. It was also pointed out that, although not reducible to expediency, the law of nature 'has the reinforcement of expediency'. Unqualified contrasts between natural law theories and theories which stress the role of utility are thus simplistic; natural law theories typically allow a significant place for utility.[136]

The main themes discussed here, which Grotius's successors take up in various ways, can be summed up as follows. Firstly, natural law is founded on the natural 'sociableness' of human beings. The *limited* sociability implicit in this notion of sociableness is shown clearly by his remark that 'it is not . . . contrary to the nature of society to look out for oneself and advance one's own interests,

---

[136] The most pronounced ex. of this is the explicitly utilitarian natural law theory of Richard Cumberland in his *De Legibus Naturae*. The argument of this ch. implies that Cumberland's theory cannot be regarded as a deviation from 'authentic' natural law. In the next ch. it will be shown that Pufendorf's account of natural law connects it even more tightly with utility than does Grotius's. The increasingly explicit role played by utility in British moral philosophy does indicate a shift away from Grotius's doctrine of rights, but there is more to Grotius (and also to Pufendorf in particular and modern natural law in general) than a theory of rights. So it does not follow that 'what was presented as natural jurisprudence [in Britain] was in fact almost from the outset a utilitarianism in disguise', as Thomas Mautner argues ('Pufendorf and 18th-century Scottish Philosophy', in id. *Samuel von Pufendorf 1632–1982: Ett rättshistoriskt symposium i Lund* (Lund: Bloms Boktryckeri, 1986), 130). Mautner is, however, quite right to see the emphasis on utility as a British, not merely English, phenomenon, and this fact vitiates Alasdair MacIntyre's attempt to show a fundamental divide between English and Scottish modes of social thought in the *18th* cent. (17th-cent. Scotland may be a different matter) in *Whose Justice? Which Rationality?* (London: Duckworth, 1988), esp. chs. 13–15.

provided the rights of others are not infringed'; and this limited sociability is behind his distinction between two sorts of moral qualities, perfect and imperfect. The former are 'legal rights strictly so called', whereas the latter are 'aptitudes', and are not enforceable. Secondly, he stresses that the original community of possession differed quite significantly from the modern notion of common ownership. Thirdly, and most importantly, private property is a late stage in a process of extensions to the *suum* by adapting and developing the original use-right. For this reason property is, in the final analysis, a system designed for the better or more effective preservation of human beings, and so cannot frustrate the use-rights of the needy. Systems of property thus have a necessary limit: they must recognize a right of necessity to use things belonging to others.

Rather little has been said about Grotius's doctrine of rights. For the purposes of this study, the important matter is that property, being a species of right, is for Grotius a power to use things without injustice. By failing to see that this power cannot include the use of other persons (as slaves) without emptying of all significance the fundamental right of self-preservation (and its corollary, the right of necessity), Grotius is led to accept the naturalness of the institution of slavery. Hobbes's acceptance of this doctrine guaranteed the centrality of this issue to later seventeenth-century political theory. Most explicitly in John Locke, the question of the possibility of slavery, given natural property, is of crucial theoretical significance.

2

Samuel Pufendorf

1. MORAL SCIENCE AND THE ELEMENTS OF LAW

If Grotius's star shines only feebly in the modern philosophical firmament, that of Samuel Pufendorf (1632–94) not uncharacteristically suffers a total eclipse.[1] In the latter stages of the seventeenth century, however, things were vastly different. Pufendorf was then the best known and, by and large, the most respected, writer on natural law, not least because he was recognized as an authoritative interpreter and defender of Grotius. A Saxon, educated at Leipzig and Jena, Pufendorf's first work on natural law, *Elementa Jurisprudentiae Universalis* (1660), owed its genesis to war between Sweden and Denmark. Employed at the time as tutor to the family of a Swedish minister at the Danish court, he was imprisoned following the outbreak of hostilities, and wrote the *Elementa* during his incarceration. The work was favourably received, particularly because of its Grotian character, and gained him academic appointments first at the University of Heidelberg, and later at Lund. Following his appointment to a chair in international law at Lund in 1670, Pufendorf published the works on which his subsequent fame depended. His main work, the massive *De Jure Naturae et Gentium* (1672), was described by Locke as 'the best book of that kind', better even than Grotius's;[2] and the short textbook based on it, *De Officio Hominis et Civis* (1673), was very widely used in courses on natural jurisprudence in the universities of Europe, and provided a model for many subsequent such books. Thus Francis Hutcheson, for example, explicitly

---

[1] e.g. C. B. Macpherson's *The Political Theory of Possessive Individualism: Hobbes to Locke* (Oxford: Clarendon Press, 1962): Grotius receives only a dismissive footnote, but Pufendorf is not mentioned at all, even though Macpherson aims to uncover the inner meaning of 17th-cent. thought.

[2] Quoted by Peter Laslett, in his editorial introd. to J. Locke, *Two Treatises of Government* (Cambridge: Cambridge University Press, 2nd edn., 1967), 74. The remark comes from Locke's *Thoughts concerning Reading and Study*, in *Works* (1801), iii. 272.

acknowledges his debt to Pufendorf in the preface to his own student textbook, *A Short Introduction to Moral Philosophy*, written over seventy years later.[3] The structural dependence of Hutcheson's textbook on *De Officio* can readily be discerned by a chapter-by-chapter comparison.

Despite such widespread acceptance, respect for Pufendorf was not universal. Possibly his sharpest critic was Leibniz, who dismissed him as 'a poor jurist and a worse philosopher'.[4] This is worth noting, not merely for the sake of recognizing the existence of a dissenting voice, but because an examination of Leibniz's main criticism helps to reveal an important and influential feature of Pufendorf's account of natural law. Prior to carrying out this task, however, some remarks on the nature of Pufendorf's enterprise are in order.

In common with many other early modern moral philosophers, Pufendorf's aim is to establish a science of morals. This description may mislead: it does not mean a body of factual knowledge, but a *systematic* body of knowledge. A science of morals in this sense seeks not only to uncover true moral principles, but necessarily true principles established by demonstration. It establishes a body of certain, demonstrable, moral truths. Thus Pufendorf speaks not only of 'the certainty of moral sciences', he also claims that 'demonstration is possible . . . in that moral science which treats of the goodness and evil of human actions'.[5] However, there is an important qualification to this claim, as will be shown below.

In treating moral science as a matter of systematic, demonstrative knowledge, Pufendorf employs the common seventeenth-century notion of *scientia*, or systematic knowledge. This Latin term was translated into English as 'science', and can be illustrated by a passage in Hobbes's *Leviathan*. In a short but important chapter, 'Of the Several Subjects of Knowledge', Hobbes distinguishes

---

[3] F. Hutcheson, *A Short Introduction to Moral Philosophy* (1747); repr. in *Collected Works* (Hildesheim: Olms, 1969), iv., p. i. Hutcheson includes Pufendorf in a select group of moderns who are fit to be ranked alongside Cicero and Aristotle.

[4] Quoted, from a letter of 1709, in L. Krieger, *The Politics of Discretion* (Chicago: University of Chicago Press, 1965), 1. Jean Barbeyrac, Pufendorf's French trans. (and influential contemporary interpreter), defended Pufendorf against Leibniz's criticisms in editorial n. to his trans. of *De Officio*. See *The Political Writings of Leibniz*, trans. and ed. P. Riley (Cambridge: Cambridge University Press, 1972).

[5] S. Pufendorf, *De Jure Naturae et Gentium Libri Octo* (1672) (hereafter *DJNG*), trans. C. H. and W. A. Oldfather (New York: Oceana Publications; London: Wildby and Sons, 1964), Bk. 1, ch. 3 (introd. headings).

knowledge of fact from knowledge of relations. The latter kind of knowledge is called 'Science', he says, adding 'this is the Knowledge required in a Philosopher; that is to say, of him that pretends to Reasoning'.[6] Pufendorf's aim is to provide this kind of knowledge.

Commonly, seventeenth-century ambitions of this kind point to the desire to emulate the method of geometry or mathematics, and Pufendorf is no exception. He was greatly impressed by that method, associating it with Descartes in particular, and with 'the new way of philosophy' in general; and describes it at one point as a matter of 'deducing everything from fixed principles and hypotheses through the mathematical mode of demonstration'.[7] His attempts to apply the method, however, indicate a progressive departure from it, or at least from any strict adherence to it. Thus the *Elementa* displays as concerted an attempt to produce a work based on the mathematical method as the subject-matter would permit: it begins with definitions and 'principles', and attempts to deduce necessarily true conclusions. For the discipline of law, the relevant principles are of three kinds—axioms derived from metaphysics, or primary philosophy; axioms based on rational intuitions; and 'experimental' principles or observations. From these principles come 'propositions', and even, in some cases, a fourth set of judgements lacking the certainty of the preceding principles. The method is mirrored in the structure of the *Elementa*: it is divided into two parts, the first dealing with definitions, the second with rational and experimental principles (axioms and observations).[8]

In *De Jure Naturae et Gentium*, however, this method is 'less explicit and less intrusive', as Krieger puts it.[9] The quasi-mathematical format has disappeared, and, although Pufendorf holds to the position that the moral sciences are indeed sciences, and thus capable of certainty, he allows a significant scope for uncertainty. Nevertheless, that a moral science is capable of certainty is implicit in the term itself, for science is 'that which we seek by means of demonstration, that is, a certain and a pure knowledge, in every way and at all times constant and free from error'.[10] Moral science manifests this certainty because

---

[6] T. Hobbes, *Leviathan*, ed. C. B. Macpherson (Harmondsworth: Penguin Books, 1968), Pt. 1, ch. 9, pp. 147–8.
[7] Quoted by Krieger, *Politics of Discretion*, 51.
[8] See ibid. 51–2.
[9] Ibid. 53.   [10] *DJNG* 1. 2. 3.

that knowledge, which considers what is upright and what is base in human actions, the principal portion of which we have undertaken to present, rests entirely upon grounds so secure, that from it can be deduced genuine demonstrations which are capable of producing a solid science. So certainly can its conclusions be derived from distinct principles, that no further ground is left for doubt.[11]

There are, however, two main aspects of moral science, of which this passage describes only one—'what is upright and what is base in human actions', that which 'concerns the rectitude of human actions in their order according to laws'.[12] This branch of moral science gives certain knowledge ('no further ground is left for doubt'), but the second branch does not. It has a more explicitly practical flavour: it 'concerns the successful management of one's own actions and those of others, with an eye to the security and welfare primarily of the public'.[13] Pufendorf recognizes that this branch of moral science is a matter of prudence, as defined by Aristotle. He approvingly quotes Aristotle's definition in the *Nicomachean Ethics* ('a true rational and practical state of mind in the field of human good and evil')[14] and in the same spirit quotes some features of Aristotle's account of the prudent man. He then sums up, reverting to his own terminology: the prudent man bases his conclusions concerning appropriate behaviour 'upon axioms drawn from a keen observation and comparison of the customs of men and the events of human history'. Pufendorf clearly accepts that the prudent man gains moral knowledge from these axioms, but because of their general reliability. They are *not* certain: 'These axioms, however, do not appear to be so firm that infallible demonstrations can be deduced from them'. Several factors contribute to the fallibility of these axioms. One is particularly relevant: the natural limits of human knowledge. These limits contribute to fallibility because 'the wit of man often goes astray in the application of those axioms, because of unforeseen events which suddenly upset all calculations'. For this and other reasons, he concludes: 'Therefore those who are engaged in the conduct of affairs do not endeavour to draw their plans to the nicety of demonstrations, but when they have used the

---

[11] *DJNG* I. 2. 4.
[12] Ibid.   [13] Ibid.
[14] Aristotle, *Nicomachean Ethics*, VI. v; quoted ibid. (The trans. given in the text of *DJNG* is that of Welldon. Cf. the 'List of Classical Authors and Translations,' *DJNG* 1369.

wisest circumspection and a kind of divination, as it were, they leave the outcome in the hands of fate.'[15]

If, as seems likely, Pufendorf's expression 'a kind of divination' means no more than a kind of predicting, or perhaps (more weakly) conjecturing, then his account of conduct based on circumspection plus divination—a process which will 'leave the outcome in the hands of fate'—exhibits some marked similarities with Locke's account of the central importance of probability, and therefore also of judgement, in practical affairs. For Locke also identifies the natural limits of our knowledge as an important constraint on our moral knowledge, forcing us to rely on probabilities:

Therefore as God has set some Things in broad day-light; as he has given us some certain Knowledge, though limited to a few Things . . . So in the greatest part of our Concernment, he has afforded us only the twilight, as I may so say, of *Probability*, suitable, I presume, to the State of Mediocrity and Probationership, he has been pleased to place us in here.[16]

Probabilities are themselves calculated by the faculty of judgement, 'which God has given Man to supply the want of clear and certain Knowledge in Cases where that cannot be had'.[17]

So not only do both Pufendorf and Locke accept the existence of demonstrable moral knowledge, they also both accept that practical knowledge is nevertheless to a significant degree uncertain, being a matter of circumspection and divination (or judgement of probabilities). What is more, the latter claim is for both a qualification of the former: there is certainty in practical affairs, but not in *all* practical affairs. Further similarities will be pointed out below, particularly on the nature of natural laws, including the question of innateness. And if, as is not unlikely, Pufendorf's views exercised some influence on the development of Locke's own, then the latter's enthusiasm for *De Jure Naturae et Gentium* is unsurprising.

[15] *DJNG* I. 2. 4. He goes on to quote Aristotle again: 'It is right, therefore, to pay no less attention to the undemonstrated assertions and opinions of such persons as are experienced or advanced in years or prudent, than to their demonstrations; for their experienced eye gives them the power of correct vision' (*Nicomachean Ethics*, VI. xi, Welldon trans.). Aristotle's point is rather stronger than Pufendorf's (more like Grotius's defence of the a posteriori method, in fact): he claims that prudence or experience gives *correct* vision, whereas Pufendorf holds only that it gives generally reliable, but fallible, conclusions.

[16] J. Locke, *An Essay concerning Human Understanding* (1690), ed. P. H. Nidditch (Oxford: Clarendon Press, 1975), IV. 14. 2.

[17] Ibid. 3.

Leibniz's verdict stands in stark contrast. His most complete discussion of Pufendorf's views occurs in a short work, originally written in the form of a letter, entitled 'Opinion on the Principles of Pufendorf',[18] in which he examines Pufendorf's shorter work, *De Officio Hominis et Civis*. He concludes that, despite its author being 'a man long renowned for his merit',[19] Pufendorf's work, 'although it is not to be despised, has nonetheless need of many corrections in its very principles'.[20] In part, Leibniz's objections to Pufendorf can be seen as part of a wider dispute. The latter's account of the foundations of natural law partly reflects the metaphysical opinions of Descartes, and, given Leibniz's opposition to Descartes's view on the relationship between the world and its creator, it is not surprising that Pufendorf's application of these views should meet similar opposition.

The objection most appropriately considered here occurs in the final two sections of Leibniz's 'Opinion'. There, Leibniz charges that Pufendorf fails to give a defensible account of the efficient cause of the law of nature. He notes that Pufendorf defines law as 'a command by which the superior obliges the subject to conform his actions to what the law itself requires'.[21] From this it follows that 'all law is prescribed by a superior',[22] and thus the state of nature, because it is a state without superiors, is a state governed by no (natural) law. In addition, this account of law appears to provide no basis for criticizing or opposing the actions that superiors in fact prescribe: 'Now, then, will he who is invested with the supreme power do nothing against justice if he proceed tyrannically against his subjects; who arbitrarily despoils his subjects . . . who makes war on others without cause?'[23] In Leibniz's eyes, then, Pufendorf's account of law, by basing law and thus justice on the command of a superior, renders the idea of justice empty. Even tyrannical acts, because they proceed from the prescription of a superior, will become lawful or just acts. Neither can Pufendorf solve this problem by calling on the divine superior, because

---

[18] G. W. von Leibniz, 'Opinion on the Principles of Pufendorf' (1706); in *The Political Writings of Leibniz*, trans. and ed. Riley, 64–75.

[19] Ibid. 65.

[20] Ibid. 75.

[21] S. Pufendorf, *De Officio Hominis et Civis Juxta Legem Naturalem Libri Duo* (1673), trans. F. S. Moore (New York: Oxford University Press, 1927), I. 2. 2; quoted in *The Political Writings of Leibniz*, trans. and ed. Riley, 70.

[22] *The Political Writings of Leibniz*, ibid.   [23] Ibid.

one must pay attention to this fact: that God is praised because he is just. There must be, then, a certain justice—or rather a supreme justice—in God, even though no one is superior to him . . . Neither the norm of conduct itself, nor the essence of the just, depends on his free decision, but rather on eternal truths, *objects of the divine intellect*, which constitute, so to speak, the essence of divinity itself . . . And, indeed, justice follows certain rules of equality and of proportion [which are] no less founded in the immutable nature of things, and in the divine ideas, than are the principles of arithmetic and geometry.[24]

In this passage Leibniz's criticism of Pufendorf depends on a Platonic picture of the relationship between God and the creation. In this respect his views are comparable to Grotius and Suárez, so it comes as no surprise to see him approvingly refer to Grotius's *etiamsi daremus* passage: 'Grotius justly observed . . . that there would be a natural obligation even on the hypothesis—which is impossible—that God does not exist, or if one but left the divine existence out of consideration.'[25] So Leibniz's opposition to Pufendorf on this issue reflects a standpoint very similar to Grotius's. Given, however, that Pufendorf explicitly rejects Grotius's position,[26] the proper evaluation of both Pufendorf and his opponents would require a consideration of not merely Pufendorf's but also other contemporary reasons for dissatisfaction with the Platonic picture. Settling the issue would therefore require a close examination of the whole seventeenth-century controversy between rationalists and voluntarists. Since that is far too large a task to tackle here, perhaps it is best to avoid it completely, and to settle with the observation that Pufendorf is not without powerful allies.

However, it is not this difference alone that prompts Leibniz's criticism. Although Pufendorf here follows the lead of Hobbes and

---

[24] Ibid. 71 (emphasis added).   [25] Ibid.

[26] See *DJNG* II. 3. 4–6, and also I. 2. 6. Briefly, Pufendorf's view is that there is a kind of necessity pertaining to natural law, but that it is a *hypothetical* necessity. It is hypothetical in so far as it is based on the free will of God, who need not have created rational and social creatures such as human beings. It is necessary because, once rational social creatures have been created, the conditions for their well-being have been thereby fixed. So natural law, although based on divine voluntary actions (and thus not eternal), can nevertheless also be described as founded in the social nature of human beings. Having allowed this much, however, it may seem odd that Pufendorf should object to Grotius's *etiamsi daremus* passage. It will be shown that his dissatisfaction reflects the conviction that law must *compel* assent.

Descartes, Leibniz does not, for the same reason, consider them bad philosophers, even though he is just as strict in his opposition to the same or related doctrines in their work. (By such doctrines, Descartes, he says, 'showed how great can be the errors of great men'.)[27] For Leibniz, Pufendorf's failings are compounded by the fact that he not only holds to this 'great error', but also fails to hold to it consistently. He falls into a contradiction because on the one hand 'he makes all juridical obligations derivative from the command of a superior' (the 'great error'), while on the other 'he states that in order that one have a superior it is necessary that they [superiors] possess not only the force [necessary] to exercise coercion, but also that they have a just cause to justify their power over my person'.[28] Pufendorf is thereby committed to holding that 'the justice of the cause is antecedent to this same superior, contrary to what has been asserted'. Leibniz concludes: 'Well, then, if the source of the law is the will of a superior and, inversely, a justifying cause of law is necessary in order to have a superior, a circle is created, than which none was ever more manifest.'[29]

In all this, it must be remembered, Leibniz is considering only Pufendorf's short textbook, *De Officio Hominis et Civis*, and, as long as only this work is taken into account, his criticisms seem perfectly just. However, if we turn to consider Pufendorf's remarks on the nature of law in general in *De Jure Naturae et Gentium*, a different picture emerges. The account provided in the latter work shows that, while Leibniz is quite right in pointing out that Pufendorf appeals to two different factors in explaining law—both power and justice—he is quite wrong to think that hopeless circularity is the result. This is because the latter work shows Pufendorf to hold that law depends for its existence on the conjunction of two different elements. He employs a version of the traditional Aristotelian notion of formal and material causes to describe the two kinds of elements by which laws are constituted.

Laws are, for Pufendorf, moral entities, which means they are a specific kind of attribute given to things, an imposition or addition to physical things or relations by intelligent beings. Moral entities are impositions on the created order of material things.[30]

---

[27] *The Political Writings of Leibniz*, trans. and ed. Riley, 71.
[28] Ibid. 73 (the reference is to *De Officio*, 1. 2. 5).
[29] Ibid. 73–4.   [30] *DJNG* 1. 1. 1–5.

(Pufendorf's account of 'moral entities' thus shows some marked similarities with Locke's account of 'archetype' ideas, in particular of 'mixed modes'.)[31] Laws, as moral entities, have a material element, in that they reflect the created order of material things, and a formal element, which is the imposition itself. For this reason Pufendorf requires of law both the will of a superior, which is necessary for the act of imposition (the formal element), and just reasons for its imposition (reflecting the order of the material element). The reasons for imposition must be *just* reasons because, in considering law, Pufendorf is concerned with explaining 'genuine' law, enactments which are just. An imposition has just reasons when it reinforces or protects the beneficial structure of natural states of affairs. The most important set of just laws are the natural laws. Unlike positive laws, their formal element lies only in the will of the divine superior. The justice of the material element is shown by the fact that, unlike positive law, natural law has a 'necessary agreement . . . with its subjects'. Natural law 'so harmonizes with the natural and social nature of man that the human race can have no wholesome and peaceful social organization without it; in other words, it has a natural benefit and utility from its own continued efficacy for the human race in general.'[32]

Pufendorf's appeal to the twin elements of the will of a superior and the existence of just reasons in his account of law is thus not, *pace* Leibniz, a confusion or vacillation about the efficient cause of law, but an attempt to specify two different kinds of elements, both of which are necessary for the existence of law. It could perhaps be said that, for Pufendorf, the will of a superior, without just reasons, is only coercion; while just reasons, without the will of a superior, are only reasons for law, but not law itself. (They are not *compelling*.) Leibniz's verdict, wholly based as it is on the abbreviated account found in *De Officio*, is thus unjustified. Pufendorf's account is more complex than his critic recognizes; and some of this complexity will be outlined in the next section.

[31] Locke, *Essay*, III. 5, especially III. 5. 12: 'the *Essences* of the *Species* of *mixed Modes* . . . are the creatures of the Understanding, rather than the works of Nature.' Pufendorf similarly refers to moral entities as 'modes' (rather than 'substances') because they 'do not exist of themselves'; and, although 'some modes flow, as it were, from the very nature of the thing itself', moral ideas differ in that they 'are superadded by intelligent agency to physical things and modes' (*DJNG* I. 1. 3). For a further discussion of mixed modes see J. Tully, *A Discourse on Property: John Locke and his Adversaries* (Cambridge: Cambridge University Press, 1980), esp. 16–18, 30–2.
[32] *DJNG* I. 6. 18.

2. THE LAW OF NATURE

Pufendorf parts company with Grotius on the question of the ultimate foundation of the law of nature. The law of nature is not, he says, independent of the divine will. Therefore, neither is it properly to be called 'eternal', since God alone is eternal. It can be called 'eternal' only in contrast to the changeability of positive law.[33] In addition, although it is true that natural law can be correctly described as a 'dictate of right reason',[34] this does not mean that it can have a 'degree of validity' if God is left out of account. This is because 'if these dictates of reason are to have the force of laws, it is necessary to presuppose the existence of God and His providence, whereby all things are governed, and primarily mankind'.[35] God is necessary for law because all law is 'the bidding of a superior'.[36] Obligation, therefore, exists only where there is a superior. There can thus be no natural law in the proper sense if God is left out of account: without a superior there is no 'degree of validity' because there is no obligation.

Pufendorf's position depends on denying the existence of any obligation where there is no law. His reason for holding this is, at least in part, because he denies that reason can of itself create obligations. Reason lacks moral power, or moral effect:

if we consider reason, in so far as it is not imbued with an understanding and sense of law, or a moral norm, it might perhaps be able to permit man the faculty of doing something more expeditiously and adroitly than a beast, and to supply sagacity to his natural powers. But that reason should be able to discover any morality in the actions of a man without reference to a law, is as impossible as for a man born blind to judge between colours.[37]

The impotence of reason, its inability to produce moral effects, is most importantly an inability to create obligations, since obligations are moral effects.[38] This is not to say that reason has no part to play in the formation of obligations: in fact, it has a crucial role. Its importance in Pufendorf's scheme is often concealed by the fact that his notion of a superior is not reducible to mere physical superiority: 'An obligation is properly laid on the mind of man by a superior, that is, by one who has both the strength to threaten some evil against those who resist him, and just reasons why he can demand that the liberty of our will be limited at his pleasure.'[39] Furthermore,

---

[33] *DJNG* I. 2. 6.   [34] Ibid. II. 3. 13, 19.   [35] Ibid. 19.
[36] Ibid. I. 2. 6.   [37] *DJNG* I. 2. 6.
[38] See e.g. ibid. IV. 4. 9.   [39] Ibid. I. 6. 9.

because obligation has these two aspects, we can speak of two kinds of obligation (as long as we remember that obligation proper requires both): thus the threat of evil, because it secures bodily compliance, can be called 'extrinsic' obligation; while the just reasons, because they 'intrinsically affect the conscience of a man', can be called 'intrinsic' obligations.[40]

This account has a great impact on later writers. For example, Francis Hutcheson distinguishes between two senses of obligation, one being 'the inward sense or conscience' (intrinsic), the other being 'a motive of interest superior to all motives on the other side', which motives 'indeed must arise from the laws of an omnipotent being' (extrinsic).[41] As the quoted passage from Pufendorf indicates, however, Hutcheson is mistaken when he goes on to claim that Pufendorf is chiefly concerned only with the latter meaning, that is, with extrinsic obligation.[42] The distinction between the two forms of obligation, and, more generally, the place of the theory of obligation in a complete science of morals, plays an important role in shaping the theories of morality and justice provided by Hutcheson and Hume. Later chapters, by making this explicit, will thereby serve to show one important aspect of Pufendorf's influence on these better-known thinkers.

Of similar importance to the later philosophers is Pufendorf's insistence on the moral inertness of reason. His view is, at bottom, an old one, reflected in Aristotle's view that reason alone cannot move us to action: as he puts it, 'intellect itself . . . moves nothing'.[43] The development this view undergoes in the hands of the 'moral sense' theories of eighteenth-century Scotland is essential for understanding the major motivations of 'moral sense' moral science. If we consider the quoted passage from Pufendorf carefully, we see first of all that reason is inert because it is essentially instrumental: reason can 'permit man the faculty of doing something more expeditiously and adroitly than a beast'. If reason is purely instrumental, then clearly it cannot move us to action, even though it can show us, in given circumstances, how to act. It will be argued below, in the last two chapters, that such an instrumental conception of reason is at the bottom of the 'moral

[40] Ibid. 10.
[41] Hutcheson, *Short Introduction*, 121.   [42] Ibid. 121–2.
[43] Aristotle, *Nicomachean Ethics*, trans. W. D. Ross (Oxford: Oxford University Press, 1980), vi. 2.

sense' school's rejection of reason as the foundation of morals. Secondly, we can see that Pufendorf's closing analogy almost invites a moral sense resolution of the issue. For reason to 'discover any morality,' he says, 'is as impossible as for a man born blind to judge between colours'. As in the physical world, then, where reason is blind without the initial input provided by the physical senses, so in the moral world reason is blind until enlightened by the activity of a prior appropriate form of sensing—moral sensing. This shows how easily the doctrine of moral sense can be grafted on to Pufendorf's account of the inertness of reason.

Pufendorf's second departure from Grotius concerns the location of the laws of nature. Grotius treats the original unwritten laws of nature as innate ideas, but Pufendorf emphatically does not—even though he is prepared to accept the apparently innatist (biblical) terminology which Grotius and many others had employed. (The law is, he allows, 'written in the hearts' of men.[44] In both doctrine and language he is thus a precursor of Locke, whose *Essay concerning Human Understanding* has usually been regarded as the *locus classicus* of the attack on innate ideas.) If we consider Pufendorf's reasons for rejecting innate ideas as the fundamental elements of natural law, we can gain some important insights into the intimate connections between nature, reason, and history in his account of natural law.

For Pufendorf, natural law is not innate:

The common saying that [natural] law is known by nature, should not be understood . . . as though actual and distinct propositions concerning things to be done or to be avoided were inherent in men's minds at the hour of their birth. But it means in part that the law can be investigated by the light of reason, in part that at least the common and important provisions of the natural law are so plain and clear that they at once find assent, and grow up in our minds, so that they can never again be destroyed, no matter how the impious man, in order to still the twinges of conscience, may endeavour to blot out the consequences of those precepts. For this reason in Scripture too the law is said to be 'written in the hearts' of men. Hence, since we are imbued from childhood with a consciousness of those maxims, in accordance with our social training, and cannot remember the time when we first imbibed them, we think of this knowledge exactly as if we had had it

---

[44] *De Officio*, I. 3. 12; cf. *DJNG* II. 3. 13.

already at birth. Everyone has the same experience with his mother tongue.[45]

Natural law is thus that law which we inevitably come to accept in our social training. Social trainings vary, of course, so it is not any or every principle we come to accept in this manner that is a part of natural law. Failure to recognize this would empty the notion of natural law of one of its characteristic elements: the denial that law is simply conventional, being founded in human nature. Only those precepts which are *inevitably* acquired through social training can be regarded as elements of natural law; such precepts are inevitably acquired because social life requires them. The necessities of social life found the principles of natural law; and this makes it possible to hold that natural law 'so harmonizes with the natural and social nature of man that the human race can have no wholesome and peaceful social organization without it; in other words, it has a natural benefit and utility from its continued efficacy for the human race in general'.[46] So, natural law reflects the fact of human sociableness. Its efficacy for the human race is its necessity for any rationally organized social life.

It is important to show the connections between the idea of natural law as that law which is necessary for social organization and social harmony, and natural law as a 'dictate of right reason'. Obviously, a law necessary for social harmony, but which none the less could be neither discovered nor achieved even if known, would be a law inapplicable to the affairs of human beings. The claim that the law of nature is a dictate of right reason is a denial of such possibilities. The law of nature does not require divine revelation to become known or effective in human affairs. Rather, it 'can be discovered and understood from the mental endowment peculiar to man, and a consideration of human nature in general'.[47] Natural

---

[45] Ibid. 1. 3. 12. Cf. *DJNG* II. 3. 13: 'we do not . . . feel obliged to maintain that the general principles of the law of nature came into and are imprinted upon the minds of men at their birth as distinct and clear rules which can be formulated by man without further investigation or thought as soon as he acquires the power of speech.' Note also Pufendorf's use of language as an ex. of something natural but not innate. In like manner Hume, in order to show that the artificial virtues are not 'unnatural', also appeals to the ex. of language. He describes language as artificial (a human artefact) but not unnatural. See D. Hume, *A Letter from a Gentleman to his friend in Edinburgh* (1745), ed. E. C. Mossner and J. V. Price (Edinburgh: Edinburgh University Press, 1967), 31.

[46] *DJNG* 1. 6. 18.   [47] Ibid.

law 'can be investigated by the light of reason'; and at least its 'common and important provisions . . . are so plain and clear that they at once find assent, and grow up in our minds, so that they can never again be destroyed'.[48] The most common and important provisions of the natural law are thus so widely recognized, and so firmly acknowledged, that they provide the basis for social interactions between human beings.

But what of the less common or important provisions of natural law? On this matter Pufendorf indicates that the requirement that natural law be a dictate of right (or 'sound') reason means that the provisions of natural law need to be discovered by the more exacting process of rational enquiry. These provisions, not being *immediately* obvious to all (they do not 'at once find assent') have to be discovered by reflection. This is achieved by rational enquiry which reflects a sensitivity to states of affairs in the world: 'the dictates of sound reason are true principles that are in accordance with the properly observed and examined nature of things, and are deduced by logical sequence from prime and true principles.'[49] Natural laws thus become established in human affairs (become recognized as natural law) through rational enquiry. Various principles might be recommended as being principles of natural law, but all such candidate-principles must be subjected to rational examination. For any such candidate-principle, its advocate's 'appeal to reason'—that is, appeal to recognition by others as rational—'will be vain if he [the advocate] is unable to prove his assertions from principles which are legitimate and agreeable with the nature of things'.[50]

Pufendorf recognizes that the 'nature of things' includes not only the nature of human beings as such, but also relevant physical and social facts:

There seems to us no more fitting and direct way to learn the law of nature than through careful consideration of the nature, condition, and desires of man himself, although in such a consideration other things should necessarily be observed which lie outside man himself, and especially such things as work for his advantage or disadvantage.[51]

So the natural law is a dictate of right reason in the sense that it is known rationally: that is, through a rational response to the specific

---

[48] *De Officio*, I. 3. 12.   [49] *DJNG* II. 3. 13.
[50] Ibid.   [51] Ibid. 14.

circumstances of human social life. Some of these laws are 'so plain and clear that they at once find assent', but others are less obvious, and can only be recognized as such through rational enquiry. Thus natural law can be characterized as having a core which is immediately obvious to all, but as also having further layers which are worked out in the course of human history, as the particular exigencies of different human situations come to bear. In this sense, Pufendorf's theory of natural law reflects a historical conception of human society. This aspect is clearly illustrated in his account of property, with its explanation of the genesis of more extensive property relations from a limited starting-point in the justified use of things for one's self-preservation.

The immediate task, however, is to spell out some of the basic features of the natural law. We have seen above that Pufendorf has not hesitated to stress the utility of natural law: 'it has a natural benefit and utility from its continued efficacy for the human race in general', and a man learns the law of nature by discovering 'such things as work for his advantage or disadvantage'. This does not mean, however, that the law of nature is founded in utility (unless we very carefully restrict its meaning). It is more accurate to say, instead, that, as it is for Grotius, the law of nature is expedient even though not founded in expediency. This is because it is founded in the social nature of human beings, in their need for an organized social existence; and at bottom in the exigencies of their self-preservation. Utility is therefore a feature of natural law, but not its ultimate foundation. In the following passage, perhaps his most emphatic treatment of the matter, he leaves no room for doubt concerning the disutility of ignoring natural law: 'not justice but injustice is supreme folly, which is of no general or lasting advantage even though a man's evil conduct may seem to him to succeed for a time.' Such temporary successes are ultimately bound to fail because they are not built firmly on sociability; they depend on failing to understand that 'all strength, indeed, comes from union with other men whom you may by no means hold together by your own strength alone . . . the safety of every man, however powerful he be, would be uncertain so long as any one thinks it to be to his advantage for him to die'.[52]

The utility of natural law lies in its accurate reflection of the

---

[52] Ibid. 10.

fundamental elements of human sociability. The law is not itself reducible to utility: Pufendorf is quite at one with Grotius on this point. His remarks have a similar flavour to Grotius's, although they are a little more sympathetic to the purveyors of the contrary view: 'differences between the laws and customs of different peoples have undoubtedly given some men excuse for alleging that there is no such thing as natural law, and that all law has arisen from the convenience of individual states, and cannot be measured in any other way.'[53] As exemplars of this viewpoint, he quotes the passage from Horace's *Satires* quoted by Grotius, and, also like Grotius, acknowledges Carneades as a famous advocate of this opposed point of view. He is more sympathetic than Grotius, however, because he implicitly acknowledges that this viewpoint can be the fruit not merely of evil motives, but of conceptual confusion. For there *is* a sense in which utility is not unjustly regarded as the foundation of natural law. The whole issue has been confused by the advocates of mere expediency, in that they 'have imposed upon the less informed by employing the ambiguous word "utility" which has a double use, as it is considered from different points of view'. The two uses are these:

One kind is what appears to be useful to the depraved judgement of disordered affections, which centre upon advantages which are for the most part immediate and fleeting, and are little concerned with the future. The other kind is judged to be useful by sound reason which not only examines what lies before its very feet, but also weighs the future consequences.[54]

Of these two senses of 'utility', the first can be called *apparent* (or short-run) utility, since the appearance of utility is rather misleading—the utility gained being an advantage which is outweighed by attendant disadvantages which emerge in the longer term. The latter, because it is 'judged to be useful by sound reason', can be called rational (genuine) utility; and since the core of the natural law is composed of such rational utilities (in dictates of sound reason which show the necessary advantages or disadvantages of various states of affairs), it is possible to say that natural law is based in rational utility. Thus it is not a mere accident that 'actions in conformity with the law of nature have . . . this characteristic, that not only are they reputable, that is, they tend to maintain and increase a man's standing, reputation, and position, but also they

[53] *DJNG* II. 3. 10.   [54] Ibid.

are useful, that is, they procure some advantage and reward for a man, and contribute to his happiness'.[55] So, for Pufendorf, there is at bottom no conflict between the demands of sociability and of a rational utility. When later writers, then, come increasingly to talk of utility—most conspicuously, writers such as Locke, Hutcheson, and Hume—it is important not to jump to the conclusion that a new approach has emerged, that the important position occupied by considerations of utility indicates the emergence of a new, more calculative rationality in human life. Shifts in terminology are not *per se* shifts in thought: whether a new picture of human society emerges with the increased prominence of the language of utility depends on the notion of utility being employed, and its implications for, or presuppositions about, the nature of the social life proper to human beings.

What is this life proper to human beings? Like Grotius, Pufendorf acknowledges the primacy of individual self-preservation, but his view is otherwise less individualistic than his predecessor's. On self-preservation, Pufendorf is at one with both Grotius and the Stoic tradition in holding that nothing is more natural than the desire to preserve oneself: 'man has this in common with all beings which are conscious of their own existence, that he has the greatest love for himself, tries to protect himself by every possible means, and tries to secure what he thinks will benefit him, and to avoid what may in his opinion injure him.'[56] Although he does not accept Grotius's defence of the a posteriori method as a legitimate means of establishing natural law,[57] Pufendorf does not hesitate to marshall support from the best of ancient authorities on this point. He refers to Cicero, Marcus Aurelius, Seneca, and yet others in support of the naturalness of the desire of self-preservation. Of course, no appeal to ancient authorities is necessary to show the instinctiveness of the desire of self-preservation, but neither is the discovery of such an instinct of crucial value in settling whether the desire is natural in

---

[55] Ibid.   [56] Ibid. 14.

[57] Ibid. 7: after quoting Cicero and Aristotle in support of the a posteriori view—which holds that agreement can provide the key to the nature of natural law—he objects that this view 'does not show at all why the law of nature was so consitituted', and it is 'also in very truth a slippery statement, involving numberless obscurities'. The situation is not helped by limiting the measure of agreement to the best of men (as Grotius does), because there will be no basis for determining who qualify as the best: 'For what people, endowed with enough judgment to preserve its existence, will be willing to acknowledge that it is barbarous?'

the requisite sense—that is, whether it is vindicated by the judgement of sound reason. Pufendorf is fully aware of this, and offers three arguments in support of the primacy of self-preservation.

The first could easily be misunderstood. At first blush it looks like nothing more than a reiteration of the original assertion:

> It should be observed . . . that in investigating the condition of man we have assigned the first place to self-love, not because one should under all circumstances prefer only himself before all others or measure everything by his own advantage, distinguishing this from the interests of others, and setting it forth as his highest goal, but because man is so framed that he thinks of his own advantage before the welfare of others for the reason that it is his nature to think of his own life before the life of others.[58]

It might seem that Pufendorf is here saying that self-love comes first because, well, it just does. But to say this would be hopelessly to confuse right and fact,[59] so it is worth asking whether a more charitable interpretation is possible. In fact, there is. Behind this passage it is possible to discern the Stoic maxim to live 'according to nature', a maxim which means not simply to do what we like, but to understand properly our nature and that of our environment, so that we do not attempt the impossible by denying what we are, and thereby do violence to ourselves. (Grotius appeals to this principle when he says that acts contrary to natural law cause violence to ourselves.)[60] Natural law is the law of action for a being with a determinate nature, and as such must be attuned to this nature. It is not a law which regards the actions of some sort of 'purely rational' being.[61] On this interpretation, Pufendorf's point is that self-love

---

[58] *DJNG* II. 3. 14.

[59] Cf. Rousseau's criticism of Grotius discussed in Ch. I.

[60] *DJBP*, Prol. 39.

[61] Natural law theories are in this respect essentially non-Kantian. They resist separating ethics from moral psychology, and so do not regard moral agents as 'noumenal choosers'. For a view of the significance of the change wrought in moral philosophy by Kant, see, in particular, A. MacIntyre, 'How Moral Agents became Ghosts, or how the history of ethics diverged from that of the philosophy of mind', *Synthese*, 53 (1982), 295–312. MacIntyre's position is summed up by his remark, in another essay that: 'the virtue of Hume's ethics, like that of Aristotle and unlike that of Kant, is that it seeks to preserve morality as something psychologically intelligible' ('Hume on "is" and "ought" ', in *Against the Self-Images of the Age* (London: Duckworth, 1971), 124). Whether MacIntyre's account is fair, it serves to emphasize that psychological intelligibility is also a non-accidental feature of Pufendorf's position; and the point is worth making because the binding role of moral psychology in natural law theories is not always remembered.

must be accorded a central place in any *workable* ethical theory regarding human beings, or indeed beings like us. For this reason it is central to natural law.

Pufendorf's second reason in support of the primacy of self-love is more readily understood. It is that recognizing the primacy of self-love reflects the undeniable good of being a responsible being, that is, of being responsible for oneself:

it is no one's business so much as my own to look out for myself. For although we hold before ourselves as our goal the common good, still, since I am also a part of society for the preservation of which some care is due, surely there is no one on whom the clear and special care of myself can more fittingly fall than upon my own self.[62]

If we are to accept responsibility for ourselves, of course, one of the central tasks of social organization will be to make it possible for us to act so as to preserve ourselves and our vital interests. And this in turn requires that we have a clear understanding of what constitutes ourselves and our vital interests. That is, there must be a notion of what is 'one's own': of the *suum* and of its legitimate (necessary or rationally useful) extensions. We shall return to this matter below: at this stage it is sufficient to note that Pufendorf's commitment to the primacy of self-love shows that his notion of human sociableness is (negatively) like Grotius's in that it is not a notion of absorption into a social whole. Human sociability requires, in fact, that we recognize and respect our separateness as individuals. (It is important to point out, however, that it requires us to recognize more than this alone. Unlike some modern theories, it does not mean that 'there are only individual people, different individual people, with their own individual lives'.)[63]

This point can serve to introduce Pufendorf's third reason for accepting the primacy of self-love: far from being in conflict with sociability, the primacy of self-love shows sociability to be necessary. It does so in this way: self-love is vital because of the very fragility of human existence, and this fragility itself makes social life necessary. As Hume would later put it, 'society becomes advantageous' because of the 'additional *force, ability,* and *security*'[64] it provides for individuals. Pufendorf puts it this way:

[62] *DJNG* II. 3. 14.
[63] As Robert Nozick puts it. See *Anarchy, State, and Utopia* (New York: Basic Books, 1974), 33.
[64] D. Hume, *A Treatise of Human Nature* (1739–40), 2nd edn., ed. L. A. Selby-Bigge, rev. P. H. Nidditch (Oxford: Clarendon Press, 1978), 485.

It is quite clear that man is an animal extremely desirous of his own preservation, in himself exposed to want, unable to exist without the help of his fellow creatures, fitted in a remarkable way to contribute to the common good, and yet at all times malicious, petulant, and easily irritated, as well as quick and powerful to do injury. For such an animal to live and enjoy the good things that in this world attend his condition, it is necessary that he be sociable, that is, be willing to join himself with others like him, and conduct himself towards them in such a way that, far from having any cause to do him harm, they may feel that there is reason to preserve and increase his good fortune.[65]

Pufendorf's account of sociability is thus distinctively less individualistic than Grotius's. He does not, as does Grotius, restrict sociability to respect for 'the rights of another', to the safeguarding for each individual of 'the possession of what belongs to him'.[66] Rather, he insists that 'by a sociable attitude we mean an attitude of each man towards every other man, by which each is understood to be bound to the other by kindness, peace, and love, and therefore by a mutual obligation'.[67] This stronger account of sociability probably reflects Pufendorf's desire to debar Hobbesian conclusions. He argues against the 'Hobbesian' position that 'nature has ordained discord and not society between men'.[68] In outline, his strategy is to argue that the 'natural state of men' is not a state of war, since the desire for self-preservation implies a limit on natural liberty.[69] He denies that 'men have both the ability and the desire to harm one another'.[70] But how does the desire for self-preservation imply a limit on natural liberty? It does not do so alone, but in conjunction with the further fact that 'a state of nature and its rule presupposes a reason in man';[71] and reason, having in the state of nature 'a common . . . an abiding, and uniform standard of judgement' is able to show men 'the nature of things, which offers a free and distinct service in pointing out general rules for living, and the law of nature', especially 'that peace to which his reason urges him'.[72] Therefore the 'Hobbesian' account of the state of nature is

[65] *DJNG* II. 3. 15.
[66] *DJBP* I. 2. i. 5.   [67] *DJNG* II. 3. 15.
[68] Ibid. 16. This is a quotation from a contemporary Hobbes critic, and represents a view Pufendorf takes to be a distortion of Hobbes's position in *De Cive*, i. 2. Pufendorf wants to debar the view *attributed* to Hobbes, whether or not it is pristine Hobbism. (For, among other things, a good survey of the main varieties of Hobbes interpretation, see R. Tuck, *Hobbes* (Oxford: Oxford University Press, 1989), Pt. 3.)
[69] *DJNG* II. 2. 3.   [70] Ibid. 6.   [71] Ibid. 3.   [72] Ibid. 9.

inadequate, because it is not the account of a state natural to a rational being: it 'was not worthy of man or true to his life, being more suitable to the life of beasts, to the nature of which both reason and speech are foreign'.[73]

In order to show what sociability does require, Pufendorf formulates his own version of the 'fundamental law of nature': 'it will be a fundamental law of nature, that "Everyman, so far as in him lies, should cultivate and preserve toward others a sociable attitude, which is peaceful and agreeable at all times to the nature and end of the human race." '[74] The requirement of this fundamental law can be determined by considering two matters: Pufendorf's remarks on the general duties of humanity, and his discussion of Cicero on the nature of sociability. The general duties of humanity are those duties which are the expression of the sociable attitude. They are summarized by the stipulation that 'a man should advance the interests of another man'. Pufendorf spells this out as follows:

A man has not paid his debt to the sociable attitude if he has not thrust me from him by some deed of malevolence or ingratitude, but some benefit should be done me, so that I may be glad that there are also others of my nature to dwell on this earth.[75]

It is not sufficient, therefore, if we live peacefully in the privative sense of not injuring others, but otherwise looking out for ourselves. For Pufendorf the general duty of humanity requires an actively helpful policy to others. He maintains this strong position in his short textbook, where he says that the duties of human beings require 'that any man promote the advantage of another, so far as he conveniently can'.[76]

Pufendorf's strong view on the requirements of sociability is echoed by later philosophers. Locke, often considered a philosopher of a strongly individualist stamp, advocates a version of it in the *Second Treatise*, where he says: 'Every one as he is *bound to preserve himself*, and not to quit his station wilfully; so by the like reason when his own Preservation comes not in competition, ought he, as much as he can, *to preserve the rest of Mankind*.'[77] This is a

---

[73] Ibid. 4.   [74] Ibid. 3. 15.   [75] Ibid. iii. 3. 1.
[76] *De Officio*, i. 8. 1.   [77] Locke, *Two Treatises*, ii. 6.

most significant passage, since it shows that, for Locke as for
Pufendorf, the requirements of sociability and of self-preservation
are intimately linked. (The account of Locke as a 'possessive
individualist' overlooks this fact.)[78] Hutcheson's views, as we shall
see below, include an even stronger notion of sociability, in that the
general good is not merely on an equal footing with the good of
individuals, but occupies a pre-eminent position. His basic
specification of the general duties of humanity is, however, directly
comparable to Pufendorf's: since 'we are formed by nature for the
service of each other, and not each one merely for himself',
therefore 'mankind, as a system, seems to have rights upon each
individual, to demand of him such conduct as is necessary for the
general good'.[79]

Pufendorf supports his position by calling on Seneca: 'We are
members of a great body. Nature has made us all akin; we are
formed of the same elements and produced to the same ends. She
has implanted in our breasts mutual affection, and made us apt for
social intercourse. She has constituted justice and equity.'[80] Seneca
goes on to explain the nature of our social interdependence by
means of an architectural metaphor. He says: 'Let us consider that
we are born for the common good. Our human society is altogether
like a vaulted stone roof, which would fall were it not held up by the
natural thrust of stone against stone.'[81] The same metaphor comes
to be appealed to in later discussions of justice, and for the same
reason—in order to bring out the mutual interdependence which is
a feature of any system of justice. Thus Hume likens justice to a
vault in his own account of justice in the *2nd Enquiry*.[82] The

[78] There is a substantial literature on this topic, spawned by C. B. Macpherson's
The Political Theory of Possessive Individualism: Hobbes to Locke; the main strands
are summarized in D. Miller, 'The Macpherson Version', *Political Studies*, 30 (1982),
120–7. A consequence of this study will be to show, in broad outline, why
Macpherson's thesis comes unstuck. By ignoring the Continental background to
17th-cent. English political thought, he both loses the opportunity to enlist the case
of Grotius in support of his thesis, and also fails to recognize the extent to which
Locke and the 18th-cent. Scottish moral philosophers have been influenced by
Pufendorf's revision of the Grotian theory, a revision in which the roles of rights and
duties have been significantly rethought, with an eye precisely to overcoming the
privative, self-possessing aspect of Grotius's view.
[79] F. Hutcheson, *A System of Moral Philosophy* (1755), in *Collected Works*, vi. 105.
[80] Seneca, Epistle xcv; quoted *DJNG* III. 3. 1.
[81] Ibid.
[82] D. Hume, *Enquiries concerning Human Understanding* (3rd edn.), ed. L. A.
Selby-Bigge, rev. P. H. Nidditch (Oxford: Clarendon Press, 1975), 305.

metaphor is well chosen, particularly from the point of view of the natural law theorist, since it neatly captures the basic fact of human interdependence on which the general duty of sociability is based. The metaphor neatly captures Pufendorf's insistence that this general duty is more than simply leaving each other alone, but requires that we contribute to the common good so that each of us 'may be glad that there are also others of [our] nature to dwell on this earth'.

Pufendorf also comments on some Ciceronian remarks on sociableness, and these help to clarify his position. However, they also indicate a possible missed opportunity. The passages in question are concerned with a feature of human nature which for Cicero is a powerful indicator of human sociableness, but which Pufendorf regards as 'less important', as 'only among the secondary reasons of sociableness'.[83] While Pufendorf accepts 'the fact that nothing is sadder for man than continued solitude', he does not accept Cicero's employment of this fact as evidence for human sociability. Cicero puts his view in a number of places. In *De Finibus* he observes that 'no one would like to pass his life in solitude, not even if surrounded with an infinite abundance of pleasures'.[84] The same view is repeated, more elaborately, in *De Officiis*. He notes there that even 'every man of excellent genius', committed to the pursuit of 'knowledge and learning', 'would fly from solitude and look for a companion in his pursuits; and would desire sometimes to teach and sometimes to learn, sometimes to listen and sometimes to speak.'[85] From our rejection of the solitary life, he concludes, 'it is easily perceived that we are born for communion and fellowship with man, and for natural association'.[86] For Pufendorf, however, this line of thought is not particularly satisfactory because human sociableness is an attitude towards others of a more purely practical kind: 'we called man a sociable creature because men are so constituted as to render mutual help more than any other creature';[87] the sociable attitude engenders 'a mutual obligation'.[88]

---

[83] *DJNG* II. 3. 15.

[84] Cicero, *De Finibus Bonorum et Malorum*, trans. H. Rackham (London: Heinemann, 1914), III. xx; quoted ibid.

[85] Cicero, *De Officiis*, trans. W. Miller (London: Heinemann, 1913), I. xliv; quoted ibid.

[86] *De Finibus*.

[87] *DJNG* II. 3. 16.

[88] Ibid. 15.

Sociableness is thus not significantly connected to the pleasure we gain from company, nor the pain of its extended absence. Pufendorf's view here is perhaps plausible, but is a missed opportunity nevertheless. It was pointed out above that the rational necessity of self-preservation was not grounded independently of the instinctive tendency to the same end. The mutual obligation of sociability could have been treated in like manner, by arguing that our natural pleasure in company, and pain at its extended absence, was a crucial aspect of our natural sociability by comprising a powerful natural motive to that end;[89] a motive which would help to explain why 'men are so constituted as to render mutual help more than any other creature'. One way of developing such an account of the motivation to sociability would be by a psychology of action which accorded a central place to mechanisms of sympathy in human behaviour. This is, of course, the general approach taken by Hume, and subsequently by Adam Smith; an approach which can thus be seen to be readily developed from Pufendorf's conception of sociability.

We are now in a position to consider how Pufendorf's account of sociability affects his view of the individual, and of the relation between the individual and society. In general outline, this issue can be dealt with rather briefly, because one of its specific elements will be considered in more detail below. We have already seen that, despite his stronger views on sociability, Pufendorf insists on the primacy of self-love, in particular on its practical aspect of self-preservation. In doing so he is following not merely Grotius, but a major strand of classical natural law thinking, stretching back to Aristotle and the Stoics. He has three reasons for insisting on this primacy: it is so central to instinctive human nature that no ethical theory can deny it and remain workable; it reflects the moral good of responsible independence; and because self-love does not conflict with sociability, but depends on the very foundation which shows sociability to be necessary—the fragility of human existence.[90]

---

[89] By 'motive' I mean a motivating force. The relationship between motivations and obligations is a central feature of the 'Newtonian' theory of moral action begun by Locke, and further developed by Hutcheson and Hume.

[90] Pufendorf occasionally waxes quite lyrical about this fragility. He says e.g., 'if you conceive a man who even in adult age is left alone in this world, and without any of the comforts and supports with which the ingenuity of men has made life more civilized and less hard, you will see an animal, naked, dumb, needy, driving away his hunger as best he can by roots and herbs, his thirst by any water he chances upon, the

The primacy of self-love is thus an ethical principle of great importance, and is expressed in the notion of an inviolable realm which surrounds the individual and whatever is (or becomes) necessary for its continued existence. This realm is the realm of 'one's own', the *suum*.

Pufendorf does not provide a concise account of the nature and limits of 'one's own', but what he does say shows his position to be very similar to Grotius's. Thus he holds that not only do we naturally seek our own preservation, but we are legitimately entitled to resist threats to it, even when these spring from the actions of other persons (who are likewise justified in preserving themselves). Thus self-defence, even violent self-defence, is lawful, provided of course that the situation is one where 'we cannot in any other way preserve our safety because of the aggression of another'.[91] Where other courses are open, injury cannot be inflicted. In contrast to Grotius, he allows no right to punish in the natural state, but this is because 'human punishment, in the proper sense of the word . . . cannot fall upon those in natural liberty'. This follows from his view that law requires the will of a superior: punishment requires legal sovereignty, but legal sovereignty does not exist in the natural state. So, despite the absence of punishment in the natural state, violent retaliation against an injuring party is perfectly justified:

in such cases we cannot only proceed to seize the other's arms, raze or occupy his fortified places, keep him in perpetual bonds, and the like, but even put him to death, if we are satisfied that his freedom will only mean another threat against our existence, and that we can find no better way to avoid him.[92]

---

severity of the weather by caves, an animal exposed to the wild beasts, and alarmed when he meets any of them'. The 'natural state' is to be distinguished from community life in that 'in the one there is the rule of passion, war, fear, poverty, ugliness, solitude, barbarism, ignorance, savagery; in the other the rule of reason, peace, security, riches, beauty, society, refinement, knowledge, good will' (*De Officio*, II. I. 9). In these more colourful passages, Pufendorf seems to have forgotten that, against Hobbes, he urges that 'the natural state of men . . . is not one of war, but of peace', even if 'this natural peace is but a weak and untrustworthy thing, and therefore . . . a poor custodian of man's safety', since even in the natural state reason can determine general laws for living, pre-eminent among which is 'that peace to which his reason urges him' (*DJNG* II. 2. 9, 12).

[91] *DJNG* II. 5. I.   [92] Ibid. VIII. 3. 2.

This procedure obviously achieves whatever punishment by a legitimate superior achieves; in the natural state this procedure is war.[93] So Pufendorf's denial of natural punishment is not a denial of the legitimacy of violent exaction of penalties or reparations, but a consequence of his theory of law. In both these cases—self-defence and exaction of penalties—the moral importance of the *suum* is shown by the fact that force is justified in preserving what is one's own.

The necessity of extending one's own to include things necessary for one's preservation means that such extensions are also necessarily legitimate, so, in the natural state, even though there is no property, there is nevertheless 'indefinite' or 'potential' property. This is a 'right . . . to things' which 'has the same effect as dominion now has, that, namely, of using things at one's own pleasure'.[94] In another place he puts the same point: 'when at the creation all things were in common, man had the right to apply to his own ends those things which were freely offered for the use of all.'[95] These remarks on the original power to use things 'at the creation' are most important: they show some of the powers contained within the *suum*. So, in order to come to an accurate understanding of Pufendorf's conception of the *suum* (and of its relation to other important concepts such as rights, duties, and sociability), it is necessary to consider these quoted passages rather carefully, and to clarify them in the light of other passages from *De Jure Naturae et Gentium*.

In the first place, Pufendorf describes the legitimacy of using things as a right. This is best understood as a simplification on his part, since the notion of a right is a legal notion: he describes 'right' as meaning either law, including 'a body or system of homogeneous laws', or (subjectively) as 'the moral quality by which we legally either command persons, or possess things, or by virtue of which something is owed us . . . Right . . . directly and clearly indicates that a thing has been lawfully acquired and is lawfully now retained.'[96] Being a matter of lawfulness, right, like law itself, requires the will of a superior. The natural state, however, being a state of natural liberty, is a state without superiors. How then can there be rights in this state? Pufendorf's answer mirrors his treatment of property

[93] *DJNG* VIII. 3. 2.   [94] Ibid. IV. 4. 3.
[95] Ibid. I. 1. 16.   [96] Ibid. 20.

itself. Just as the original property in things in the natural state is only 'potential' property, so the original right to use things in that state is no more than a 'potential' or 'indefinite' right: 'God allowed man to turn the earth, its products, and its creatures, to his own use and convenience, that is, he gave men an *indefinite* right to them.'[97] An 'indefinite' right becomes a right in the fullest sense only through mutual consent or agreement: 'assuming an original equal faculty of men over things, it is impossible to conceive how the mere corporal act of one person can prejudice the faculty of others, unless their consent is given, that is, unless [a] pact intervenes.'[98] A pact is necessary because, without it, human actions do not have a moral effect, do not create obligations on the part of others.[99] Obligations bind the will, and, where there is no superior, the will can be bound only by consenting to be, because consent is a form of voluntary submission of the will.[100] So rights, including rights to use things, arise through agreements wherever there is no established sovereign, or where the sovereign's edicts do not extend. Pufendorf is at pains to point out, however, that agreements need not be express agreements: for example, property, like other rights, 'presupposes absolutely an act of man and an agreement, whether tacit or express'.[101] (In tacit agreements, consent is 'inferred': it 'is not shown by the signs which men regularly make use of in their transactions, but . . . is clearly to be gathered from the nature of the business and other circumstances'. An example of this is the case of a foreigner entering a country friendly to foreign visitors. The

---

[97] Ibid. IV. 4. 4 (emphasis added). Cf. ibid. III. 5. 3: 'A right to all things, precious to every human deed, must be understood not exclusively, but only indefinitely, that is, not that one man may claim everything for himself to the exclusion of the rest of mankind, but that nature does not define what particular things belong to one man, and what to another before they agree among themselves on their division and allocation.'   [98] Ibid. IV. 4. 5.

[99] See ibid. III. 5. 3: 'not every natural faculty to do something is properly a right, but only that which concerns some moral effect, in the case of those who have the same nature as I. Thus . . . when a man takes inanimate objects or animals for his use, he exercises only a purely natural faculty, if it is considered simply with regard to the objects and animals which he uses, without respect to other men. But this faculty takes on the nature of a real right, at the moment when this moral effect is produced in the rest of mankind, that other men may not hinder him, or compete with him, against his will, in using such objects or animals.'

[100] See K. Olivecrona, *Law as Fact* (London: Stevens & Sons, 2nd edn., 1971), 12; and *DJNG* I. 6. 12; III. 5. 3.

[101] Ibid. IV. 4. 4.

foreigner, provided he understands what the laws of the country are, by entering thereby shows 'his willingness to conduct himself by the laws of that state'.)[102] The position of human beings in the natural state, with respect to the created order, can, therefore, be summed up as follows:

> man has by nature a faculty to take for his use all inanimate objects and animals. But that faculty, thus exactly defined, cannot properly be called a right, both because such things are under no obligation to present themselves for man's use, and because, by virtue of the natural equality of all men, one man cannot rightfully exclude the rest from such things, unless their consent, expressed or presumed, has let him have them as his very own. Only when this has been done, can he say that he has a proper right to the thing.[103]

The original *suum*, then, includes no rights. It includes a natural faculty or power to take and use things, especially those things needed for preservation, but rights proper arise only through agreements between human beings. Pufendorf draws some important conclusions from this doctrine. Firstly, Hobbes must be mistaken in holding that there is an original right to all things.[104] Secondly, because rights arise as a result of agreements, and such agreements' typically bind the other party to corresponding obligations, rights and duties are commonly (but not necessarily) correlative. The existence of an obligation entails the existence of another's right, but, although the existence of a right typically corresponds to another's obligation, this is not always the case.[105] From a modern perspective, it is also worth noting that on this account rights function only weakly as a limit on, or bar to, specific kinds of social organization. Pufendorf's position is sharply different from modern libertarians like Nozick,[106] and also different, though much less

---

[102] *DJNG* III. 7. 2.   [103] Ibid. 5. 3.

[104] See ibid. 2–3, where Pufendorf discusses Hobbes's views in *De Cive*.

[105] *DJNG* III. 5. 1: 'when an obligation arises for one person, there springs up in another its corresponding right . . . Although the opposite of the case does not always hold: that is, when one man has a right, there is at once an obligation in another; for instance, sovereigns have a right to exact punishment, but the criminal is under no obligation to undergo it.' He points out that correlativity can be achieved if we understand 'right' in a certain way; but he does not argue that we need, or should prefer, to understand the term in that way.

[106] Nozick opens *Anarchy, State, and Utopia* with a strong statement of the natural rights of individuals, and then goes on to pose the question whether these rights

sharply so, from Locke. The latter difference will show up most clearly in the case of slavery.

On the question of rights, some matters need pointing out. The first is that, despite being themselves a social creation, rights in Pufendorf's scheme are nevertheless, in an important sense, *natural* rights. They are natural in just the sense that the law of nature is natural: that is, they are either necessary to peaceful social existence, or possess a rational utility to that end. Being generated through agreements is no bar to naturalness of this kind, for not only does the law of nature approve of all agreements 'which have been introduced about things by men, provided they involve no contradiction or do not overturn society', it in fact *requires* agreements (tacit or express). With respect to the role of agreements in the development of property, for example, Pufendorf says that 'natural law clearly advised that men should by convention introduce the assignment of such things to individuals, according as it might be of advantage to human society'.[107] The right to property is natural, then, because it arises necessarily in human social life. Its introduction is inevitable because of the great advantages it provides for the peaceful management of such life.

By showing the naturalness of the right of property, however, Pufendorf does not mean either to justify unlimited private property, or to deny the rectitude of common possessions. He clearly believes that *some* things must become 'proper' to individuals (a view which reflects his insistence that self-preservation is indeed rightly understood as *self*-preservation), but beyond this he requires only that distinctions of possessions in particular societies must be clearly settled. The precise nature and extent of property rights is settled differently in different societies:

it was left to men themselves, to determine by the forethought of sane reason what measures must be taken to prevent discord from arising among mankind from the use of that right . . . the manner, intensity, and extent of this power [over things] were left to the judgement and disposition of men; whether, in other words, they would confine it within certain limits, or within none at all, and whether they wanted every man to have a right to

preclude the possibility of a just political authority. See p. ix: 'How much room do individual rights leave for the state?'

[107] *DJNG* iv. 4. 4. In order to avoid confusion with Hume's notion of convention, I have employed the term 'agreements' rather than (as does the trans.) 'conventions' in the discussion of this passage.

everything, or only to a certain and fixed part of things, or to be assigned his definite portion with which he should rest content and claim no right to anything else.[108]

So, recognizing a natural right to property, or, in like manner, any other right which is natural in this sense, does not prescribe a particular form of society or polity. It does prescribe some necessary conditions, but these are rather weak. Slavery is a case in point. Pufendorf's doctrine of natural right does not remove the possibility of slavery; it merely places limitations on how slavery can legitimately arise, and the extent of the power that can be legitimately exercised over a slave. The former of these limitations presupposes that there are no 'slaves by nature', as Aristotle had held, because slavery arises only through 'the intervention of some act of men'.[109] In this sense, slavery is not a natural but an *adventitious* state.[110] The view 'handed down from the Greeks', that there are 'slaves by nature', is unacceptable because, 'if taken in so crude a form, [it] is directly at odds with the natural equality of men';[111] and such equality is a precept of natural law.[112] Rather, slavery originates in consent, later being extended—justly or otherwise—through war.[113] Pufendorf does not provide any historical support for this account of the origin of slavery, so perhaps he is considering only the origin of legitimate slavery, which, because it is the creation of a right over another person, *must* have originated in an act of will.[114]

The second limitation, the power legitimately exercised over a slave, depends on Pufendorf's view (presumably based on the doctrine of the natural equality of human beings) that the slave is not to be regarded as akin to a material object. Rather, the right to rule over slaves needs to be understood as akin to the rights of sovereigns over their subjects. Therefore 'it cannot properly be said that the men themselves are alienated, but only the right to rule over them'. It is not a precept of the law of nature, but because 'the

---

[108] *DJNG* IV. 4. 4.   [109] Ibid. VI. 3. 2.

[110] See ibid. I. 1. 7: 'That is an *adventitious* state which comes to men . . . by virtue of some human deed.'

[111] Ibid. III. 2. 8.   [112] Ibid. I.

[113] Ibid. VI. 3. 5–6. Pufendorf's reasoning in VI. 3. 5, which concludes 'Therefore, the origin of slavery was due to willing consent and not to war', is extremely difficult to follow. Most of VI. 3. 5. appears to be evidence for the contrary view.

[114] The question of the legitimacy of slavery will be considered in sect. 5 of this ch.

brutality of many nations has gone to such lengths', typically slaves 'are numbered among . . . material possessions, and are treated not as subjects for their master's sovereignty, but as objects for his violence'.[115] In the same spirit Pufendorf denies the common doctrine that the slave, because his or her rights have been alienated, can be done no injury.[116] In these ways, then, Pufendorf spells out the legitimate boundaries of the institution of slavery; that is, the extent to which it does not conflict with the law of nature. In identifying such limitations, he differs significantly from Grotius, who, despite regarding slavery as a base condition, none the less failed to provide any account of the 'natural limits' of slavery. In contrast to Locke, however, he does not hold that slavery is incompatible with the natural liberty or equality of human beings.[117] The important question of whether consent to slavery is ever necessary—agreement, it must be remembered, presupposes the use of reason[118]—will be considered in section 5, where the implications of the right of necessity will be examined further.

For Pufendorf, rights are best understood as *secondary* phenomena. Unlike many modern theories which accord rights a pre-eminent position by treating duties as phenomena generated by rights, for Pufendorf rights are generated by agreements because such agreements are necessary for society, and thus reflect the fundamental duties of sociableness. How then do such fundamental duties arise? In order to answer this question, it is first necessary to remember that, being a fundamental part of the law of nature, duties have both a formal and a material element. Pufendorf's short definition of a duty in *De Officio* reflects this requirement: 'duty is here defined by me as man's action, duly conformed to the ordinances of the law, and in virtue of obligation.'[119] In being conformed to 'the ordinances of the law', duty is conformed to the will of a superior, so this part of the definition shows us the formal element from which duty is generated. The material element must therefore be sought in the obligation, which is distinct from the duty

[115] *DJNG* VI. 3. 7.   [116] Ibid. 8.
[117] Locke does, of course, allow household servants. Presumably these are not lifelong servants, but wage labourers: if not, his position would not differ markedly from Pufendorf's. The form of slavery he has in mind, however, is not one kept within specific limits, but the more thoroughgoing form of subjection he discerns in Filmer's defence of absolutism and denial of natural liberty in *Patriarcha*.
[118] *DJNG* III. 6. 3.
[119] *De Officio*, I. 1. 1. (trans. slightly amended).

itself. (For Pufendorf, the difference appears to be that our duty is what we must do, whereas obligation is what binds the will, i.e. what compels us to do our duty.) The matter is complicated further by the fact that Pufendorf divides obligations into 'intrinsic' and 'extrinsic'. Extrinsic obligation is, however, the formal element of obligation, the external law, so to isolate the material element necessary to fill out the account of duty we must examine the nature of intrinsic obligation. This, the material element of obligation, is that part of obligation which affects the conscience. It can even be described as a natural feeling of obligation.[120]

What is the source of such feelings? Pufendorf provides an answer in his account of sociability: 'we called man a sociable creature because men are so constituted as to render mutual help more than any other creature.'[121] In the same vein he approvingly quotes Seneca: Nature 'has implanted in our breasts mutual affection, and made us apt for social intercourse'.[122] This feature of the human constitution, our natural mutual affection, is the source of the feeling of obligation; hence Pufendorf is able to conclude that social life engenders 'a mutual obligation'.[123] The point is that we are so constituted that we seek to assist, and be assisted by, other human beings, even in aiming only at our own preservation. Mutual help of this kind produces the recognition of mutual dependence, and therefore the recognition, in specific circumstances, that particular actions are required for the maintenance of a rational social order, or social harmony. And this recognition, which is the experience of conscience, is the material element of obligation and also of duty; and thereby shows duty to be more than the mere following of a rule.

Duties arise, then, through the natural mutuality of human life, sanctioned by law. The fundamental role of duties in Pufendorf's scheme—most visibly perceived in the structure of *De Officio*, which is divided up according to the various duties of human beings—reflects his stronger account of sociability. Duties are fundamental not merely because human beings live in groups, and need to do so, but because they have a social nature which ordains mutual intercourse.

---

[120] The Humean overtones here are not accidental. In Ch. 5 it will be argued that Hume's principal concerns are with *intrinsic* obligation and motivation.
[121] *DJNG* II. 3. 16.   [122] Ibid. III. 3. 1.   [123] Ibid. II. 3. 5.

The mutuality of social life is not, however, all of a piece. Although the sociable attitude is a general duty of humanity, the requirements of sociability fall into two distinct groups. This division reflects an important distinction in social life:

if a man does me no good turn, and does not join with me even in the ordinary duties, I can still live in all tranquillity with him, provided he hurts me in no way. Nay, we desire nothing more than this from most of mankind, mutual assistance being rendered only within a limited circle. But how can I live at peace with him who does me injury . . . ?[124]

Those general duties of humanity which are necessary for social peace are obviously vital, whereas those which enrich social life but are not absolutely necessary for social harmony are less important. Failure to perform some duties threatens social life itself, while failure to perform others impoverishes society but does not threaten it. The difference here can be put in terms of the necessity of protecting the *suum*. Because the *suum* must be protected for there to be social life at all, those duties which are concerned with protecting the *suum* are enforceable, i.e. they are appropriately enforced. Thus the appropriateness of enforcement can be used to distinguish between the two kinds of obligation: those requirements of sociability which reflect the primary necessity of protecting the *suum* differ from those which do not, in that the former can be legitimately enforced whereas the latter cannot. Pufendorf calls these requirements, respectively, perfect and imperfect obligations:

a thing may be owed us in two ways, either by a perfect, or by an imperfect obligation, to which a perfect and an imperfect right correspond respectively, [differing in that] damage which another is bound to restore can be done us only in things owed us under the first category, but not in things owed us under the second category.[125]

It is noteworthy that Pufendorf also speaks here of perfect and imperfect rights. The distinction, and the terminology, is adapted from Grotius, who distinguishes perfect moral qualities (rights) from imperfect moral qualities (aptitudes). Grotius does not, however, speak of 'imperfect rights'; that Pufendorf is prepared to speak this way shows his willingness to broaden the notion of a right, by detaching it from its legal foundation. (This tendency is reflected also in Locke and, especially, Hutcheson.) Neither does

[124] Ibid. III. 1. 1.   [125] Ibid. 3.

Grotius speak of obligations as perfect or imperfect. Pufendorf's way of drawing this distinction is a hint in the direction of modern distinctions between law and morals: between what we can be compelled to do by others, on the one hand, and, on the other, what our own humanity should compel us to do, without external enforcement.

Putting the distinction in this way is revealing, because it indicates that perfect obligations differ from imperfect in that, while the former have both an extrinsic and an intrinsic component (both a formal and a material element), the latter have only the intrinsic element. Imperfect obligation arises only *within* the agent, unaccompanied by any external power to compel action. As Pufendorf puts it: 'these last duties ought to be performed upon a kind of voluntary impulse arising from a man's good nature, and [there is] no faculty to force him to perform them.'[126] The 'voluntary impulse' here is the operation of the conscience, which is the source of intrinsic obligation. Imperfect obligation is centrally a matter of conscience, and this is shown by the appearance, in the quotation above, of that most distinctive of conscience-affecting words: the word 'ought'. Pufendorf explicitly identifies this word as capturing the essential quality of imperfect obligation: its capacity to bind inwardly the otherwise free (undirected) will of the human mind: 'what the people *ought* to do is contrasted with what it *could* do, the word 'ought' being used for that less perfect obligation, whereby we are supposed to undertake the exercise of every virtue.'[127] So, for Pufendorf, the word 'ought' pre-eminently expresses the nature of imperfect obligation. Later chapters will show that, for Hutcheson and Hume also, the word 'ought' and the notion of obligation are both best understood in the light of this account of imperfect obligation—that is, as *intrinsic* obligation. Making this feature explicit is also an important aid to understanding Hume's division of the virtues, and thus of his account of our obligations concerning justice.

3. VARIETIES OF NATURAL STATES

Before proceeding further, it will be helpful to clarify some potential sources of confusion. Pufendorf makes an important

---

[126] *DJNG* III. I. 3.   [127] Ibid.

distinction between natural and adventitious states. 'The state of men,' he says, 'is either natural or adventitious'.[128] where an adventitious state is a state which arises 'by virtue of some human deed'.[129] This appears to raise a problem. It has been argued that some kinds of human actions, because necessary for the harmony of society, are properly understood as natural, and so give rise to natural states of affairs. But these states of affairs arise by the actions of human beings, so they must be classed as adventitious states. The problem is that Pufendorf's division of states into *either* natural *or* adventitious, if it is to be taken at face value, precludes this possibility. Such states, of which property is one, cannot be both natural and adventitious, unless Pufendorf uses 'natural' in more than one way.

In fact, this is what he does, and quite self-consciously. He distinguishes three senses of 'natural': 'the natural state can be considered . . . either in relation to God the Creator, or in relation to individual men, as regards themselves, or as regards other men.'[130] As this remark suggests, the second and third senses can be regarded as variations on a common theme, so, for purposes of exposition, the economical course is to group them together, and contrast them with the first sense.

Pufendorf describes the first sense thus:

Viewed in the first way, the natural state of man is that condition in which he was placed by the Creator, when He willed that man should be an animal superior to all the rest. From this state it follows that man should recognize and worship his Author, and marvel at all His works; and also *pass his life in a very different manner from the brutes*. Hence this state is contrasted with the life and condition of the brutes.[131]

In this sense, what is natural to human beings is what marks them off as creatures of a special kind. The idea is of what is properly appropriate to human beings, or human societies. In this sense of 'natural', then, any course of action which is a necessary response to the requirements of human sociability will be a natural course of action, and will produce natural states of affairs. It is in this sense that Pufendorf and Grotius speak of the development of property as a natural development. However, in this first sense, the opposite to a natural state is not an adventitious state (since most such natural

---

[128] *De Officio*, II. 1. 2.   [129] *DJNG* I. 1. 7; cf. *De Officio*, II. 2. 1.
[130] *De Officio*, II. 1. 2.   [131] Ibid. 3 (emphasis added).

states will also be adventitious), but an *unnatural* (a 'brutish') state.
The failure to be natural in this sense is a failure to be fully human,
or fully appropriate to human life. Alternatively, it might be said
that, since the natural state of human beings is a rational state, to
fail to be natural in this sense would be to fail in rationality, and
hence to be arbitrary. So, in this sense, the opposite of a natural
state is any state which is unnatural or arbitrary.

   The second and third senses of 'natural' are, however, appropriately
contrasted with adventitious states of affairs. In the second sense,
'natural' is understood in this way:

> we can consider the natural state of man, if we imagine what his condition
> would be, if one were left entirely to himself, without any added support
> from other men, assuming indeed that condition of human nature which is
> found at present . . . in this sense the natural state is opposed to a life
> improved by the industry of men.[132]

Such a state, Pufendorf notes, is one 'more wretched than that of
any wild beast', because of the weakness and vulnerability of human
individuals, without the power of collective action. In this sense,
property is clearly not natural, since it is generated by the
appropriative acts of human beings, and is maintained by their
mutual agreement (even if tacit). In its more sophisticated forms, it
reflects the variety and extent of 'the industry of men'. As such, it is
an adventitious state. It is not, however, an unnatural or an
arbitrary state of affairs.

   The same can be said of the third sense. In this sense,

> we consider the natural state of man according as men are understood to be
> related to each other, merely from that common kinship which results from
> similarity of nature, before any agreement or act of man, by which one
> came to be particularly bound to another . . . In this sense the natural state is
> opposed to the civil state.[133]

So, in this sense, the natural state is the state of natural liberty,
where 'all men and individual men' are 'bound to other men by
nothing but the bond of a common humanity'.[134] Since property
binds, or obligates, by an agreement of human beings, it is not
merely the bond of a common humanity. It is, rather, part of a civil
state, a specifically social institution characteristic of civil society.

---

[132] *De Officio*, II. 1. 4.   [133] Ibid. 5.   [134] *DJNG* II. 2. 1.

So, in the third sense as in the second, property is not natural but adventitious. And, as also in the second, in the third sense it is equally misguided to conclude that, because property is not natural, it is therefore unnatural or arbitrary. The distinction of possessions is rather a necessary feature of the social life of civil societies, being an integral part of 'a suitable order [for] mankind's existence'.[135]

So property can be regarded as either natural or adventitious, depending on the sense of 'natural' employed. This is important for the proper understanding not only of Pufendorf, but also of other philosophers who employ his distinctions for their own ends. Most notable among these is David Hume, so it will be instructive if we leap ahead briefly, and consider some of Hume's views in the light of Pufendorf's distinctions.

In *A Treatise of Human Nature*, Hume argues that justice is not a natural, but an *artificial* virtue. His point (which will be considered in more detail below) is that justice is among those virtues which 'produce pleasure and approbation by means of an artifice or contrivance, which arises from the circumstances and necessities of mankind'.[136] Such artificial virtues, being the result of artifice and contrivance, reflect both the 'industry of men' and the agreements (or conventions) which are necessary to the social life. Hume's notion of an artificial virtue is thus that of a virtue characteristic of, in Pufendorf's terms, an adventitious state. His distinction between the natural and the artificial is, in outline, the same as Pufendorf's distinction between the natural and the adventitious.

The point is supported by recognizing that Hume, in distinguishing the artificial from the natural, is careful to note that this is connected to only *one* sense of 'natural', a sense which corresponds to Pufendorf's second and third senses. He is careful to point out that there is another sense in which justice is indeed natural. For this reason he insists that, although artificial, justice is not unnatural,[137]

<hr/>

[135] Ibid.   [136] Hume, *Treatise*, 477.

[137] In his letter to Francis Hutcheson of 17 Sept. 1739, Hume stresses that he has 'never called justice unnatural, but only artificial'. His aim in this part of the letter is to resist Hutcheson's teleological notion of 'natural'—it is, he says, 'founded on final causes', which are 'pretty uncertain and unphilosophical'. He illustrates his preferred notion of 'natural' with a quotation from Horace (*Satires*, I. iii. 98) which stresses the role of utility in distinguishing the naturally good. He then concludes that 'Grotius and Pufendorf, to be consistent, must assert the same'. See letter no. 13 in *The Letters of David Hume*, ed. J. Y. T. Greig (Oxford: Clarendon Press, 1932). The letter is also printed in D. D. Raphael (ed.), *British Moralists 1650–1800* (Oxford: Clarendon Press, 1969), ii. 109–10.

nor is it arbitrary.[138] In another place, he says that justice is artificial as opposed to natural 'in the same Sense' as 'Sucking is an Action natural to Man, and Speech is artificial'.[139]

Pufendorf has in mind the other sense of 'natural' when, in denying an innate basis to natural law, he says that natural law is natural in much the way that language is.[140] Hume agrees that in *this* sense, justice, like language, is indeed natural: 'Justice, in another Sense of the word, is so natural to Man, that no Society of Men, and even no individual Member of any Society, was ever entirely devoid of all Sense of it.'[141] This is because the sense of justice necessarily arises in the development of human society, and 'In so sagacious an animal, what necessarily arises from the exertion of his intellectual faculties may justly be esteemed natural.'[142] The sense of 'natural' Hume has in mind here is clearly Pufendorf's first sense, since the sense in which justice is artificial rather than natural is the sense which Pufendorf employs in showing that property is adventitious rather than natural. So, rather than, as is sometimes held, being a decisive break from the tradition of natural law, Hume's account depends crucially on distinctions already established by Pufendorf. To underscore the connection, we need only consider Hume's concluding remarks to his first account of the artificiality of justice:

To avoid giving offence, I must here observe, that when I deny justice to be a natural virtue, I make use of the word *natural*, only as oppos'd to *artificial*. In another sense of the word . . . no virtue is more natural than justice. Mankind is an inventive species; and where an invention is obvious and absolutely necessary, it may as properly be said to be natural as any thing that proceeds immediately from original principles, without the intervention of thought or reflexion.

He then adds that it is not improper to describe the rules of justice as natural laws, provided this expression is understood in a particular way:

Tho' the rules of justice be *artificial*, they are not *arbitrary*. Nor is the expression improper to call them *Laws of Nature*; if by natural we

---

[138] *Treatise*, 484.
[139] Hume, *A Letter from a Gentleman*, 31.
[140] *De Officio*, I. 3. 12.
[141] Hume, *A Letter from a Gentleman*, 31.
[142] *Enquiries*, 307; cf. *DJNG* II. 2. 2, where Pufendorf attributes the improvements generated in adventitious states to 'the sagacity of men'.

understand what is common to any species, or even if we confine it to mean what is inseparable from the species.[143]

Pufendorf's account of the senses of 'natural' shows such Humean remarks to be fairly orthodox, and not implicit criticism of established notions of the naturalness of natural law. We can also note in passing that, contrary to those interpretations of Hume which detect in his writings a scepticism which touches all human thought and practice, his discussion of, and distinctions concerning, the varieties of the natural and their opposites provides good reason for accepting that he has indeed a genuine desire 'to avoid giving offence'. There is no need or justification for looking for the sceptic's irony in such passages; they are most happily understood as the reiteration of concepts and distinctions already established in some quarters of the intellectual world. In the final chapter, the nature of Hume's relationship to natural law will be considered more fully. This particular matter can be summed up by observing that, by distinguishing between several senses of 'natural', and thus allowing that, in different respects, property can be said to be both natural and adventitious, Pufendorf establishes a distinction with important subsequent employments. In the next section his explanation of the development of property will be considered in detail, in particular his account of the circumstances and actions which conspire to generate complex property relations from more simple antecedents.

4. THE NATURAL NECESSITY OF PROPERTY

The vulnerability of human life requires the specification of the personal realm, the realm capable of suffering injury. This realm is called 'one's own', the *suum*. The necessity of using material things in order to preserve oneself, and the transferable nature of these

---

[143] *Treatise*, 484. Cf. also the concern in the *2nd Enquiry* to play down the whole question (almost certainly evidence of Hume's frustrations over the misinterpretation of the *Treatise*): 'The word *natural* is commonly taken in so many senses and is of so loose a signification, that it seems vain to dispute whether justice be natural or not' (*Enquiries*, 307). The preceding discussion is evidence enough that Hume's remarks here are not an attempt to remove the facade of natural law from a basically utilitarian theory (as Macpherson claims in *The Political Theory of Possessive Individualism: Hobbes to Locke*, 270).

things (they can be removed from one's possession by the action of others, without being destroyed in the process),[144] requires that the *suum* be extended to include these things; and these things thereby become proper to oneself, one's property. Such extension of the *suum* is necessary for the maintenance of peaceful social life, so in this sense the development of property is a natural process. Property is natural to human life.

In outline, this is Pufendorf's position. A more detailed exposition of his views thus appropriately begins by observing the nature and implications of human vulnerability: 'Such is the constitution of man's body that it cannot live from its own substance, but has need of substances gathered from outside, by which it is nourished and fortified against those things which would destroy its structure.'[145] For this reason God has willed that human beings have a general power to use things. The exercise of this power is unproblematic in so far as it concerns plants and other insensate things, since they are unable to 'suffer any ill'.[146] The use of animals is admittedly a more delicate matter, but Pufendorf holds that human beings can without injustice use animals for their own ends since there is no moral community between human beings and animals. There is 'no right of obligation . . . between men and beasts', but a 'practical state of war'.[147] Nevertheless there are limits on how this power is to be used: cruelty is to be rejected—but not for the sake of the animals.[148]

It has already been shown that the original power to use things is not to be understood as a right. Nevertheless it *is* a moral power, since it produces a moral effect, an effect on the legitimate actions of other human beings. Unlike most moral effects, however, which arise only as the result of an agreement, this particular effect arises directly from the original *suum*: since to take or destroy another's

---

[144] Cf. *Treatise*, 487–8.
[145] *DJNG* IV. 3. 1.   [146] Ibid. 3.
[147] Ibid. 5. This implies, incidentally, that animals can in turn use human beings for *their* ends without injustice. Pufendorf recognizes the implication: he does not hold that the beasts were created *for* human beings, in the sense of having an obligation to submit to human purposes. On the general question of the relationship between human beings and animals in the thought of the period, see in particular K. Thomas, *Man and the Natural World: Changing Attitudes in England 1500–1800* (Harmondsworth: Penguin Books, 1984).
[148] *DJNG* IV. 3. 6: 'a useless and wanton destruction of animals tends to the hurt of all human society, and to the dishonour of the Creator and Author of such a gift.'

food, or even to prevent the other from gathering food, is to interfere with the fundamental necessity of self-preservation, and thereby to cause injury. However, if there is an original moral effect which precedes human agreements, then this must be expressible as an original moral relation between human beings, with respect to the physical world. Pufendorf recognizes this implication, and expresses it by saying that human beings had an original community of possession of all things. He is anxious that the nature of this original community not be misunderstood. He joins with Grotius in holding that the original community differed markedly from modern notions of common possession. The difference can be caught by distinguishing two kinds of community of possession, negative and positive.

Positive community is the developed notion of common ownership: 'Common things, by the . . . positive meaning, differ from things owned, only in the respect that the latter belong to one person while the former belong to several in the same manner.'[149] Positive community does not differ from private property 'in the manner and force of dominion', only in 'the subject in which it terminates'. Private dominion, or property, 'terminates' in one man, while common dominion, or positive community, terminates in several. Positive community thus has two important features.

In the first place, it cannot be changed without agreements. Since none of the co-owners

has a right extending, as it were, over the whole thing, but having power only over a part of the thing, such part still remaining undivided, it is obvious that one person cannot of his own right dispose of the entire thing, but only of his share; and that if any decision is to be reached in the whole thing, the consent and authority of each person concerned in it must be secured.[150]

So, while individuals can renounce their shares in a positive common possession, positive community of possession cannot itself be abandoned without agreement. Changing to a system of private property in parts of the whole, for example, cannot occur without the consent of 'each person concerned'. (Pufendorf does not tell us whether, in such cases, *tacit* consent is possible.)

The second feature of positive community is that, like proprietor-ship, it presupposes the exclusion of others: 'Positive community as

----

[149] Ibid. 4. 2.   [150] Ibid.

well as proprietorship imply an exclusion of others from the thing which is said to be common or proper, and therefore presupposes more men than one in the world.'[151] Positive community is, in other words, a right shared by a group of human beings who are only a part of the entire population, the remaining portion being excluded from the possessions in question. Clearly, this means that positive community is not the original community of possession shared by all human beings in the earliest days of the Creation. The original community must therefore have been *negative* community:

> Therefore, just as things could not be said to be proper to a man, if he were the only being in the world, so the things from the use of which no man is excluded, or which, in other words, belong to one man no more than to another, should be called common in the [negative] and not in the [positive] meaning of the term.[152]

Since the original community of possession was negative in character, positive community, like private property, was a later development: 'things were created neither proper nor common (in positive community) by any express command of God, but these distinctions were later created by men as the peace of human society demanded.'[153]

So, to understand the nature of the original community of possession, it is necessary to explain Pufendorf's concept of negative community. He describes it briefly in one passage as a state in which 'all things lay open to all men, and belonged no more to one than to another'.[154] He offers a more extensive treatment in another passage. In a state of negative community, he says,

> things are said to be common, according as they are considered before the interposition of any human act, as a result of which [acts] they are held to belong in a special way to this man rather than that. In the same sense such things are said to be nobody's, more in a negative than a positive sense; that is, that *they are not yet assigned to a particular person*, not that they cannot be assigned to a particular person. They are, furthermore, called 'things that lie open to any and every person'.[155]

Negative community is thus a thoroughly *inclusive* state. Unlike positive community, which presupposes the exclusion of some

---

[151] *DJNG* IV. 4. 3.   [152] Ibid.
[153] Ibid. 4.   [154] Ibid. 5.
[155] Ibid. 2 (emphasis added).

group of others, negative community necessarily excludes none.

Pufendorf's remark that in negative community things are not yet assigned to particular individuals is important, and deserves closer examination. He is not merely saying that, as a matter of fact, there are no private owners in such a state. Rather, the 'not yet' is the key to understanding negative community *as* community, and not merely as a state where there is no private property. A state without private property is not a state in which private property does not yet exist unless it contains within it the germ from which such property arises. This is just what negative community must contain, since it must reflect the fact that human beings can legitimately use things for their own preservation. Negative community is thus the state of the openness of the world to use and appropriation; there is an original negative community of things not because there is a mere possibility of using things (because they are not already owned), but because there is a moral necessity of such use. Negative community expresses the nature of the relationship between human beings and the world. It reflects the fact that, in an important sense, the world is for the use of human beings: in using the world for their own ends, human beings are not strangers (or trespassers) on a foreign soil. They are at home.[156] (The world is not for them in any stronger sense, however, especially not in the sense that it is in any way under an obligation to submit. This is important for the proper understanding of the moral position of animals.)

The negative community that human beings originally had in the physical world can best be understood by analogy with the situation of invited guests at a buffet banquet.[157] The food at such an occasion is for the guests, but no particular item is for any particular guest. Nor is the food as a whole only for the guests as a whole, since they do not first have to come to agree about who should get what. They do not each have a right, shared with others, to all the food provided. Rather, the food is just there for the taking: each guest is free to take what he or she wishes, and wrongs nobody by so doing,

[156] It is important to recognize this feature of negative community, since it shows a difficulty in secularizing any theory founded on it. The relation is not simply one of confronting a world of things, so the question of appropriation of what is negatively common is not simply a matter of how unheld things come to be held, of how an unowned thing comes to be owned. Robert Nozick overlooks this feature in his treatment of Locke's theory of appropriation in *Anarchy, State, and Utopia*, 174 ff.

[157] A number of natural law writers employ this sort of ex. One possible source is the parable of the banquet in Luke 14: 16–24.

provided what is taken has not already been claimed by someone else, and provided the taking itself involves no violence or injury. In such a situation, it is of utmost importance to have a clear understanding of what is necessary in order to have successfully removed some of the available food from its initial common status. Successful removal must be publicly recognizable, in order to maintain peace, especially by preventing unintended violations of what is no longer common. At a banquet, these matters are usually solved rather easily: placing food on a plate, and drink in a glass, are usually recognized as acts of removal. Whether the act is successful just because of the act itself, or because of the acceptance of the act as appropriate, is another matter. On the former understanding, the act is successful just because of its quality as an act. Successful removal could in this case be described as being due to the exercise of labour. On the latter understanding, the act is successful because it is *seen* to be an appropriate solution to the problem, and so is not interfered with. In this case, successful removal could be described as being due to (tacit) agreement.

These alternatives rarely trouble the guests at such functions, but the issue is an important one for Pufendorf, and indeed for other philosophers who understand the original condition of human beings with respect to things to be a negative community. In fact, the problem of how to remove anything from the original common, so that it can become the private property of individuals, is the central problem of an account based on negative community. The origin of private property is a question that can be raised no matter what the original relation of human beings to the world happened to be, but the question takes different forms according to the understanding of the original relation. If the original relation was one of no community whatsoever, but merely a number of human beings confronting a mass of things, then there is no question of how to remove from a common. Instead there is the question of how to make property out of nothing (as it were): how to make a moral relation out of an initially merely physical relation. (It may even be asked: Is such a development possible?)[158] If the original relation

---

[158] Denying community amounts to denying that the world can be regarded as made *for us*, even in a weak sense. Instead of being related to a world as guests to a banquet, we instead confront a world of things *as strangers*. From such a premiss, it could then be argued that the rise of property reflects only the exercise of force over the world, and not the sophistication of an original moral relation. Thus the more

was of a positive community—a relation which is best understood as akin to a legal partnership, where each partner has specific rights—then there is no way to remove from the common but by agreement.[159] There is in such a case no issue about how to remove from the common. The important issue, if positive community is assumed, is, rather, how legitimate use is to be made, by individuals, of what is owned in common, without recourse to agreements.[160]

Since Pufendorf holds that the original community of possession is negative, the task of explaining the origin of property becomes a matter of explaining the nature of 'the steps of departure'[161] from negative community. So we should now consider his account of the main aspects of this departure from the original community.

First of all, it is important to keep in mind that 'the steps of departure' from primitive community are indeed *steps*, and that they are not unnatural. They are steps because 'men left this original negative community of things . . . not, indeed, all at once, and for all time, but successively, and as the state of things, or the nature and number of men, seemed to require'.[162] In so doing, they were not acting unnaturally, or contrary to natural law, for two distinct reasons. Firstly, the naturalness of negative community does not imply that it must be preserved:

when we assert that by nature all things were negatively common, we do not mean that the law of nature commands us to maintain that state of things for all time, but only that things considered without any previous act of men were of such a nature that they belonged no more to one man than to another.[163]

Negative community is thus natural in the sense that it is not adventitious. As we have seen, there is another sense of 'natural', in which some social institution or state of affairs can be natural even if adventitious. In this sense, an institution is a part of natural law

pronounced forms of 'environmental philosophy' could be seen as springing from a denial of any original community of possession.

[159] *DJNG* IV. 4. 2.
[160] That Locke puts the question of how property in things arises in terms of how to *remove* things from their original community I take to be evidence that he assumes an original negative community. The issue will, however, be discussed fully in the next ch.; Locke speaks of removing from the common at *Two Treatises*, ii. 27, 28, 30.
[161] *DJNG* IV. 4. 6, heading.
[162] Ibid.   [163] Ibid. 13.

because 'sane reason, upon a consideration of the general state of social life, advises that this be set up and established among men'.[164] It is this sense of 'natural' which provides the second reason for the naturalness of the departure from negative community. The departure from negative community is natural because it is recommended by sane reason. In fact, sane reason recommends not only that negative community be left behind, but that it be left behind only in a series of steps, rather than all at once. It recommends that negative community be left behind, and systems of property generated, in order to prevent rivalry and preserve peace among human beings:

And truly the peace and tranquillity of mankind, the maintenance of which is the first concern of the law of nature, made no uncertain suggestion as to what might be the most salutary arrangement by men in this regard. For after the human race had multiplied and acquired a cultural mode of life, the peace of men did not suffer that there should remain for every man an equal power over all things, that is, that all things should be open to all for the promiscuous use of every man . . . Since innumerable conflicts could not avoid arising from the ·rivalry of many persons over the same thing, which could not suffice for all of them at one time, especially in view of the fact that such is the nature of the vast majority of things, that they can be of service to but one person at one time.[165]

Although the development of property was necessary in order to avoid quarrels and preserve peace, the preservation of peace was not served by the total abandonment of all negative community when its abandonment was necessary with respect to some things. Rather, total abandonment would have been pointless and arbitrary. Among other things, it would have involved the appropriation of some things which, because of either their natural abundance or some other features, ought not at any time to be appropriated. This is true of, in particular, the air and the open sea.[166] (In respect of the latter, Pufendorf accepts the view expounded by Grotius in *Mare Liberum* and *De Jure Belli ac Pacis*.)[167] So negative community should be abandoned progressively,

---

[164] *DJNG* IV. 4. 14.   [165] Ibid. 6.
[166] Ibid. 5. 2, 9.
[167] Pufendorf says, among other things, that 'peaceful navigation of the ocean extends to all men and is free', a principle which allows peaceful navigation for the purposes of trade (ibid. 10). Cf. also *DJBP* II.2. iii; II. 2. xiii. 5; and of course *ML*.

as required by the need to maintain peace in the face of particular
social developments:

> when we say that reason suggested the departure from the community, we
> do not mean to imply that it was necessary for all things to pass under
> proprietorship at one moment, but only as considerations of men, of things,
> and of places required, and as the best means were found to remove causes
> of dispute.[168]

Natural law thus does not enjoin that everything should be made
proper to individuals. Rather, it 'enjoins the observance of
whatever things work to the end of the dominion instituted'. It does
enjoin proprietorship, but proprietorship is not thereby uniformly
nor universally required across all human societies; rather,
'proprietorship . . . has been introduced as the peace of men seemed
to require it'.[169]

By holding that property arises in a series of steps which reflect
prevailing circumstances in particular social situations, Pufendorf
allows that the history of property is not everywhere the same. The
nature and number of the steps from primitive negative community
must vary according to the different circumstances of different
human groups. His position is simply that the nature and extent of
property is a matter for human beings to settle, by their use of sane
reason to determine what is necessary for social peace: 'the law of
nature approves all conventions which have been introduced about
things by men, provided they involve no contradiction or do not
overturn society.' Although natural law advises the introduction of
property, it does so 'on the condition that it would rest with the
judgement of men, whether they wanted all things to be proper or
only some, or would hold some things indivisible and leave the rest
open to all, yet in such a way that no one might claim them for
himself alone'.[170]

Having stressed the stepwise development of property, we need
now to consider the factors which require steps to be taken, or
which determine the order or character of the steps to be taken. The
first of these factors Pufendorf adjudges to be the relative scarcity of
necessary goods in the natural (i.e. primitive) state:

> Most things which are of use to men immediately and are employed to
> nourish them and protect their bodies, are not produced everywhere by

---

[168] *DJNG* IV. 4. 13.   [169] Ibid. 14.
[170] Ibid. 4.

nature and without cultivation in such abundance that they fully suffice for everyone. Therefore, an occasion for quarrels and wars lay ready at hand, if two or more men needed the same thing, and individuals tried to appropriate for themselves the same thing, when it was not enough for all.

Property is then a solution to the quarrels and conflicts which arise over the allocation of relatively scarce goods. It is an institution which functions to preserve peace. This factor, says Pufendorf, 'also shows the falsity of the old saying: "Mine and thine are the causes of all wars". Rather it is that "mine and thine" were introduced to avoid wars.'[171] The point of introducing the institution, and its success in this role, are two different matters, of course; but Pufendorf's defence of property as an aid to social peace remains important and relevant, given the influence, in its recent guises, of that old saying on twentieth-century political thought and life.

But to return to the beginnings of things: if it was a primitive relative scarcity which caused the introduction of property, this puts the lie to the common view that there was an original Golden Age. The belief in the existence of such a time Pufendorf attributes to nostalgia for the simple life. He observes that the old have a tendency to praise the past, particularly the time of their own youth. So those who were forced by circumstances to abandon primitive simplicity for the more industrious life, with its property and developing refinement, 'took such a change of habits very hard, and many a time longed for their nuts and idleness'. Later generations, remembering 'this complaint of their forebears' (and not untouched by nostalgia themselves) thereby came to construct 'those dreams about a Golden Age'.[172] Pufendorf thus adopts a position quite distinct from Grotius's: for the latter, the idea of the Golden Age is employed uncritically in *Mare Liberum* (although this could perhaps be regarded as a heuristic device), and the transition to property relations in *De Jure Belli ac Pacis* is a response not to scarcity but to the inconveniences and quarrels which are seen as an unavoidable part of the collection and distribution of a product which is physically scattered, heterogeneous (and so not readily commensurable), and the fruit of unequal contributions.[173] Pufendorf does, however, recognize the role of this last factor, the inequality of individual contributions in creating the consumable products. It is the second factor he recognizes in the development of property.

[171] *DJNG* iv. 4. 6.   [172] Ibid. 8.
[173] See *ML* 23 (*DJPC* 227); *DJBP* ii. 2. ii. 2–4.

The physical necessities of life, even in the simplest of human societies, have to be collected; and, in more complex social orders, they have to be produced. So, to possess even the basic necessities of life, a society depends on the contribution of each member; and this contribution is labour. Social peace is not likely to be maintained if unequal expenditure of labour on the part of individuals is not reflected in some way in the allocation of resources. But the simplest way to maintain a rough parity between amount of labour expended and amount of returns—at least, one which avoids quarrels—is to institute a system of private property. This is especially so either for those things which are consumed by use (such as food), or for those exhaustible resources readily attributable to individuals (such as most mobile goods, and some kinds of immobile goods, for example, permanent dwellings). Pufendorf sums up the basic requirements of this factor thus:

> most things require labour and cultivation by men to produce them and make them fit for use. But in such cases it was improper that a man who had contributed no labour should have right to things equal to his by whose industry a thing had been raised or rendered fit for service. Therefore, it was advantageous to peace among men that, as soon as men multiplied, there should be introduced dominion of mobile things, especially such as require labour and cultivation by men, and, among immobile things, dominion of those which are of immediate use to men, such as places for dwelling.[174]

In another passage, he points out the role of labour in the original acquisition of things. In the original negative community, 'the bodies of things belong to no one, but their fruits after gathering are proper . . . An oak tree belonged to no man, but the acorns that fell to the ground were his who had gathered them.'[175]

Thus Pufendorf allocates an important role to labour. His position is quite similar to Grotius's view in *Mare Liberum*, where it is said that nature has willed that some things 'through the industry and labour of each man became his own'.[176] None the less, it is not true for either that labour *makes* property, since agreement plays a crucial role in both theories. For Pufendorf, although labour may be a necessary part of the process in which property is generated, property is a moral quality which can only be brought into existence

[174] *DJNG* iv. 4. 6.
[175] Ibid. 13.
[176] *ML* 2.

by those actions which can have a moral effect.[177] Property does not come into being as a result of labour, or in some other way dependent on labour but not agreements (as Locke and Hutcheson later contend)[178] but depends on agreements, whether express or tacit:

although there appears to be some reason why . . . things should belong to some men rather than to others [i.e. because of labour expended], yet the dominion of the one group, involving, as it does, the exclusion of the next, had to be confirmed at least by a tacit pact, which contained at the same time a tacit renunciation on the part of the rest; because, when things have been assigned to one person, the rest of mankind do not care to advance any claim to them on the alleged ground that the earth, as the common home of men, has contributed to those same things their substance and nourishment.[179]

So, should men fail to protest at particular acts of seizure or other forms of labour, they can be held to have tacitly renounced any claim to goods thus acquired, and have tacitly consented to the acquisition.

For 'immobile things produced by nature without the labour of man, such as fields', the situation differs in one important respect:

[177] *DJNG* IV. 4. 1: 'proprietorship and community are moral qualities which have no physical or intrinsic effect upon things themselves, but only produce a moral effect in relation to other men.' In *A System of Moral Philosophy*, Hutcheson stresses that 'the difficulties of dealing with this subject', that is, of understanding the genesis of property, 'arise from some confused imagination that property is some *physical* quality or relation produced by some action of men', whereas it is in fact a moral relation (*Collected Works*, v. 318; emphasis added). Among his targets he may intend Locke, who at one point in his treatment of the origin of property, considering the very ex. of the gathering of acorns employed above by Pufendorf, argues that the acorns must belong to the person nourished by them because 'No Body can deny but the nourishment is his' (*Two Treatises*, ii. 28). The nourishment is undoubtedly a physical effect, but hardly a moral effect—esp. when it is remembered that nourishment is gained even when self-preservation is not at stake, and also that not only honest gatherers, but also thieves, are equally well nourished by the acorns they come to consume.

[178] Hutcheson argues that, if there is an original negative community, consumable goods can be appropriated 'without consulting the rest of mankind . . . Thus we need not have recourse to any old conventions or compacts, as with Grotius or Pufendorf, in explaining the original of property' (*System*, in *Collected Works*, v. 331). In arguing thus he is following Locke, of course; but it will be argued in the next ch. that Locke, although he certainly rejects the need for compacts, does not thereby reduce successful appropriation merely to the exercise of labour. Rather, he makes property dependent on *rational* labour, labour in accord with the divine purposes for the creation.

[179] *DJNG* IV. 4. 6.

unlike those things already considered, these are not scarce, but abundant. For this reason they come to be appropriated by individuals not all at once, but progressively. They become proper by occupation, and occupation is limited in extent because it is a matter of what can be *used*. In the case under consideration, that of fields, this limit is expressed in the equation of the extent of occupation with the extent of cultivation:

regarding the immobile things produced by nature without the labour of man, such as fields, they were so extensive that they abundantly provided for the small number of early men, and for that reason at first only so much of them was occupied as men judged to be suitable for their uses, while the rest was left in a state of original negative community, so that every man who wished to was free in the future to take it . . . fields should belong to those who cultivated them.[180]

Here, in embryo, is Locke's requirement that appropriation from the original community be limited by the capacity to use the things appropriated. For Locke, a man may appropriate anything as long as it stays 'within the *bounds*, set by reason of what might serve for his *use*'. In this way also peace is preserved (as the natural law requires): 'there could then be little room for Quarrels or contentions about Property so established.'[181] Applied to the land itself, the use-criterion limits appropriation, as it does for Pufendorf, to what is cultivated: '*As much Land* as a Man Tills, Plants, Improves, Cultivates, and can use the Product of, so much is his *Property*.'[182] Unlike Pufendorf, Locke provides an explicit test for unsuccessful usage—the 'spoilage condition'. However, although Pufendorf affirms what Locke denies by requiring a pact to generate the necessary moral effect, his pact has a similar effect to Locke's spoilage condition because it has a necessary content. It affirms occupation by use, restricts occupation to what is used, and so leaves unclaimed land for future occupation:

hence it is understood that a pact was agreed upon, to the effect that such fields as had been assigned to one person by the express convention of the rest of men, or such as the rest could be held tacitly to have withdrawn from, in view of the fact that one man alone had been allowed to enjoy them in peace, while they had claimed for themselves other fields on the same basis—that such fields should belong to those who had cultivated them.

---

[180] Ibid.   [181] *Two Treatises*, ii. 31.
[182] Ibid. 32.

'And finally, that what was left should pass to those who would hereafter occupy the fields.[183]

These passages show us the extent to which Pufendorf provides a foundation for Locke to build his own theory of appropriation.

We can now also offer a more detailed consideration of Pufendorf's relationship to Grotius. He indicates his own view of the relationship by remarking that, apart from 'what he [i.e. Grotius] adds against the accepted doctrines of our churches, which have been already censured enough by others',[184] he is in substantial agreement with Grotius. He understands himself to be refining and clarifying Grotius's views, thereby avoiding some of the latter's confusions. He sees his main contributions to be, firstly, establishing a clear distinction between negative and positive community, and, secondly, providing an improved explanation of why a pact was necessary to establish property. Some of his observations on these matters will now be examined, since they serve to clarify aspects of his theory.

Pufendorf comments on Grotius's account of the original divine donation of the earth to human beings as follows:

[Grotius] says: 'Soon after the creation of the world, and a second time after the Flood, God conferred upon the human race a general right over things of a lower nature'. This we accept in the sense that God allowed men a right to use the things of this earth 'in a general way', that is, He did not determine at that same time what things should be held individually, and what in common, but this He left to the judgment of men, that they should dispose of the matter according as it seemed to work for peace. But no credit should be given to any such idea as that God at the beginning instituted a positive community, from which men later withdrew on their own initiative, but rather, so far as it concerned God, such things were left open to the uses of men.[185]

This passage raises two important matters. First, Pufendorf's interpretative strictures—that original community, established by divine donation, be understood negatively rather than positively—should not be taken to signal a disagreement with Grotius. He makes it clear that Grotius's view implies negative community, but that the failure to distinguish clearly between the two types of community sometimes leads him (Grotius) into confusion. Thus he commends Grotius for recognizing that the original community

---

[183] *DJNG* IV. 4. 6.   [184] Ibid. 9.   [185] Ibid.

required human beings to live a simple life, to be 'content to live upon simple fruits', etc., whereas refinement required the introduction of property. Negative community, but not positive community, has this implication, since the former precludes the accumulation and division of a *social* product. Under negative community, each person simply takes what he or she needs, whereas under positive community a system of accumulation and distribution may be established by an express pact. Since only positive community depends on a system of mutual regard, Pufendorf criticizes Grotius for thinking that the original community depended in any way on affection: 'But when he adds that community could have endured "if men had lived on terms of mutual affection such as rarely appears", he confuses negative community with positive.'[186]

The second important matter is indicated by the denial of any original positive community, 'from which men later withdrew on their own initiative'. There is something a little odd about this remark, and attending to it will help to bring into clearer focus a feature of natural law theory. The oddity is that positive community can only be withdrawn from by agreement: 'if any decision is to be reached on the whole thing, the consent and authority of each person concerned in it must be secured.'[187] This consent must be expressly given (as will be shown below). So positive community can only be successfully withdrawn from in the earliest ages of human society, before the number and geographical extent of human beings made an express agreement of the entire human population impossible. Unless such an express agreement took place, then, contrary to the fact of positive laws concerning . property, an original positive community of things (if such there was) would still be in force. To suppose an original positive community is thus to raise the possibility that distinctions of ownership by positive law are in fact not justified. And, given that this possibility can only be removed by supposing a primitive express agreement of which there is no known record, to suppose an original positive community is to call sharply into question the entire edifice of the positive law of property. This would be, for Pufendorf, such a profoundly disturbing possibility that it is surpising that he seems not to consider it. He appears simply to take

[186] Ibid.   [187] Ibid. 2.

it for granted that, if there was an original positive community, it no longer exists, but was withdrawn from successfully. Why does he accept this?

It may be that the answer lies right at the heart of the natural law enterprise, neatly caught in the seventeenth-century conception of natural law as moral science. The idea of moral science, as outlined in section 1, is the idea of a systematic body of knowledge of the relations between moral phenomena, in just the way that physical science is a systematic body of knowledge of the relations between physical phenomena. As such, moral science depends, like physical science, on the reality of its phenomena. Natural law, as moral science, thus has the task of explaining the moral phenomena we in fact have. It is, in this respect, a rather conservative enterprise. It does not ask, What sort of moral world ought there to be?, but What is the origin of the moral world (we have)? This is what is at issue in the question concerning the origin of property. A natural law explanation of the origin of property is an explanation both of how property can arise from a state without property, and how the history of property is a natural (rational) process which leads to the distinctions of property we recognize. In this spirit, it appears that Pufendorf rules out the revolutionary possibility that there is in fact no private property, but a positive community, at the very beginning of his enterprise. By accepting the naturalness of law he thereby rejects the 'sceptical' theories. Provided that we do not press the term too hard, we can say that a natural law theory is a 'common-sense' theory, in that it does not undermine the views widely established in a society.

Pufendorf sees his second main advance on Grotius's views to be the clarification of the nature and role of pacts in establishing property. He agrees with Grotius that a pact, whether express or tacit, is necessary to establish a moral relation between human beings, because moral effects depend on public acts. If there is no public act, there can be no moral effect, since in such cases 'others were not able to know what a man wished to be his own, that they might refrain from it'. Therefore, as Grotius puts it, 'things at the first passed into proprietorship not by a mere act of will'. An act of seizure is thus a necessary part of staking a claim to some unpossessed thing, but a pact is also necessary, because the act of seizure is not of itself sufficient to create a moral effect, but does so when it is not resisted by others, or is expressly consented to by them. In explaining this, Pufendorf shows that, while a tacit pact is adequate for establishing property from negative community, positive community can not be generated without express consent. To establish property, he says:

> there was need of an external act or seizure, and for this to produce a moral effect, that is, an obligation on the part of others to refrain from a thing already seized by some one else, an antecedent pact was required and an express pact, indeed, when several men divided among themselves things open to all; but a tacit pact sufficed when the things occupied at that time had been left unpossessed by the first dividers of things. For it is understood that these men agreed that those things which in the first division had not been assigned to a definite individual should pass to him who was the first to take possession of them.[188]

Property for immediate use arises out of negative community by a tacit pact of non-interference with acts of seizure, but more extensive and sophisticated forms of property (including, most importantly, positive community) arise out of a division, and this cannot occur without an express pact.

Pufendorf thus differs from the rather relaxed approach to explicit agreements exhibited by Grotius, an approach which reflects the latter's heavy reliance on sacred history. Pufendorf has no quarrel with sacred history, but he is led to his conclusions more by considerations of theoretical necessity than by following the patriarchal narratives of the Book of Genesis. In his theory, history still occupies an important place, as is shown, for example, by his insistence that the character and extent of a system of property is entirely a matter for the human actors who produce it, as long as in producing it they act according to the rational necessities of the situation, rather than violently going against nature. In addition, his insistence that property arises not all at once, but in steps, is part of this requirement. Pufendorf's account of property, like that of Grotius before him, can be called natural (in that it arises necessarily according to the requirements of human sociableness) and historical (in being the product of human actions over time). Like Grotius, his aim is to produce a natural history of property.

[188] *DJNG* iv. 4. 9.

5. NECESSITY, SLAVERY, AND INDUSTRY

In this section, Pufendorf's treatment of the important question of
the right of necessity will be examined. The task 'is to inquire what
force the necessity of safety has to free some act from the obligation
of general laws',[189] in particular, of general laws of property. He
acknowledges that there is widespread support for the view that
necessity has such a force:

The power of necessity is a phrase upon the lips of all men, because it lacks
the restraint of law, and is understood to form an exception in all the rules
of men, while it carries the right to do many things which, apart from it,
were held to be forbidden.[190]

Pufendorf accepts that there is such a right, but stresses that it
cannot be taken for granted.[191] It does not apply to all things, since
the creation depends for its order on its laws. Exceptions may
threaten or endanger this order, so they can only be allowed within
specific limits. The nature of the limits which concern the property
of others will be explained below.

   Since the question at issue is whether there is a right of necessity
which overrules positive laws of property, Pufendorf frames his
discussion in terms of positive law. He holds that positive laws must
be understood to make an exception in the case of necessity,
because the legislators' positive actions must be understood in a
particular way: the legislators, 'since they had as their purpose the
promotion through these laws and institutions of men's safety or
convenience, are supposed always to have had before their eyes the
weakness of human nature, and how man cannot help avoiding and
repelling whatever tends to his destruction'. Extreme necessity is of
course a paradigm case, so 'most laws, and especially positive laws,
are understood to make an exception of a case of necessity, or to lay
no obligation, when such an obligation will be attended by some
evil, destructive of human nature, or too great for the common
constancy of mankind'.[192]

---

[189] *DJNG* II. 6. 1. For Pufendorf necessity affects not only safety but also honour;
however he refers to the complications caused by considerations of this kind only in
passing.
[190] Ibid.   [191] Ibid. 2.
[192] Ibid. IV. 4. 2. Pufendorf adds 'unless such a case is included expressly, or in the
nature of the matter'. It is not clear why such exceptions are permissible. Given that such
laws ignore the 'weakness of human nature', do they not do violence to that nature?

Why does Pufendorf hold that positive law must, in the general run of things, 'make an exception of a case of necessity'? To explain his position, he focuses attention on the mind of the legislator(s): the legislators 'had as their purpose the promotion . . . of men's safety or convenience'. If we ask, Why did the legislators have this purpose? (or, alternatively, How do we know that they had this purpose?), Pufendorf's answer appears to be, Because we must believe that they did. That is, he seems to appeal to interpretative charity. This is not entirely a satisfying solution, since it requires us to believe of the original legislators what may well not be true. Law would then be founded on a convenient fiction, or noble lie. It is therefore worth looking at the matter a little more closely.

The strongest evidence for understanding Pufendorf to be employing a principle of interpretative charity is provided by his remark that 'it is presumed from the benevolent mind of the legislator, and from the consideration of human nature, that a case of necessity is not included under a law which has been conceived with a general scope'.[193] An appeal to 'the benevolent mind of the legislator' does indeed look like interpretative charity. However, it will be argued that it is not; and that, in any case, nothing relevant depends on the issue, because exceptions in the case of necessity can be established independently.

In the first place: in the quoted passage, Pufendorf is not relying on a principle of interpretative charity because it is not the benevolence of the legislator's mind which is being presumed. Rather, for reasons which will be given below, this is taken to be a simple fact. What is being presumed is that, given the legislator's benevolent mind, and given also human nature, a particular conclusion follows—that necessity constitutes an exception to a law 'which has been conceived with a general scope'. The presumption, in other words, concerns the validity of a particular deduction from a set of premises which include a factual claim about the legislator's mind. The presumption is not *about* that mind (or state of mind). So neither is it an instance of interpretative charity.

What of Pufendorf's other claim—that the legislator's purpose is 'the promotion . . . of men's safety or convenience'? This view admits of the same treatment. It might at first appear to be a charitable presumption about the legislator's purposes, but in fact

[193] Ibid.

Pufendorf is simply asserting that this *is* the legislator's purpose. What leads him to make such a bold claim? Why should the legislator's purpose be the promotion of safety and convenience?

The short answer is that it is so because it *must* be. The legislator's purpose must be so because it follows 'from the consideration of human nature'. How can the consideration of human nature demonstrate the nature of the legislator's purposes? Before showing how this can be so, it should be noted that, if it can be successfully demonstrated, then it is also established that the exceptions to general laws generated in cases of necessity can be derived directly from the consideration of human nature. No special recourse to the legislator's mind would then be necessary, so neither would it matter what is attributed, charitably or otherwise, to that mind. Pufendorf's view that the legislator's purpose is to promote safety and convenience is simply the view that law has this function—that is, that it in fact has this function, not merely that it ought to (but does not). It has this function simply because it does promote safety and convenience. The rule of law, while it does not guarantee the peace and safety of human society, none the less promotes such peace and safety. Of course, particular laws—especially those that proceed from despotism or tyranny—are quite able to destroy social peace and safety. So what reason is there to be confident that the rule of law in general has a peaceful tendency?

The question can be answered in two distinct but complementary ways. Firstly, laws (and indeed societies) are subject to the forces of natural selection. (Pufendorf would not have put it this way, of course, but his extensive knowledge of ancient history would provide him with ample reasons for accepting the principle in question.) That is, laws are tested both internally by their subjects and externally by neighbouring societies. Laws which fail to unify and organize adequately the members of a society make that society easy prey when it comes into conflict with a society which, through more effective laws, has solved such problems. And laws which fail to gain the acceptance of the subjects of the laws are constantly subject to pressure for change through the non-compliance or otherwise dissenting activities of the subjects. In other words, those positively promulgated laws which have the highest survival value are just those laws which do promote the peace and safety of the members of the society. Laws with a high survival value, then, are those laws which so harmonize with human nature that 'the human race can have no wholesome and peaceful social organization'[194] without them. That is, laws with a high survival value are, or approximate, natural laws. So, although we are here dealing with positive laws, which *need* not be natural, we see that the social forces which produce such laws also provide a reason for believing that positive law will, in the main, conform to the patterns of natural law.

The second reason for holding that the rule of law has a peaceful tendency springs more directly from a consideration of the classical conception of human nature on which Pufendorf, like so many of his predecessors, relies. The influence of the classical conception shows itself in his stress on the social tendencies of human beings, and more specifically in his understanding of societies, and their laws, as the fruit of agreement between rational social beings. On this conception, apart from those (tacit) agreements which may be necessary to establish social institutions, institutions are maintained or revised as the result of rational politics. Politics of this kind has been described as 'the science of freedom, the public activity of free men, who come to agreement through discussion, compromise, conciliation and bargaining, through reconciling diverse interests and defining particular common interests'.[195] In fact, it is a process with a peaceful tendency, because it reconciles diverse interests and serves to establish common interests. So, by understanding the social processes of law-making in this light, Pufendorf readily comes to accept the peaceful tendencies of the rule of law. These are the peaceful purposes of the legislator.

(It might be queried, if the account of the legislator's mind is translatable without distortion into an account of law itself, why Pufendorf complicates—or apparently complicates—matters by talk of the legislator's mind? A plausible answer is that his concern is to capture the (for him) necessary formal element of law—that it arises from the will of a superior. By speaking of the legislator, the superior will, Pufendorf is able to underline his view that laws are not merely eternal rational principles, but require the superior's coercive power to establish their obligatory character.)

This brief account of the process of agreement through discussion, compromise, and so on, of rational beings is an

---

[194] *DJNG* I. 6. 18.

[195] E. Kamenka, 'Marxism and Politics', *Bulletin of the Australian Society of Legal Philosophy*, 10 (Mar. 1986), 20. Kamenka is offering an account of that 'older tradition, deriving from Aristotle and revived in recent years by Bernard Crick' (ibid.).

important aid to understanding Pufendorf's account of necessity, and the difference it makes. If law is the fruit of such a rational political process, it is shaped by what rational beings could be imagined to assent to. Thus we can understand not only why an exception is recognized in the case of necessity, since a rational view of human nature will include the awareness of its vulnerability to a wide range of possible misfortunes, not excluding those of human origin;[196] we can also understand why necessity establishes a right; why the right has, in Pufendorf's account, what may otherwise appear to be a rather curious collection of constraints; and why Pufendorf is able to insist that even positive law, if it is to generate obligations, presupposes an important general principle. The principle in question is a further indication of a close link between positive law and natural law, so it should be considered before examining Pufendorf's account of the right of necessity and its specific limitations.

The general principle presupposed by positive laws is this: 'the nature of affirmative commands requires that, in order for a man to be obligated here and now to the performance of some act, they presuppose the opportunity, matter, and ability necessary for an action.'[197] The principle can be summed up as: obligation presupposes capacity. Its importance for moral philosophy is difficult to overstress, since it is the principle underlying the Kantian dictum 'ought implies can'. Pufendorf is conscious of its significance, and provides a second formulation: 'to obligate ourselves it is required that we have the moral and physical faculty to perform some thing or action, in other words, that the performance is not beyond our strength and no law forbids it.'[198] It is the nature of affirmative commands to presuppose the moral and physical capacity to comply because it is in the nature of affirmative commands to obligate. Affirmative commands are thus not merely imperatives, but are expressions of the will of a rational superior, in that they arise through the rational[199] agreement of rational beings to establish legislative power. Obligation itself requires the capacity

---

[196] See e.g. *De Officio*, I. 3. 7: 'man is indeed an animal most bent upon self-preservation, helpless in himself, unable to save himself without the aid of his fellows, highly adapted to promote mutual interests; but on the other hand no less malicious, insolent, and easily provoked, also as able as he is prone to inflict injury upon another.'

[197] *DJNG* II. 6. 2.   [198] Ibid. III. 7. 1.   [199] Ibid. II. 6. 3.

to comply because rational beings would not freely agree to subject themselves to laws they could not be capable of keeping.

The most obvious example of such a law is, of course, that which endangers or denies one's preservation, or, more commonly, those cases where, because of the specific circumstances, keeping or endeavouring to keep an otherwise acceptable law endangers one's preservation. Thus the various kinds of capacities ('opportunity, matter, and ability') necessary for obligation 'are always understood to be wanting, when something cannot be done unless I perish in the doing, for the casting away of love and care for oneself is classed among things which are impossible, and which surpass the ordinary constancy of men'.[200] This passage helps to illustrate an important connection: to make an exception of necessity is to affirm the fundamental importance of self-preservation. Thus the principle necessary for positive laws to be obligating, that obligation presupposes capacity, is at bottom a commitment to the fundamental importance of self-preservation. The obligation of positive laws is therefore tied to their (implicit) recognition of the fundamental importance of self-preservation. But the recognition of the fundamental importance of self-preservation is, as has been argued above, one of the distinguishing marks of natural law. Therefore, to generate obligations, positive law must not conflict with this most important feature of natural law. For at least all those natural laws which govern adventitious states, the same must be true. (Such laws, since they concern only the social, not the cosmic, order, can be limited to human capabilites without threatening to undermine the order of creation.) This means that such natural laws likewise allow exceptions in the case of necessity:

But it should be observed, in connexion with those laws which cover the mutual duties of men, that there are certain precepts of natural law which presuppose some human deed or institution, that, as any one clearly recognizes upon a consideration of its end, should not be extended to a case of extreme necessity; and therefore the same exception also is in the law.[201]

The law of property, being a precept of natural law which presupposes 'some human deed or institution', must therefore recognize exceptions in cases of extreme necessity. That is, the law of property must recognize a right, arising out of necessity, to take from the property of others what is required for one's preservation.

---

[200] Ibid. 2.   [201] Ibid.

Pufendorf's account of the nature and extent of this right can now be examined.

It was said above that, by recognizing that laws arise out of the free agreements of rational beings, we can understand both that necessity generates a right, and what the extent and limitations of this right are, especially in so far as it affects the property of others. First of all, the exception of the case of necessity can properly be said to generate a right of necessity because it is a definite moral effect generated by rational agreement. The right has one general limit, a limit which reflects the primacy of self-love: it does not require that the situation of the necessitous be relieved if by so doing the giver is reduced to like necessity. As Pufendorf puts it, 'I am not expected to give bread to a drowning person, if I myself need it . . . Nor, if another is in danger of drowning, am I bound to draw him out, if I must perish in his place.'[202]

In the case of rights over the property of others, Pufendorf recognizes a range of special restrictions. Although an apparently heterogeneous lot, they reflect the limitations rational agents are presumed to require in order to arrive at agreement. The most important constraint on what can be agreed upon in the case of necessity, with respect to the property of others, is that imposed by the original rationale for establishing property. The exceptions to be allowed in the case of necessity must not be such that they frustrate the point of property relations. The sorts of exceptions which can be generated by necessity can thus be determined only by keeping in mind the reasons for the introduction of ownership. Pufendorf therefore summarizes the main reasons for property at this point. He says, 'The most important advanced are, [1] that thereby the quarrels arising from the original community of ownership are avoided, and [2] that the industry of men is increased, in that each man has to secure his possession by his own efforts.'[203] Rights of necessity over the property of others must thus be limited by the necessity to avoid quarrels (and, more generally, to preserve peace), and by the necessity to secure the fruits of industry in the hands of the industrious.

The first reason for property is reflected in the fact that the right

---

[202] *DJNG* II. 6. 2.

[203] Ibid. 5. It will be shown below that recognition of the increasing sophistication and productive power of modern societies leads to the second of these factors being stressed, while the first tends to disappear from view.

of necessity must be constrained by due process. The right does not, in the first instance, empower the necessitous simply to take from the goods of another. Rather, a man in need must first make a formal demand of the owner, and only if this is refused can he resort to more direct means. But even in this case he cannot simply take what he needs: he must, wherever possible, seek a court ruling in his favour. (This is not always possible, of course: as Pufendorf observes, quoting an ancient proverb: 'Necessity keeps no holidays.')[204] Only if a court ruling cannot be gained, or if the relevant institutions refuse to recognize his case, can he resort to directly taking what he needs. In this situation, the right of necessity allows him to take what he needs from what is another's, without thereby committing a crime. Pufendorf spells out the implications of the right as follows:

a person may not himself lay hands at once on property owed him by another, but should demand of the owner that he hand it over to him of his own accord. If, however, the owner refuses of his own accord to meet his obligation, the power of ownership is by no means so great that property owed another may not be taken from an unwilling owner, through the authority of a judge in commonwealths, or, in a state of natural liberty, by the might of war . . . But if such a precaution is not taken for the poor in some particular commonwealths . . . would you have him die of hunger? Can any human institution have such power that, if another neglects to do his duty toward me, I must perish rather than depart from the customary and usual manner of procedure? I should not feel, therefore, that a man has made himself guilty of the crime of theft if when he has, through no fault of his own, fallen into extreme want [of the necessities of life] . . . he should make away with them by violence or by stealth; and especially so if he intends to make good their value whenever a kindlier fortune may smile upon him.[205]

Although an eloquent defence of those in need, this passage also indicates two other limitations on the exercise of the right of necessity, limitations which reflect the constraint imposed by the second reason for property. These limitations are, firstly, that the want should have arisen 'through no fault of his own', and, secondly, that the case for taking what is needed is considerably strengthened if the taker intends to restore what has been taken 'whenever a kindlier fortune may smile upon him'. In a later passage Pufendorf adopts a stronger version of this second

[204] Ibid. 2.   [205] Ibid. 5.

requirement, holding that 'restitution *must* be made', and castigates Grotius on the ground that the latter's account of necessity implies that restitution need not be made (even though Grotius asserts that it must—i.e. his account is both inadequate and inconsistent). Pufendorf then proceeds to weaken this claim (presumably thinking of those who cannot—and therefore ought not to—make actual restitution), by concluding that one who seizes another's goods is thereby put under an obligation, but this obligation is 'either of gratitude, or of making good the value of the object involved'.[206] Clearly, this requirement serves to protect the industrious. It does so in two ways: by helping to prevent frivolous claims on the goods of another, since the obligation to repay where possible removes the incentive to make claims where there is no pressing need; and by minimizing the extent to which claims on the goods of the industrious constitute permanent losses of their possessions, thereby minimizing any disincentive to accumulate a surplus, a disincentive which would arise on a too-liberal interpretation of the right of necessity.

Similarly, the 'no fault' limitation is designed to protect the industrious from the reckless and, especially, the idle. In this case the reason does not have to be inferred, since Pufendorf explicitly makes the connection:

A distinction should be made between the case in which a man fell under such necessity through no fault of his, and that in which his own sluggishness and negligence are to blame. Unless such a distinction is drawn, a right is apparently given to lazy scoundrels who have fallen upon want through idleness, whereby they may appropriate to themselves by force what has been secured by the labour of others; and so, since their idleness maintains their want, they put the industrious under the necessity of maintaining against their will such a useless herd.[207]

This possibility is intolerable, because it would allow the incentive to industry to be completely destroyed. To tolerate it would transform the right of necessity from a safety net for the victims of misfortune to a manacle on social development. Moreover, in this passage Pufendorf shows that the right of necessity is not of such an unrestricted scope: for rights depend on agreements, and, to be binding, agreements must be rationally consented to. In this case

[206] *DJNG* II. 6. 6.   [207] Ibid.

any such consent is clearly lacking, since, in such circumstances, the industrious maintain the 'useless herd' against their will. Pufendorf considers obtaining the consent of rational beings to maintain such a state of affairs to be unimaginable. So, by keeping in mind that the right of necessity, like all rights, depends on the agreement of rational agents, it becomes evident that Pufendorf's conclusion (which may otherwise seem damagingly *ad hoc*) faithfully reflects his commitments. He concludes: 'the proper reply to lazy drones is that which the ant, as the fable has it, gave in the winter to the lazy grasshopper.'[208]

Pufendorf's position is that in order to maintain the purpose of property relations, limitations of this kind on the right of necessity are unavoidable. He therefore rejects Grotius's view that in the event of necessity the original use-right revives. Although, on the latter's view, it may be possible to exclude the claims of the lazy, the other protective limitations Pufendorf requires could not be maintained. To allow the revival of the original use-right is to imply that necessity causes the rights of property-holders to lapse; in effect to deny the existence of property-holders. Since Pufendorf's further limitations presuppose that there are property-holders whose rights guarantee them special consideration, Grotius's interpretation cannot accommodate them. Reviving original use-rights would rule out the possibility of applying the method of due process, would recognize no owner to whom restitution should be made (or even gratitude owed), and would be unable to apply the principle of the primacy of self-preservation, by which an owner is entitled not to give to another if he will thereby fall into necessity. It is not hard to imagine that, for Pufendorf, Grotius's proposal is best regarded as a cure worse than the disease it seeks to treat. In fact, its major failings—its lack of safeguards for the efforts of the industrious, and its inability to overcome not only quarrels but also lingering resentments which would constitute a permanent threat to peace—are so serious that it must be regarded as contrary to natural law: it could not be accepted by rational beings reflecting on these questions. So, despite its apparently *ad hoc* features, Pufendorf's account of the right of necessity conforms better to the requirements of natural law.

How does the right of necessity bear on the question of slavery?

---

[208] Ibid. (The reference is to Aesop.)

Does extreme necessity ever require self-enslavement? That is, are there any cases of dire necessity for which the only solution is self-enslavement, or does the right of necessity rule out such possibilities? Pufendorf holds that slavery first arose through contract, through acts of self-enslavement.[209] Were these acts necessary? He clearly envisages one kind of case where he believes they were, for, in a passage which refers to some biblical cases of necessity, he remarks that 'the man who had no further means of maintaining himself was supposed to sell himself into slavery'.[210] However, the man who has no further means of maintaining himself has, through the right generated by necessity, no need to sell himself into slavery, provided the necessary limitations of that right are observed. The important limitation, in this case, is the requirement that the man's condition be no fault of his own. If his need is due to laziness, the right of necessity can offer him no protection, so, in such a case, self-enslavement is indeed necessary. In one of the important senses of 'natural', then, some cases of slavery can have a natural origin. (In the other main sense of 'natural', of course, no slavery is ever natural, since it does not arise independently of human actions.[211] In this sense, human beings are all naturally free.)

There is something curious here. It appears that those cases where individuals are not protected by the right of necessity are precisely those cases where the attempt to enter slavery is least likely to be successful. If only the lazy must enslave themselves, only the lazy are available as slaves. What incentive could there be, then, for taking on a slave? Pufendorf's answer would probably be as follows: granted that only the lazy or incompetent are available as slaves, none the less under the proper direction—including a discipline 'more rigorous' than that applied to a son[212]—the slave can be made productive. In fact, he recognizes that slaves typically spring from the ranks of the least industrious. He accounts for the development of slavery in this way:

Our idea on the origin of slavery is as follows. When in early days men departed from their original simple manner of living and began to devote more efforts to the elaboration of life . . . it is highly probable that the more sagacious and more wealthy invited the more sluggish and the poorer sort to hire themselves out to them.

[209] *DJNG* VI. 3. 4.   [210] Ibid. II. 6. 5.
[211] Ibid. VI. 3. 2.   [212] Ibid. I.

Then, 'when *both* parties came to realize the advantage of this', there was established a permanent system of 'goods for work': 'And so the first beginnings of slavery followed upon the willing consent of men of poorer condition; and a contract of the form of "goods for work"; I will always provide for you, if you will always work for me.'[213] Significantly, what is explained here is the origin of a particular form of economic order, including an uneven division of responsibility. What is not explained is the origin of a rightless state. This is not merely accidental: if Pufendorf is to account for the origin of slavery by contract, then what is contracted must be capable of rational consent if the contract is to be binding. A rightless state, subject to the arbitrary, perhaps brutal, acts of a master is clearly not within the bounds of rational consent—no rational being could consent to being made morally powerless, any more than being made physically powerless. So Pufendorf must hold that slavery is not properly regarded as a state where the slave is denied the status of a moral being. This he does: he insists, as already mentioned, that slaves are not owned by their masters in the same manner as are physical objects; the relation of master to slave is rather that of sovereign to subject. Slaves alienate only the right to rule over them.[214] They remain beings capable of receiving an injury, and so masters do not escape duties towards their slaves.[215]

The facts of history do not measure up, of course, and Pufendorf acknowledges that this is so: the 'brutality of many nations' leads to slaves being 'numbered among . . . material possessions'.[216] The power of the master in these cases becomes 'extended to the point that not only the labour but also the body of the slave is understood to belong to his master'.[217] Pufendorf is quite critical of such extensions of power, but not so critical as to reject them as violations of the natural (as contrary to what is capable of rational agreement). As a result, he ends up accepting that, even in the most severe versions of slavery, the children of slaves (who certainly are not guilty of laziness or incompetence, having had no opportunity to be either) are required, by the effective necessity of the mother (who has nothing of her own with which to sustain them), to be enslaved as well.

This case shows the extent to which the institution of slavery has strayed from the original agreement of 'goods for work', an

---

[213] Ibid. vi. 3. 4 (emphasis added).   [214] Ibid. 7.
[215] Ibid. 8.   [216] Ibid. 7.   [217] Ibid. 9.

arrangement advantageous to both parties. There is no indication that the goods received by the enslaved mother are at all apportioned to her work value, or even that she receives anything other than subsistence goods, since she is unable to accrue even that small surplus of goods necessary to support her child. She is conceived to be in a state of permanent necessity, with no opportunity to provide her children with a better or even an alternative life. In this sort of case, then, slavery loses any resemblance to the original system of mutual advantage—it has become an avenue of despair. It is quite implausible to imagine that such a one-way arrangement could be agreed to by rational beings.

Pufendorf himself concedes that his attempt to give slavery something of a human face is not successful. After comparing the relation of master to slave with that of sovereign to subject, he is forced to concede that there is a fundamental difference: the subject's subjection to the sovereign is, properly conceived, a subjection to general laws; the slave, on the other hand, is subject simply to the master's arbitrary will. The great disadvantage of slavery, he says, is that

free men need obey only the state and its general laws, and need fear no punishment but what is defined in them, while in all else they hold it their special delight to suit their own will. But slaves serve one who is even a fellow citizen, are subject to his special orders, penalties, and restraints, and are forced to bear his harshness; which is all the more irksome the more frequent and intimate the contact between them. And this is all the harder because the laws of the state rarely come to the assistance of servants against their masters, save when their harshness comes to a head in some outrageous savagery.[218]

Except in the most extreme circumstances, then, the slave's state is not governed by law, but by the arbitrary will of the master. As such, it cannot be compared with the situation of the subject under the sovereign, nor can it be understood as an agreement in which some rational advantage is embodied. Rather, the brutality which has been such a feature of the history of slavery must be seen as a permanent possibility, inherent in the nature of the master–slave relation itself. Pufendorf thus effectively shows that the institution of slavery is an institution of violence, not a law-governed condition. It therefore cannot be recognized by natural law.

[218] *DJNG* vi. 3. 10.

So, not only are most forms of self-enslavement unnecessary, arising as they do in circumstances already protected by the right of necessity, but also those other forms which are not protected thereby must be rejected, since slavery, because of its inherent tolerance of violence, is a state contrary to natural law. The lazy and incompetent are not thereby spared from any penalty, however, nor must the right of necessity over the goods of others be extended to cater for them. The latter cannot be, since to do so would be to undermine the whole purpose of property relations. Pufendorf's most promising avenue of resolution would appear to be this: although they cannot be compelled to enter slavery, willingly or otherwise, it does not follow that they cannot be compelled to enter some law-governed form of compulsory servitude. Such servitude, provided it is constrained within limits sufficient to prevent the violence of slavery, and avoid its perpetuity (especially with respect to the children of slaves), could resolve the problem of the lazy and incompetent without undermining the safeguard to industry that is part of the purpose of any system of property. A controlled form of compulsory labour is undoubtedly better than simply outlawing the lazy or the economically incompetent, and would provide them with a stable status. Where no other solution is possible, such a system, unlike slavery, would not be contrary to natural law.

Of course, a far better solution would be to engineer a society in which laziness and incompetence could be avoided. Perhaps the most promising path to achieving such a goal would be to provide strong positive incentives to industrious activity, and for just this reason Pufendorf holds a secure system of property to be necessary. It is not, however, sufficient. Equally necessary is a rational science of domestic management and wealth creation, including a sensitive measure of the values of goods, in order to facilitate commercial exchanges. By developing a science of this kind, the way would be open to overcoming the problem of necessity. The recognition of this possibility, and of its importance, is a distinctive feature of the social theories of Pufendorf's successors: as they develop an increasingly sophisticated appreciation of the productive powers of human labour and of commercial exchanges—an appreciation which leads to the new science of political economy—so their concern with the state of necessity, and of its rights, steadily diminishes. The right of necessity loses its explicit function—as a limitation on the exercise of rights over things—in later theories, but this does not of itself imply a weakened concern for the well-being of the economically (and thus morally) vulnerable. Rather, it is the predictable outcome of a strategy thought to provide a powerful—albeit indirect—solution to the problem of necessity, and its presumed causes in laziness and carelessness. For theories of this kind, commercial society has a built-in 'maximin' tendency, in that it functions steadily to improve the lot of the (non-irretrievably) worst off.[219] The view is strongly defended by Locke in a famous passage, where he says that, in America, 'a King of a large and fruitful Territory there feeds, lodges, and is clad worse than a day Labourer in *England*'.[220] And Hume, although he admits that commercial society must encourage avarice,[221] holds none the less that 'the ages of refinement are both the happiest and the most virtuous'.[222] If avarice serves to cure the vices that cause poverty, it may well be thought a small price to pay for a general improvement in the lot of humankind.

Pufendorf shows himself to be aware of some aspects of this outlook, especially when discussing prices and money. He recognizes a strong correlation between the absence of a money economy and the absence of civilization: 'It is perfectly plain that those nations which are unacquainted with the use of currency have no part in the advances of civilization.'[223] The correlation reflects the fact that in sophisticated societies simple ways of measuring the values of things do not suffice. The 'ordinary price' of a thing or action is 'the aptitude of a thing or action, by which it can either mediately or immediately contribute something to the necessity of human life, or to making it more advantageous or pleasant'.[224] The ordinary price of a thing is its use-value. Measuring value in this way did not long suffice for human life, however, since the division of labour made the different use-values of things, practically speaking, incommensurable. So it became necessary for human beings to establish a new means of measuring values:

In view of the fact that things subject to proprietorship differed in nature and did not afford the same service to human necessities . . . therefore, by

---

[219] For the 'maximin' rule of measuring the justice of outcomes, see J. Rawls, *A Theory of Justice* (Oxford: Oxford University Press, 1972), 152–3.

[220] *Two Treatises*, ii. 41.

[221] D. Hume, 'Of Commerce', in *Essays Moral, Political, and Literary*, ed. T. H. Green and T. H. Grose (London, 1882), i. 295: 'it is requisite to . . . animate [men] with a spirit of avarice and industry, art and luxury.'

[222] 'Of Refinement in the Arts', ibid. i. 300.

[223] *DJNG* v. i. 11.   [224] Ibid. 4.

the agreement of men some measure had to be set upon things, according to which measure things of different nature could be compared to and made equal with each other.[225]

This measure of value, because it is both established by agreement and is also the measure of the proper prices of other things, Pufendorf calls the eminent price. The eminent price needs a sensitive system of measurements of value, so to this end money is introduced. And, since money measures the value of *all* goods, it has a stable value which does not decay with the spoiling or wearing out of particular goods. Money is thus 'a sort of . . . sponsor or surety' of value.[226]

If it is to fulfil its function as a convenient medium of exchange, money must possess certain qualities: it must be durable, easily transportable, and scarce. (Scarcity is necessary because it allows 'the values of many things' to be 'compressed' into something of manageable size.) For these reasons the rare metals were established as the most appropriate forms of money: 'it seemed the most convenient thing to the majority of nations to take the more noble and comparatively rare metals, such as gold . . . silver, and bronze.'[227] Thus the needs of sophisticated society generate a system of metal money, a system established by agreement, and which provides a stable measure of value.

Locke takes over this view of money in the *Second Treatise*, explaining the invention of money in terms of the sophistication of society.[228] He also accepts Pufendorf's account of the nature of the just price. Pufendorf holds that the just price cannot be established independently of market forces. Neither is it simply the market price, however, since the latter is, or can be, shaped by too various a set of forces. Rather, 'it is a just price which is commonly set by those who are sufficiently acquainted with both the merchandise and the market'.[229] The just price thus admits of a certain 'latitude', or variation; what it most importantly excludes is any price variation established by deception or extortion. Locke's treatment of the just price likewise explains it in terms of fair and informed market forces. Markets are neither essentially just nor essentially unjust. *Fair* markets, however, establish just prices.[230]

---

[225] Ibid. 1.   [226] Ibid. 12.   [227] Ibid. 13.

[228] *Two Treatises*, ii. 37.   [229] *DJNG* v. 1. 9.

[230] Locke's treatment of just price is contained in 'Venditio 95', published as an app. to John Dunn's 'Justice and the Interpretation of Locke's Political Theory',

Pufendorf's observations on price and money reflect his awareness of the importance of industry in human society. He contends that by securing the fruits of industry to the industrious, a source of conflict is avoided. Further, the security thus achieved is itself a spur to increased industry, and so a means of overcoming the problems of necessity—including the slave economy it tends to generate. His inheritors develop this increased concern with the fledgling study of political economy. They also show an accompanying decrease in explicit discussion of the question of necessity and its rights (and thus also of self-enslavement), especially in the stable political climate of mid-eighteenth-century Britain. At the end of the seventeenth century in England, however, political questions quite distinct from the problem of necessity brought the issue of slavery to the fore. And, whereas the Continental Natural Lawyers hesitated from directly attacking slavery, even when some of their fundamental principles required nothing less, the sharply different political climate in late-seventeenth-century England encouraged a different tone altogether. The desire to avoid the perceived threat of political slavery discouraged vacillation about the acceptability of enslavement, including those forms generated by necessity. This shift in attitude is shown clearly in the political writings of John Locke.

Locke unequivocally holds that the right of necessity, which he understands in terms of a right of charity, shows enslavement to be always unnecessary as well as morally unacceptable:

Charity gives every Man a Title to so much out of another's Plenty, as will keep him from extream want, where he has no means to subsist otherwise; and a Man can no more justly make use of another's necessity, to force him to become his Vassal, by with-holding that Relief, God requires him to afford to the wants of his Brother, than he that has more strength can seize upon a weaker, master him to his Obedience, and with a Dagger at his Throat offer him Death or Slavery.[231]

The next chapter will show how Locke is able to reject slavery in all its forms by arguing that the obligation to preserve oneself requires that the *suum* be inalienable. This doctrine has significant consequences for his account of property, but slavery does not loom large as an economic (rather than political) problem. For Locke, the problem of necessity is solved by rational industry.

Political Studies, 16 (1968), 68–87. (This fragment also points out that charity places on us more far-reaching demands than does justice.)

[231] *Two Treatises*, i. 42.

3
John Locke

1. THE FOUNDATION OF NATURAL LAW

In the *Two Treatises of Government*, Locke claims that his fundamental principles are drawn from, and his arguments accord with, the requirements of the law of nature. He appears to recognize no problems concerning our knowledge of this law: 'the Law of Nature [is] plain and intelligible to all rational Creatures.' It is an unwritten law, 'and so no where to be found but in the minds of Men', but it is nevertheless plain to all because a man's knowledge of it 'is *grounded on* his having *Reason*, which is able to instruct him in that Law he is to govern himself by'. For this reason, it can truly be said that 'the Law of Nature . . . is the Law of Reason'.[1] As such, the law of nature is a source of knowledge of the human condition which is distinct from, but in accord with, divine revelation. Thus Locke holds that natural reason and revelation provide alternative, independent justifications of the right of self-preservation:

Whether we consider natural *Reason*, which tells us, that Men, being once born, have a right to their Preservation, and consequently to Meat and Drink, and such other things, as Nature affords for their Subsistence: Or *Revelation*, which gives us an account of those Grants God made of the World to *Adam*, and to *Noah*, and his Sons, 'tis very clear, that God, as King David says, *Psal.* CVX. xvj. *has given the Earth to the Children of Men*, given it to Mankind in common.[2]

Locke's point is that natural reason, and so natural law, enables us to arrive at conclusions concerning the human condition which are plain to all who seek them out, and fully independent of divine revelation. Natural law is a system of natural knowledge which is the yardstick for assessing human actions and institutions, and it is

[1] J. Locke, *Two Treatises of Government* (1690), ed. P. Laslett (Cambridge: Cambridge University Press, 2nd edn., 1967), i. 101; ii. 63, 124, 136.
[2] Ibid. ii. 25. The precise nature of the grant in common made to all mankind will be addressed in the 3rd sect. of this ch.

to this system that he appeals in formulating the doctrines of the *Two Treatises*. The frequent references to natural law in this work reflect, in both content and frequency, the fundamental position it allots to natural law.

However, in the *Essay concerning Human Understanding* (published in the same year as the *Two Treatises*), the situation seems rather different. References there to the law of nature are extremely scarce—it is mentioned only three times in a work of considerable length. Moreover, although the reality and importance of natural law is not denied, Locke's remarks on the topic are considerably more circumspect than the bold assertions of the *Two Treatises*.

The *Essay* makes only three claims about natural law. In the first place, natural law is said to be generally acknowledged, because it follows from the knowledge of God's existence: 'the existence of God, is so many ways manifest, and the Obedience we owe him, so congruous to the Light of Reason, that the great part of Mankind give Testimony to the Law of Nature.'[3] The naturalness of the natural law is thus not its independence of any theological commitments, but the fact that it is discerned by natural methods, methods which also show the truth of certain theological beliefs. Secondly, Locke stresses that his attack on innate ideas is not a rejection of natural law: 'there is a great deal of difference between an innate Law, and a law of Nature; between something imprinted on our Minds in their very original, and something that we being ignorant of may attain to the knowledge of, by the use and due application of our natural Faculties.'[4] This second remark tells us rather more than the first. It not only affirms that the law of nature is the law of natural reason, as maintained in the *Two Treatises*, it also draws out the implication that such laws are not innate, but *discovered*.

Locke's third remark in the *Essay* is that natural law belongs to one of three sorts of moral rule 'to which Men generally refer, and by which they judge of the Rectitude or Pravity of their Actions.' The three sorts of moral rule are: the Divine Law, the Civil Law, and the 'Law of *Opinion* or *Reputation*, if I may so call it'.[5] Natural

[3] J. Locke, *An Essay concerning Human Understanding* (1690), ed. P. H. Nidditch (Oxford: Clarendon Press, 1975), I. 3. 6.   [4] Ibid. 13.

[5] Ibid. II. 28. 6–7. In the 1st edn. of the *Essay*, the 3rd law was called the *philosophical* law'.

law is part of the Divine Law, because Divine Law is 'that Law which God has set to the actions of Men, whether promulgated to them by the light of Nature, or the voice of Revelation'.[6] The law promulgated by 'the voice of Revelation' is divine positive law; but the law promulgated by 'the light of Nature' is the law of nature. Both these laws are properly regarded as Divine Law, because both are given by God, and rightfully given:

> That God has given a Rule whereby Men should govern themselves, I think there is no body so brutish as to deny. He has a Right to do it, we are his Creatures: He has Goodness and Wisdom to direct our Actions to that which is best: and he has Power to enforce it by Rewards and Punishments, of infinite weight and duration, in another Life: for no body can take us out of his hands.[7]

In this passage, two quite distinct reasons are given to show that God's rule over us is rightful: he has the power to enforce it, and he has 'Goodness and Wisdom to direct our Actions to that which is best'. These two aspects of God's rule can once again be explained as its formal and material elements, respectively. Locke sometimes forgets or plays down the material element, with its emphasis on the good for human beings in obeying it, but in this passage (and in others considered below) the importance of the material element is recognized.

Locke's explicitly theological framework can sometimes mislead the reader, especially concerning the place of natural law in his system. One instructive example is Peter Laslett's misconception of the scope of Locke's 'Divine Law'. In his editorial introduction to the *Two Treatises*, Laslett mistakenly claims that, for Locke, 'when it comes [II. xxviii. 7–] to the description of the laws or rules which men actually refer their actions to, no natural law is mentioned'. Since, in the schema of the *Essay*, all actions are measured only by Divine Law, Civil Law, or the Law of '*Opinion* or *Reputation*', he concludes that 'The *Essay* has no room for natural law.'[8] Laslett's mistake springs from his failure to notice that 'Divine Law' includes both divine positive law and natural law. For Locke, natural law is a part of Divine Law because the obligation to obey it depends directly on God. As pointed out above, natural law is distinguished by the manner in which it is known; but, like divine positive law, the obligation to obey it is not independent of the divine will. Rather,

---

[6] Ibid. 8.   [7] Ibid.   [8] P. Laslett, introd. to *Two Treatises*, 81.

the obligation to obey natural law is grounded in the formal and material elements of the divine will, and the natural law is a distinct rule for human action only because the necessary knowledge of God is accessible to 'the Light of Reason'. Presumably, Laslett has overlooked the fact that, for Locke, natural law does not bind independently of knowledge of God's existence. Like Pufendorf, Locke rejects Grotius's 'rationalistic' *etiamsi daremus* clause; like Pufendorf, he bases the obligation to obey the natural law on both the formal and material elements of the divine will.

So Locke's position in the *Essay* is that natural law is part of the Divine Law; that it is knowable by the use of our natural rational faculties, and so is not dependent on a doctrine of innate ideas; and that our obligation to obey it depends on the (naturally knowable) twin elements of the divine will. From a work of the magnitude of the *Essay*, this is not a very substantial return, particularly when it is remembered that the original aim of the *Essay* was to settle some difficult questions concerning 'the Principles of morality and reveal'd Religion'.[9] Nevertheless, it is sufficient to show that, as a matter of fact, the *Essay* does find a place for natural law.

Is the *Essay* consistent in doing so? A number of commentators have held that it is not—von Leyden, and also Laslett and John Dunn.[10] The latter two, however, do little more than repeat the former's conclusion, with a general approving reference to his discussion of the issue, so it should be sufficient to consider some

[9] From a marginal note by James Tyrrell to his copy of the *Essay*, quoted by R. S. Woolhouse, *Locke* (Brighton: Harvester Press, 1983), 7. Locke himself remarks, in 'The Epistle to the Reader', that the *Essay* had its beginnings when 'five or six Friends meeting at my Chamber, and discoursing on a subject very remote from this [i.e. from the workings and extent of the human understanding], found themselves quickly at a stand, by the Difficulties that rose on every side'. To resolve the problem, it was agreed that 'before we set our selves upon Enquiries of that Nature, it was necessary to examine our own Abilities, and see, what Objects our Understandings were, or were not fitted to deal with' (*Essay*, 7). The original aim of the *Essay* was therefore to determine whether the limited capacities and operations of the understanding were capable of discerning moral and religious knowledge. The passages already quoted on natural law show that Locke's conclusion is affirmative, so it is not inappropriate to complain that it says so little on the matter. His intention appears to have been to conclude it with an account of the principles of morality, but he abandoned the attempt—it remained in an unfinished and unpublished form in a paper entitled 'Of Ethick in General'. See W. von Leyden's editorial introd. to J. Locke, *Essays on the Law of Nature* (Oxford: Clarendon Press, 1954), 69–71. (The *Essays* will subsequently be cited as *ELN*.)

[10] See *ELN* 71–82; Laslett, introd. to *Two Treatises*, 79–83; J. Dunn, *The Political Thought of John Locke* (Cambridge: Cambridge University Press, 1969), 187–8.

main features of von Leyden's position. Specifically, von Leyden claims that two of the *Essay*'s doctrines are inconsistent with accepting the existence of natural law, and these 'explain why Locke did not more fully discuss natural law in the *Essay*'. They are 'his growing belief in hedonism, and his scepticism about language'.[11] The problem created by his views on language is clear enough: it is certainly not easy to see how he can hold both that the law of nature is 'plain and intelligible to all rational Creatures' and that, because of the 'imperfection' and 'abuse' of words, 'in the interpretation of Laws, whether Divine, or Humane, there is no end', and that therefore 'in Discourse of Religion, Law, and Morality, . . . there will be the greatest difficulty'.[12]

Hedonism is not so obviously a problem. John Colman, for example, has argued that Locke's hedonism is not inconsistent with his account of natural law. For Locke, moral qualities, although justified by reason, are not intuited by reason alone. Rather, 'it is discursive reason working with data given in experience which finds out what the moral law demands'.[13] Locke holds that pleasure and pain, or their prospect, are the mainsprings of human action, and moral behaviour depends on rational reflection on how pleasure is achieved, or pain avoided. There is no natural harmony of this-worldly interests, however, so human beings sometimes show a lack of conviction in moral matters. Moral practices do not always measure up to moral professions:

if we will not in Civility allow too much Sincerity to the Professions of most *Men*, but think their Actions to be the Interpreters of their Thoughts, we shall find, that they have no such internal Veneration for these Rules, nor so *full a Perswasion of their Certainty* and Obligation. The great Principle of Morality, *To do as one would be done to*, is more commended, than practised.[14]

This lack of 'internal Veneration' for moral rules would destroy morality itself, were it not for the other-worldly pleasures and pains of divine rewards and punishments. Hedonistic motivations are not

---

[11] Von Leyden, introd., *ELN* 75.
[12] *Two Treatises*, ii. 124; *Essay*, iii. 9. 9, 22. Cf. von Leyden's discussion of this point, *ELN* 73.
[13] J. Colman, *John Locke's Moral Philosophy* (Edinburgh: Edinburgh University Press, 1983), 236. (The next sect. will show that Locke emphasizes this point in the 4th essay on natural law.)
[14] *Essay*, I. 3. 7.

inconsistent with natural law because 'the true ground of Morality'
is 'the Will and Law of a God, who sees Men in the dark, has in his
Hand Rewards and Punishments, and Power enough to call to
account the Proudest Offender'.[15] Von Leyden's view, that there is
a tension (if not an outright contradiction)[16] between the hedonism
of the *Essay* and Locke's natural law doctrines, depends on his
interpretation of Locke's early *Essays on the Law of Nature*. In his
editor's introduction to those essays, he says:

> From what Locke has to say in his sixth essay it appears that he regards
> natural law as a set of commands proceeding from the will of God and that
> it is on this account that this law is righteous and binding. The position he
> adopts in that deep-reaching question of scholastic controversy concerning
> the essence of law is that of the Nominalists, represented by the so-called
> 'voluntarist' theory, i.e. he adopts a legislative ethics. Yet . . . his position
> shifts and inclines towards the 'intellectualist' theory of the Realists,
> according to which law has its foundation in a dictate of Right Reason, in
> the essential nature of things, and is thus independent of will.[17]

John Dunn's understanding of the *Essays on the Law of Nature*
appears to be heavily indebted to von Leyden's interpretation. In
similar vein, he remarks that the *Essays* 'present the mind at work
and not merely the finished results of such work'.[18]

These views are, I believe, mistaken. Locke does not shift from a
voluntarist to a rationalist (or 'intellectualist') account of natural
law. Rather, he consistently maintains a voluntarist position
(although he does not consistently maintain the same voluntarist
position throughout). To appreciate Locke's position properly, it
will be helpful to consider John Colman's reply to von Leyden.
Colman holds that von Leyden is mistaken because Locke 'does not
waver between a voluntarist and an intellectualist theory of law, but
consistently maintains the former. Nevertheless, it is true that
Locke is not a voluntarist with respect to the content of the moral

---

[15] *Essay*, 1. 3. 6.
[16] 'To hold a belief in an ultimate moral law, or law of nature, and to maintain that
"good and bad, being relative terms, do not denote anything in the nature of the
thing, but only the relation it bears to another, in its aptness and tendency to produce
in it pleasure or pain", is to express two doctrines which, if not altogether
incompatible, are bound to produce vacillation and vagueness in the mind of him
who holds them.' Von Leyden, introd., *ELN* 72. The internal quotation is from
Locke's unpubl. MS 'Of Ethick in General', sect. 7.
[17] Von Leyden, introd., *ELN* 51.
[18] Dunn, *Political Thought of John Locke*, 21.

law. His voluntarism is strictly a theory of moral obligation.'[19]
Colman is half right: his distinction between moral obligation and
the content of the moral law overdraws a distinction which is best
understood as identifying different sides of the one coin. It is best
understood as the distinction between the nature of obligation, and
its extent. What Colman calls the theory of moral obligation is best
described as the theory of the nature of obligation. The content of
the moral law is in fact how far this obligation extends—what things
we are obligated to do, or to refrain from doing. Taken together,
these two aspects of obligation constitute the law of nature.

Locke devotes little space to clarifying his position on these
issues, but the little he does say shows him to be in accord with
Pufendorf's view that obligation has both a formal and a material
aspect. His account begins from the claim that our obligation to
conform to the requirements of natural law derives from the will of
God. The divine will has two aspects, formal and material. The
formal aspect is God's creative power, and thus also his power over
his creatures. As Locke puts it in the *Essays*, 'it is the decree of a
superior will, wherein the formal cause of a law appears to
consist'.[20] However, this formal element is not sufficient to
constitute an obligation: a full account of obligation needs to specify
'what is and what is not to be done, which is the proper function of a
law'. When it contains these two elements, the law possesses 'all
that is requisite to create an obligation'.[21]

The second of the elements is the material element of the divine
will. Properly describing this element is no easy matter. It can be
described as the content or even the fruit of the divine will; but its
material character is better displayed by recognizing that it is the
creation itself. However, it is not just the creation as a set of brute
facts, since thinking of it in this way would eclipse the divine
purpose for the creation. The material element of the divine will is
thus the whole creation, understood teleologically. It provides a
necessary part of the foundation of natural law because it provides a
teleological understanding of human nature—the part of the
creation to which natural law applies. (Locke acknowledges that
there is a natural law only in so far as there is human nature: 'human
nature must needs be changed before this law can be either altered
or annulled . . . natural law stands and falls together with the nature

---

[19] Colman, *John Locke's Moral Philosophy*, 32.
[20] Essay I, *ELN* 111–13.   [21] Ibid. 113.

of man as it is at present.')[22] So unlike the formal element, the material element of the divine will is not a coercive will standing over against the natural world; it is, rather, the natural world itself.

For this reason a voluntarist account of natural law in which the divine will is understood to include both formal and material elements is best understood as an attempt to subsume rationalism, not to deny it.[23] And, as such, an account of this kind can make use of locutions which may have been thought to be ineluctably rationalist. So Locke cannot be charged with inconsistency when he explains natural law in terms strongly reminiscent of Cudworth. For example: natural law 'does not depend on an unstable and changeable will, but on the eternal order of things . . . certain essential features of things are immutable, and . . . certain duties arise out of necessity and cannot be other than they are'; it is 'a fixed and permanent rule of morals, which reason itself pronounces, and which persists, being a fact so firmly rooted in the soil of human nature'.[24]

Given language of this kind, it is not surprising that von Leyden and others should conclude that Locke comes to desert the voluntarist ship. However, his meaning is clarified by a subsequent passage in the same essay. Although, he says,

[22] Essay VII, *ELN* 199, 201. Cf. von Leyden's introd.: 'the bonds of natural law are coeval with the human race' (p. 51).

[23] It is not possible to provide a thorough account of the dispute between voluntarists and rationalists (or 'intellectualists'), or of its wider significance. My suggestion here, that the voluntarism of Pufendorf and Locke makes use of the Aristotelian distinction between formal and material causes in order to subsume, rather than oppose, rationalism, is based on hints contained in their discussions of the basic issue of obligation, which hold out the promise of harmonizing their otherwise disparate remarks. The suggestion implies a certain untidiness in a different respect, in that it implies that ancient notions were pressed into service in order to overcome some apparently unpalatable implications of modern voluntarism. The untidiness should not be surprising, however, since in the realm of 'practical' (rather than 'speculative') philosophy, intellectual revolutions find it difficult to dispense with ideas that continue to be serviceable, even if of very doubtful parentage. For the classical treatment of the rise of theological voluntarism and its impact on the natural sciences, see M. B. Foster, 'The Christian Doctrine of Creation and the Rise of Modern Natural Science' and 'Christian Theology and Modern Science of Nature II', *Mind*, 43 (1934), 446–68, and 45 (1936), 1–28. For a recent discussion of the broad features of the voluntarist–rationalist dispute in which the implications for morals and politics are discussed (albeit without allowing for the weaker, or more harmonizing, form of voluntarism suggested here), see J. Tully, 'Governing Conduct', in E. Leites (ed.), *Conscience and Casuistry in Early Modern Europe* (Cambridge: Cambridge University Press, 1988), 12–71 (esp. 33–56).

[24] Essay VII, *ELN* 199.

certain essential features of things are immutable . . . this is not because nature or God (as I should say more correctly) could not have created man differently. Rather, the cause is that, since man has been made as he is, equipped with reason and his other faculties and destined for this mode of life, there necessarily result from his inborn constitution some definite duties for him, which cannot be other than they are.[25]

Humankind was not necessarily made in a certain way—the divine will was unconstrained—but nevertheless has been made with a certain character. (Human nature can thus be said to display, in Pufendorf's terms, a hypothetical necessity.) God's formal will is necessary for there to be a created world at all; God's material will makes the world the kind of world it is. The law of nature depends directly on (our recognition of) God's existence, in that it requires the formal foundation of God's power over us. The material foundation of the law is human nature itself, conceived teleologically: a nature 'equipped with reason and his other faculties and destined for this mode of life'. By keeping in mind that the divine will has both formal and material elements, then, it is possible to explain Locke's account of natural law in consistently voluntarist terms.

However, although consistently voluntarist, Locke's voluntarism is not itself always consistent: he sometimes forgets the necessity of the material element. For example, at one point in the *Second Treatise* Locke holds that human beings are unreservedly subject to the divine will because 'they are his Property, whose Workmanship they are, made to last during his, not one anothers Pleasure'.[26] This may overstate the case. As long as God is in control of his own creation, we must be in his power, and in this sense can be said to last during his pleasure. But dependence of this kind does not justify arbitrary ('wilful') interventions in the course of the world: it merely emphasizes our impotence before the divine will (whether manifested in miraculous interventions, or in the face of natural—created— forces). Since Locke also holds that the divine will is not unstable and changeable, but manifest in 'the eternal order of things', an order of things which necessitates certain duties because of the material constitution of the world,[27] it should be concluded that God's 'pleasure' is quite unlike our own, because it excludes arbitrariness. It cannot be separated from the divine purpose for the creation. So, if we accept that we are dependent creatures, made to

[25] Ibid.   [26] *Two Treatises*, ii. 6.   [27] Essay VII, *ELN* 199.

last during God's pleasure, we are not entitled to conclude (as Locke seems tempted to do) that, if he so chooses, God can legitimately dispose of us as we might choose to dispose of some unvalued possession. (Incidentally, neither would we be necessarily entitled to conclude that a divine disposal of this sort would be wrong. If, as Locke holds, the moral law applies only to human beings, there is no room for ascribing wrongdoing in such a case. However, restricting the scope of the moral law to human beings does not imply abandoning grounds for complaint. Such complaints could be of the form 'If God were human, his actions would be wrong', or 'God does not treat us as well as he requires us to treat each other.')

A second, and more complete, example of forgetting the difference the material element makes occurs in the seventh of the *Essays on the Law of Nature*. When countering objections to his view that the binding force of natural law is eternal, Locke discusses an attempted refutation in the following way:

A proof that the binding force of the law of nature is not everlasting and universal can be given in this way: namely by showing that, though by general agreement it is a law of nature that every man should be allowed to keep his own property, or, if you like, that no one may take away and keep for himself what is another's property, yet at God's command the binding force of this law can lapse, for this actually happened, as we read, in the case of the Israelites when they departed from Egypt and journeyed to Palestine. To this we reply by denying the minor premiss: for if God should order someone not to restore something he has received on loan, the ownership of the thing itself, but not the binding force of natural law, would cease; the law is not violated, but the owner is changed, for the previous owner loses together with the possession of the thing his right to it. In fact, the goods of fortune are never so much ours that they cease to be God's: that supreme Lord of all things can, without doing wrong, give of His property to anyone as He pleases by His sovereign will.[28]

This will not do. Of course God can do whatever he pleases, without doing wrong, since Locke has limited the law of nature to human actions. So the assertion that God does no wrong in performing a particular action is not a moral judgement—nor even any kind of judgement of the relevant action. This is evidenced by the fact that it would be equally true to say of the action that God did not act *rightly* in doing it. So, if Locke's ambition in this passage is, even in

[28] Essay VII, *ELN* 201–3.

part, to justify the ways of God to human beings, he does not succeed: the appearance of justification depends on an equivocation on 'without doing wrong'. If Locke's aim is not justificatory, the observation that God does no wrong is no more than a reminder that certain kinds of objects cannot possess certain kinds of qualities.

Locke's difficulties arise because he has forgotten the material element. It cannot be true that 'the ownership of the thing itself, but not the binding force of natural law, would cease': the binding force of natural law reflects not only God's formal act of willing, but also the material content of that act, manifested concretely in the world itself. The law 'does not depend on an unstable and changeable will, but on the eternal order of things';[29] it is the 'rational apprehension of what is right [that] puts us under an obligation'.[30]

Locke neglects the material element in a number of other passages. The problems generated are well illustrated by considering two passages from the sixth essay. He says, at one point, that 'God has created us out of nothing and, if He pleases, will reduce us again to nothing: we are, therefore, subject to Him in perfect justice and by utmost necessity.'[31] God's power over us means that we are indeed subject to him by utmost necessity; but if the natural law does not apply to God, what can it mean to say that we are subject to him in perfect justice? Since no reference is made to the nature of God's material will, the claim amounts to no more than a reiteration of the extent of the divine power. However, Locke obviously wants to say more than this, as another passage in the same essay shows: 'since nothing else is required to impose an obligation but the authority and rightful power of the one who commands and the disclosure of his will, no one can doubt that the law of nature is binding on men.'[32] So obligation requires not merely power but 'authority and rightful power'. It also requires disclosure of the will of the authority, since without adequate disclosure we could know neither the fact nor the extent of the obligation. (In recognizing this requirement, Locke shows himself to accept that obligation depends on capacity; that 'ought' implies 'can'.) In the case of natural law, the disclosure of the divine will must be naturally knowable—discernible by 'the light and principles of nature', the light of reason. But a mere disclosure of will is not sufficient: the will

---

[29] Ibid. 199.   [30] Essay VI, ibid. 185.
[31] Ibid. 187.   [32] Ibid.

disclosed must be recognizable as one of rightful power, of perfect justice. This cannot be done unless the material element of the divine will, as revealed in the created order, is kept clearly in view.

Even this stipulation may seem to be insufficient. For how can recognizing the structure and purposes of the creation reveal that God's power is rightful, or that his activity is perfectly just, when the natural law applies only to human beings? Through the features of the created order, including our own most important capacity to reflect rationally on the world and our place in it—we can come to an understanding of the nature of rightful power and perfect justice with respect to ourselves. This is exactly what it is to come to an understanding of the natural law. So central notions of natural law, such as rightful power and perfect justice, indeed depend on the material element of the divine will. They do not, however, apply to the divine will, and so cannot be employed to describe divine actions. On Locke's own terms, the conclusion seems irresistible. Is there any way around it?

Strictly speaking, there is not. Perhaps the best approach, in order to reduce the tension between Locke's restriction of natural law to human beings while ascribing moral qualities to God, is to appeal to analogy. Since divine volitions or actions display specific features which correspond more or less closely to features of human volitions or actions, they are best described in analogous terms. The latter are subject to natural law, and so can be accounted just or unjust, right or wrong, etc.; the former, although not subject to natural law, are to some degree analogous to actions that are, and so are analogous to acts of justice or injustice, and so on. And the actions of the stable and unchanging divine will can be seen, by the light of reason, to correspond to those actions which, among human beings, are best described as just and right. In this way it is possible to speak of divine volition and actions *as if* they are subject to natural law, even though they are not. In this way the correspondence of divine volitions or actions with the goods apprehended by the light of reason make it possible to speak of God's justice, goodness, and so on. The part played by the material element requires that it be possible to speak in this way, that our judgements of divine actions, however poorly understood, show these actions not to be contrary to the principles embodied in the natural law. Locke's appeals to considerations of divine goodness when filling out the ground of natural human obligations, even though he sometimes forgets them or underrates their importance, need to be explained along lines such as these. Some passages where he brings material factors to the fore can serve to close off the issue.

In the *Essay concerning Human Understanding*, Locke, as previously observed, justifies God's right over us not merely by reminding us of the extent of our dependence on divine power, but also by pointing out that God 'has Goodness and Wisdom to direct our Actions to that which is best'. A number of similar passages occur in the *Essays on the Law of Nature*. In the first essay, he holds that the law is not only the enactment of a superior power, but also 'implanted in our hearts'.[33] It is thus something we acknowledge to be just, and not merely a requirement of prudence. Later on in the same essay, Locke defends the existence of the law of nature in two ways. Firstly, he appeals to Aristotle's account in the *Nicomachean Ethics* of human functioning as a matter of 'the active exercise of the mind's faculties in accordance with rational principle' in order to conclude that 'man must of necessity perform what reason prescribes'.[34] Secondly, he says that the existence of the law of nature 'can be derived from men's consciences', and offers Juvenal in support: 'no one who commits a wicked action is acquitted in his own judgement.'[35] Both these arguments show the law of nature to be dependent on our own nature as beings of a determinate kind, and so on the material element of the divine will. They show us to be judges of what is and what is not in accordance with the law of nature, and therefore not merely objects at the free disposal of an inscrutable omnipotence.

Most of the other passages where Locke invokes the material element of obligation occur in the sixth essay. This is not surprising, since the sixth essay directly addresses the question of our obligation to obey natural law. Several of these passages have been quoted above, so one further example should be sufficient. Not only, says Locke, does God's absolute power over us mean that 'we are bound to observe the limits He prescribes', but also that 'it is reasonable that we should do what shall please Him who is omniscient and most wise'.[36] The second part seems to have been

[33] Essay I, *ELN* 111. What is meant by describing the law as 'implanted' will be explained below.

[34] Ibid. 113. The quotation, from *Nicomachean Ethics*, i. 7, is taken from the trans. of H. Rackham. (See von Leyden's editorial footnote, p. 113.)

[35] Ibid. 117. The quotation is from *Satires*, xiii. 2–3; the trans. is apparently von Leyden's own.   [36] Essay VI, *ELN* 183.

added as something of an afterthought, but even so it draws our attention to the material element of the divine will. God is 'omniscient and most wise', and so when Locke appears to invoke divine power alone as the source of obligation, this is not because power itself constitutes obligation, but because the power of 'Him who is omniscient and most wise' is always *rightful* power: 'no one can oblige or bind us to do anything, unless he has *right and power* over us; and indeed, when he commands what he wishes should be done and what should not be done, *he only makes use of his right*.'[37] Right is not power *simpliciter*. The formal command of a superior is not itself sufficient to constitute obligation, even though it is necessary. (It is necessary because without such commands, there are no obligations—only reasons for action.) Obligation requires both the superior's will, and the superior's right to command obedience through the justice and goodness of his (material) will. For Locke, God is the superior who satisfies both conditions: therefore his rule over us is rightful. This rule is the 'Divine Law' referred to in the *Essay concerning Human Understanding*; and the law of nature is that part of the Divine Law which is knowable by the 'light of Nature'.[38]

2. THE CHARACTERISTICS OF NATURAL LAW

Since, for Locke, natural law is ultimately grounded in both formal and material elements of the divine will, his position is clearly similar to Pufendorf's. This is especially true of his later views, which probably reflect Pufendorf's influence. However, his earlier views, developed independently—the *Essays on the Law of Nature* were written before the publication of *De Jure Naturae et Gentium*—also display a broadly similar understanding of natural law, preserving many of the general features of the natural law tradition outlined in the preceding chapters.[39] This is not to say that Locke makes no useful contribution to that tradition, instead

[37] Essay VI, *ELN* 181–3 (emphasis added).

[38] *Essay*, II. 28. 7.

[39] The treatment of natural law in the *Essays* shows a significant difference of vocabulary from the brief discussions in the later works—the influence of Aquinas (and in fact St Paul) are clearly visible—but differences in content are less pronounced. (The roles assigned to utility and self-preservation in the law of nature are two differences that will be illustrated below.)

merely recapitulating established doctrines. Quite the opposite is true: he makes a major contribution to spelling out the material foundation of natural law. The early *Essays* provide a sketch of this foundation, but the *Essay concerning Human Understanding* is a major—albeit incomplete[40]—attempt to specify the material grounds of natural obligations.[41] To examine the doctrines of the *Essay* is, however, a task too large to undertake here, so it will be necessary to settle for the sketch offered in the *Essays on the Law of Nature*.

The essential orthodoxy of Locke's account of natural law in the *Essays* can be shown by a brief summary. Firstly, as Grotius had done, and Pufendorf would shortly do, Locke identifies Carneades as the archetypal enemy of natural law. Carneades had held that there is 'no law of nature, for all men . . . are driven by innate impulse to seek their own interests', and in particular that there is no natural justice, 'or, if it exists, it is the height of folly, inasmuch as to be mindful of the advantages of others is to do harm to oneself'.[42] Locke observes, however, that 'this most harmful opinion' of Carneades and his followers 'has . . . always been opposed by the more rational part of men, in whom there was some sense of a common humanity, some concern for fellowship'.[43] The reply is an important one, because it identifies three typical features of natural law. The defenders of natural law against the sceptics are 'more rational', have a sense of 'common humanity', and show a concern for 'fellowship'. In more characteristic terminology, this is to say that natural law is a 'law of reason', or a 'dictate of right reason'; is founded in human nature; and thereby implies, in some way, the necessity of social life, of 'sociableness'. This cluster of characteristics require explanation.

[40] In fact, it has commonly been thought to be quite misconceived. John Colman, *John Locke's Moral Philosophy*, is more sympathetic than most. For a firm (if not argued) opinion that the attempt 'is not in principle possible', see John Dunn, *Political Thought of John Locke*, 25, 187. Dunn cites the support of Hume's *Dialogues concerning Natural Religion*, and also the views of von Leyden. His most recent treatment of the issue—in *Locke* (Oxford: Oxford University Press, 1984), ch. 3—remains critical, but is less dismissive.

[41] It was noted above that the aim of the *Essay* was to examine the sources of knowledge in order to determine its extent and limits, not for its own sake, but in order to resolve problems of religion and morality.

[42] Essay viii, *ELN* 205. Von Leyden suggests, quite plausibly, that Grotius is Locke's source (p. 204 n.).

[43] Ibid.

The law of nature is a dictate of right reason. Locke approvingly refers to this description of natural law in the second essay: 'the law of nature is most often called right reason itself and the dictate of right reason.'[44] He is not entirely happy with the term, however, because it seems to make reason and its dictates self-sufficient. Reason needs to be understood as an activity which requires raw materials: 'Nothing indeed is achieved by reason, that powerful faculty of arguing, unless there is first something posited and taken for granted.'[45] Describing natural law as a dictate of right reason may obscure this fact, so Locke expresses misgivings about the terminology. Natural law, he says,

appears to me less correctly termed by some people the dictate of reason, since reason does not so much establish and pronounce this law of nature as search for it and discover it as a law enacted by a superior power and implanted in our hearts. Neither is reason so much the maker of that law as its interpreter . . . nor indeed can reason give us laws, since it is only a faculty of our mind and part of us.[46]

This means that, although the law is 'in conformity with rational nature'[47]—without which it would not be binding—the role of reason is essentially to discover the law within us, to explicate and clarify all that is in conformity with our nature as rational social beings. For this reason Locke tends to avoid speaking of natural law as a dictate of right reason. Like Pufendorf, he holds that the requirements of natural law are worked out by human beings employing the process of reasoning.

Unlike Pufendorf, however, he is gripped by a powerful metaphor of 'enlightenment': knowledge is an activity which brings objects out of darkness into the light. Thus he refers to reason as 'the light of nature'; and because reason can search it out, the law is 'discernible by the light of reason'. Pufendorf, in contrast, speaks rather colourlessly of 'sound reason': terminology which safely catches his meaning, that the law of nature comes to be known as the result of a process of ratiocination in which logical or moral pitfalls are avoided. Locke's metaphorical language invites

[44] Essay II, *ELN* 125; cf. also Essay v, ibid. 161.
[45] Ibid.
[46] Essay I, ibid. 111.
[47] Ibid. Cf. Essay VII, ibid. 191: violation of natural law is loathsome to 'those who think rightly and live according to nature'. This (Stoic) formulation has already been encountered in Grotius and Pufendorf.

the possibility that the conception of the role of reason may be shaped by the picture implicit in his choice of language. Does this happen?

He is anxious to stress that it does not:

> while we assert that the light of nature points to this law, we should not wish this to be understood in the sense that some inward light is by nature implanted in man, which perpetually reminds him of his duty and leads him straight and without fail whither he has to go. We do not maintain that this law of nature, written as it were on tablets, lies open in our hearts, and that, as soon as some inward light comes near it (like a torch approaching a notice board hung up in darkness), it is at length read, perceived, and noted by the rays of that light.[48]

Rather, to say that something is known by the light of nature is to hold only that it is known by the exercise of our own faculties: 'we mean nothing else but that there is some sort of truth to the knowledge of which a man can attain by himself and without the help of another, if he makes proper use of the faculties he is endowed with by nature.'[49] Perhaps he protests too much, because there is some evidence that the metaphor does exert an influence. One indication is his belief that what is investigated by reason must be within us: 'implanted in our hearts'; 'not written, but innate, i.e. natural'; 'an inborn, i.e. natural, law'.[50] The metaphor invites conclusions of this kind because, if knowledge is pictured as a process of casting light on objects that are indistinct or hidden in darkness, then coming to know must be a process of discovering what is already physically present. It thus encourages thinking of natural law as something within us. But there is no need to think in this way. One can hold that natural law is founded in human nature, or is in conformity with our nature, without holding that it is actually within us. If natural law is understood as the conclusion of sound reason, as does Pufendorf, then natural law can be founded in our (rational) nature without having to be already within us. The point can be illustrated as follows. Our obligation to observe natural law depends on recognizing the existence of God. But the knowledge of God's existence is not implanted within us: it arises instead from a rational apprehension of the order and design of the created universe. Although we are ourselves a part of this order, the

---

[48] Essay II, *ELN* 123. [49] Ibid.
[50] Essay I, ibid. 111, 117; Essay II, ibid. 131.

obligation is in conformity with our nature because our nature is rational, and because the obligation is rationally perceived. So the binding force of natural law, without which it is not a law at all,[51] is not within us, but arises from reflection on the nature of the world and our place within it. Locke's tendency to think of the law as, in some way, within us thus appears to be at least reinforced by his choice of metaphor.

By reinforcing the tendency to speak of natural law as 'implanted', Locke's metaphor generates difficulties for his account of natural law, specifically because he denies that the law is a set of innate ideas in the mind. It is not 'inscribed in the minds of men'; there are 'no principles either practical or speculative, . . . written in the minds of men by nature'.[52] It is tempting, given these remarks, to conclude that the law of nature is implanted not in our minds, but in our *hearts*. However, this possibility (if indeed it is coherent) is blocked off, because he does not provide a clear separation of hearts from minds. The arguments against the 'inscription' (in our minds) thesis are introduced by the statement that the arguments 'show that there exists no . . . imprint of the law of nature in our hearts'.[53]

It is unlikely that there is any completely tidy resolution of the issue, given the obscurities of his metaphorical language. Clearly, he denies that our knowledge of natural law is innate, a set of ideas 'inscribed in the minds of men'. Rather, knowledge of natural law arises through the employment of our own rational faculty, reflecting on our sense-experience.[54] This depends on our having the kind of constitution we have (and which could be said to be implanted in us), so knowledge of natural law at least depends on what is implanted in us. In this way at least it is founded in our human nature. The natural law itself, however, is only very misleadingly described as being within our hearts: although it depends on what is within our hearts, it is not itself within us. When he avoids metaphor Locke recognizes as much. He acknowledges, for example, that natural law depends on reflection which regards both our own inner constitution, and also the purpose of the whole created order: 'what it is that is to be done by us can be partly

[51] Essay I, *ELN* 111–13.
[52] Essay III, ibid. 137, 145.
[53] Ibid. 137.
[54] Essay IV, ibid.

gathered by the end in view for all things . . . Partly also we can infer the principle and a definite rule of our duty from man's own constitution and the faculties with which he is equipped.'[55] Here there is no talk of anything implanted within us. The law of nature is discovered by rational reflection, and in this sense can be called a dictate of right reason. In addition, the object of reflection includes our own constitution, and so is (partly) founded in human nature. However, Locke draws back from the view that our natural instincts are an accurate guide to the content of the law. It is mistaken, he says, to 'seek the principles of moral action and a rule to live by in men's appetites and natural instincts', because such an approach cannot provide 'the binding force of a law'—it is an approach which mistakenly holds that 'that was morally best which most people desired'.[56] Locke is thus at odds with Grotius, who had followed the Stoics on this point by holding that reason shows the essential rectitude of the most fundamental instincts. For Locke, reason plays a more critical role. Natural law's foundation in human nature is for him less a matter of instincts, and more strongly a matter of reflection on our situation in the universe.

For this reason Locke is not, in the *Essays on the Law of Nature*, entirely happy with the common doctrine that the natural law has its foundation in the necessity of self-preservation. He says, for example, that 'if the source and origin of this law is the care and preservation of oneself, virtue would seem to be not so much man's duty as his convenience, nor will anything be good except what is useful to him'.[57] This would be to found natural law in expediency, which is impossible, since such a 'law' would have no binding force: 'whenever it pleases us to claim our right and give way to our own inclinations, we can certainly disregard and transgress this law without blame, though perhaps not without disadvantage.'[58] However, if we take a larger view, and think not merely of our private advantage and preservation, but reflect on our constitution and its place within the divinely created order of things, it is evident that self-preservation has a fundamental role because we cannot avoid recognizing that we are under an obligation to preserve ourselves. (This doctrine is, of course, a linchpin of the argument of

[55] Ibid. 157.
[56] Essay VIII, ibid. 213.
[57] Essay VII, ibid. 201.
[58] Ibid.

the *Second Treatise*.)[59] The obligation to preserve ourselves does not justify all our instinctive forms of self-preserving behaviour, but it does affirm that self-preserving instinct which contributes to sociableness: a man 'feels himself . . . to be impelled by life's experience and pressing needs to procure and preserve a life in society with other men'.[60]

Locke recognizes sociableness as one of the fundamental principles of natural law, and the passage above shows him to recognize that society is necessary for individual survival. However, like Grotius and Pufendorf, he sees that society is not simply something entered into by human beings for purely pragmatic or self-interested considerations. Rather, human beings are peculiarly fitted for social life. Sociableness is a part of human nature itself: a man is 'urged to enter into society by a certain propensity of nature, and to be prepared for the maintenance of society by the gift of speech and through the intercourse of language, in fact as much as he is obliged to preserve himself'.[61] Whether his use of 'urged' in this passage refers to an obligation or merely to natural instinct, it is clear that Locke understands sociable instincts to be in accord with the dictates of natural law. This is indicated by the conclusion of the quotation: we are urged to enter into society as much as we are obliged to preserve ourselves. This is only slightly stronger than the doctrine of the *Second Treatise*, which holds that we are bound to preserve others as long as by so doing we do not impair our own preservation: 'Every one as he is *bound to preserve himself*, and not to quit his Station wilfully; so by the like reason when his own Preservation comes not in competition, ought he, as much as he can, *to preserve the rest of Mankind*.'[62] Although weaker than the above remark from the *Essays*, this passage from the *Second Treatise* indicates a stronger commitment to the social life than

[59] *Two Treatises*, ii. 6: 'Every one . . . is *bound to preserve himself*.' Locke also affirms a right of preservation (ii. 25), but, unlike the *Essays*, where right is sharply distinguished from law in a Hobbesian manner (Essay I, *ELN* 111; cf. *Leviathan*, ch. 14), in the *Two Treatises* the right of preservation appears to mean the freedom to do what the obligation implies. (Cf. T. Mautner, 'Natural Rights in Locke', *Philosophical Topics*, 12 (1982), 73–7.) The transformation of Locke's view can plausibly be attributed to the influence of Pufendorf. As Ch. 2 has shown, in Pufendorf's scheme rights are not fundamental moral entities, but are implied by the fundamental duties of sociableness. Locke's view is best understood in the same light—as the discussion below of the 'workmanship model' will show.

[60] Essay IV, *ELN* 157.

[61] Ibid. 157–8. Cf. e.g. *DJBP*, Prol. 5–7.

[62] *Two Treatises*, ii. 6.

Grotius's in *De Jure Belli ac Pacis*.[63] Irrespective of the way Locke orders the relationship between caring for oneself and caring for others, however, he is confident that the two obligations do not conflict: 'the duties of life are not at variance with one another, nor do they arm men one against another.' Stated more fully,

virtuous actions themselves do not clash nor do they engage men in conflict: they kindle and cherish one another. Justice in me does not take away equity in another, nor does the liberality of a prince thwart the generosity of his subjects. The moral purity of a parent does not corrupt his children, nor can the moderation of a Cato lessen the austerity of a Cicero.[64]

Abiding by natural law is thus the guarantee of social peace, the provision of a social environment in which the virtuous life can flourish. At least partly for this reason, Locke connects the observance of natural law to happiness: the law concerns how to reach happiness.[65] The law is thus without point if a modicum of happiness is not possible. He outlines the nature of this modicum in the *Essay*, when he says that 'the lowest degree of what can be called *Happiness*, is so much ease from all Pain, and so much present Pleasure, as without which any one cannot be content'.[66] The possibility of this level of contentment is undeniable, since it can be observed to occur, at least on occasions. Locke does not say this, of course, but his discussion of the question of happiness seems to take for granted some such common-sense approach. He is not interested in arguing for the pessimistic classical thesis that happiness does not exist.[67]

---

[63] *DJBP* I. 2. i. 6.

[64] Essay VIII, *ELN* 213. Locke's conception of the virtue of self-preservation and its relation to other virtues thus cannot be squeezed into Macpherson's framework. Not only does self-preservation not imply that the individual 'owes nothing to society', Locke's conception of an overall *harmony* between the various forms of virtue canot be fitted into a simple market model of society, with its essentially competitive, self-interested structure. Cf. C. B. Macpherson, *The Political Theory of Possessive Individualism: Hobbes to Locke* (Oxford: Clarendon Press, 1962), 263–4.

[65] Essay V, *ELN* 175: ' . . . about how to reach happiness, that is, about the law of nature.' Cf. Essay IV, ibid. 147: 'that height of virtue and felicity whereto the gods invite and nature also tends.'

[66] *Essay*, II. 21. 42.

[67] In his Censor's Valedictory Speech, delivered in Oxford in 1664, he treats this classical doctrine (particularly common amongst the tragedians) respectfully but not seriously. He gives a mock funeral oration in which he observes that, since life is nothing but a miserable prison, a man 'is best advised to make an end of himself' (as von Leyden puts it in his editorial summary, *ELN* 218). This is *not* a doctrine to be found in any of Locke's serious works!

If natural law is concerned with how to reach happiness, then clearly it promotes utility. Locke accepts that it does, but, in common with Grotius and Pufendorf, he rejects the idea that the law is grounded in utility: 'Utility is not the basis of the law or the ground of obligation', but 'the consequence of obedience to it'. Therefore 'the rightness of an action does not depend on its utility; on the contrary, its utility is a result of its rightness'.[68] For this reason, Pufendorf, as shown in the previous chapter, holds that there is therefore a particular kind of utility, which was referred to as 'rational utility', on which the law can be said to be grounded. Locke makes no comparable move, because he typically thinks of utility in terms of private interest. This is indicated by his argument that to found law in utility would be to destroy the benefits of society.[69] He does not see this result, as we would be inclined to do, as a conflict between narrower and wider conceptions of utility; instead, he simply concludes that utility is thereby discredited as a possible foundation for law.

In summary, then, Locke's account of the basic features of natural law is in general agreement with the views of Grotius and Pufendorf, if in some respects a little more cautious and reserved. He affirms, against the Carneadean sceptic, that there is a natural law, a non-arbitrary law grounded (if not ultimately grounded) in human nature. Human nature is a rational nature, so the law can also be said to be a dictate of right reason, as long as this is understood to mean that reason searches out or interprets the law— it does not invent it or dictate what it must be. Human beings are sociable creatures, by both nature and necessity, so the natural law is also a law of sociability. It is not a law based on 'utility' (on private interest), but it none the less serves the interests of all individuals. Neither is it a law founded on private instincts of self-preservation; nevertheless there is a duty of self-preservation, as there is a duty to preserve others wherever possible. (The relative importance of self-preservation appears to be greater in the *Two Treatises* than in the earlier *Essays*, although an accurate judgement of the matter is not easy, since explicit remarks are few and scattered.)

Like Pufendorf, Locke rejects two Grotian doctrines. In the first place, he rejects Grotius's a posteriori defence of natural law. The general consent of men, even of the best of men, is no guide to the

---

[68] Essay VIII, *ELN* 215.   [69] Ibid. 213.

content of natural law. Secondly, he rejects Grotius's account of obligation as summed up in the *etiamsi daremus* passage. It is not true that the natural law could have any degree of validity if God does not exist. The obligation to conform to the dictates of natural law depends on the divine will. It does not, however, depend on an arbitrary divine command, in the sense of a command (or commands) simply set over against the nature of the created world. Rather, obligation depends on both formal and material elements of the divine will. Finally, although natural law can be said to be, in some sense, implanted in our hearts, it is not inscribed in our minds. The natural law is not a cluster of innate ideas, but is discovered by rational reflection on sense-experience.

This last point makes it possible to raise the problem of natural law and history. In the next section, it will be argued that, in his account of property, Locke shows a historical conception of the development, or progressive uncovering, of natural law. In common with Grotius and Pufendorf, he has an essentially 'two stages' conception of human social history: of primitive simplicity followed by developed society (the latter distinguished by a money economy). This does not mean that history has only two steps, because development and change is possible within each stage, particularly in the latter.[70] Before turning to these questions, however, it is worth recognizing that, by holding the knowledge of natural law to be the result of rational reflection on sense-experience, Locke has made the necessary space for an account of society and social institutions in which historical development is an integral part. This is simply because sense-experience occurs over time: not merely in the lifetimes of individuals,[71] but also in the much

---

[70] Locke recognizes the different modes of subsistence later developed by Adam Smith into the 'four stages' theory—gathering and hunting, pastoral, agricultural, and commercial—but it is doubtful that he saw these in terms of an evolutionary sequence; and, in any case, the vital development is the invention of money. Cf. R. Meek, *Social Science and the Ignoble Savage* (Cambridge: Cambridge University Press, 1976), ch. 1, and N. Wood, *John Locke and Agrarian Capitalism* (Berkeley, Calif.: University of California Press, 1984), 51. Wood's view is similar to that defended here in that he also interprets Locke's theory as an attempt to provide a natural history of property. However, by failing to recognize the importance of utility in the modern natural law theories, he unnecessarily separates natural history from natural law (e.g. pp. 50, 72).

[71] Locke is particularly aware of the influence of early childhood learning, and, like Pufendorf, sees the very earliness of the learning as the source of the mistaken belief that our knowledge of natural law is innate. He says: 'opinions about moral rightness and goodness which we embrace so firmly are for the most part such as, in a

larger time span of the history of human society. In the *Essays on the Law of Nature*, he is not particularly concerned with the latter, and does not consider it directly; in fact, he may well not have thought of the matter in these terms. However, the 'two stages' conception of social history which is so essential to the argument of chapter 5 of the *Second Treatise* clearly implies that significant changes in social circumstances—that is, significant changes in the content of sense-experience for whole societies in historical time—require that social rules themselves undergo changes, as judged necessary by rational reflection on the changed circumstances. So natural law, because discovered by reasoning about sense-experience, must be sensitive to historical epochs. Whether conceived of as a timeless law hidden in the nature of things, in the nature of the created order (as Locke thinks in the *Essays*),[72] or more simply as the determinations of rational reflection on sense-experience (as he may hold in the *Two Treatises*), natural law must be understood to be, at least in its finer judgements, context sensitive. For Locke, as for Grotius and Pufendorf, natural law is a historical law, specifying different rules in different circumstances. In many instances this will not generate important practical differences; but we should not expect this to be true when considering the different historical epochs envisaged by the 'two stages' theory.

Finally, rational reflection on sense-experience can be done either rightly or wrongly. Reason does not merely construct plausible arguments for holding various beliefs, nor does it admit of antinomies. It is a chain which leads the mind from things known to things previously unknown: 'reason is . . . the discursive faculty of

still tender age, before we can as yet determine anything about them or observe how they insinuate themselves, stream into our unguarded minds and are inculcated by our parents or teachers or others with whom we live . . . And at last, because in this way and without our notice these opinions have crept into our minds with but little attention on our part, striking roots in our breasts while we are unaware either of the manner or the time, and also because they assert their authority by the general consent and approval of men with whom we have social intercourse, we immediately think we must conclude that they are inscribed in our hearts by God and by nature, since we observe no other origin of them', Essay III, *ELN* 141–3. (This shows, incidentally, that natural law is not necessarily *learnt* by rational processes. Its rationality is not impugned, however, since the important point is that it is justified by rational reflection; that what we learn, however we learn it, is in accord with right reason.)

[72] This is shown most clearly in Essay IV, *ELN* 149 ff., where reason and sense-experience discover the design and purpose of the world created by God.

the mind, which advances from things known to things unknown and argues from one thing to another in a definite and fixed order of propositions.'[73] Alternatively, Locke thinks of reason as a light which dispels the darkness, which brings things previously hidden 'to light'. According to this picture, reason shows, or leads to, the truth. Reason is right reason as long as it is not false reasoning—that is, as long as there are no logical or factual errors, whether admitted innocently or through corrupting special interests. So, to hold that natural law is known by reason and sense-experience, and that it is therefore a historically sensitive law, is not at all to cast doubt on what natural law requires (in any given time or place), nor on our capacity to know it. If we possess the facts, and make no fallacious inferences, we can arrive at a clear and certain knowledge of the requirements of natural law. In particular, we can determine what the law requires with respect to the keystone of a just social order, the law of property and its foundation.

3. PROPERTY: ITS ORIGINS AND DEVELOPMENT

3.1 Labour, Workmanship, and Preservation

If we approach Locke's account of property and its origins through an examination of his views on natural law, one feature stands out. In contrast to the *Essays on the Law of Nature*, the *Two Treatises of Government* quite cheerfully accept the legitimacy of self-interested self-preserving behaviour. Locke does not come to espouse an uncaring individualism—it remains our duty to preserve others, even though self-sacrifice is not to be commended—but self-preservation enjoys a priority which it is denied in the *Essays*. In the explanation and defence of private property, this is a shift which cannot but be of momentous import. Private property fits far more happily into a scheme of life based on the injunction to secure the basic concerns of others *after* one has secured one's own, than on an alternative scheme based on the injunction to regard equally the basic concerns of oneself and others. So to explain this shift in Locke's thought should be to provide the key to his account of property, and of its importance in political society; and to

[73] Ibid. 149.

understand why an author anxious for anonymity nevertheless
could have held that 'property I have nowhere found more clearly
explained, than in a book entitled, Two Treatises of Government'.[74]

The key insight which distinguishes the *Two Treatises* from the
Essays is that the productive capacity of human labour increases the
supply of goods available for human life, and thereby improves
human life. The attempt to satisfy needs is not a competition for
fixed resources, not a 'zero-sum game',[75] as the *Essays* suppose:

Victuals, clothes, adornments, riches, and all other good things of this life
are provided for common use. And so, when any man snatches for himself
as much as he can, he takes away from another man's heap the amount he
adds to his own, and it is impossible for anyone to grow rich except at the
expense of someone else.[76]

The picture painted in the *Two Treatises* could hardly be more
different. Property arises, in accord with the dictates of natural law
(which include the rule that 'Men, being once born, have a right to
their Preservation'),[77] directly through the labour of individuals.[78]
Labour is able to play such a fundamental role not because it is an
unpleasant activity which deserves compensation—although Locke
was not unsympathetic to considerations of this kind[79]—but
because it is an activity in accord with the purposes of God. It is
purposeful activity, directed to useful ends, and which secures
preservation in the primitive state and improves human life once
basic necessities have been met. Understood in this way, it
therefore adds to the value of resources by increasing their
productivity. Chapter 5 of the *Second Treatise* is full of such
connections: ''tis *Labour* indeed that *puts the difference of value* on
every thing'; in fact, '*labour makes the far greatest part of the value* of

---

[74] Locke, in a letter to his younger relative the Revd Richard King, dated 25 Aug.
1703. See Laslett's introd., in *Two Treatises*, 3–7.
[75] For this way of putting the difference I am indebted to I. Hont and M. Ignatieff,
'Needs and Justice in the *Wealth of Nations*: An Introductory Essay', in id. (eds.),
Wealth and Virtue: The Shaping of Political Economy in the Scottish Enlightenment
(Cambridge: Cambridge University Press, 1983), 41 n.
[76] Essay VIII, *ELN* 211.
[77] *Two Treatises*, ii. 25.
[78] In contrast to Grotius and Pufendorf, Locke bypasses the question of consent
altogether. This is crucial to his critique of Sir Robert Filmer's *Patriarcha*, which will
be considered in more detail later in this ch.
[79] See e.g. *Two Treatises*, ii. 34, where one who seeks to benefit by the fruits of
another's labour thereby desires 'the benefit of another's Pains, which he had no
right to'.

things, we enjoy in this World'; a conservative estimate is that 'of the *Products* of the Earth useful to the Life of Man 9/10 are the *effects of labour*'.[80] The appropriation of land by labour is an appropriation 'by improving it'; to leave some land unclaimed is to leave it available for another, to leave it 'for his Improvement'; land already appropriated by another is not available to us because it is 'already improved by another's Labour',[81] and so on. The doctrine of the origin of property through labour will not properly be understood if it is not recognized that Locke thinks of labour as a rational (or purposeful), value-creating activity. Labour is not any exercise of energy on objects in the world—acts of destruction or mere amusement certainly do not qualify—but those actions directed towards the preservation or comfort of our being. One passage in the *Second Treatise* makes the connection in some detail:

As much Land as a Man Tills, Plants, Improves, Cultivates and can use the product of, so much is his *Property* . . . God, when he gave the World in common to all Mankind, commanded Man also to labour, and the penury of his Condition required it of him. God and his Reason commanded him to subdue the Earth, *i.e.* improve it for the benefit of Life, and therein lay out something upon it that was his own, his labour.[82]

So labour is to be understood as the activity of improving for the benefit of life, an activity commanded by God as the result of the Fall.[83] Labour is the means whereby property is acquired, both because of the role human beings play in God's larger purposes for the whole created order, and because labour is the improving, value-adding activity required by the duty to preserve oneself and others. These two aspects are neatly conjoined if labour is thought of as workmanship, the human activity which mirrors the divine creative act, and which accords with its purposes. For convenience, this conception of human activity and its importance will be referred to as the 'workmanship model'.[84]

---

[80] Ibid. 40, 42. [81] Ibid. 33, 34.
[82] Ibid. 32.
[83] See Gen. 3: 17–19, God's curse on Adam: 'cursed is the ground for thy sake . . . in the sweat of thy face shalt thou eat bread' (KJV).
[84] The notion of workmanship and the 'workmanship model' are derived from J. Tully, *A Discourse on Property: John Locke and his Adversaries* (Cambridge: Cambridge University Press, 1980), esp. chs. 1 and 3. However, the account of workmanship provided here differs from the views of Tully (and also Dunn). It has substantially weaker implications: in particular, it does not imply that Locke rules out the legitimacy of the wage relation, as Tully argues (see pp. 135–45).

Once it is recognized that Locke's account of the origin of property through labour calls on the workmanship model of human life, it becomes possible to avoid a common misunderstanding, and also to clarify other features of his position. In the first place, Locke's interpreters not infrequently fall into error by placing too much weight on the metaphor of appropriation by means of mixing labour with things. It is certainly true that he treats the appropriative acts of individuals as a process by which things in common (that is, things *not yet* private)[85] become private property by being mixed with, or joined to, something which is private—the labour of the bodies of particular individuals. But this whole picture depends on the workmanship model in that it recognizes only improving activities as labour, and also by presupposing an original community designed specially to meet the needs of the workmanship model. So it is a misconception to interpret Lockian appropriation as simply a process whereby the mixing of 'held' with 'unheld' things forms a larger group of (inexplicably) 'held' things.[86]

Secondly, the workmanship model helps to put Locke's important remarks about rationality and industry in a proper perspective. The world is not meant to remain 'common and uncultivated', because God gave the world 'to the use of the Industrious and Rational, (and *Labour* was to be *his Title* to it;) not to the Fancy or Covetousness of the Quarrelsom and Contentious'.[87] *Contra* Macpherson, industry and rationality are not connected here by the 'assumption that unlimited accumulation is the essence of rationality'.[88] While it is true that Locke places no limits on how much can be accumulated once primitive simplicity has been abandoned, he is not thereby committed to a defence of unlimited accumulation. Quite apart from his denunciation of covetousness, remarks scattered throughout his unpublished manuscripts, in particular, show him to be concerned to limit the extent of industry in favour of education, for

[85] It will be argued below that the things in common are to be understood to be in an original *negative* community.

[86] Cf. R. Nozick, *Anarchy, State, and Utopia* (New York: Basic Books, 1974), 174–5. It should be clear that the workmanship model excludes exs. such as the can of tomato juice spilt into the sea. Nozick has been effectively criticized by Onora O'Neill for ignoring the importance of the notion of improvement: see 'Nozick's Entitlements', *Inquiry*, 19 (1976), 476–9 in particular.

[87] *Two Treatises*, ii. 34.

[88] Macpherson, *The Political Theory of Possessive Individualism: Hobbes to Locke*, 237.

the general social benefits such change would bring.[89] The workmanship model can serve to remind us that Locke's concern is not accumulation *per se* (unlimited or otherwise), but improvement. Accumulation and industry are rational in so far as they are improving activities. Of course, Locke accepts that, by and large, they *are*, but this is entirely a contingent matter. Where accumulation or industry do not improve (where, for example, they foster avarice or ignorance), they are not defensible, nor are they rational.

The positive side of this stance is visible in the defence of private property itself, and can be shown by comparing some passages in the *Second Treatise* with the passage quoted above from the *Essays on the Law of Nature*. In the *Essays*, Locke holds that to take for oneself is to reduce the stock available for others, but in the *Two Treatises* this is not so. Appropriating is no longer harmful:

Nor was this *appropriation* of any parcel of *Land*, by improving it, any prejudice to any other Man, since there was still enough, and as good left; and more than the yet unprovided could use. So that in effect, there was never the less left for others because of his inclosure for himself. For he that leaves as much as another can make use of, does as good as take nothing at all.[90]

In this passage, appropriation does no harm because appropriation for use leaves the original bounty (available for others) intact. Some subsequent passages show that the effect of improvement is, in certain important respects, even advantageous to the unpropertied. The process is as follows.

First of all, it is necessary to grasp the full implications of the power of productive labour, the source of appropriation, if the value of appropriation is itself to be properly understood:

Nor is it so strange, as perhaps before consideration it may appear, that the *Property of labour* should be able to over-ballance the Community of Land. For 'tis *Labour* indeed that *puts the difference of value* on every thing . . . I think it will be a very modest Computation to say, that of the *Products* of the Earth useful to the Life of Man 9/10 are the *effects of labour*: nay, if we will rightly estimate things as they come to our use, and cast up the several Expences about them, what in them is purely owing to *Nature*, and what to *labour*, we shall find, that in most of them 99/100 are wholly to be put on the account of *labour*.[91]

---

[89] This issue is thoroughly dealt with by J. Dunn, *The Political Thought of John Locke*, ch. 17. See esp. the Locke MSS quoted at 231 n. and 235–6 n.

[90] *Two Treatises*, ii. 33.   [91] Ibid. 40.

For this reason, the appropriation of the earth into private possessions amounts to a productive act—an expansion of the available social resources. Private appropriation in accord with the workmanship model is the path to a social bounty of goods.[92] Of course, such a bounty cannot be effectively stored until the development of a money economy, since property is limited to what is not spoiled. Only with the development of money, specifically gold—'*a little piece of yellow Metal*, which would keep without wasting or decay'[93]—could a bounty be preserved.

Locke is well aware that any such bounty is not enjoyed equally, but goes principally to the propertied. Thus to establish, by consent, a money economy is to consent to inequality of goods:

since Gold and Silver, being little useful to the Life of Man in proportion to Food, Rayment, and Carriage, has its *value* only from the consent of Men, whereof Labour yet makes, in great part, *the measure*, it is plain, that Men have agreed to disproportionate and unequal Possession of the Earth.[94]

Nevertheless, the inequalities produced by labour and subsequently entrenched (perhaps even extended)[95] in a money economy do not leave the unpropertied untouched. Locke does not go into the causes, but he clearly envisages some sort of 'trickle-down' effect. The bounty produced by the propertied extends to the unpropertied, improving their condition, so that they actually benefit from the appropriative acts of the propertied. This is shown by a comparison of the unpropertied in a money economy with the wealthiest members of a society where primitive community still reigns: among the 'several Nations of the Americans . . . a King of a large and fruitful Territory there feeds, lodges, and is clad worse than a day Labourer in England'.[96] Since 'in the beginning all the World

---

[92] Locke's argument is thus a defence of enclosure, and on grounds remarkably similar to those that had been employed *against* enclosure in Tudor times. See Wood, *John Locke and Agrarian Capitalism*, 58–68.

[93] *Two Treatises*, ii. 37.

[94] Ibid. 50.

[95] Locke sees no need to argue that 'the inequality created by the emergence of money was a faithful reflection of natural differentials in human industry' (Hont and Ignatieff, 'Needs and Justice in the *Wealth of Nations*', 39). His concern is with the improvement of society, and with the resultant fate of the poor. He only minimally possesses what Nozick calls a 'patterned' conception of distributive justice (see *Anarchy, State, and Utopia*, 155–60); e.g. *Two Treatises*, i. 42, shows him to regard inheritance as a just process—but it is not a process in which differentials of industry are preserved.

[96] *Two Treatises*, ii. 41.

was *America*',[97] the institution of private property, despite establishing dramatic inequalities of wealth, has served to improve the condition of the worst off because of the productive power of labour it nurtures and protects.[98]

This interpretation of Locke's account of appropriation makes it possible to recognize fully the importance of the two conditions he places on appropriation—the 'spoilage' condition and the 'enough, and as good left for others' condition. First of all, spoilage: Locke restricts the application of this condition to the stage of primitive simplicity (the pre-money economic stage), where it prevents excessive accumulation:

It will perhaps be objected . . . That if gathering the Acorn or other Fruits of the Earth, &c. makes a right to them, then any one may *ingross* as much as he will. To which I Answer, Not so. The same Law of Nature, that does by this means give us Property, does also *bound* that *Property* too. *God has given us all things richly*, 1 Tim. vi. 17 is the Voice of Reason confirmed by Inspiration. But how far has he given it to us? *To enjoy*. As much as any one can make use of to any advantage of life before it spoils; so much he may by his labour fix a Property in. Whatever is beyond this, is more than his share, and belongs to others. Nothing was made by God for Man to spoil or destroy.[99]

Here we see the connection between the spoilage condition and the overall workmanship model nicely revealed. The workmanship model implies that, in the age of primitive simplicity, accumulation is limited to what can be used without spoiling. The spoilage condition is not, then, an *ad hoc* condition tacked on in an effort to avoid undesirable consequences generated by a gap in the labour theory. Rather, the Lockian theory of the role of labour, properly understood (as workmanship), requires that accumulation be limited along these lines.

The advent of a money economy means that the spoilage condition no longer applies, because surpluses stored in the form of money do not spoil or decay. Locke apparently regards the surplus of money thus stored quite simply as a stock of wealth, thereby revealing the impact of mercantilist assumptions about money and

---

[97] Ibid. 49.

[98] Locke thus defends private appropriation on approximately 'maximin' grounds: the institution is justified because it is advantageous to the worst off. See J. Rawls, *A Theory of Justice* (Oxford: Oxford University Press, 1972), sect. 26.

[99] *Two Treatises*, ii. 31.

wealth on his account of property. This is worth explaining a little
more fully. From a mercantilist point of view, money—that is,
precious metal—is just stored-up wealth. As Adam Smith notes in
one of his brief remarks on Locke's writings on interest and money,
'His notions were . . . founded upon the idea that public opulence
consists in money, tho' he treats the matter in a more philosophical
light than the rest [of the mercantilists].'[100] If instead it were held, ·
with Smith, that 'riches do not consist in money, but commodities',
and that 'the consumptibility . . . of goods is the great cause of
human industry',[101] then it would have to be concluded that, on the
workmanship model, storing up money is not storing up wealth but
a form of waste, of preventing the accumulation of wealth. If, as
Smith holds, money 'may be compared to the high roads of a
country, which bear neither corn nor grass themselves but circulate
all the corn and grass in the country', then money is wasted unless it
is used, and it is most useful—most efficient—where the proportion
of money to goods is low.[102] If wealth lies in 'the great abundance of
the necessaries of life', and not in money, then to store up money is
to misuse it, to fail to employ it in the creation and circulation of
wealth: 'every unnecessary accumulation of money is a dead stock
which might be employed in enriching the nation.'[103] These
Smithian observations indicate that the place of money in Locke's
account of property is due not only to the workmanship model with
its picture of a harmonious relationship between divine and human
purposes—it also reflects a mercantilist theory of money and
wealth. The employment of a more modern economic theory would
shift the emphasis away from money to the question of the most
efficient usage of productive goods. The workmanship model, with
its anti-spoilage, anti-wastage requirements, could then be more
effectively implemented.

To return to Locke's own picture. The spoilage condition
operates to restrict accumulation in the stage of primitive simplicity,
but not thereafter. For this reason it has sometimes been thought
that the 'enough, and as good' clause plays the same role in the
advanced money economy. Robert Nozick, for example, speaks of
this clause as 'the Lockean proviso'.[104] There is some reason to

[100] A. Smith, *Lectures on Jurisprudence*, ed. R. L. Meek, D. D. Raphael, and P. G.
Stein (Oxford: Clarendon Press, 1978), LJ(B) 254.
[101] Ibid. 255.   [102] Ibid. 245.   [103] Ibid. 245, 258.
[104] *Anarchy, State, and Utopia*, 174–82.

think views of this sort mistaken, although the evidence is not decisive. The 'enough, and as good' clause may not operate as a limit on appropriation at all, and thus may not be a proviso in the relevant sense. Examining those passages where the clause occurs will show how this could be so.

It is introduced in a passage dealing with original accumulation in the stage of primitive simplicity: '*Labour* being the unquestionable Property of the Labourer, no Man but he can have a right to what that is once joyned to, at least where there is enough, and as good left in common for others.'[105] The 'enough, and as good' clause functions as a proviso on legitimate appropriation if it is a necessary condition for successful appropriation by labour: that is, appropriation is successful *only* if there is enough and as good left. However, the clause can equally well be taken to be specifying a sufficient condition: 'at least where' may mean 'wherever', and the clause then asserts that *wherever* there is enough and as good left for others, there appropriation of the fruits of the earth is legitimate. The impulse to read it as a necessary condition is natural enough, since the reader may expect Locke to address the question, What happens when land (or other appropriable resources) runs out? If the clause specifies a sufficient condition, he offers no answer to that question. Is this a serious problem?

Since it is reasonable to expect Locke to address the question of the rights that obtain under conditions of necessity, as Grotius and Pufendorf do, it would appear that it is. However, the interpretation of appropriation by labour as workmanship, and thus as a method of increasing the social bounty, can overcome the problem of necessity by ending the persistent social problem of necessity. (Individual cases of necessity will still occur on occasions, of course.) If this is Locke's view, then he need not be expected to offer a detailed account of the right of necessity in his theory of just property; and the sufficient condition interpretation of the 'enough, and as good' clause would then allow him legitimately to sidestep the obstacle of necessity. It would do so by giving the following account of appropriation.[106]

---

[105] *Two Treatises*, ii. 27.

[106] This account of the 'enough, and as good' clause, and its implications for reading Locke's theory (including the role allotted to charity), derives from J. Waldron, 'Enough and As Good Left for Others', *Philosophical Quarterly*, 29 (1979), 319–28. The view is further defended in id., *The Right to Private Property* (Oxford: Clarendon Press, 1988), 207–18. This interpretation is dubitable, but not because it

The Book of Genesis records that there was a bountiful provision for human needs in the original primitive state. Therefore, appropriation in the state of primitive simplicity was indeed legitimate. Locke thus has no need to consider what might have been the proper course if, in the original primitive state, there had not been 'enough and as good left'. Sacred history tells us that the original state was bountiful, that 'in the beginning all the World was *America*'. Appropriation made no appreciable impact on the original bounty, since it did not prevent there being 'enough, and as good': 'Nor was this appropriation of any parcel of Land, by improving it, any prejudice to any other Man, since there was still enough, and as good left.'[107] With the development of a money economy, inequalities become entrenched, but are justified because the productive power of the new economy brings advantages even to the worst off. However, the productive power of this economy steadily leads to the appropriation of all available land, so that some come to be excluded from possession altogether. Is there then no longer enough and as good left? If the question asks whether there is any of the original common available for others, the answer must be in the negative—but if the issue concerns the ready availability of a stock of goods for the self-preserving use of the worst off, the answer is quite different. For, even in those 'parts of the World, (where the Increase of People and Stock, with the *Use of Money*) had made Land scarce',[108] there are enough and as good resources available, as is shown by the condition of the day-labourer—being better off than the king in America. In other words, 'enough, and as good' can be understood to be satisfied even after the introduction of the money economy, not because parts of the original common remain unappropriated, but because the appropriation of land and other resources increases the social bounty, both in quantity and availability. The worst off, the day-labourer, thus has enough and as good of those things necessary for his preservation—'Meat and Drink, and such other things as Nature affords for . . . Subsistence'.[109] Interpreted in this way, then, the 'enough, and as good' clause regards unclaimed land or goods in common only in so far as these are the means of subsistence—as

generates any incoherences in the overall picture it ascribes to Locke. The problem is, rather, that 'at least where' is a slippery expression, and cannot happily be made to bear too much weight.

[107] *Two Treatises*, ii. 33.   [108] Ibid. 45.   [109] Ibid. 25.

they are in the pre-money economy. In the money economy, however, subsistence, and even flourishing, becomes (for most people) no longer dependent on landed property, nor on the existence of an unappropriated common, but on deriving an income sufficient for life's purposes. So the purpose of the 'enough, and as good' clause, in the stage of the money economy, is satisfied if incomes provide a reasonable living. The case of the day-labourer shows that they do.

The 'enough, and as good' clause in Locke's account of property can thus be understood as a sufficient condition on appropriation, and as a condition which suffices in another sense because it is always satisfied. From an initial bounty, the operations of a system of private appropriation through the improving acts of human labour thereby not only maintain, but actually increase, the supply of goods useful and available for human life—even for the worst off. In this way 'the *Property of labour*' is able to 'over-ballance the Community of Land'.

Even the most productive and humane of economic systems, however, is not immune to disruptions, whether private misfortunes or more general social catastrophes, such as famines. So, despite developing a theory designed to overcome necessity as a general problem, Locke does not ignore the plight of those in serious need. Instead of appealing to the 'enough, and as good' clause, or some variant on Grotius's view, he directly invokes the right of charity all men can legitimately claim against one another:

As *Justice* gives every Man a Title to the product of his honest Industry, and the fair Acquisitions of his Ancestors descended to him; so *Charity* gives every Man a Title to so much out of another's Plenty, as will keep him from extream want, where he has no means to subsist otherwise.[110]

Locke's choice of language here—that charity, like justice, gives a *title* to another's surplus—is not accidental. Charity is not to be understood merely as an imperfect duty of humanity (i.e. of humane benevolence), but as 'a Right to the Surplusage of . . . Goods'. For the needy person, such goods 'cannot justly be denied him, when his pressing Wants call for it'.[111] If the right is to have any significant practical application, charity must overrule justice—otherwise considerations of justice could always be invoked to nullify any attempt to enforce the right of charity. Although Locke

[110] Ibid. i. 42.   [111] Ibid.

does at one point provide a ranking of the virtues which puts justice ahead of charity,[112] he is not there judging on which virtue should overrule when conflict arises between them, but on their comparative necessity for social life—a standard whereby justice must prevail. For justice is necessary for society to exist at all, whereas charity, although perhaps always useful or desirable, is necessary only in specific circumstances. So it is possible to hold that, all things considered, charity is a virtue somewhat less important than justice, but which nevertheless overrides justice when the two come directly into conflict.

Of course, a view of this kind would be short on plausibility if charity had frequently to be invoked in order to maintain the social fabric. Since this is not so—the high productivity of the system of private appropriation keeps cases of necessity rare, and Locke restricts the operations of charity to 'extream want' or 'pressing Wants', where no other means of survival is available[113]—the right of charity does not play a major role in Locke's system of justice. Still, it should not be overlooked, providing as it does a buffer against extreme necessity. For this reason the right of charity can be regarded as Locke's version of the right of necessity acknowledged by Grotius and Pufendorf. The Lockian version is quite distinct, however: unlike Grotius, he does not base the right on a revival of original community, and, unlike Pufendorf, neither does he base it on the duties to the poor that can be agreed upon by rational agents. Having, in the *Two Treatises*, resolved his earlier doubts about the legitimacy of self-preservation, Locke founds the right directly on the natural inclination to self-preservation. He quite forcefully affirms the reliability of this inclination as a guide to action in the following passage from that work:

For the desire, strong desire of Preserving his Life and Being having been Planted in him, as a Principle of Action by God himself, Reason, *which was*

---

[112] See Locke's MS note 'Moralists', quoted by Hont and Ignatieff, 'Needs and Justice in the *Wealth of Nations*', 38 n.: 'Justice the greatest and difficultest duty being thus established the rest will not be hard. The next sort of virtues are those which relate to society and so border on Justice . . . such as are Civility, Charity, Liberality.'

[113] Cf. Locke's position in Essay VII. *ELN* 195: 'we are not obliged to provide with shelter and to refresh with food any and every man, or at any time whatever, but only when a poor man's misfortune calls for our alms and our property supplies means for charity.' Of course, our property can supply means for charity only if it is firmly secured by the rules of justice. (This passage from the *Essays* is (mis)quoted by Hont and Ignatieff, 'Needs and Justice in the *Wealth of Nations*', 37.)

the Voice of God in him, could not but teach him and assure him, that pursuing that natural Inclination he had to preserve his Being, he followed the Will of his Maker.[114]

It is now possible to sum up. The workmanship model, with its focus on human activity as an important part of the larger divine purposes of the created order—and in particular on the vital role of improving human labour, driven by the strong, divinely implanted, desire for self-preservation—is the foundation on which Locke builds his account of property in the *Two Treatises of Government*. By overcoming the limitations imposed by the static, or 'zero-sum', picture of available resources he had accepted in the *Essays on the Law of Nature*, Locke is able to give a full and almost free rein to self-interested behaviour without pernicious consequences for the social order. In the stage of primitive simplicity, the spoilage condition implied by the workmanship model of the created order prevents the accumulation of excessively large estates. In the developed stage of a money economy, the productive capacity of labour guarantees that the initial bounty of God's provision for human beings is always maintained, so that no matter how scarce usable land becomes, there is always 'enough, and as good' of the means of subsistence for all—in fact, there is more for even the worst off. (For this reason Locke may intend the 'enough, and as good' clause to specify a sufficient, rather than a necessary, condition on successful appropriation.) This harmonious system is not immune to natural disasters, so, in common with Grotius and Pufendorf, Locke provides a safety net in the form of the right of charity, his version of the right of necessity.

3.2 *Property and Political Liberty*

Considered simply as a theory of appropriation and prosperity, Locke's account of property in the *Two Treatises* is a significant achievement. However, to portray it wholly in such terms would be to overlook the theory's central political achievement: its defence of the property rights of individuals against the encroachments of arbitrary royal power, without recourse to any contentious doctrine of original consent. Although Grotius (and, following him,

---

[114] *Two Treatises*, i. 86. (To describe reason as the voice of God within, as Locke does here, is to bring out sharply the central place his theory allocates to God's material will.)

Pufendorf) had held that successful appropriation required some form of consent, whether tacit or express, this doctrine was not one Locke could easily accept. Sir Robert Filmer, writing in defence of absolute monarchical power against the views of the Whig party (which included amongst its number Locke's employer and benefactor the first Earl of Shaftesbury), had mounted a strong attack on the credibility and binding power of any form of original consent. So, by providing an account of the rise of property from an original community of possession, Locke removed a source of embarrassment for Whig (and related) defences of individual property against the arbitrary encroachments of monarchical power. (The point here is that a theory of property premised on an original community of possession is thereby committed to take seriously the claims of all human beings to the bounty of the earth. Except for the Hobbesian solution, in which original community is voluntarily abandoned in an attempt to secure individual safety through the protective power of an absolute sovereign, theories premised on an original community typically seek to preserve a sphere of individual freedom by preventing the possibility of absolute monarchical possession of the earth, its fruits, and its inhabitants.)

An examination of Filmer's attack on the idea of an original agreement, and Locke's response, will serve to clarify some important features of the Lockian theory. Filmer brings two arguments against Grotius's view that consent played an important role in the origin of property, first in *Observations concerning the Original of Government*, and then again in *Patriarcha* ('a defence of the natural power of kings against the unnatural liberty of the people').[115] Filmer's first argument is that, to be binding on all, consent must be unanimous—but unanimity is not historically credible. He observes ironically:

Certainly it was a rare felicity, that all the men in the world at one instant of time should agree together in one mind to change the natural community of

---

[115] *Patriarcha and other Political Works of Sir Robert Filmer*, ed. P. Laslett (Oxford: Basil Blackwell, 1949). The quotation is the subtitle of *Patriarcha*. The literature on Filmer is not extensive, although it has grown substantially since Laslett's introd. to the *Two Treatises* brought him firmly into the spotlight (see pp. 45–78). For extended discussions of Filmer's views, see J. Daly, *Sir Robert Filmer and English Political Thought* (Toronto: University of Toronto Press, 1979), and G. Schochet, *The Authoritarian Family and Political Attitudes in 17th-Century England: Patriarchalism in Political Thought* (New Brunswick, NJ: Transaction Books, 1988).

all things into private dominion: for without such a unanimous consent it was not possible for community to be altered: for if but one man in the world had dissented, the alteration had been unjust, because that man by the law of nature had a right to the common use of all things in the world; so that to have given a propriety of any one thing to any other, had been to have robbed him of his right to the common use of all things.[116]

However, Grotius's position is less vulnerable to this charge than Filmer supposes, partly because consent in his scheme is not simply a once-and-for-all matter. His dependence on the Genesis patriarchal narratives allows him to offer a less structured account than Filmer recognizes. For example, he can allow that consent was achieved in and for different regions at different times. Furthermore, he is able to treat the very question of consent in a rather free-and-easy fashion: following Genesis, he holds that some innovations occurred as the result of agreement, whereas others did not. The rise of private property is a case in point. According to Grotius, common ownership was abandoned because changes in the way of life made it necessary to do so, and private property replaced it because such a system of property solved the problems at hand. However, since private ownership is not merely a private relation between an individual and a thing, but a social relation between individuals with respect to things, some public recognition of this new relation is essential for its existence.[117] It is in this context that Grotius speaks of consent, but even here it need not be an express act: property is established 'by a kind of agreement, either expressed, as by a division, or implied, as by occupation'. So the necessary consent is gained even if no actual agreement is made between the affected parties—all that is needed is that everybody respect each other's acts of occupation. By adding that when 'as yet no division had been made, it is to be supposed that all agreed, that whatever each one had taken possession of should be his property',[118] Grotius is not committed to the view that some meeting occurred of all living (adult male) human beings. His point is simply that private property grew as the result of particular acts of occupation, which became established as a result of tacit acceptance by the other interested parties. He does not hold that all the men in the world agreed at any one time to change the original community of things: tacit agreement will do the job perfectly well.

[116] *Observations*, in *Patriarcha*, ed. Laslett, 273.
[117] *DJBP* II. 2. ii. 4–5.　　　　　[118] Ibid. 5.

Why does Filmer fail to see this? The best explanation is that he
misunderstands Grotius's conception of the original community.
For Grotius, the original community was a state in which 'each man
could at once take whatever he wished for his own needs, and could
consume whatever was capable of being consumed'.[119] It therefore
was not, as Filmer conceived it, a state in which 'man by the law of
nature had a right to the common use of all things in the world'.
Rather, the original common state was one in which, by the law of
nature, man had a common right (or, a right in common) to the use of
all things in the world. In other words, the original community was a
community of equal right to things, not a state of positive community
of things. As Grotius imagines it, it is that form of community which
Pufendorf subsequently termed negative community. Although
Grotius's conception of the original community is perhaps not too
clearly stated in *De Jure Belli ac Pacis*, he had previously stressed
the point in *Mare Liberum*—the original meaning of common
property is there described as not being a matter of joint ownership
but of the absence of private property.[120]

If the original community was negative, everything then simply
lay open for use. The important issue, given such a situation, would
then be how to maintain harmony; and this would be achieved by
the stipulation that appropriative acts be publicly recognized. As
long as appropriative acts were public, then, the onus would not be
on the appropriator to make good his claim, but on the other
interested parties to show that the appropriative act was, in some
way, not successful. In a scheme of this kind, agreement need only
be tacit, in contrast to the situation if an original positive community
is supposed. In such a case, agreement must play a crucial role,
because the onus would be on the intending appropriators, not on
the non-appropriators to resist specific acts of appropriation. In
positive community, all men are joint owners, and so their explicit
consent is needed before any part can be removed from the
common. It cannot be presumed that they have consented as long as
they do not object: to allow positive community to be departed from
without express agreement would be to fail to take seriously the
ownership rights of the joint owners. Filmer's stipulation concerning
the agreement to depart from the original common state thus shows
him to take for granted that the original community was a positive

community. Grotius, however, neither shares nor needs to share this assumption—so Filmer's first criticism of the original community thesis is unsuccessful.

Before examining Filmer's second criticism of the role of consent in Grotius's account, it will be instructive to relate Filmer's first criticism to some Lockian remarks. Although it is not clear why he should have failed to do so, Locke makes no clear distinction between negative and positive community. Instead, he speaks indifferently of things belonging to all in common. He even attempts to illustrate original community by reference to '*Commons*, which remain so by Compact',[121] without considering whether the two kinds of common are the same. He apparently fails to see the importance of distinguishing carefully between the two kinds of community. In fact, it seems that, in the passages where he rejects the necessity of an original agreement—'if such a consent as that was necessary, Man had starved, notwithstanding the Plenty God had given him'[122]—it is Filmer's version of the original community thesis, not Grotius's or Pufendorf's, that he has in mind. Those passages therefore amount to Locke asserting that the original community must have been negative: to insist on an explicit agreement, with its threat of starvation for the earliest human beings, is mistakenly to believe that the original community of possession was a positive community. Locke's theory should thus be understood as a defence of the established natural law position against a misdirected attack. Although the form of the defence requires some revisions to the established theory, Locke is not engaged in a major reconstruction in order to save the theory from a damaging attack. Filmer's attack is not damaging because it is premised on a misconception; and Locke's purpose is partially obscured by his failure to take advantage of the conceptual tool (the negative–positive distinction) most useful for the task. This interpretation of Locke's position is not uncontentious, however, so the question of the form of the original community will be considered in more detail below.

To return to Filmer. His second objection to Grotius is this: even if there was an original consent, why should it bind posterity? He sees no reason why subsequent generations should not possess the same freedom to choose available to their early forebears:

---

[121] *Two Treatises*, ii. 28.
[122] Ibid.; and cf. ibid. 29.

If our first parents, or some other of our forefathers did voluntarily bring in property of goods, and subjection to governors, and it were in their power either to bring them in or not, or having brought them in, to alter their minds, and restore them to their first condition of community and liberty; what reason can there be alleged that men that now live should not have the same power? So that if any one man in the world, be he never so mean or base, will but alter his will, and say, he will resume his natural right to community, and be restored unto his natural liberty, and consequently take what he please and do what he list, who can say that such a man doth more than by right he may? And then it will be lawful for every man, when he please, to dissolve all government, and destroy all property.[123]

This argument fails for much the same reasons as the first. Once again, Filmer sees agreement simply as a matter of express free choice, a choice which can be withdrawn from even by members of the initial consenting party, not to mention by any one of their descendants. And, once again, the reason for this conception of agreement is the assumption of an original positive community, with human beings understood to be joint owners of the earth. In fact, he must take it to be not merely an original, but a *permanent* positive community of possession, since he does not allow that the original common was simply given up by its joint owners.[124] But Grotius's view is that an original negative community of possession was given up because of a change in social circumstances, because men no longer wished to live the simple life to which common possession was tied. It was rational reflection on experience which showed that the original community no longer sufficed, and the agreement to abandon common property was no more than the (express or tacit) rational recognition of this fact. So on this view it is not possible to withdraw from private property, once established, precisely because property was necessary for maintaining a harmonious social order. Since any withdrawal from private property would endanger society at large, withdrawal is contrary to the rational dictates of natural law. So Filmer's argument depends

---

[123] *Observations*, in *Patriarcha*, 274; cf. also 65.

[124] Filmer's stance on this point may indicate the background influence of biblical conceptions. At least, given the biblical picture, this view is readily explicable: if God gave the world to mankind in common, it is very inviting to understand this gift not as a mere historical fact, but as timeless, as identifying a permanent condition of human life. James Tully believes this also to be true of Locke's position: the common right of all mankind 'is not tensed' (*A Discourse on Property*, 60–1). Locke's language is apparently untensed, but whether this indicates a doctrine of timeless common possession is not settled thereby.

on mistakenly attributing to Grotius a doctrine of original (and enduring) positive community. This is one aspect of a more general tendency in Filmer's interpretation of Grotius—as James Tully points out, Filmer attributes to Grotius a cluster of *Hobbesian* doctrines.[125]

Locke does not directly address these issues. His critique of Filmer in the *First Treatise* is almost entirely concerned with the question of Adam's title to sovereignty over the earth and its inhabitants,[126] and, by accounting for original appropriation without recourse to consent, makes a direct reply unnecessary. One feature of Filmer's argument is noteworthy, however: the intimate connection he supposes to exist between government and property. In his view, a central problem with any attempt to found both government and property by means of consent is that the revocability of consent renders both government and property unstable. If consent is the foundation of justice and politics, then 'every man, when he please', can 'dissolve all government, and destroy all property'. Although Filmer's claims here depend on misconceiving the role of consent in Grotius's theory, as argued above, his remarks nevertheless serve to show Locke's political achievement: by establishing property independently of any agreement, he protects it from even the threat of insecurity. And, although he allows that governments do depend crucially on consent, by arguing that the 'great and *chief end* therefore, of Mens uniting into Commonwealths, and putting themselves under Government, *is the Preservation of their Property*',[127] he shows that the propertied, at least, have no motive to render government insecure. Thus Locke connects the fate of government and property, but avoids Filmer's criticism by doing so in a way that makes both of them more secure.

The full extent of Locke's political achievement at this point can be illustrated by considering a possible objection: what motive have

---

[125] Tully, *A Discourse on Property*, 127.

[126] He tells us that large parts of the *First Treatise* were lost, so it is possible that some relevant issues may have been discussed there. See the Preface to the *Two Treatises*, 155: 'Reader, *Thou hast here the Beginning and End of a Discourse concerning Government; what Fate has otherwise disposed of the Papers that should have filled up the middle, and were more than all the rest, 'tis not worthwhile to tell thee.*'

[127] *Two Treatises*, ii. 124; cf. also ibid. 94: 'Government has no other end but the preservation of Property.'

the unpropertied for the preservation of government? Locke's
answer neatly synthesizes several previously disparate strands in the
natural law tradition. He could reply in this way: the unpropertied
may have no motive to preserve government, but the issue is of little
importance. A society whose government conforms to the 'True
Original, Extent, and End of Civil Government',[128] in a sense
abolishes the unpropertied state. This is because 'every Man has a
Property in his own *Person*'.[129] This dictum implies that, for all men
alike, government is essential because it preserves property; and
also that, because this most fundamental of properties, like all
property, does not depend on consent, neither can it be lost or even
alienated. Under just government, then, men are neither enslaved
by others, nor can they enslave themselves—the law of nature
forbids slavery. So in one move Locke shows both that all men have
a strong interest in preserving government because their own self-
preservation enjoins it, and that slavery cannot exist in a society
regulated by just principles. He therefore rejects self-enslavement
even through necessity—an issue which had proved very awkward
for Grotius and Pufendorf. He also turns the close connection
between government and property, assumed by Filmer, against the
latter's own conclusions; and so is able to show, as he had intended,
that 'Slavery is so vile and miserable an Estate of Man . . . that 'tis
hardly to be conceived, that an *Englishman*, much less a
Gentleman, should plead for't.'[130] Being himself both an Englishman
and a Gentleman,[131] Locke is well fitted to show the vileness and
miseries of slavery; and through his account of property also shows
it to be incompatible with a just social order.[132]

---

[128] From the title-page of the *Second Treatise*, 283. See also Laslett's notes on the
history of the titles of the work, p. 284.

[129] *Two Treatises*, ii. 27.

[130] Ibid. i. 1.

[131] The title-page to the 2nd (and subsequent) edns. of the *Essay* assure us that the
work is 'Written by JOHN LOCKE, Gent.'—see p. 1, and nn to the title-page, p. 2.

[132] If a man should step outside these just relations, and thus put himself in a state of
war with other men, then he has forfeited his right of self-preservation. Such a man
can be enslaved, because slavery is nothing but 'the State of War continued' (*Two
Treatises*, ii. 24). Presumably he would have defended his own colonial interests
along these lines. Indeed, it is not implausible to hold that a state of war existed
between plantation owners and slaves in the New World—but Locke must argue that
this state was initiated by the *slaves*, which is another matter entirely. For an account
of the tensions in Locke's theory of slavery, and also of his practice concerning it, see
R. W. Grant, *John Locke's Liberalism* (Chicago: University of Chicago Press, 1987),
66–83.

Locke's account of property has two important features. The first has been widely recognized: he uses the term 'property' in a broad sense, to mean not merely material goods but 'Life, Liberty, and Estate'.[133] The second is indicated by the fact that Locke understands life and liberty to be inalienable rights, and thereby is committed to rejecting the view that property is a right of absolute control over things. He holds property to be neither reducible to a set of mere things, nor essentially a right of control. He is thus at odds with modern usage, and even with Grotius and Pufendorf.[134] His view is nevertheless not to be interpreted as a conceptual break with the natural lawyers. It is certainly a terminological variation, but it is not a conceptual break because, like Grotius and Pufendorf, Locke thinks of property in terms of the *suum* and its extensions. This is the second important factor referred to above, and the key to understanding Locke's otherwise curious doctrine that every man has a property in his own person. If this connection is clarified, it is then possible to provide a full account of how the different elements in Locke's theory fit together.

The idea of a property in one's person is introduced in this way: 'every Man has a *Property* in his own *Person*. This no Body has any Right to but himself. The *Labour* of his Body, and the *Work* of his Hands, we may say, are properly his.'[135] A man has property in his person because his person (including any action which proceeds from it) is properly his, and is so because he has an exclusive right to it: 'no Body has any right . . . but himself.' This is exactly how Grotius speaks of the *suum*: ' "own" implies that a thing belongs to some one person in such a way that it cannot belong to any other person.'[136] In Grotian terms, then, Locke's notion of a property in

---

[133] Most explicitly stated at *Two Treatises*, ii. 87, but evident in many other places. For the significance of this meaning of 'property' for Locke's political theory as a whole, see A. Ryan, 'Locke and the Dictatorship of the Bourgeoisie', *Political Studies*, 13 (1965), 210–30.

[134] See, among others, Hont and Ignatieff, 'Needs and Justice in the *Wealth of Nations*', 35. They also claim, with Tully (*A Discourse on Property*, 60–1), that Locke uses 'property' also to mean a 'common right to use'. Locke does on occasions use the term in this way, but it will be argued below that his notion of property in one's person will not do the political work it is clearly intended to do (in particular, to ban slavery) unless property is understood to be a right to *exclude* others in some way. Tully is quite correct, however, when he insists that for Locke property is not a right of 'use, abuse, and alienation' (ibid. 61)—although this does not imply that 'it is a right of use only'. It is, rather, a right of exclusive possession.

[135] *Two Treatises*, ii. 27.

[136] *ML* 24.

one's person is simply that we are each our own: we belong to ourselves in a way that we cannot belong to others. If we ask, In what way do we thus belong to ourselves?, we are seeking an answer to the question, What is it that is one's own? Grotius's answer is this: 'By nature a man's life is his own, not indeed to destroy, but to safeguard; also his own are his body, limbs, reputation, honour, and the acts of his will.'[137] If we count body and limb as parts, or at least supports, of one's life, and recognize that the acts of our will can be redescribed as the freedom to act according to our will, then Grotius's version of the *suum* amounts to life, reputation, and liberty. When the *suum* is extended to include those things necessary for survival, it is then composed of life, reputation, liberty, and estate.

The strong similarity with Locke is evident. Aside from questions of reputation (with which he seems little concerned), Locke's extended notion of property parallels Grotius's account of the *suum*. In fact, the foundation of his account of property, the property in one's own person, can be shown to be simply the central natural law concept of the (unextended) *suum*: that one's life and liberty belong only to oneself, not to anyone else. In accord with Grotius, Locke accepts that this does not mean that one's life is simply at one's free disposal. Rather, because one's life is one's own 'not indeed to destroy, but to safeguard', one's liberty is not to be understood as modern negative liberty—the absence of restraints—but as the freedom to pursue whatever courses of action are not in conflict with the safeguarding of one's life. In Lockian terms, because our life is our own to safeguard, we have a duty to preserve ourselves: 'Everyone . . . is bound to preserve himself.'[138] The natural liberty which is our own is the freedom to act in whatever ways do not conflict with this duty, or with the associated duties of natural law: 'The *Natural Liberty* of Man is . . . to have only the Law of Nature for his Rule.'[139] However, in so far as this liberty *is* ruled by the law of nature (i.e. where the liberties in question are to act in accordance with the dictates of natural law, rather than simply not conflicting with them), the liberty has the force of a right. This applies pre-eminently to the actions necessary for self-preservation:

---

[137] *DJBP* ii. 17. ii. 1.   [138] *Two Treatises*, ii. 6.

[139] Ibid. 22. The law of nature is sensitive to those acts of will in which we voluntarily bind ourselves. So, as long as a polity is consented to, all the laws of that polity are protected by the law of nature (cf. ibid. 57).

'Men, being once born, have a right to their Preservation, and consequently to Meat and Drink, and such other things, as Nature affords for their Subsistence.'[140] The property in one's person thus has a dynamic quality, in that it needs to grow to survive—it requires the acquisition of certain things. The *suum* must be extended—'mixed' with things—in order to be maintained.

The idea of the necessity of extending the *suum* is thus the best explanation of Locke's attraction to the 'mixing' metaphor in his account of appropriation. The metaphor certainly creates difficulties, but it is not necessary to go into the issue in detail. At least some of the apparent problems can be attributed to the preconceptions of modern interpreters, rather than to the 'mixing' arguments themselves. For example, the arguments seem very strange if he is thought to be trying to show how a cluster—or 'bundle'—of rights can be transferred from one object to another.[141] But to interpret him in this way is to fail to take him at his word. He wants to know how things can become mine, not through positive legal acts of human societies, but naturally. Some things do become mine naturally because there are natural processes by which things become a part of me—hence the remark that 'The Fruit, or Venison, which nourishes the wild Indian . . . must be his, and so his, i.e. a part of him.' It must be his, have become a part of him, since 'No Body can deny but the nourishment is his.'[142] Locke is certainly trying to show the origin of a legal relation, but his commitment to natural law is, like Grotius's, a commitment that legal relations arise by mirroring natural relations. As Grotius puts it, 'When property or ownership was invented, the law of property was established to imitate nature.'[143] (These remarks are not meant to suggest that the problems can all be made to disappear.[144] Quite the contrary. In fact, it will be argued below that Locke's argument works rather better if all talk of 'mixing' is set aside, and appeal is made directly to the right to preserve oneself—a right which itself depends directly on the property one has in one's person.)

[140] Ibid. 25.
[141] Some modern readers of Locke assume that he must be doing this, since on their *own* analyses the concept of property is represented as a 'bundle' of rights. See e.g. L. Becker, *Property Rights: Philosophic Foundations* (London: Routledge & Kegan Paul, 1977).   [142] *Two Treatises*, ii. 26, 28.
[143] *ML* 25; cf. *DJPC* 229: ' . . . this law was patterned after nature's plan.'
[144] For an illustration of some of the difficulties that arise, see Waldron, *The Right to Private Property*, 184–91.

It is possible to provide an independent line of support for the claim that Locke's notion of property in one's person is equivalent to the natural law notion of the *suum*. Doing so will show both the conceptual continuity between the natural law notion and property in one's person, and also the high degree of continuity between Locke's terminology and that of his English predecessors.

The initial evidence is provided by Karl Olivecrona. In his article 'Appropriation in the State of Nature: Locke on the Origin of Property', he argues convincingly for the equivalence of the notions of *suum* and property in one's person, and further that the Latin *suum* was typically translated into seventeenth-century English as 'propriety'.[145] For example, he points out that Hobbes discusses the Scholastic adage, that justice is *suum cuique tribuere*, as follows: 'the ordinary definition of Justice in the Schooles [is] that *Justice is the constant Will of giving to every man his own*. And therefore where there is no *Own*, that is, no Propriety, there is no Injustice.'[146] So for Hobbes, *suum*, or one's own, is one's propriety. His list 'of things held in propriety', discussed later in *Leviathan*, reinforces the connection. Things held in propriety are there shown to be layered, as is the *suum*: 'those that are dearest to a man are his own life, & limbs; and in the next degree, (in most men,) those that concern conjugall affection; and after them riches and means of living.'[147]

With the same Scholastic adage in mind, Locke affirms the connection between propriety and justice in the first edition of the *Essay*: '*Where there is no Propriety, there is no Injustice*, is a Proposition as certain as any Demonstration in Euclid.'[148] So both this one and the Hobbesian passage quoted above give solid support to Olivecrona's claim that 'propriety' was the common English translation of *suum*.[149] Furthermore, in seventeenth-century usage, 'propriety' and 'property' were often used interchangeably, so it is safe to conclude that *suum* and 'property' were at least roughly equivalent. The interchangeability of 'propriety' and 'property' is

[145] K. Olivecrona, 'Appropriation in the State of Nature: Locke on the Origin of Property', *Journal of the History of Ideas*, 35 (1974), 221–30.
[146] T. Hobbes, *Leviathan*, ed. C. B. Macpherson (Harmondsworth: Penguin Books, 1968), ch. 15.
[147] Ibid., ch. 30. This passage also shows, somewhat surprisingly, that Hobbes, like Grotius but unlike Locke, incorporates social factors into his account of the *suum*.
[148] *Essay*, IV. 3. 18 n.
[149] Olivecrona, 'Appropriation in the State of Nature', 219.

well illustrated by Locke himself: after showing an initial preference for 'propriety' in much of his work, he changed many references to 'property' in later versions.[150] Thus in later editions of the *Essay* the passage quoted above becomes '*Where there is no Property, there is no Injustice*',[151] and 'propriety' is replaced by 'property' in a number of late revisions to the *Two Treatises*.[152] Not in all places, however: in the chapter on property itself, Locke says at one point that by labouring on things one comes to '*acquire a Propriety in them*'.[153] In addition, the distinctively Lockian expression 'a property in one's person' is clearly prefigured in a work by Richard Baxter, *The Second Part of the Nonconformist's Plea for Peace* (published in 1680, but 'mostly written many years past'). Baxter speaks there in very Lockian terms of a propriety in oneself which can be legitimately extended:

Every man is born with a propriety in his *own members*, and nature giveth him a propriety in *his Children*, and his food and other just *acquisitions* of his industry . . . And men's *lives* and *Liberties* are the chief parts of their propriety. That is the people's just *reserved Property*, and *Liberty*, which neither *God taketh from them* . . . nor is *given away* by their *own* foresaid consent.[154]

These examples all help to show that the equivalence between Locke's notion of property in one's person and the natural lawyer's notion of the *suum* is not surprising. Not only was *suum* commonly translated as 'property' or 'propriety'; the idea of generating property in things through property in one's person is equivalent to the established idea of the necessity of extending the *suum* to include things requisite for its maintenance, and is also observable in other political writers of the late seventeenth century. Locke's doctrine of the property in one's person can therefore be regarded as something of a commonplace—an interpretation, shared by contemporaries, of a central doctrine of the major European natural lawyers.

[150] See *Two Treatises*, introd. 101–2 and nn., and the n. to ch. 5 of the *First Treatise*.

[151] *Essay* iv. 3. 18 and n.

[152] See *Two Treatises*, introd.

[153] Ibid. ii. 37.

[154] See Laslett's editorial footnote, *Two Treatises*, ii. 27. Note that, despite the strikingly similar cast of Baxter's thought, one aspect of his view is distinctively anti-Lockian—he allows that a man has a propriety 'in *his Children*', a position Locke explicitly rejects (see *Two Treatises*, ii. 60–7, 170).

It was suggested above that Locke's notion of 'mixing' one's labour with things reflects the idea of extending the *suum* to things—the *suum* laps over its original boundaries and mixes with parts of the world—but that Locke's theory does not require, and even can be better stated without, resorting to this metaphor. The reason is this: although the idea of extending the *suum* encourages thinking of it as a kind of physical realm, as some sort of special substance, it is in fact a moral realm: that realm which cannot be encroached upon by others without doing an injury. Locke draws the conclusion that, because property in things is necessary for protecting property in one's person, the right to preserve oneself extends to an exclusive right to use things, as long as such uses conform to natural law, as interpreted by the workmanship model of the creation and its purposes.[155] And, since the workmanship model justifies self-preserving actions because they represent the minimum interpretation of the duty to improve the created order in accordance with divine purposes, it also justifies more complete interpretations of this general duty. Therefore, since Locke holds that an extensive system of unequal private property linked to a money economy is in accord with a more complete interpretation, limited rights of private property generated by the right of self-preservation can be extended to such extensive systems of property.

If this general line of thought is applied to the individual case in the state of nature, 'mixing' ceases to play any important role in legitimate appropriation. A man who by his labour acquires those things necessary for his preservation (and, of course, for the preservation of his family) acts in accordance with the duties imposed by natural law. He has a right to act in this way, and does no injury to others by so doing. And no one can take these necessary things from him without doing him an injury. He thus has an exclusive right to them: 'no Body has any Right . . . but himself.' They are therefore his property. No more need be said. The 'mixing' metaphor only complicates the issue. Perhaps its principal function has been to lead too many readers astray.

We are now in a position to spell out Locke's fundamental doctrines on the right of preservation and its implications, and thereby to show the inseparable connection between natural liberty and property, with its specific implications for slavery. To begin, it is

---

[155] See, in particular, *Two Treatises*, ii. 57.

necessary to consider Locke's assertion of the right of self-preservation in context. He says:

Whether we consider natural *Reason*, which tells us, that Men, being once born, have a right to their Preservation, and consequently to Meat and Drink, and such other things, as Nature affords for their Subsistence: Or *Revelation*, which gives us an account of those Grants God made of the World to *Adam*, and to *Noah*, and his Sons, 'tis very clear, that God, as King *David* says, *Psal.* CXV. xvj. *has given the Earth to the Children of Men*, given it to Mankind in common.[156]

The world is given to mankind in common in such a way that it initially belongs to no one in particular—the original meaning of 'common' identified by Grotius, and termed negative community by Pufendorf. Locke insists that the world has been given in common in order to reject Filmer's doctrine that the world is the private property of Adam and his heirs: the world has not been given only 'to *Adam*, and his Heirs in Succession, exclusive of all the rest of his Posterity'. There was an original community because 'no body has originally a private Dominion, exclusive of the rest of Mankind'. Locke is then faced with the problem of how, given an original community, private property arises. It must arise because it is necessary—'there must of necessity be a means to appropriate . . . before [things] can be of any use, or at all beneficial to any particular Man'—and it in fact arises through the improving acts of human labour and the beneficial effects of developed economies. The task is then to show the political implications of an original community which has been 'given to Men for the Support and Comfort of their being'.[157]

We can best approach this question by considering an important passage which appears to deny that the world is given to men in common, because the world and all that is in it belongs to God. The passage has previously been referred to in brief. It runs as follows:

For Men being all the Workmanship of one Omnipotent, and infinitely wise Maker; All the Servants of one Sovereign Master, sent into the World by his order and about his business, they are his Property, whose Workmanship they are, made to last during his, not one anothers Pleasure.[158]

This passage must be treated with caution. It has already been argued that, because God's will is not changeable, being materially

---

[156] Ibid. 25.   [157] Ibid. 26.   [158] Ibid. 6.

embodied in the world, including in our own selves,[159] our being made to last during God's pleasure must not be understood to mean that the laws of nature can be changed. Nor is it the case that, by being God's property, human beings cannot belong to themselves, or cannot successfully appropriate the earth and its fruits. Rather, Locke's point is that we are God's property because we belong to him: we are part of God's creation, and are therefore subject to divine purposes. This implies that, in the first place, to be God's property is simply to be subject to natural law. In the second place, however, to recognize ourselves as God's property is to recognize that we belong to no one else. God has an exclusive right over men, so no human being can have any such right. So Locke's concern here is not, despite the language of ownership, to enslave men, but to free them; to free them from each other through the rule of natural law. This is clearly shown by the immediate context of the quoted passage, which is concerned with securing political liberty. The sentences immediately preceding and immediately following the quoted 'workmanship' passage are these:

The *State of Nature* has a Law of Nature to govern it, which obliges every one: and Reason, which is that Law, teaches all Mankind, who will but consult it, that being all equal and independent, no one ought to harm another in his Life, Health, Liberty, or Possessions . . . And being furnished with like Faculties, sharing all in one Community of Nature, there cannot be supposed any such *Subordination* among us, that may Authorize us to destroy one another, as if we were made for one anothers uses, as the inferior ranks of Creatures are for ours.[160]

The state that 'all Men are naturally in' is therefore a state of subjection to natural law alone. It is 'a *State of perfect Freedom* to order their Actions, and dispose of their Possessions, and Persons as they think fit, within the bounds of the Law of Nature, without asking leave, or depending upon the Will of any other Man'.[161]

However, although it is a state of perfect freedom, the natural state of men is not without its inconveniences. In particular, the lack of an independent authority to settle any disputes that may arise means that, although '*the State of Nature, and the State of War* . . .

---

[159] Esp. in our reason, which is in mankind '*the Voice of God*' (*Two Treatises*, i. 86).
[160] Ibid. ii. 6.
[161] Ibid. 4. Cf. ibid. 22: 'The *Natural Liberty* of Man is to be free from any Superior Power on Earth, and not to be under the Will or Legislative Authority of Man, but to have only the Law of Nature for his Rule.'

are as far distant, as a State of Peace, Good Will, Mutual Assistance, and Preservation, and a State of Enmity, Malice, Violence, and Mutual Destruction are one from another',[162] there is always the possibility that disputes will lead to the state of nature breaking down, and giving way to the state of war. So, in order to avoid the state of war, men establish political society:

> To avoid this State of War ... is one great *reason of Mens putting themselves into Society*, and quitting the State of Nature. For where there is an Authority, a Power on Earth, from which relief can be had by *appeal*, there the continuance of the State of War is excluded, and the Controversie is decided by that Power.[163]

This is perhaps reasonable enough, but what of the state of perfect freedom? Is the liberty of the natural state simply abandoned in favour of security in the political state? Locke's answer is in the negative: the '*Natural Liberty* of Man' is exchanged for the '*Liberty of Man, in Society*'. He holds that men do not give up their liberty when they enter society because society is founded on consent, and therefore on a legislature which passes laws 'according to the Trust put in it'. Political society, rightly conceived, involves no subjection to 'the inconstant, uncertain, unknown, Arbitrary Will of another Man'. It can be understood to generate not a superior, but a *common*, power—and therefore involves no diminution of freedom. Instead, it produces '*Freedom of Men under Government*', which is 'to have a standing Rule to live by, common to every one of that Society, and made by the Legislative Power erected in it', and, outside the purview of such rules, 'A Liberty to follow my own Will'. To satisfy these conditions is to guarantee the '*Liberty of Man, in Society*'.[164]

Is Locke just playing fast and loose? Do notions like the freedom of men under government, or the liberty of man in society, simply obscure the fact that they refer to a condition which is a kind of unfreedom? If, by 'liberty', Locke means that condition of being free from all restraints Isaiah Berlin has called 'negative liberty',[165] then he is certainly guilty of obfuscation. However, in an important passage he shows himself to be aware of the 'paradox of

---

[162] Ibid. 19.
[163] Ibid. 21.
[164] Ibid. 22.
[165] I. Berlin, 'Two Concepts of Liberty', in id., *Four Essays on Liberty* (Oxford: Oxford University Press, 1969).

freedom'[166]—that, to be maintained, freedom depends on restraints which preserve and foster it. Freedom, he says, depends on law:

For *Law*, in its true Notion, is not so much the Limitation as *the direction of a free and intelligent Agent* to his proper Interest, and prescribes no farther than is for the general good of those under that Law. Could they be happier without it, the *Law*, as an useless thing would of it self vanish; and that ill deserves the Name of Confinement which hedges us in only from Bogs and Precipices. So that, however it may be mistaken, *the end of Law* is not to abolish or restrain, but *to preserve and enlarge Freedom*: for in all the states of created beings capable of Laws, *where there is no Law, there is no Freedom*.[167]

The enemy of freedom is not law, but being 'subject to the arbitrary will of another'. And, since the consent on which legitimate political society is built precludes any such subjection, the liberty of man in society is genuine liberty.

Locke needs to be able to maintain this, because such liberty is crucial to the exercise of the right of self-preservation. Without liberty, self-preservation cannot be effectively pursued, so much so that to lose liberty is to lose the control necessary even for staying alive. Unfree men are simply at the mercy of others: 'I have no reason to suppose, that he, who would *take away my Liberty*, would not when he had me in his Power, take away everything else.'[168] And from this it follows that '*Freedom* from Absolute, Arbitrary Power, is so necessary to, and closely joyned with a Man's Preservation, that he cannot part with it, but by what forfeits his Preservation and Life together.'[169] Further, no man can 'forfeit his Preservation' because no man has the power to forfeit his own life—the right of self-preservation is built upon the duty to preserve oneself prescribed by natural law. Every man 'is *bound to preserve himself*, and not to quit his Station wilfully'.[170] Freedom under natural law therefore does not allow suicide, nor does it permit self-enslavement. In fact, the latter is similar to the former, in that it effectively amounts to giving up one's life:

A Man, not having the Power of his own Life *cannot*, by compact, or his own Consent, *enslave himself* to any one, nor put himself under the

---

[166] See, in particular, K. Popper, *The Open Society and its Enemies* (London: Routledge, 1945).
[167] *Two Treatises*, ii. 57.
[168] Ibid. 18.   [169] Ibid. 23.   [170] Ibid. 6.

Absolute, Arbitrary Power of another, to take away his Life, when he pleases. No body can give more Power than he has himself, and he that cannot take away his own Life, cannot give another power over it.[171]

Nor, it need hardly be said, can a man be forcibly enslaved by anyone else. Since liberty is necessary for self-preservation, to deprive another of liberty is to exercise power over his life—a power which one does not legitimately possess, since each and every man has a property in his own person. Slavery must be ruled out completely: men have power over their own lives in order to preserve themselves (and to improve the general lot, by providing for 'the Support and Comfort of their being');[172] and this power can be exercised only over their own lives (not of others), but *must* be exercised over their own lives (i.e. cannot be given up). The twin doctrines of the right of self-preservation and the property in one's own person thus deny any place for slavery within a just social order. No form of slavery is possible in a political society conformed to the principles of natural law. Slavery is, in its 'pure' form at least, 'nothing else, but *the State of War continued, between a lawful Conquerour, and a Captive*',[173] and, since one great reason for entering political society is precisely to avoid the state of war, the justification for political society is lost if slavery is allowed to have a place within it. Locke implies as much in his principle that 'the great and *chief end* therefore, of Mens uniting into Commonwealths, and putting themselves under Government, *is the Preservation of their Property*', because 'the general name, *Property*' refers not merely to things but to 'Lives, Liberties, and Estates'.[174] If the task of civil government is to preserve property, then, among other things, it is to protect its citizens from all forms of slavery.

3.3 *The History of Property: Word and Object*

It is not uncommon for modern philosophers, concerned with the contemporary political question of the justifiability of modern systems of private property, to begin their enquiries by examining 'traditional' arguments for property—of which Locke's 'labour theory' is a leading example. Approaches to Locke's theory from this sort of perspective commonly go astray on two counts. One has been already indicated: the role played by labour in Locke's scheme

---

171 Ibid. 23.　　172 Ibid. 26.
173 Ibid. 24.　　174 Ibid. 124, 123.

is only properly understood if it is seen as an activity in accord with the general requirements of the workmanship model. Modern accounts frequently go astray at this point.[175] The second error is no less common, and is implicit in the preceding conclusion concerning property and slavery. It can be brought out by recognizing that if slavery is excluded because of the property that all men have in their own persons, it can only be because this basic form of property cannot be alienated (voluntarily or otherwise).[176] Further, if our appropriation of what is *necessary* for our subsistence (that is, leaving aside the questions of surpluses, and also of traded goods) depends on our duty to preserve ourselves, then neither will these appropriations be alienable. So Locke accepts that at least some forms of property—including the fundamental form from which more extensive properties are derived—are not alienable. This is sufficient to set his concept of property apart from the modern conceptions that preoccupy the philosophers in question. It is a mistake to assume, then, that Locke's arguments for property are arguments for that cluster of rights which many modern philosophers regard as constituting property.

However, it would also be mistaken to think that Locke's arguments all concern a phenomenon quite distinct from modern property. His account of property is historical in two senses: he deals not only with the advent of property, but with the elaboration and specification, over time, of the meaning of property relations themselves. Improving labour begins property in things in a historical sense—it starts a process of extension and elaboration (through rational reflection on sense experience) of an originally rather amorphous relation of exclusively belonging to,[177] into a complex and sophisticated notion of positive law in which a cluster, or bundle, of rights comes to be accepted as constituting property. Furthermore, although Locke accepts that there is development in the nature of property relations (which may or may not be a smooth,

---

[175] Nozick's treatment of Locke's theory in *Anarchy, State, and Utopia* (pp. 174–8) has already been mentioned; but a better (more detailed) ex. of the tendency is Becker's *Property Rights*.

[176] The issue will be complicated by questions of the legitimacy of punishment, but the point here is not affected by being restricted to innocent parties.

[177] Although Locke does sometimes use 'property' to mean forms of common ownership as well, it is this exclusive sense he has in mind in the ch. on property. Every man has a property in his own person because 'this no Body has any Right to but himself'. Cf. also *DJNG* IV. 4. 2.

continuing process—in fact, his 'two stages' theory may imply only two forms of property), he is not committed to the particular concept of property implicit in modern British property law. This can readily be indicated. In order to show that property allows a wide range of powers over things, he points out that 'Property, whose Original is from the Right a Man has to use any of the Inferior Creatures, for the Support and Comfort of his Life, is for *the benefit and sole Advantage* of the Proprietor, so that he may even destroy the thing, *where need requires*.'[178] This passage shows that, in Locke's view, even the widest powers a man has over a thing are constrained (or, better, directed)[179] by considerations of need or advantage. Wilful destruction is not within the purview of property right; property does not bestow absolute control over a thing.

This is most important, given the widespread modern tendency to identify the power of absolute control as the very essence of property right. Lawrence Becker, following the influential analysis by A. M. Honoré,[180] calls the right of absolute control over a thing the right to the capital. It is 'the power to alienate the thing and to consume, waste, modify, or destroy it'.[181] Of the 'bundle' of rights discernible in the complex modern notion of property, the right to the capital is the 'fundamental' right: 'One who has all the rights in the list save that of capital may own the thing in a derivative sense, but the one who has the right to the capital is "fundamentally" the owner.'[182] If this is 'fundamentally' what ownership is—and if ownership and property are identical[183]—then Becker is correct to conclude that arguments of a Lockian type, although they might establish some kind of rights, do not establish *property* rights.[184] Locke's arguments do not aim to establish the right Becker has 'fundamentally' in mind. In fact, should we accept the latter's conception of property, we would be forced to conclude that Locke is not really talking of property at all. However, we need not be

[178] *Two Treatises*, i. 92 (emphases added).　　　[179] Ibid. ii. 57.
[180] A. M. Honoré, 'Ownership', in A. G. Guest (ed.), *Oxford Essays in Jurisprudence* (Oxford: Clarendon Press, 1961); repr. in A. M. Honoré, *Making Law Bind* (Oxford: Clarendon Press, 1987).
[181] Becker, *Property Rights*, 19.
[182] Ibid. 20. Becker's use of scare quotes here is rather puzzling: presumably he does not intend to empty the meaning.
[183] For Becker they are (ibid. 18). For a more detailed account of the relationship between the 2 concepts, see A. Reeve, *Property* (London: Macmillan, 1986), ch. 2.
[184] Becker, *Property Rights*, 40–1.

moved to such a drastic solution. It suffices to insist that Becker and
Locke employ different concepts of property, and that the failure of
Locke's arguments to establish Becker's concept of property is
therefore unsurprising.

There is a good deal to be gained by making this difference clear.
By further clarifying a feature of Locke's concept of property, it aids
in the assessment of an important recent interpretation of Locke's
thought. Before turning to that interpretation, it will be helpful if
the most relevant aspects of the position being advanced here are
briefly summarized, and supported with some further considerations.
Locke's central use of 'property' is to mean exclusive belonging.
'Property' can thus have a wide and a narrow meaning, depending
on whether what is being referred to is *all* that is mine, or the *things*
(other than me) that are mine. (This scope difference can in its turn
be related to the *suum*. The broad meaning identifies property with
the *suum* and its extensions; the narrow meaning limits the
reference of 'property' to the extensions alone.) The important
point, though, is that Locke must have an exclusive right in mind
because his arguments for political liberty and against slavery
depend on it. The whole thrust of his account of the relation
between government, property, and liberty is to guarantee that men
belong only to themselves, that they can in no way be 'subject to the
inconstant, uncertain, unknown, Arbitrary Will of another Man'.[185]
To prevent such subjection, the exclusive rights inherent in private
property are crucial. The same point is made in the *Essays on the
Law of Nature*. In arguing against personal interest as the
foundation of natural law, Locke is none the less anxious to stress
that natural law aims precisely at protecting personal interest, in
particular by protecting private property. He says:

We do not wish to be understood to say that the common rules of human
equity and each man's private interest are opposed to one another, for the
strongest protection of each man's private property is the law of nature,
without the observance of which it is impossible for anybody to be master of
his property and to pursue his private advantage. Hence it will be clear to
anyone who candidly considers for himself the human race and the
practices of men, that nothing contributes so much to the general welfare of
each and so effectively keeps men's possessions safe and secure as the
observance of natural law.[186]

[185] *Two Treatises*, ii. 22.
[186] Essay VIII, *ELN* 207.

In this passage we see exactly the same connections—between natural law, private property, individual liberty (in the necessity to pursue one's own advantage), and the general welfare—as are evident in the *Two Treatises*. For Locke, private property is a bulwark against slavery, the keystone of political freedom and the key to general material prosperity.

It is thus no small surprise to find a recent interpretation of Locke's theory which denies that it is a defence of private property at all, but an argument for individual use-rights arising out of an original *positive* community. This is the burden of James Tully's book, *A Discourse on Property: John Locke and his Adversaries*. It would lead too wide of the main purposes of this study to engage in a detailed examination of Tully's dense book, but, because of the very different picture he draws of Locke's position, it is necessary to consider some central features of his position.[187]

The very idea of an original positive community is rather odd, and especially so in the case of Locke's theory of property. This is because of some of the characteristics of positive community as described by Pufendorf. He says, in the first place, that positive community, like proprietorship, implies 'an exclusion of others from the thing which is said to be common'.[188] A positive community is a group of joint owners, marked off from an (in the relevant respect) unpropertied remainder of humankind. Obviously, this could not be true of an original positive community, for in such a state there are no non-owners. Pufendorf's conception of a positive community is of a relation which could not have been the original relation between human beings and the earth. For Pufendorf, positive community, like private property, arises in the course of human history as the result of consent.

This serves to introduce the second oddity. Since Locke's account of appropriation is designed to avoid recourse to consent, it is odd to explain his position by means of a relation which apparently arises through consent. Tully is aware of the oddness, and seeks to overcome it by claiming that Locke *redefines* positive community.[189] However, there is a further problem regarding the role of consent if

---

[187] Tully's book has provoked some sharp responses. Two of the more extensive replies to his thesis are Waldron, *The Right to Private Property*, ch. 6, and Wood, *John Locke and Agrarian Capitalism*, ch. 5.

[188] *DJNG* IV. 4. 3.

[189] Tully, *A Discourse on Property*, 127. The success of the claim will be determined below.

Locke's theory is premised on a kind of original positive community. This is due to the fact that changes to a system of positive community require consent by all owning parties—in this case, all human beings. In a system of positive community, says Pufendorf, 'it is obvious that one person cannot of his own right dispose of the entire thing, but only of his share; and that if any decision is to be reached on the whole thing, the consent and authority of each person concerned in it must be secured'.[190] It might not immediately be clear why this passage should indicate a problem for Tully's interpretation of Locke, since he holds only that Locke's is an account of legitimate use, not of converting an original common into private property. And indeed, consent raises no difficulties at this point. There is a problem, however, with the establishment of a money economy. In the pre-money stage, there is no problem about the specification of one's share: this is fixed by the necessity of preserving oneself. But the advent of money makes this no longer true. The money economy introduces possessions which go well beyond the original share, so, for the establishment of the money economy, 'the consent and authority of each person concerned in it must be secured'. Now it may be thought that there is no problem here, since Locke not only holds that money is introduced by consent, but also that 'disproportionate and unequal Possession of the Earth' is thereby consented to.[191] The problem, however, is indicated by the fact that Locke clearly has in mind a tacit consent only; and it has been argued above that tacit consent, while it is well suited to the burdens consent must bear given an original negative community, does not seem nearly sufficient for dissolving (or even restructuring) positive communities. Filmer's argument, that abandonment of original community required an explicit and universal consent (and was therefore inconceivable), was dependent, it was argued, on positing an original positive community. If Locke also begins from an original positive community, then he needs a stronger form of consent than he provides—the departure from 'natural shares' that is such a feature of the money economy is otherwise a prima-facie case of unauthorized taking from joint owners. (At this point it is worth remembering Proudhon's famous remark, that 'property is theft':

---

[190] *DJNG* IV. 4. 2.
[191] *Two Treatises*, ii. 50.

property is indeed theft when it is constituted by unauthorised departure from a positive common.)

Admittedly, Locke does accord an important role to express consent in his complete account of property: he holds that 'in Governments the laws regulate the right of property',[192] and the establishment of governments depends on express consent ('compact').[193] So, although '*Labour, in the Beginning, gave a right of property*', the contemporary disposition of property is not explicable without recourse to express agreements. By establishing political societies in order to avoid the ills of the state of war, men have (among other things) '*by Compact and Agreement, settled the Property* which Labour and Industry began'.[194] However, even settling property by consent in this way remains vulnerable to a Filmerian criticism (if we suppose that it is this agreement which initiates the move away from 'natural shares') since such consent is not universal, but arises in particular parts of the earth as the need arises. So the idea of an original positive community is not without problems, problems which are magnified if it is supposed that such a state underlies Locke's conception of the original common and the method of departure from it.

Tully recognizes that positive community theories were subjected to telling criticism in the seventeenth century, but he holds that Locke was aware of these criticisms, and met them by redefining positive community. We need to examine Tully's account of this redefinition rather carefully. He says this:

Locke's solution . . . is to redefine positive community. Although the common belongs to everyone in the same manner, it belongs to them to use for the duty of acquiring the means necessary for support and comfort. Their inclusive rights refer to these means which are due to each. Thus, each right does not refer to every item on the common. Indeed, *it does not refer to any item on the common* but, rather, to items made from the common.[195]

In order properly to assess this passage, it is first necessary to examine Tully's claim that the original right to self-preservation in

---

[192] Ibid.

[193] Ibid. Locke equates compact with express consent in this passage by maintaining that the value of money is established by 'tacit agreement', that is, 'without compact'.

[194] Ibid. ii. 45.

[195] Tully, *A Discourse on Property*, 127 (emphasis added).

Locke's theory is an inclusive right (a right not to be excluded). This is, I believe, quite misleading. To see why, it is first necessary to remember that Locke envisages the original state of the world as a state of plenty. The natural bounty of the earth far exceeds the limited self-preserving needs of the first human beings (and their want of money prevents the long-term storing of wealth, so that needs do not expand), so the 'economic problem' is simply a matter of gathering the acorns that have fallen from the oak trees, or gathering apples from the trees in the wood.[196] Since 'in the beginning all the world was *America*', it follows that the principal concern of the first inhabitants was to limit their improving acts (cultivation, enclosure, etc.) to what was needed to 'supply the Conveniences of Life'. Whatever was beyond this was useless, so if cultivation, for example, had extended beyond needs, it would have been wasted effort, and would have been given up by its improvers, and allowed to return 'to the wild Common of Nature'.[197] In such a situation of plenty, with everything lying ready to hand, as it were, how is exclusion from the common possible? The fact is, it is not possible—at least, not without enslaving, imprisoning, or otherwise denying the natural liberty of mankind. Men in natural liberty have no need for a specific right not to be excluded, since exclusion is not possible without violating natural law. All they need is the right to take what is there for the taking. This is what the right of self-preservation entails. And, since what is taken can serve no self-preserving purpose if it is not secure from being taken away by others, the right of preservation, if it is to be efficacious, must also imply a right to exclude others from what is taken. But it is not itself an exclusive right, nor an inclusive. It is simply a right to act in a certain way, a way which neither includes nor excludes others. It can be described as a legitimate power to act in the ways necessary to preserve oneself; a legitimate power because, in exercising it, one does no wrong.

We are now in a position to see Tully's central mistake. He correctly holds that, although the right to self-preservation is not an inclusive right, it is a right to the *means* of preservation, and hence is not a right to particular items of the common: 'it does not refer to any item on the common.' The right to self-preservation thus implies that the original common is common in such a way that,

---

[196] *Two Treatises*, ii. 28.
[197] Ibid. 49, 48.

while it is open to the use of all, it belongs to nobody. But this is just what it is to be negatively common. Tully quite rightly insists that 'the restructuring of common rights so their reference does not conflict is the answer to all the critics of positive community';[198] but if such a restructuring removes all reference to the actual items of the original common, the critics of positive community have been met by asserting negative community. This is Locke's response, and Tully shows it to be so.

Tully's very detailed account of Locke's theory of property deserves a more thorough treatment than it can be accorded here. Having shown the claim that Locke posits an original positive community to be unsustained, we shall have to settle for a rather brief discussion of its companion doctrine—that by 'property' Locke means common property, not private property.[199] Tully's view depends on his account of Locke's reply, in the *First Treatise*, to Filmer's argument that God's grant to Adam of 'Dominion' over every living thing (Genesis 1: 28) made Adam monarch and proprietor of the whole world. Locke's reply is two pronged: that the passage in question concerns property alone; and that the grant given to Adam was not private but in common with all mankind. As he puts it: 'by this Grant God gave him not *Private Dominion* over the Inferior Creatures, but right in common with all Mankind; so neither was he *Monarch*, upon the account of the Property here given him.'[200] Locke's point here is that God's grant to Adam concerns property alone (and not sovereignty), and that the property given to Adam was not private, but a right in common with others. So Locke is here using 'property' in a broad sense to mean both 'Private Dominion' and 'right in common'—i.e. the sense we employ when distinguishing private property from common property. Tully, however, draws the remarkable conclusion that this passage shows that, for Locke, 'property is not private dominion'.[201] The passage means only that the property given to Adam was not private dominion. Tully converts a historical into a conceptual point, and thereby lays the foundation for an ingenious but misleading interpretation.[202]

---

[198] Tully, *A Discourse on Property*, 127.   [199] Ibid. 61.
[200] *Two Treatises*, i. 24.   [201] Tully, *A Discourse on Property*, 60.
[202] At several points Tully's argument here (ibid. 60–1) is rather too quick; e.g. he says that 'Filmer calls private dominion "property" ' whereas Locke calls dominion *in common* 'property'. But this is not true. Locke uses 'property' to include Filmer's 'private dominion', as one passage shows clearly: 'this Grant of God gave *Adam*

This tendency, to read a historical account of the origin and development of property as a conceptual analysis, is possibly the most characteristic failing of interpretations of Locke's theory. Perhaps it is not surprising, since the ideological context of the *Two Treatises of Government* required that the question of the origin of property be discussed in considerable detail. However, the preoccupation with origins should not obscure the fact that Locke, like Grotius and Pufendorf, attempts what I have called a natural history of property—an account of the natural causes that produce it, and of the subsequent developments that are necessitated by the natural duties to preserve and improve the whole created world. An inability to take off 'analytical' spectacles when confronted with natural history has frequently obscured from modern philosophers the fact that when Locke speaks of the origin of property he is not thinking of a first principle from which a priori deductions can be made, but a historical beginning which is rational in the sense that it is a reflection of intelligent divine purposes and tailored to human ends, and which therefore is able to develop naturally (predictably and non-violently) into more extensive and sophisticated systems of property through free and rational deliberation on changes in historical circumstances. To underline the point, this chapter can be concluded with a brief résumé of the natural history of property implicit in the *Second Treatise*.

In the beginnings of human society, God gave the world to mankind in common, for the support and comfort of their being. The earliest human beings, being not very numerous, enjoyed a great natural bounty which enabled them immediately to appropriate whatever they needed. Although such appropriations removed things from the original common, this was no injustice to anyone because things were common only in a 'negative' sense—they belonged to nobody in particular, and so they simply became the property of whoever took them (for use). The bounds of any person's use were the bounds of what that person could legitimately appropriate, and such appropriations were legitimate because they were taken for use. To take from what others had taken for use was thus to do them injury, to endanger their preservation. Such takings

Property, or as our A—— calls it, *Private Dominion* . . .' (*Two Treatises*, i. 23). This passage also shows that Locke does not restrict his use of 'property' to mean only right in common.

were not necessary (because of the natural bounty), and, because injurious, could be punished.

This state continued until men established, by agreement, money in the form of precious metals. This made a profound change. No longer was appropriation limited to immediate use, since the produce of labour could now be changed for metal which did not decay, and hence could be stored indefinitely. This made much larger properties possible, especially large estates which could produce a saleable surplus. By allowing large estates to develop, the use of money thus greatly accelerated the rate at which land was occupied, and thereby also allowed the development of great inequalities of wealth. This was no harm to the poor, however, since by working on the estates of the rich they could be better clothed and fed than was possible in the independent but poorer state in the pre-money society. The improvement in general living standards was due to the great increase in productivity brought about by liberating the immense capacities of human labour from the constraint of satisfying only immediate needs.

The increase in the size of estates, and also of population, made possible by the use of money also made land scarce in various parts of the world. Land therefore became considerably more valuable, leading the different societies to settle on boundaries for their distinct territories, and to establish legislatures in order to regulate the property of their members. So, although in some parts of the world a natural common may still obtain, in other parts of the world property has come to be regulated by laws established by governments.

Locke's account comes to a rather abrupt halt at this point, because he has fulfilled his purpose of sketching in the development of property from original appropriation to modern legal relations. He does not specify what these modern relations must be, since they are determined by the different legislatures. As long as the legislatures themselves are constituted by consent, they can pass laws concerning the nature and extent of property. Of course, no radical undermining of private property could be consented to, since the productivity of the system, and hence the wealth of the whole people, depends on maintaining the security of possessions. Nevertheless it is true that in such stable, developed societies, property becomes whatever the law makes of it. It must, in order to be property, remain exclusive possession, but the precise character and extent of the rights encompassed in property become a matter of (tacit) general agreement, entrenched in legal rules. In such societies property can become a 'bundle' of rights. But Locke's account makes it clear that the original property we have in our persons, and the property established in things for use in the early stages of human history, are no such thing. The establishment of civil government is the decisive move towards modern legal notions of property: 'For in Governments the Laws regulate the right of property, and the possession of land is determined by positive constitutions.'[203] This important passage should not be taken to imply that the establishment of government results in a 'spill'—that property has to be renegotiated. Locke is unlikely to have differed from Grotius's view that 'it is to be supposed that all agreed, that whatever each one had taken possession of should be his property',[204] and this suggestion is supported by Locke's claim that civil governments *settle* property.[205] Property arises naturally through the self-preserving activities of human beings, and the more sophisticated notions of property that develop in civil society are a continuation of this natural process, being adaptations to changed circumstances or refinements introduced for the further improvement of human life.

[203] *Two Treatises*, ii. 50.
[204] *DJBP* II. 2. ii. 5.
[205] See *Two Treatises*, ii. 45: 'Men . . . by *Compact* and Agreement, *settled the Property* which Labour and Industry began.'

4

Francis Hutcheson

1. MORAL SCIENCE AND MORAL SENSE

Locke bequeathed to his successors a complex inheritance. The *Two Treatises* hinged on the inalienability of the property in one's person. Not only did this rule out the more explicit forms of slavery, it also excluded *political* slavery: any political system which placed its citizens under an unregulated, or arbitrary, will. This led Locke to the conclusion that government is a trust instituted by and for the people, and therefore dependent on their (revocable) consent. In addition, the *Two Treatises* had clearly indicated the great importance of labour for the creation of wealth, thereby benefiting even the worst off, and serving to overcome self-enslavement through necessity—perhaps the most lingering cause of slavery. The *Essay concerning Human Understanding* left an equally powerful impression, and not merely in the realm of speculative philosophy. Its concern with both the foundations of knowledge and the efficient causes of human action led to an upsurge of interest in moral epistemology and psychology, and thereby to the first attempts to give a sophisticated account of the natural jurists' commonplace that the natural law has its foundations in human nature. The complex task facing Locke's inheritors was to find a way to unify these different themes from the *Two Treatises* and the *Essay*, and it is in this context that the work of Francis Hutcheson (1694–1746) is such a striking achievement. In this chapter, Hutcheson's synthesis of Lockian and other themes will be outlined, concluding with an analysis of the crucial weakness in his account of justice—a weakness which throws substantial light on Hume's purposes in Book III of the *Treatise*.[1]

[1] Far too long neglected, Hutcheson is now starting to gain some of the attention he deserves. For some recent studies which discuss his work in an appropriate context, see D. F. Norton, *David Hume: Common-Sense Moralist, Sceptical Metaphysician* (Princeton: Princeton University Press, 1982); R. F. Teichgraeber III, *'Free Trade' and Moral Philosophy* (Durham, NC: Duke University Press, 1986); A. MacIntyre, *Whose Justice? Which Rationality?* (London: Duckworth, 1988); and

First of all, however, it will be useful to skirt a common pitfall. The account of Locke's views provided in the previous chapter follows the bulk of recent scholarship in holding that Locke's theological commitments play a crucial role in his overall position. They are not mere window-dressing, and so it cannot be assumed that to remove them is no more than to clear away unhelpful obstructions to the clear presentation of the essentials of his moral and political position. However, neither can it be assumed that the opposite is true—that the theological premisses are so crucial that to tamper with them is to destroy the theory, or that the theory can bear no close relation to any secular political view. The former assumption seems often to lie behind modern attempts to present Locke as the first modern liberal, while the latter attends the more zealous attempts to rebut the former. The former holds Locke up as the fountain-head from which the whole liberal tradition flows, while the latter offers the rather unexpected view that, in sharp contrast to a widespread belief, Locke's influence on the political thought of the eighteenth century was of little significance.[2]

The interpretation of Locke's views provided in the preceding chapter provides a bridge between these extremes. By recognizing that Locke's theological voluntarism essentially includes both formal and material elements, it becomes possible to concentrate attention on the material element, and thereby to produce genuinely secular variants of the original theory. Thus, for example, Locke's doctrine that we are God's property has, for its material component, the doctrine that we are not and cannot be the property of each other. This component can therefore be transformed into a secular doctrine of individual rights—that the natural liberty of human beings is an inalienable right. Interpreted in this way, Locke's theory is indeed a direct ancestor of some influential eighteenth-century doctrines.[3]

V. Hope, *Virtue by Consensus: The Moral Philosophy of Hutcheson, Hume, and Smith* (Oxford: Clarendon Press, 1989).

[2] The account given here of Locke's impact on early 18th-cent. Scotland owes much to J. Moore, 'Locke and the Scottish Jurists', an unpubl. paper delivered to the Conference for the Study of Political Thought (1980). The view that Locke's influence in the 18th cent. was quite limited is espoused in particular by John Dunn. See 'The Politics of Locke in England and America', in J. Yolton (ed.), *John Locke: Problems and Perspectives* (Cambridge: Cambridge University Press, 1969).

[3] Although it should also be noted that the resulting theories—whatever the virtue of their comparative metaphysical parsimony—are not therefore the stronger; e.g. the secular version of the doctrine of negative community—that the unoccupied

Such general questions aside, there is no doubt that Locke's specific influence on the philosophers of the Scottish Enlightenment was extensive and profound. It was also of a particular colour: he was there read and understood as an interpreter and defender of the modern natural law of Grotius and Pufendorf. Thus, as exemplified by Hutcheson, his theory of the origin of property was read as a theory of the manner of occupation of an original negative common.[4] And because read in this way, Locke's distinctive metaphor of appropriation through mixing part of oneself with things was passed over as unimportant, except as evidence of a regrettable confusion about the nature of property.[5] The previous chapter has argued, of course, that this is not merely a possible interpretation of Locke's theory, but the one we should prefer.

This view of Locke, as a contributor to the conception of modern natural law developed by Grotius and Pufendorf, is clearly illustrated in the work of Gershom Carmichael, a significant if little-known figure in the development of the social theory characteristic of the Scottish Enlightenment. His historical significance is summed up in James McCosh's observation that his work is 'the bond which connects the old philosophy with the new in Scotland'.[6] Appointed

world lies simply there for the taking—may seem not merely an improvement, but an obvious truth. However, the secular version lacks both the theological justification *and* the attendant theologically based limits to such taking. It therefore stands in danger of becoming mere dogma, and untethered dogma at that. The absence of foundations could of course be endured, even enjoyed, were it not that the disutilities of the dogma—in the shape of modern environmental degradation—are beginning to press home irresistibly.

[4] Hutcheson incorporates distinctively Lockian features in his account of property, including the pivotal role of labour (rather than consent), and the workmanship model's requirement that appropriation be tied to some form of improvement. This will be spelt out in more detail below, but it is worth noting that in both these respects he (and Locke) stress elements that are present, if rather undeveloped, in Pufendorf's account of the origin of property. Pufendorf holds that occupation requires physical contact—it 'begins with the joining of body to body immediately or through a proper instrument'—and also the intention to improve by productive use—'it is the customary thing, that occupancy of movables be effected by the hands, of land by the feet, *along with the intention of cultivating it*' (*DJNG* iv. 6. 8; emphasis added).

[5] 'The difficulties upon this subject arise from some confused imagination that property is some physical quality or relation produced by some action of men', as Hutcheson puts it in *A System of Moral Philosophy* (1755) i. 318. Cf. also i. 346, and *A Short Introduction to Moral Philosophy* (1747), 152. Both these works are repr. in F. Hutcheson, *Collected Works* (Hildesheim: Olms, 1969).

[6] J. McCosh, *The Scottish Philosophy* (London, 1875), 36; quoted in J. Moore and M. Silverthorne, 'Gershom Carmichael and the Natural Jurisprudence Tradition in

in 1727 as the first Professor of Moral Philosophy in the University of Glasgow (having been a Regent there since 1694),[7] and thus Hutcheson's immediate predecessor, Carmichael introduced Pufendorf's *De Officio Hominis et Civis* 'into the centre of Scottish moral philosophy'.[8] Given the profound influence that Pufendorf's work was to enjoy in eighteenth-century Scotland, this was itself of considerable account. However, Carmichael's principal contribution to Scottish intellectual life was as a commentator on Pufendorf's textbook. His lectures on *De Officio* included significant amendments to Pufendorf's views, and he included these as editorial commentary in his own editions of the work (the first was published in Glasgow in 1718, the second in Edinburgh in 1724). The commentary achieved independent fame, as Hutcheson eloquently testifies: 'that worthy and ingenious man the late Professor Gershom Carmichael of Glasgow, by far the best commentator on that book, has so supplied and corrected [*De Officio*] that the notes are of much more value than the text.'[9]

The notes thus praised have a powerful Lockian component. As Moore puts it, 'Carmichael referred his readers repeatedly to improvements made by Locke on themes addressed by Pufendorf', improvements which consistently defended the individual against the power of the magistrate:

In his discussions of the state of nature, of the family, of master and servant relations, of the causes of civil society, of the duties of magistrates and the rights of subjects Carmichael amended Pufendorf's texts by notes, supplements and appendices which provided the reader with an understanding of the duties of man and the citizen which was much more insistent on the rights of individuals and less indulgent towards the power of magistrates than the text of Pufendorf; the authority most frequently invoked for these amendments was Locke's *Second Treatise*.[10]

Eighteenth-Century Scotland', in I. Hont and M. Ignatieff (eds.), *Wealth and Virtue: The Shaping of Political Economy in the Scottish Enlightenment* (Cambridge: Cambridge University Press, 1983), 73.

[7] Ibid. 75. For an account of the Regent system, and an attempt to explain some of the reasons for, and broader implications of, its abandonment in early 18th-cent. Scotland, see MacIntyre, *Whose Justice? Which Rationality?*, 237–59.

[8] T. A. Horne, 'Moral and Economic Improvement: Francis Hutcheson on Property', *History of Political Thought*, 7 (1986), 115.

[9] Hutcheson, *Short Introduction*, p. i.

[10] Moore, 'Locke and the Scottish Jurists', 4. (For the same reason he showed no affection for Jacobitism, describing it as 'the perverse and malignant spirit which inspires evil citizens among us to unsettle the public happiness'. Its popularity, he went on, 'has

So Carmichael's improvements on Pufendorf are, to a significant degree, explicitly Lockian, and it is reasonable to suppose that such Lockian elements play a conspicuous part in Hutcheson's estimation of the value of Carmichael's notes. Certainly, for his part, Hutcheson makes liberal use of a number of Lockian concepts and distinctions, even though his own political theory, especially in its later manifestations, moves a long way from Locke's conclusions.

Explaining this tension in Hutcheson's work—his employment of Lockian concepts to serve quite un-Lockian ends—is a central concern of this chapter. Although, as mentioned, his differences from Locke are most clear-cut in the later works, they are present even in the earliest, because they arise in the process of elaborating his distinctive doctrines in moral psychology and moral epistemology, doctrines which were—at least in part—designed to *rebut* Lockian theses. They are, however, also shaped by Lockian doctrines, in that Hutcheson's concern with moral psychology and epistemology is a direct (and complex) response to Locke's investigations in the *Essay*. The moral sense theory, as developed by Hutcheson and his contemporaries, is inconceivable without Locke's attention to the nature of moral goodness and the springs of moral action in the *Essay*.

It is important that this be recognized. The reason is not simply that by so doing we identify the intellectual origins of the theories of moral sense or moral sentiment which dominate moral philosophy in eighteenth-century Scotland, but also that we thereby become better able to understand their point—to provide a genuine science of morals. As such, they are the inheritors of a concern characteristic of seventeenth-century natural law theories. A brief sketch will show how this is so. It was shown in Chapter 2 that one of Pufendorf's aims was to establish a science of morals in the sense of a demonstrative system of morals. He thought this a genuine possibility in part because moral notions, and moral institutions, are produced by human activity. Locke's account of moral ideas as archetype ideas has affinities with Pufendorf's account of moral entities, and similarly allows the conclusion that a demonstrative

no other source . . . than ignorance of the true principles of natural law'. Quoted by Horne, 'Moral and Economic Improvement', 116, from J. Moore and M. Silverthorne's unpub. *The Political Writings of Gershom Carmichael*.)

system of morals is possible.[11] He offers a famous example (quoted in part above) in support of this doctrine: *'Where there is no Property, there is no Injustice*, is a Proposition as certain as any Demonstration in *Euclid.*'[12] He also recognizes, however, that a system of demonstratively true propositions is not a moral science in any useful sense, because in such a scheme 'the force of morality is lost and evaporates only into words disputes & niceties'.[13] Rather, a science of morality worthy of the name should include an account of the efficient causes of morals. It should provide an account of the psychology of moral action, and thereby provide an answer to the question: What is it that drives us to moral action?

Locke's concern with this question, and, more generally, with the science of moral action, can be attributed to the influence of natural law theorizing. This can be shown in the following way. The modern natural law theories show an awareness of historical development, even if only a rudimentary one which divides human history, and therefore human societies, into simple and sophisticated stages. This in turn implies the possibility of a kind of natural history of moral conceptions and social institutions. In this history, the knowledge of the requirements of natural law arises over time through rational reflection on sense-experience. However, the natural history of morals is not merely a history of moral knowledge, but of moral *practice*. The fact of moral practice shows that there must be natural processes in us which move us to moral actions (even if, as the history of *immorality* shows, they do not infallibly move us). The seventeenth century's new natural philosophy, with its characteristically dualistic metaphysics, denied that the motive force of moral actions could be performed by reason alone (even though reason plays a vital role in discriminating between possible courses of action). Rather, because action is bodily action, it requires both reason and bodily forces or processes. So the rise of the new natural philosophy, together with the

[11] The affinities with *The New Science* of Giambattista Vico (1668–1744) are also striking, as is noted by J. Tully, *A Discourse on Property: John Locke and his Adversaries* (Cambridge: Cambridge University Press, 1980), 24.

[12] *Essay*, IV. 3. 18.

[13] 'Of Ethick in General', quoted in J. Colman, *John Locke's Moral Philosophy* (Edinburgh: Edinburgh University Press, 1983), 167. As Colman also notes, this shows that Locke concurs with Berkeley's critical assessment of the demonstrative system: 'To demonstrate Morality it seems one need only make a Dictionary of Words & see which includes which at least. This is the greatest part & bulk of the Work.'

established concerns and explanations of natural law theory, produced the need for an account of the forces that move us to action, and to moral action in particular. This conjunction produced, in other words, the distinctively eighteenth-century quest for the 'springs' of action. This quest is nothing other than the attempt to work out in detail, with the aid of the new natural philosophy, the precise meaning of the natural lawyers' commonplace that the law of nature is founded in human nature.

The theory of the moral sense is one such attempt to provide an account of the springs of action in human nature. It is best understood if seen against the background of Locke's account in the *Essay*, since it is a reaction to the perceived inadequacies of the Lockian theory. Since it would detract too much from the main thread of this chapter to include more than a skeletal account of the responses to Locke's theory, a more extended version has been provided in the Appendix.[14] So here it is sufficient to begin with the fact that the theory of the moral sense has its origins in the writings of Locke's own pupil, the third Earl of Shaftesbury. In Shaftesbury's view, Locke's attempt to derive all human action from self-love, at the same time dispensing with innate ideas, amounts to a complete denial of moral virtue. His ire is particularly directed at the latter: because, for Locke, virtue and vice are not 'naturally imprinted on human minds', says Shaftesbury, they therefore cannot be 'anything in themselves'.[15] But virtue *is* something, is innate in our minds, and is perceived by a special sense—the moral sense.

Hutcheson's sympathies are with Shaftesbury's positive doctrine, rather than his reasons. He presents himself as a defender of Shaftesbury, and similarly attacks the self-love theory of morals—represented by both Hobbes,[16] and 'the Author of the Fable of the

---

[14] Although more extensive, the account there is still limited by the concerns of this ch.—it is not an account of the general reception of Locke's concerns with the springs of action.

[15] *Letters of the Earl of Shaftesbury to a Student at the University* (1716); quoted in J. Aronson, 'Shaftesbury on Locke', *American Political Science Review*, 53 (1959), 1103. Cf. also Norton, *David Hume*, 35.

[16] The doctrine that 'all the desires of the *human Mind*, nay of all *thinking Natures*, are reducible to *Self-Love*, or *Desire of private Happiness*' is the doctrine of 'the old *Epicureans*', now revived by Mr. *Hobbes*, and followed by many better Writers' (*An Essay on the Nature and Conduct of the Passions and Affections, with Illustrations on the Moral Sense* (1728), in *Collected Works*, ii. 207–8).

Bees'[17]—but he detaches the doctrine of the moral sense from the defence of innate ideas. In fact, he explicitly denies that innate ideas play a role in his account of the moral sense: 'We are not to imagine that this *moral Sense*, more than the other Senses, supposes any *innate ideas, Knowledge, or practical Proposition.*'[18] Partly for this reason, Hutcheson does not share Shaftesbury's hostility to Locke. In fact, he appears to owe a substantial Lockian debt. Thus, not only does he detach the doctrine of moral sense from any appeal to innate ideas, his account of moral perception has many Lockian echoes. As will be shown more fully below, he explains the perception of moral qualities in terms strongly reminiscent of Locke's account of the perception of secondary qualities. This has prompted Tom Campbell to the view that he 'deploys a Lockian epistemology' to counter the self-love account of morality.[19] If this position can be maintained, it would be a little ironic, since Locke's own theory is itself one such account. The claim has not gone unchallenged.[20] But it is certainly true that there are Lockian elements in Hutcheson's theory; and, if we employ Locke's account of the perception of secondary qualities as a guide to Hutcheson's

[17] *An Inquiry concerning Beauty and Virtue* (1st edn., 1725), subtitle; in *Collected Works*, i.
[18] *An Inquiry concerning Beauty and Virtue* (2nd edn., 1726; repub. New York: Garland Publishing, 1971), 135. Unless noted otherwise, all subsequent references to the *Inquiry* are to this edn. See also, esp. for the rev. and expanded discussion of the nature of moral perception, the 4th edn., 1738 (Farnborough: Gregg International, 1969), 129–31.
[19] T. D. Campbell, 'Francis Hutcheson: "Father" of the Scottish Enlightenment', in R. H. Campbell and A. S. Skinner (eds.), *The Origins and Nature of the Scottish Enlightenment* (Edinburgh: John Donald, 1982), 168.
[20] See, in particular, E. Michael, 'Francis Hutcheson on Aesthetic Perception and Aesthetic Pleasure', *British Journal of Aesthetics*, 24 (1984), 241–53, and a number of works by D. F. Norton: 'Hutcheson on Perception and Moral Perception', *Archiv für Geschichte der Philosophie*, 59 (1977), 181–97; *David Hume*, 55–93; and 'Hutcheson's Moral Realism', *Journal of the History of Philosophy*, 23 (1985), 397–418. In this context, Hutcheson's rejection of innate ideas needs to be stressed. This is not because it shows him to be a Lockian—since Pufendorf also denies that moral knowledge arises from innate ideas (e.g. *De Officio*, I. 3. 12)—but because it shows how *not* to interpret his account of moral ideas as 'concomitant ideas'. On this question see, in particular, 'Hutcheson's Moral Realism', although Norton's case for interpreting Hutcheson to be anti-Lockian is, I think, rather overdrawn. The dissatisfactions Hutcheson registers concerning 'those, who after Mr. LOCKE have rejected *innate Ideas*' (*Inquiry*, 81; 4th edn., 78–9) are of 2 kinds: he objects to the careless conclusions drawn from this doctrine (*Inquiry*, 81), and he exhibits the frustrations of the moralist at the intricate but, practically speaking, useless theorizings of the epistemologist (Hutcheson, *Passions and Affections*, 198). He does not show any affection for innatist doctrines.

account of moral perception, we can approach an understanding of Hutcheson's position, and see also that the doctrine of moral sense is strengthened by being detached from innatist doctrines. This will be shown in the next section.

An equally important reason for Hutcheson's more accommodating attitude to Locke's views is that, unlike Shaftesbury, he does not interpret the attempt to found morality in self-love as an attack on morals itself. The self-love theory fails not because it undermines morality but because it does not measure up to the facts. It is forced to provide tortuous stories for the most simple and familiar of unselfish acts. In treating of 'our Desires or Affections', the self-love theorists have been forced to make 'the most generous, kind, and disinterested of them, to proceed from Self-Love, by some subtle Trains of Reasoning, to which honest Hearts are often wholly Strangers'.[21]

However, his denial that morality is founded in self-love does not lead Hutcheson to hold that acting morally is contrary to our self-interest. He notes that many self-love theorists, in their efforts to support their hypothesis, point out the various ways in which moral actions can be seen to serve our interests. He then correctly observes that this appearance, even if veridical, in no way shows that such actions are founded in, or motivated by, considerations of self-interest. Concerning the efforts of those 'ingenious speculative Men, in their straining to support an Hypothesis',[22] he says: 'Allow their Reasonings to be perfectly good, they only prove, that after long Reflections, and Reasoning, we may find out some ground, even from Views of Interest, to approve the same Actions which every Man admires as soon as he hears of them.'[23] Here we see a familiar natural law theme, only in a different dress. Principles of morals are not founded in private interest, but they are nevertheless not contrary to private interest, because founded in human nature. The new twist, however, is that the sociable principles of morality are founded not in the instinct of self-preservation, not in self-love, but in a fundamental sociable principle of human nature—the benevolent affections of the moral sense.

To suppose a fundamental principle of benevolence in human nature cannot help but have profound consequences for the theory

[21] Preface to Hutcheson, *Passions and Affections*, p. vi. See also the introd. to *Illustrations*, 209.
[22] Introd. to *Illustrations*, 209.
[23] *Inquiry*, 125.

of natural law, especially concerning the nature of our obligation to obey it. For, if we naturally approve of, and are motivated to pursue benevolent courses of action in ourselves, and to reward them in others, there appears to be less need to call on the divine power to enforce moral behaviour. It seems that the true ground of morality is not 'the Will and Law of a God who sees men in the dark, has in his Hand Rewards and Punishments, and Power enough to call to account the Proudest Offender'.[24] Rather, human nature itself, even if not ineluctably moral, is at least enlivened by a fundamental moral principle. It is therefore possible to explain human moral practice without referring to the laws of a superior (whether human or divine). The upshot of the attempt to identify a set of distinctively moral psychological processes within the human frame is thus a social theory which, whatever its metaphysical orientation, effectively fulfils the ambitions of Grotian rationalism. The theory of the moral sense promises the vindication of the *etiamsi daremus* passage.

Hutcheson is well aware of this. He deliberately sets out to explain 'how we acquire more particular Ideas of *Virtue* and *Vice*, abstracting from any *Law*, *Human*, or *Divine*'.[25] It is the moral sense which makes this possible, because it provides a foundation for natural law which obviates the need to incorporate a formal element in the obligation to follow the requirements of natural law. At least in the ideal case,[26] natural law is efficacious without the need for divine rewards or punishments, because the benevolent affections of the moral sense allow us to recognize and act on the law's dictates. So the obligation to observe the natural law can be grounded directly on the material element, on human nature itself, in the form of the benevolent affections of the moral sense. If the formal element of obligation can be thus set aside, however, then it is indeed true to say that the dictates of the natural law have 'a degree of validity', even were it to be allowed that 'there is no God, or that the affairs of men are of no concern to Him'. So, in this way, the development of the doctrine of the moral sense rehabilitates the Grotian conception of an obligation to obey the dictates of natural law that is independent of belief in God. Hutcheson draws back from holding that this (material) obligation is sufficient to ensure

---

[24] *Essay*, I. 3. 6. [25] *Inquiry*, 266.

[26] The formal element is required in Hutcheson's full account because in real cases it is true that our moral sense can be weak, our selfishness 'grown strong', and our understanding weak (see *Inquiry*, 268).

obedience, given the weaknesses of our nature and the limits to our understanding, so the laws of a supreme being are still necessary in the end. However, the divine role has thus been substantially curtailed. Instead of guaranteeing the very possibility of the moral law, by providing the coercive power necessary to make the perception of obligation efficacious, God's *explicit* role is reduced to reinforcement, and thus to holding the system together at its weak points.[27] In the common course of social life, the benevolent operations of the moral sense will suffice to remind human beings of their duties, and, where special circumstances do not interfere, to lead them to act accordingly.

If it should then be further argued that, although the complete efficacy of natural law requires a coercive power to accommodate those cases where natural motivation fails, this coercive power can be achieved by instituting, entirely through human action, a civil power, then the way is open for an account of the reinforcement of natural law in which God's power is no longer necessary. Thus Hume's theory can be seen to be a development of Hutcheson's, in which moral obligations have their origins in the moral sense, but are guaranteed by the strictly enforced rules of the civil power. In addition, one respect in which that theory can be seen to be a return to a Grotian theory is also evident. But this is merely to provide a tantalizing sketch. To comprehend fully the impact of the theory of moral sense, it is necessary to spell out just what this sense is, what it recommends, and the consequences it has for the account of natural law and the obligation to obey it. This is the task of the next section. It will then be possible to set out the main elements of the political edifice—the theory of rights and property—Hutcheson stands on that foundation. This in turn will help to identify the principal weakness of the moral sense as a foundation for social order: its inability to guarantee a secure system of justice.

2. MORAL SENSE AND MORAL SENSIBILIA

Hutcheson's argument for the moral sense is part of a larger argument about our perceptual capacities. He first argues for the

---

[27] Hume's objection to Hutcheson's teleology may perhaps be read as the charge that God plays an important *implicit* role in the structure of Hutcheson's moral theory. But it should not be too quickly assumed that teleological theories are metaphysics in disguise.

existence of a sense of beauty, holding that our aesthetic responses
to objects depends on a form of distinctively aesthetic perception,
and that this form of perception can be described as a sense of
beauty. 'Were there no Mind with a *Sense* of Beauty to contemplate
Objects,' he says, 'I see not how they could be call'd *beautiful*.'[28]
After developing this thesis, he then offers a parallel account of the
moral sense. His method is not mere idiosyncrasy, nor an attempt to
buy acceptance of a less plausible thesis by tying it to one more
plausible. Rather, the parallelism of the two arguments is meant to
reveal features of our perceptual capacities that more parsimonious
accounts of these capacities overlook. It thereby provides solid
supporting evidence for his more general 'sentimentalist' (or anti-
rationalist)[29] position. In a nutshell, his position is that not only do
we perceive directly the beauty of objects, we also perceive the
beauty of actions, which latter beauty we denote as moral virtue.
Judgements of moral goodness have their foundation in the
perception of a peculiar kind of beauty, which we call moral beauty.
It is appropriate, then, that we follow Hutcheson's order of
exposition, and consider the foundations of aesthetic judgements
before turning to consider the foundation of moral virtue in the
moral sense.[30]

---

[28] *Inquiry*, 15.

[29] These terms are meant to be taken broadly. Amongst the sentimentalists or
anti-rationalists I mean to include the moral sense philosophers and their
sentimentalist successors: that is, all those moral philosophers who denied that
reason can alone provide a *sufficient* explanation for the phenomena of morals.
Against the rationalists (principally Cudworth, Clarke, and Wollaston), they argued
that, although reason could perhaps discern the nature of the good, it could not
explain why we approve of it, or more generally, why morals is a practical matter.
This issue, including the pivotal role of the notion of obligation, will be considered
more fully below.

[30] Hutcheson's position is thus distinct from the more familiar contemporary
defences of moral knowledge which exploit the analogy with non-primary perceptual
qualities (represented, most notably, by John McDowell) in several ways. Unlike
McDowell, Hutcheson rejects the view that reason is intrinsically motivating, and his
perceptual argument is not so closely tied to parallels with the experience of
secondary qualities such as colour. Rather, Hutcheson's exposition, although
developed against the background of Locke's account of secondary qualities, is
nevertheless an *extension* (not merely an application) of Locke's argument. It can be
described as an attempt to establish the existence of a further distinctive set of
perceived qualities (*tertiary* qualities): beauty and moral beauty (virtue). The
distinguishing feature of these qualities is that they are *pleasing* sensations, so there
are definite limits on the extent to which they can be illuminated by analogies with
qualities like colour, the perception of which are not essentially pleasing. For
McDowell's view, see e.g. his 'Values and Secondary Qualities', in T. Honderich

Beauty, says Hutcheson, is one idea amongst a number commonly neglected by philosophers: 'The only Pleasure of Sense, which our Philosophers seem to consider, is that which accompanys the simple Ideas of Sensation: But there are vastly greater Pleasures in those complex Ideas of Objects, which obtain the Names of *Beautiful, Regular, Harmonious.*'[31] Since the pleasures of sense play a vital part in shaping the courses of action we naturally pursue, the neglect is rather surprising. So Hutcheson sets himself to remedy the fact. Although, as noted above, the Lockian connection can be overplayed, Hutcheson's exposition frequently relies on characteristically Lockian concepts. Thus, as in the quoted passage, he contrasts simple with complex ideas, and employs a broad notion of pleasure to bring out the attractive (or distasteful) features of a very wide range of our sensory experiences. This extends to the treatment of the sense of beauty and the moral sense, where his choice of language shows close affinities with Locke's account of the primary and secondary qualities. Whether these affinities run deep is not easily resolved. Norton has argued that Hutcheson's epistemology, when carefully examined, shows him to have adhered to a distinctive Scottish epistemology for which a theory of concomitant ideas functioned as an alternative to Locke's corpuscularian-spirited distinction between primary and secondary qualities.[32] The issue is a difficult one, but can perhaps be avoided, since, although Hutcheson may have held to an epistemology of much less Lockian colour than often supposed, there is ample textual evidence to support a compatibility thesis. He does not appear to regard his account of the senses to be in competition with Locke's views. Instead, he is willing to employ important elements of Locke's account of primary and secondary qualities in presenting his own views, a fact which supports a compatibilist reading of the issue. The following discussion will show the background presence of Lockian features.

Our recognition of the beauty of objects shows that 'there is some

(ed.), *Morality and Objectivity* (London: Routledge & Kegan Paul, 1985). This difference is all the more striking because McDowell also argues for a realist view of aesthetic qualities, in 'Aesthetic Value, Objectivity and the Fabric of the World', in E. Schaper (ed.), *Pleasure, Preference and Value* (Cambridge: Cambridge University Press, 1983).

[31] *Inquiry*, 7.
[32] See the works referred to in n. 20 above.

sense of *Beauty natural* to Men'.[33] Beauty itself is an *'Idea rais'd in us'*, and the sense of beauty is *'our Power of receiving this Idea'*.[34] However, although our idea of beauty is always the idea of the beauty of an object, it is wrong to suppose that our idea arises because of something in the object which is itself beautiful. Rather, beauty

is not understood to be any Quality suppos'd to be in the Object, which should of itself be beautiful, without relation to any Mind which perceives it: For Beauty, like other Names of sensible Ideas, properly denotes the *Perception* of some Mind; so *Cold*, *Hot*, *Sweet*, *Bitter*, denote the Sensations in our Minds, to which perhaps there is no resemblance in the Objects, which excite these Ideas in us, however we generally imagine that there is something in the Object just like our Perception.[35]

This is precisely the manner in which Locke distinguishes our ideas of secondary qualities from those of primary qualities. The former, unlike the latter, do not resemble the 'Patterns [which] do really exist in the Bodies themselves'.[36] The secondary qualities are always connected to 'the Perception of some Mind' because they are powers in (or of) objects: 'Powers to produce various Sensations in us by their primary Qualities, *i.e.* by the Bulk, Figure, Texture, and Motion of their insensible parts, as Colours, Sounds, Tasts, *etc.*'[37]

For Hutcheson, beauty can be understood in similar terms. In the first place, like all such qualities, it must be perceived, or sensed. In fact, his decision to speak of a sense of beauty, rather than making the simpler claim that beauty is sensed, is, he says, for reasons of convenience:

---

[33] *Inquiry*, p. xvii. Stated thus, his view is of course inadequate. That we perceive some things to be beautiful no more establishes a distinct sense of beauty than perceiving some things to be green establishes a distinct sense of (or for) greenness. However, Hutcheson need not be disturbed by this objection. What matters for him is not so much the constitution of our sense-organs (he does not suppose that the sense of beauty or the moral sense are discrete sensory apparatuses like our *external* sense-organs), but that beauty and moral virtue are, like colours or sounds or tastes, *perceived*, and are therefore ideas which correspond to specific qualities in (or *of*) objects or actions.

[34] *Inquiry*, 7.

[35] Ibid. 14.

[36] *Essay*, II. 8. 15.

[37] Ibid. 10. In this passage Locke adds that the secondary qualities 'in truth are nothing in the Objects themselves', but this is best treated as a piece of carelessness. His standard position is that the secondary qualities are powers of objects, reducible to specific configurations of the primary qualities, which thereby cause in us the ideas they do.

It is of no consequence whether we call these Ideas of *Beauty* and *Harmony*, Perceptions of the *External Senses* of Seeing and Hearing, or not. I should rather chuse to call our Power of perceiving these Ideas, an INTERNAL SENSE, were it only for the Convenience of distinguishing them from other Sensations of Seeing and Hearing, which men may have without Perception of *Beauty* and *Harmony*.[38]

The sense of beauty can properly be called a sense because, like all senses, it is independent of the will: in sensing 'the Mind . . . is passive'. That is, it 'has not Power directly to present the Perception or Idea, or to vary it at its Reception, as long as we continue our Bodys in a state fit to be acted upon by the external Object'.[39] Thus a sense is nothing more than a 'Determination of the Mind' to receive impressions of a specific sort. The sense of beauty is our (passive) ability, the 'determination', or constitution, of our mind to perceive beauty in the objects of our experience. Hutcheson goes on to add that beauty is essentially a matter of '*Uniformity amidst variety*'.[40] The experience of beauty is the particular pleasure we derive from the recognition of uniformity amidst variety, and it is generally excited by '*Forms, Proportions, Resemblances, Theorems*'.[41]

Once the existence of the sense of beauty has been recognized, it is readily discernible that it is not the only 'internal sense': 'If the Reader be convinc'd of such *Determinations* of the Mind to be pleas'd with *Forms, Proportions, Resemblances, Theorems*, it will be no difficult matter to apprehend another *superior Sense, natural* also to Men, determining them to be pleas'd with *Action, Characters, Affections*. This is the *moral Sense*.'[42] Thus we arrive at the moral sense. It is that passive ability of the mind to perceive the moral goodness of actions, characters, and affections. Moral goodness can be understood as those qualities of actions, characters, and affections which cause an observer to approve of them by 'pleasing a *moral Sense*'. The notion of pleasing the moral sense is the notion that 'certain *Affections* or *Actions* of an Agent, standing in a *certain Relation* to other Agents, is approved by every *Observer*, or raises in him a *grateful Perception*, or moves the Observer to *love* the Agent'.[43] This means that there can be no explication of moral judgement which excludes reference to an observer. So in this way as well Hutcheson's account of virtue is comparable to the Lockian account of the secondary qualities, since

---

[38] *Inquiry*, 8.   [39] Ibid. 2.   [40] Ibid. 17 and *passim*.
[41] Ibid., p. xvii.   [42] Ibid.   [43] *Illustrations*, 252.

the latter are powers in objects to produce the relevant 'Idea' in an appropriately placed observer.[44]

Does this mean that moral virtue is simply in the (moral) eye of the beholder? Hutcheson has been taken to mean so, but there is good reason for thinking this interpretation stems from a too-hasty judgement about the implications of the secondary qualities model. His position can be best understood by contrasting it with a remark of Hume's, in which this common interpretation of secondary qualities is evident. The remark occurs in a frequently quoted letter to Hutcheson in 1740 (part of a passage apparently extracted from the then forthcoming third book of the *Treatise*), in which Hume compares 'vice and virtue' to 'sounds, colours, heat and cold, which according to modern philosophy, are not qualities in objects but perceptions in the mind'.[45] This is not Hutcheson's position, nor is it Locke's.[46] The secondary qualities are not perceptions in minds rather than qualities of objects. It is the *ideas* of secondary qualities that are perceptions in minds, but then so are the ideas of *primary* qualities. The secondary qualities are qualities of objects, but qualities which, unlike the primary qualities, do not 'resemble' the ideas they generate in the perceiving mind. So, for *this* reason, accounts of secondary qualities must take account of the perceptions of a mind in order to show what the idea of a secondary quality is like. Because the ideas of primary qualities resemble the qualities themselves, the account of primary qualities has no need to refer to the observer. None of this implies that secondary qualities are merely in the mind. Since they are specific configurations of the primary qualities, qualities which are uncontentiously in the object, then so must they be also. And, in this spirit, Hutcheson speaks of beauty and harmony as 'being excited upon our *Perception* of some *primary Quality*'.[47]

[44] *Essay*, ii. 8. 10.

[45] David Hume to Francis Hutcheson, 16 Mar. 1740; letter no. 16 in *The Letters of David Hume*, ed. J. Y. T. Greig (Oxford: Clarendon Press, 1932). Repr. in D. D. Raphael (ed.), *British Moralists 1650–1800* (Oxford: Clarendon Press, 1969), ii. 110. (Cf. *Treatise*, 469.)

[46] There is also room for doubting that it was *Hume's*. In *David Hume: Common-Sense Moralist, Sceptical Metaphysician*, D. F. Norton argues for a weakly realist interpretation of Hume not too dissimilar from the interpretation of Hutcheson's position offered here. Although not committed to it, the account given of Hume in the next ch. is broadly compatible with Norton's interpretation.

[47] *Inquiry*, 14–15.

So the proper account of beauty and, indeed, other forms of internal sensing, requires a part to be played by both object and perceiving mind. Undoubtedly, some of the confusions that have arisen concerning the proper understanding of secondary qualities, and our ideas of them, can be traced to uncertainties in Locke's exposition. Nevertheless, Hutcheson clearly wants to avoid a purely subjectivist account of beauty and virtue. He stresses this in later formulations of the theory. In the 1738 edition of the *Inquiry* he says

The Quality approved by our moral Sense is conceived to reside in the Person approved, and to be a Perfection and Dignity in him . . . The Perception of the Approver, tho' attended with Pleasure, plainly represents something quite distinct from this Pleasure; even as the Perception of *external Forms* is attended with Pleasure, and yet represents something distinct from this pleasure. This may prevent many Cavils upon this Subject.[48]

And in *A System of Moral Philosophy* he points out that

Tho' the approbation of moral excellence is a grateful action or sensation of the mind, 'tis plain the good approved is not this tendency to give us a grateful sensation. As, in approving a beautiful form, we refer the beauty to the object; we do not say that it is beautiful because we reap some little pleasure in viewing it, but we are pleased in viewing it because it is antecedently beautiful. Thus, when we admire the virtue of another, the whole excellence, or that quality which by nature we are determined to approve, is conceived to be in that other; we are pleased in the contemplation because the object is excellent and the object is not judged to be therefore excellent because it gives us pleasure.[49]

Despite this insistence on the reality of beauty and virtue, one particular feature of an account of moral virtue couched in terms dependent on an account of secondary qualities appears to vitiate the claim. The problem is this: although secondary qualities are not mere perceptions, but powers possessed by objects, these powers are the effect of primary qualities, and, most importantly, produce ideas in us which do not resemble those (patterns of) primary qualities. Rather, the ideas of secondary qualities seem to be the product of a thoroughly contingent relation between the primary qualities of objects and our perceptual capacities, a relation which naturally leads us to believe that objects are coloured, etc., in just the way they are extended or solid. So it seems necessary to

[48] *Inquiry* (4th edn., 1738), 130–1.   [49] *System*, i. 53–4.

conclude that a moral theory dependent on parallels with secondary qualities will in fact support some form of scepticism about moral judgements because, like the secondary qualities, they inevitably involve us in a form of error. Secondary qualities, it could be said, are 'deceitful', because they systematically mislead us about their nature; and the same judgement could likewise be applied to judgements of moral virtue. But if moral virtue is deceitful, is not this to undermine morality after all? So, on such an account, what can remain of natural law?

Henry Home, Lord Kames, an older relative of Hume, addresses this question, at least in so far as it concerns the recognized secondary qualities. In his *Essays on the Principles of Morality and Natural Religion* (1751), a set of essays mainly directed to responding to Hume's *Treatise*, he does refer to secondary qualities of objects as deceitful, but attempts to defuse the issue. His solution is to appeal to the providential teleology of the workmanship model. We are, he says, made for a certain providential purpose, and as long as this purpose is not violated, the precise relation, or resemblance, between our ideas of objects and the qualities of the objects themselves is a matter on which no sceptical argument can gain a foothold. Given the similarity of doctrine and purpose of his and Hutcheson's moral theories, it is reasonable to employ Kames's argument as a possible elaboration of Hutcheson's position.

Kames grounds his argument on a Lockian view of the purposes of human life, and thereby of the bounds of knowledge:

It was not intended that man should make profound discoveries. He is framed to be more an active than a contemplative being; and his views both of the natural and moral world are so adjusted, as to be made subservient to correctness of action rather than of belief.[50]

From this point of view, secondary qualities are not deceitful because they do not cause us to act wrongly, even though we may be quite mistaken about the nature of, for example, coloured surfaces. So, despite widespread false beliefs about the precise nature of secondary qualities, human beings are not in the least misled about those things that are their proper concern. On the contrary, the ends of life and action are better provided for by such artifice, than if these perceptions were more exact copies of their objects.[51] This is

[50] Lord Kames, *Essays on the Principles of Morality and Natural Religion* (1751) (New York: Garland Publishing, 1976), 152.   [51] Ibid. 152–3.

because, for example, colours enable us to distinguish more easily between objects, thus facilitating the execution of particular courses of action. But the hand of Providence is displayed most clearly in the fact that the secondary qualities do more than facilitate our practical purposes: they enrich all aspects of our experience. Kames stresses the difference that colours make to our world:

Colour in particular is a sort of visionary beauty, which nature has spread over all her works. It is a wonderful artifice, to present objects to us thus differently distinguished: to mark them out to the eye in various attires, so as to be best known and remembered: and to paint on the fancy, gay and lively, grand and striking, or sober and melancholy scenes: whence many of our most pleasurable and most affecting sensations arise.[52]

In Hutcheson's view also, moral experience satisfies both of these features. Not only does it, in the strongest way possible, facilitate our practical purposes—since, by being necessary for social life, it is also necessary for self-preservation—it is also at bottom a sort of beauty, since moral perception is the perception of the beauty of action.

The providential supposition that human beings are intended to be active rather than contemplative beings can thus serve as a bulwark against the potentially damaging implications of an account of moral virtues and vices that draws substantially on terms and distinctions borrowed from the Lockian account of secondary qualities. Although our ideas of secondary qualities, because they do not resemble the configurations of primary qualities that cause them, may in one sense be described as deceitful, our patterns of acting in the world are not undermined. For this reason the perception of moral virtue is not deceitful in any relevant respect, because morals is not so much a matter of correct beliefs about the nature of the world as of appropriate action within it. (If the providential teleology is removed, the situation is not so felicitous. We are then faced with the bare fact of inconsistencies between the beliefs we naturally depend on for acting within the world, and the beliefs we arrive at through study and reflection: a conflict, that is, between natural beliefs and philosophy. This is Hume's situation. His solution, to ease the tensions through a practical philosophy of human nature in which 'moderation' and

[52] Ibid. 154.

'mitigated scepticism' play central roles, will be considered more fully in the next chapter.)

To this point, we have been concerned in this section to show what Hutcheson understands the moral sense to be. It is now appropriate to make some brief remarks on what it is that pleases the moral sense, in order to show the impact of the doctrine of the moral sense on Hutcheson's theory of property, and of politics in general—a theory which, as noted above, has initially a markedly Lockian spirit.

What does our moral sense lead us to approve? Hutcheson's answer is very simple:

'tis plain that the primary objects of this faculty are the affections of the will, and that the several affections which are approved, tho' in very different degrees, yet all agree in one general character, of tendency to the happiness of others, and to the moral perfection of the mind possessing them.[53]

Benevolence is the affection of the will which desires the happiness of others, so benevolence lies at the heart of all moral action: 'some sort of benevolent affections, or some dispositions imagined to be connected with them, are the natural objects of approbation.'[54] This means, significantly, that we have a natural tendency to approve, and therefore also reward (in others) and perform (ourselves) benevolent actions. For this reason Hutcheson is led to endorse important elements of a politics of virtue, rather than of strict adherence to rules. This is implicit in his early works, but is quite explicit in the later *System*. For example, he accepts there that the duties of the citizens cannot be spelt out in detail, but can—in fact, *must*—be determined by the virtuous (benevolent) citizenry themselves:

It is superfluous to heap up common-place maxims, well known, but of difficult application to particular cases; a good man's heart will always be zealous for the interest of any innocent association for a publick interest, in which, by the Divine Providence, he is engaged; and will look upon this situation of his fortunes as the voice of God directing him to that part of his fellows who should be more peculiarly the objects of his affectionate concern.[55]

This marked shift away from a rule-based system of politics is certainly odd for a theory which is worked out within the framework

---

[53] *System*, i. 62.   [54] Ibid. 63.   [55] Ibid. ii. 375–6.

of natural law. For Hutcheson's intellectual inheritors, Kames and (especially) Hume, it was not merely odd, but unacceptable— especially as it concerned the realm of justice properly or narrowly conceived, the realm of property relations.

A further oddity (at least to modern ears) stems from Hutcheson's programme of deriving the more complex moral notions, including that of obligation, from the moral sense. Since the moral sense naturally approves of benevolence, Hutcheson concludes that we have an obligation to be benevolent.[56] This seems strange because it appears to violate the maxim that 'ought' implies 'can': although obligation binds the will, and the will governs our actions, the will has little influence over our states of mind. So, if we do not feel benevolent, little can be achieved in that direction by an effort of will. This means that, while it is unproblematic to speak of an obligation to beneficence, benevolence is an entirely different kettle of fish. It will be argued in the next chapter, however, that Hutcheson's conception of an obligation to benevolence is not due to confusion, and, further, that understanding his point provides the key to explaining a famous Humean observation on moral reasoning.

3. NATURAL LAW AND THE VARIETIES OF RIGHTS

The doctrine of the moral sense grounds an account of natural law in which the role of formal obligation has been so drastically curtailed that Hutcheson allows it to drop out of view altogether. In his view, the task of moral philosophy is to explain 'how we acquire our more particular ideas of *Virtue* and *Vice*, abstracting from any *Law*, *Human*, or *Divine*'. So moral philosophy is essentially a naturalistic enterprise, in that it is (or at the very least aims to be) independent of any particular set of religious or metaphysical beliefs. He thus offers an account of natural law essentially based on the moral sense and the implications that can be drawn from it with the aid of ordinary (non-metaphysical) reasoning.[57]

---

[56] *Inquiry*, 249–50.

[57] A caveat and a criticism are in order here. The caveat is that, as mentioned previously, Hutcheson does recognize the reinforcing effect that religious belief can have in prompting obedience to the moral law when private interest or weakness obtrude (*Inquiry*, 268), and his teleology may be thought (as apparently by Hume) defensible only when supported by further metaphysical beliefs. Nevertheless, his

In outline, Hutcheson's grounding of natural law in the moral sense proceeds as follows. He begins from the observation that 'many have high Notions of *Honour, Faith, Generosity, Justice*, who have scarce any Opinions about the DEITY, or any Thoughts of *future Rewards*; and abhor anything which is *Treacherous, Cruel,* or *Unjust*, without any regard to *future Punishments*.'[58] The essential selflessness of the moral sense allows it to provide a direct foundation for human sociability: 'we are determin'd to common Friendships and Acquaintances, not by the sullen Apprehensions of our *Necessitys*, or Prospects of *Interest*; but by an incredible variety of little agreeable, engaging Evidences of *Love, Good-nature,* and other *morally amiable Qualities* in those we converse with.'[59] And since human sociability is the foundation of the natural law, the moral sense is also the ultimate foundation of natural law. The natural law is a system of 'maxims, or rules of conduct' derived from the moral sense. It derives *naturally* from the moral sense both because it arises necessarily, and because it does not depend on any supernatural commitments. Rather, it is moral philosophy which,

intentions are certainly naturalistic. This serves to introduce the criticism. In *Whose Justice? Which Rationality?*, Alasdair MacIntyre distinguishes between 'Scottish' (metaphysical) and 'English' (interest-based) modes of social theorizing. He claims that the former affirmed, while the latter denied, the following view of justice: 'to pursue justice one must be able . . . to transcend both whatever moves one to pursue one's own self-interest and also whatever moves one to consult the interest of any group of others, *no matter how enlarged*. To distribute justly is to distribute *according to desert*, not according to interest, and justice thus conceived cannot be shown to be the interest of anyone and everyone, whether on a Hobbesian view or even on one derived from Shaftesbury's more generous conception of human nature' (p. 277, emphases added). In arguing thus, MacIntyre overlooks the difference made to Scottish thought by the advent of modern natural law as introduced by Carmichael and popularized by Hutcheson. For Hutcheson, the informed moral sense (based on 'Shaftesbury's more generous conception of human nature') consults *precisely* the public interest ('a good man's heart will always be zealous for the interest of any innocent association for a publick interest', *System*, ii. 376); and justice, because it must recognize the category of 'external' rights (to be described below), is thereby committed to *violating* canons of desert, again for reasons of public interest. MacIntyre's account of Scottish thought is perhaps a reliable guide to the pre-Enlightenment period, but he misunderstands the variety and direction of the intellectual forces at work within 18th-cent. Scotland. Specifically, he overlooks the Pufendorfian identification of the dictates of natural law with those of rational utility. As a result he misunderstands not only Hutcheson but Hume as well. This ch. and the next will serve to show that, rather than constituting an 'Anglicizing subversion' of Scottish (including Hutchesonian) social thought, Hume's moral philosophy is shaped by, and responds to, the problematic achievements of Hutchesonian natural law.

[58] *Inquiry*, 128 (Theories of a Lockian kind are clearly the target here.)
[59] Ibid. 257.

by reflecting on the approbations of the moral sense, establishes what is the content of natural law. The maxims of conduct approved by the moral sense are established 'as far as it can be done by observations and conclusions discoverable from the constitution of nature, without any aids of supernatural revelation: these maxims, or rules of conduct are therefore reputed as laws of nature, and the system or collection of them is called the LAW OF NATURE.'[60]

It is perhaps somewhat odd that Hutcheson should speak of the moral sense as explaining our particular ideas of virtue and vice, without reference to a law, and then to call the system of such ideas the *law* of nature. However, there is no substantial issue here. The laws of which the law of nature is independent are the commands of any superior being, and hence of the formal element of a voluntarist account of obligation (thus the reference to laws '*Human*, or *Divine*'). The moral sense can found natural laws only if those laws are understood in non-voluntarist terms—as indeed Hutcheson understands them. Recognizing this is sufficient to dispel the appearance of paradox in his remarks about law and the moral sense. Additionally, this helps to explain why Hutcheson's notion of law should turn out to be significantly weaker than that of his predecessors. The absence of a coercive power to secure compliance allows, and the implicit commitment of the moral sense point of view requires, a considerably enhanced scope for individual judgement, and thus for defeasible law. The benevolent perspective of the moral sense will require that, in extreme circumstances such as dire necessity (and perhaps in less extreme circumstances as well), particular rules be set aside. The rules of conduct which comprise the natural law, then, although not merely rules of thumb, cannot be indefeasible. A hint of this position can be detected in Hutcheson's appeal to 'the good man's heart' quoted above—its further implications will be considered below.

The natural law specifies the particular rules of conduct, and therefore obligations, of social life. So it is surprising that Hutcheson does not speak much of obligations. Rather, he holds that from the moral sense 'we derive our Ideas of RIGHTS'[61]—and he then proceeds to spell out the content of the natural law principally in terms of such rights. However, his use of this key notion is very distinctive, and shows the powerful influence of the benevolent

---

[60] *System*, i. 1.   [61] *Inquiry*, 277.

affections that please the moral sense. His position cannot be accommodated in the recent idea of a 'right-based' theory.[62] Rather, since the moral sense shows that 'some sort of benevolent affections' are the foundation of all moral goodness, the rights espoused are defined in terms of the overall public good:

Whenever it appears to us, that *a Faculty of doing, demanding, or possessing any thing, universally allow'd in certain Circumstances, would in the whole tend to the general Good,* we say that any Person in such Circumstances, has *a right to do, possess, or demand that Thing.* And according as this Tendency to the *publick Good* is *greater* or *less,* the *Right* is *greater* or *less.*[63]

In this passage, Hutcheson's indebtedness to Grotius's definition of a right is evident—a right is defined as a faculty, a power to act with a moral effect. However the content is different in two ways. In the first place it shows the influence of Pufendorf's reconstruction of rights in terms of duties, so the notion of a right as a power to act with a moral effect is cashed out as a power to act rightly, as indeed it is for Locke. Secondly, Hutcheson transforms the notion of a right by his extremely restricted conception of what counts as a moral effect. On his view all moral effects can be reduced to one, to the tendency to enhance the general good, so a right is simply the power of acting to enhance the general good. This has a striking implication, the effects of which are felt throughout Hutcheson's moral and political theory: since the general good is not identical to the individual good, the notion of a right has become detached from its previous foundation in the *suum,* the realm of one's own. As a result, Hutcheson's system leaves the *suum* vulnerable to encroachment or invasion.[64]

---

[62] Ronald Dworkin offers a tentative division of political theories into *right-based, goal-based,* and *duty-based* theories. See *Taking Rights Seriously* (London: Duckworth, 1977), 171–2; and see also J. Mackie, 'Can there be a Right-Based Moral Theory?', and J. Raz, 'Right-Based Moralities', both in J. Waldron (ed.), *Theories of Rights* (Oxford: Oxford University Press, 1984). (On this kind of classification, interestingly, Hutcheson's position would be best described as an uneasy mixture of goal-based and duty-based elements.)   [63] *Inquiry,* 277.

[64] The important issues here are carefully discussed by T. Mautner, 'Pufendorf and 18th-century Scottish Philosophy', in id., *Samuel von Pufendorf 1632–1982: Ett rättshistoriskt i Lund* (Lund: Bloms Boktryckeri, 1986), 125–30. The account provided here is indebted to Mautner's, but differs on the position occupied by Pufendorf: he assimilates Pufendorf's position to Grotius's, and places them in equal opposition to Hutcheson, whereas the account of Pufendorf given in Ch. 2 places him in an intermediate position betwee the other two.

The full implications of this development will become clearer below. At this stage, the relevant feature is that, by explicating rights in terms of their contribution to the general good, Hutcheson is able to organize different rights into a hierarchy, according to their different degree of contribution. Thus, as he puts it, rights may be 'greater' or 'less'. The greater rights need not necessarily override lesser rights, but they are certainly more important, more admirable. Greatness is judged not in terms of the value of each particular exercise of a given right, but of the right in general: hence the greatness of a right is a function of its inseparability from the general good. The greatest rights, those which are not separable from the general good, he describes, employing Pufendorf's terminology, as perfect rights:

The *Rights* call'd *perfect*, are of *such necessity to the publick Good, that the universal Violation of them would make human Life intolerable*; and it actually makes those miserable, whose *Rights* are thus *violated*. On the contrary, to fulfill these *Rights* in every Instance, tends to the *publick Good*, either *directly*, or by promoting the innocent Advantage of a *Part*.[65]

The observance of these rights is essential for achieving the common good, so the moral sense cannot but approve of all reasonable means for securing them, including enforcement. So in the exercise or protection of the perfect rights the use of force is justified. The justification of enforcement introduces no new complexities, because that justification is itself in terms of the public good: 'as to the general Consequences, the universal Use of Force in *a State of Nature*, in pursuance of *perfect Rights*, seems exceedingly *advantageous* to the *Whole*, by making every one dread any attempts against the *perfect Rights* of others.'[66] In other words, perfect rights are those moral powers the exercise or possession of which not merely tends to the general good, but is absolutely inseparable from its maintenance or increase. Therefore their enforcement, or 'violent Defence, or Prosecution',[67] also tends to the general good, and so perfect rights can be legitimately enforced. Thus Hutcheson adapts Pufendorf's distinctions to his own ends.

Which rights are so closely tied to the general good that they can appropriately be regarded as perfect rights? Hutcheson gives a short list:

---

[65] *Inquiry*, 277.   [66] Ibid. 278.   [67] Ibid. 277.

Instances of *perfect Rights* are those to our *Lives*; to the *Fruits* of our
Labours; to demand Performance of *Contracts* upon valuable Considerations,
from men capable of performing them; to *direct* our own Actions either for
publick, or innocent *private Good*, before we have submitted them to the
Direction of others in any measure; and many others of like nature.[68]

Of these four rights, the first is a right to life, the last a right to
natural liberty, while the second and third are rights to acquisition
and contract. Given that acquisition and contract are those forms of
free action which are, for the purposes of physical preservation at
least, perhaps the most important kinds of liberty, Hutcheson's
short list of perfect rights can be explained in terms of Locke's right
of original property in one's person (i.e. to life and liberty), from
which all other properties (estate) are derived. In the *System*,
Hutcheson explicitly invokes the Lockian conception when he
remarks that 'each man is the original proprietor of his own
liberty',[69] but in the passage quoted above, and at other points, the
notion of self-proprietorship is discernible even in the *Inquiry*.[70]

This notion is, of course, traceable to Grotius and Pufendorf,
since, as has been shown above, the idea of being proprietor of
oneself testifies to the ongoing influence of the important notion of
the *suum*.[71] The debt to Pufendorf in particular should be stressed
at this point, since Hutcheson follows Pufendorf also in distinguishing between natural and adventitious rights. The latter arise, it will
be remembered, as a result of 'some previous acts of man'[72]—so,
since they necessarily involve human actions, the rights to 'the
Fruits of our Labours' and to 'demand Performance of *Contracts*'
must be classified not as natural but as adventitious rights. And,
since these two rights are the most important elements of justice, of
giving to each his due, Hutcheson must conclude that justice is
essentially concerned with adventitious rights.[73]

[68] *Inquiry*, 278.
[69] *System*, ii. 211.   [70] See, in particular, *Inquiry*, 283.
[71] Grotius, in fact, holds that even the institution of promising depends on our
being proprietors of our actions (see *DJPB* II. 11. i. 3)—although it is important to
remember that his meaning is that our actions *belong to us*, are part of our *suum*.
[72] *De Officio*, II. 2. 1.
[73] Hutcheson does not employ these distinctions in the earlier *Inquiry*, but in the
System he simply applies Pufendorf's concepts (see i. 293 ff.). (Note also that this
conclusion, that justice is a matter of adventitious rights, is equivalent to saying, in
Humean language, that the virtues of justice are *artificial*—Hume's terminology
differs principally because of his more explicit motivational concerns, as the next ch.
will show.)

The second major category of rights are the imperfect rights. Like all rights, they 'tend to the improvement and increase of *positive* Good in any Society', but they are to be distinguished from perfect rights because they 'are not *absolutely* necessary to prevent universal Misery'. By violating them, one does not deprive human beings of any good they previously enjoyed, but 'only disappoints Men of the Happiness expected from the Humanity or Gratitude of others'. For this reason, 'a violent Prosecution of such *Rights* would generally occasion greater *Evil* than the Violation of them'.[74] So imperfect rights, even though they tend to the general good of society, cannot be justly enforced. In fact, some of them are impossible to enforce, such as the imperfect right to acts of kindness. Kindness enforced is kindness no longer: as Hutcheson puts it, it 'would cease to appear amiable'.[75]

Imperfect rights are most frequently adventitious, since they are usually appropriate to quite specific situations shaped by human actions, as Hutcheson's examples indicate: 'Instances of *imperfect Rights* are those which the *Poor* have to the Charity of the Wealthy; which *all Men* have to offices of no trouble or expense to the Performer; which *Benefactors* have to returns of Gratitude, and such like.'[76] One other aspect of the distinction between imperfect and perfect rights has something of a contemporary flavour. Roughly, the former are not enforceable because they correspond to omissions of positive goods, whereas the latter are enforceable because they involve commissions of actual evils. However, Hutcheson's account only roughly corresponds to this familiar distinction because he is as concerned with motivations as with actual performances. The violation of imperfect rights is best tolerated, he says, because it 'only argues a Man to have such weak *Benevolence*, as not to study advancing the *positive Good* of others, when in the least opposite to his own'. In contrast, the violation of perfect rights cannot be tolerated because it 'argues the *injurious Person* to be *positively evil* or *cruel*; or at least so *immoderately selfish* as to be indifferent about the *positive Misery* and *Ruin* of others, when he imagines he can find his *Interest* in it'.[77] Violating the former shows merely 'a weak Desire of *publick Happiness*,' whereas violating the latter shows the violator to verge on being 'entirely negligent of the *Misery* of others'.[78] Persons of the latter

[74] *Inquiry*, 279. [75] Ibid. [76] Ibid.
[77] Ibid. 279–80. [78] Ibid. 280.

kind must be restrained in their actions, because such neglect of the condition of others shows them to be completely deficient in the moral sensitivities underlying all social affections, and on which social life itself depends.[79]

The third kind of right distinguished by Hutcheson is the most removed from the general good. Called an 'external' right, it is best understood as a degenerate perfect right: perfect because it can be justifiably enforced; and degenerate because it has lost its connection with the general good. In the *System* it is described as 'rather a shadow of right than any thing deserving that honourable name',[80] and, although this and other remarks in the later work appear more harsh than those in the *Inquiry*, the two works display a similarly grudging attitude towards rights of this kind. In fact, this attitude seems to be reflected in the very choice of terminology: the point seems to be that these rights are 'external' because they are no more than the shell or husk of a right. They have the outer appearance of a right, and must in the ordinary run of things be treated as such; but they remain defective or degenerate, in that they are lacking the core of a right—the tendency to promote the general good. External rights are rights which have lost their *telos*.

If rights have a *telos*, to promote the general good, and external rights lack precisely this, how can they be regarded as rights at all? To say the least, this is rather odd. However, Hutcheson appears to have two reasons for living with the oddity, rather than dispensing with external rights altogether. He mentions only one of these, but the second is implied by his own examples. They can be brought to light by examining his account of these degenerate rights.

External rights are enforceable rights which conflict with imperfect rights. They arise 'when *the doing, possessing, or demanding of anything is really detrimental to the Publick in any particular Instance, as being contrary to the imperfect Right of*

---

[79] Hutcheson's discussion of the relationship between perfect and imperfect rights can thus be fruitfully compared with Philippa Foot's distinction between negative duties (to avoid injury) and positive duties (to bring aid). Note that for Foot, as for Hutcheson, there is a rough (but *only* rough) correlation between these duties and the distinction between omissions and actions. See 'The Problem of Abortion and the Doctrine of the Double Effect', in *Virtues and Vices* (Oxford: Basil Blackwell, 1978), 26–30. Hutcheson's distinction is given a more thorough grounding by Adam Smith in *The Theory of Moral Sentiments*. For an account of the use Smith makes of the distinction see K. Haakonssen, *The Science of a Legislator* (Cambridge: Cambridge University Press, 1981), ch. 4.

[80] *System*, i. 259.

another'.[81] Why then should they be observed? Firstly, since violations of imperfect rights 'give no *Right* to force',[82] the fact of such violations alone is not sufficient ground for abandoning external rights. Secondly, and more importantly, although each individual external right is detrimental to the general good, honouring external rights as a whole is just the opposite: '*the universally denying Men this Faculty . . . would do more mischief than all the Evils to be fear'd from the Use of this Faculty.*'[83] He adds that it is always 'more *humane* and *kind*' not to exercise one's external rights, even though denying their legitimacy would be 'vastly more *pernicious*'.[84] But why should this be so? The answer can be gleaned by examining some of his examples: 'Instances of *external Rights* are these; that of a *wealthy Miser* to recall his Loan from the most industrious poor Tradesman at any time; that of demanding the Performance of a *Covenant* too burdensome on one side . . . ',[85] and so on. The significant feature of these examples is their specificity. The problem is not, for example, with contracts *per se*, but with contracts of a particular sort. This specificity is in fact the key to understanding the external rights: they are all undesirable special cases of desirable general rules. That loans should be repaid, and covenants fulfilled, are both desirable general rules because without such transactions between human beings an entire form of social life could not be maintained. However, both allow special cases which are anything but worth while, as Hutcheson's examples show. If such rules are to be socially efficacious, parties bound by them cannot be left at liberty to decide where or when it should bind. This would be to render all rules unenforceable, and would undermine even such perfect rights as the right to 'demand Performance of *Contracts*'. Consequently, all the undesirable special cases of important general rules should be treated, not simply on their own merits, but in the light of the relevant general rule. This is the situation of external rights. As *undesirable* instances of more general perfect rights, they conflict with imperfect rights. However, as undesirable *instances* of general perfect rights, they remain enforceable rights. They cannot be denied without simultaneously denying perfect rights. And, given the necessity of perfect rights for the maintenance and improvement of

---

[81] *Inquiry*, 280.
[82] Ibid. 282.   [83] Ibid. 280–1.
[84] Ibid. 282.   [85] Ibid. 281.

social life, the denial of external rights is therefore 'vastly more *pernicious*' than recognizing their legitimacy.

This line of argument, although reasonable on its own terms, nevertheless creates difficulties for Hutcheson. It is quite at odds with the *System*'s trust in the virtuous citizenry, as shown in the quotation at the end of section 2 above. A fully-fledged politics of virtue would weaken significantly, and perhaps even abolish, external rights. The extent of the problem can be underscored by recognizing that the benevolent affections of the moral sense will, in each particular case, prompt us to act in opposition to external rights. Hutcheson's sympathetic critics, particularly Kames and Hume, picked out precisely this weakness in his theory. The system of justice depends on recognizing external rights, but such rights can be maintained only by appealing to the sense of duty. However, the sense of duty cannot be grounded in the benevolent affections of the moral sense, because that sense, it will be remembered, is simply a passive determination of the mind to approve of benevolent actions or characters—and neither external rights, nor the sense of duty, display any such benevolent characteristics. So Hutcheson's theory illustrates by default the necessity of finding or creating a separate foundation for acting from the sense of duty.[86]

Hutcheson's notion of external rights also sharply points up the difference between his conception of rights and more familiar conceptions, particularly as it concerns social harmony and the situation of the individual. It was observed above that the *telos* of rights in Hutcheson's system is to promote the general good. He understands this connection very inclusively, such that any class of action which serves the general good, either directly or (as with external rights) indirectly, is thereby a right. This allows a great number and variety of rights. However, it also implies that, provided the general good can be accurately specified, the catalogue of rights will tend to constitute a harmonious system. Only in those specific cases where external rights are generated can there be conflict *between* rights. And, since external rights are rights which *ought not to be exercised* (because it is always 'more *humane and kind*' not to exercise them), the exercise of rights in

---

[86] Kames objects to Hutcheson's account of duty and Justice in *Essays on the Principles of Morality and Natural Religion*, 55–7; and see Hume's account of the artificiality of the sense of duty in *Treatise*, 477 ff.

Hutcheson's system should work together to produce a harmonious social good.

He is conscious of this feature of his account, emphasising its lack of internal conflicts. Perfect rights, since they are all necessary for the general good, form a mutually supporting system. Hence, he concludes, they cannot come into conflict: 'there can be no Opposition of *perfect Rights* among themselves'. Similarly, perfect rights cannot conflict with imperfect rights, and '*external Rights* cannot be opposite among themselves'.[87] Of these three claims, however, only the second is obviously true—but its truth is at the price of vacuity, since any otherwise perfect right which conflicts with an imperfect right, it has been argued, is *ipso facto* an external right. The first can be defended, if appropriately interpreted. Hutcheson cannot mean that my right to contract cannot interfere with your right to contract, since conflicts of this sort are almost inevitable. If he is instead taken to mean that the rights to life, liberty, and free contract do not themselves come into conflict, he appears to be on safer ground. Even here, however, problems remain: he must hold, for example, that contracting into slavery can never be for the general good. This is certainly not obvious. And the third claim, that external rights cannot come into conflict, is also puzzling. The important point, however, is that Hutcheson appears confident that his theory of rights fits together into a coherent and (largely) harmonious whole, a whole which, by defending the general good, defends the good of all.

If this really is his view, the attempt to show the harmony of his system unwittingly reveals how little is the protection offered to the individual. For the general or public good is not always served by respecting or promoting the good of each individual, and on some occasions may even require substantial interferences with it. For just this reason, theories of rights tend to specify not social goods but the good of individuals, and may even conceive the former to be the principal threat to the latter. While these dangers are often exaggerated (threats to individual goods, because they stem frequently from putative social goods, do not thereby stem from social goods), it is undeniable that individual and social goods are not identical, and that, whether individually or collectively, human beings pose an implicit threat to one another. So theories of rights,

---

[87] *Inquiry*, 282.

which aim at protecting individuals from this sort of implicit threat, typically proceed by marking individuals off from one another, and defining a sphere of inviolability. As the natural law account of the *suum* and its legitimate or necessary extensions shows, the task of the theory of rights need not be exhausted by protecting the individual's person, but can be extended to include a more thorough account of right action. The extensions, however, cannot replace the concern for the person. The problem with Hutcheson's theory is that he has created just this possibility. His preoccupation with the general good has left the individual good at risk; and this feature of his position becomes evident in his account of property and politics.

4. PROPERTY AND POLITICAL CONSTITUTION

Hutcheson's account of property and politics can be approached by first considering his account of the alienability of rights. He allows that rights are alienable provided two conditions are met: (a) the alienation must be *possible*, and (b) it must 'serve some valuable Purpose'.[88] The first of these conditions shows that the '*Right of private Judgement*, or of our *inward Sentiments*, is *unalienable*', since we cannot conform our inmost thoughts to anyone else's will. The second condition guarantees both freedom of worship and an inalienable right to liberty: 'a *direct Right* over our *Lives* or *Limbs*, is not *alienable* to any Person; so that he might at Pleasure put us to death, or maim us.'[89] Hutcheson thus introduces the central inalienable right of Locke's political theory: the inalienable natural right to life and liberty, the property in one's person. The Lockian echoes here are quite strong (most notably, the reference to being put at another's 'pleasure'),[90] and, as with Locke's theory, the function of this right in Hutcheson's scheme is to ban slavery.

The two views differ quite sharply, however, on the question of a fundamental right of self-preservation. In Locke's theory, this right plays a pivotal role, but Hutcheson does not refer to it at all. It appears that this is not an oversight, but further evidence of his commitment to the general good. Self-preservation, as distinct from the preservation of human society, ceases to be a fundamental right. So, having asserted the existence of the right to liberty, Hutcheson

---

[88] *Inquiry*, 282–3.
[89] Ibid. 283.   [90] *Two Treatises*, ii. 6.

immediately introduces a further right which is sharply at odds with *self*-preservation, since its exercise cannot but put individual life and liberty at risk. It may require not only that we risk our lives, but that we surrender our liberty, to the extent of abandoning power over our lives to the authority of others:

> We have indeed a *Right* to hazard our Lives in any good Action which is of importance to *the Publick*; and it may often serve a most valuable end, to subject the direction of such perilous Actions to the Prudence of others in pursuing a *publick Good*; as *Soldiers* do to their *General*, or to a *Council* of *War*.[91]

He adds 'so far this *right* is *alienable*'—and thereby shows that this particular right can justifiably be invoked in order to override the general '*Right* over our *Lives* or *Limbs*'.

Hutcheson clearly has rather exceptional circumstances in mind here, but it is nevertheless hard to imagine Locke concurring with his solution. The right to hazard one's life and limb, even to the extent of placing that life and limb into the hands of another, is so far from the spirit of the *Two Treatises* that it is hardly possible to imagine Locke allowing it at all; and certainly not without introducing strong caveats. So it is difficult to resist the conclusion that here we see Hutcheson accepting a basic Lockian concept, only immediately to reshape it to fit his fundamental commitment to advancing the general good. Nor is this the only place in Hutcheson's theory that this tendency can be discerned. It is also evident in his account of the origins of the institutions vital for human society: that is, of the foundation of property, and of the formation of a civil polity from a state of nature. Examining these two aspects of Hutcheson's view will bring the characteristic tendencies of his theory into sharp relief.

The basic starting-point of Hutcheson's account of property can be regarded in either of two (roughly equivalent) lights: as a Lockian revision of Pufendorf, or as an attempt to produce a naturalized (and thus secular) version of Locke's theory.[92] He affirms that the original condition of the first human beings with respect to the earth and its bounty was, as Pufendorf had said, a

[91] Ibid.

[92] These 2 alternatives are only equivalent, of course, if Locke's theory is understood as a development of Pufendorf's natural jurisprudence, as argued for in Ch. 3. As indicated above, this is how Carmichael and Hutcheson did understand him.

negative community; and he implicitly demonstrates how that notion underlies Locke's theory, by erecting a substantially Lockian theory on that foundation. To suppose an original negative community, he holds, is to imply that the original establishment of property required neither an agreement, as Grotius and Pufendorf had supposed, nor an explicit (divine) parental grant, as Filmer had argued.[93] Rather, property arose from the original negative community directly through labour. Unlike Locke, however, he does not attempt to trace this development to, or justify it in terms of, any theological imperative. He does not, for example, appeal to the divine command to Adam to labour.[94] Instead, as his account of the law of nature implies, he appeals only to the material advantages for human life that stem from the improving activity of labour and the proper securing of its fruits. He is quite critical of one aspect of Locke's argument, however. He castigates those who mistakenly conceive of property as a 'physical quality or relation' rather than a moral quality,[95] and it is pretty clear that here he has in mind Locke's argument that property in a thing could be established by the thing becoming 'part of oneself'.[96] He may have thought the trouble stems from Locke's broad notion of property, because, even though he defends an original and inalienable right over our lives and limbs that is functionally equivalent to Locke's notion of a property in one's person, he does not employ the Lockian term. With rare exceptions, he restricts the meaning of 'property' to rights over external things (Locke's 'estate').

Once the terminological differences and theological absences are set aside, however, Hutcheson's profoundly Lockian outlook is evident. The key to his theory is the value for human life of '*Labour and Industry*'.[97] In fact, so great is the weight placed on the effects of labour that it is clear he gives his whole-hearted assent to Locke's dictum that '*labour makes the far greatest part of the value* of things, we enjoy in this World'.[98] In some places he even seems simply to

---

[93] *System*, i. 330–1.   [94] Cf. *Two Treatises*, ii. 31; Gen. 3: 17–19.
[95] *System*, i. 318, 346; ii. 12. He insists that, because property is a kind of right, it is a moral quality 'competent to some person' (i. 253), and is therefore founded entirely in justice, that is, in the law of nature (i. 346–7). Perhaps Locke's uncertainty on this point can be traced to Pufendorf, because the latter at one point remarks, in terminology which appears to encourage Locke's confusion, that 'ownership . . . is the right by which the substance, so to speak, of a thing belongs to a man' (*De Officio*, I. 12. 3).
[96] Cf. *Two Treatises*, ii. 26.   [97] *Inquiry*, 284.
[98] *Two Treatises*, ii. 42.

paraphrase Locke's account. For example, Locke claims in the *Two Treatises* that: 'I think it will be but a very modest Computation to say, that of the *Products* of the Earth useful to the Life of man 9/10 are the *effects of labour*'.[99] Hutcheson concurs entirely with this 'modest Computation': 'That we may see the Foundation of some of the more *important rights of Mankind* let us observe, that probably nine Tenths, at least, of the things which are useful to Mankind, are owing to their *Labour* and *Industry*'.[100] His justification of property depends entirely on these useful effects, or, to be more precise, on the necessity of securing them against threats. In outline, his view is as follows.

Having distinguished property from the original right over our lives and limbs, Hutcheson has no need to argue that property is either necessary for, or implied by, the eating of an acorn or an apple in the wild.[101] The original right is in such circumstances all that is necessary. In holding this he follows Grotius and Pufendorf; but his explanation for why property arises diverges considerably from theirs. They attributed the origin of property to a shift to a more refined mode of life, but Hutcheson argues that property becomes necessary with the advent of scarcity, and thus of competition for limited resources—whether these resources are natural or generated by industry. The chief cause of scarcity, he says, is population increase:

when once Men become so numerous, that the *natural Product* of the Earth is not sufficient for their Support, or Ease, or innocent Pleasure, a necessity arises, for the support of the increasing *System*, that such a *Tenour* of Conduct be observ'd, as shall most effectually promote *Industry*; and that Men abstain from all Actions which would have the contrary effect.[102]

Among the factors which work to this end are general benevolence, the strong ties of blood and friendship, and the desire for honour.[103] They are not, however, sufficient, because all such mutually supporting passions and affections are undermined when a person is not confident of securing 'the Fruits of his own innocent Labour'. This is because, where the fruits of industry are not protected, 'it exposes the *Industrious* as a constant prey to the *Slothful*, and sets *Self-love* against *Industry*'.[104] In such circumstances, even the most benevolently inclined will quickly weary of their efforts providing,

---

[99] Ibid. 40.   [100] *Inquiry*, 284.   [101] Cf. *Two Treatises*, ii. 28.
[102] *Inquiry*, 284.   [103] Ibid.   [104] Ibid. 285.

not resources for advancing either public or private goods, but a pool to be plundered by those not prepared to contribute to either their own or the general welfare. Self-love will then counsel against industrious activity, because there will be no room for confidence that effort will secure any reward.

So, without the adequate protection of the fruits of industry, all practical endeavour is in vain. The great benefits to be gained, not merely by protecting, but by stimulating, the members of society to productive activity, urge the creation of a system of property. Property is introduced to protect industry, and is justified entirely in terms of its ability to do so. As Hutcheson puts it, without property 'we could scarce hope for any *Industry*, or anything beyond the Product of uncultivated Nature'. The manifold advantages of cultivation and industry thus require us to recognize 'the Ground of our *Right* of *Dominion* and *Property*, in the *Fruits* of our *Labours*'.[105]

Hutcheson goes on to argue that the value of such industry will be achieved only if there is not only protection for, but also unhindered disposal of, any surplus beyond our needs. Thus he concludes that the right of property in things implies also the rights to accumulate, to trade, to donate, and to dispose of by testament.[106] His view appears to be not only that incentives for industry require protection for the fruits of industry, but that such incentives (and thus the social good) are maximized when power over the fruits of industry is itself maximized. If this is his reasoning, it is open to a range of possible objections; although it is not to the point to pursue them further here.[107] The important matter is the central role Hutcheson assigns to the protection and promotion of

[105] *Inquiry*, 285. Cf. D. Winch, *Adam Smith's Politics* (Cambridge: Cambridge University Press, 1978), 49–50, for a discussion of Hutcheson's position.

[106] *Inquiry*, 286.

[107] One possible objection can be illustrated by Adam Smith's response to his rather breezy 'derivation' of testamentary succession. Smith points out that testamentary succession is a late and sophisticated development in the history of property, and is so because incentives for industry are satisfactorily protected if the property passes to those who have made a significant contribution to the development and maintenance of the property. Legal succession of this kind, which normally favours next of kin is 'not so much on account of their relation to the father as on account of the labour they had bestowed' in acquiring and developing the property. So the history of legal succession indicates an explicit regard for protecting the industry of the family and others *against* the whims of the owner. See Adam Smith, *Lectures on Jurisprudence*, ed. R. L. Meek, D. D. Raphael, and P. G. Stein (Oxford: Clarendon Press, 1978), LJ(B) 156.

industry. The system of property is justified entirely in terms of the advantages that such a system can bring to the members of the society as a whole. Provided the system does stimulate industry and protect its fruits, or does so better than any imaginable rival, it pleases the moral sense, and so is justified.

The inequalities generated by a system of property are thus also to be judged by their effect on human industry: 'as property is constituted to encourage and reward industry, it can never be so extended as to prevent or frustrate the diligence of mankind.'[108] In this passage, Hutcheson's principal concern is to prevent any person or society from acquiring a right in 'a vast tract of land quite beyond their power to cultivate'. If limitations of this kind are not imposed, 'the caprice or vain ambition of one state might keep half the earth desolate, and oppress the rest of mankind'.[109] So the key role played by industry in Hutcheson's scheme means that the theory provides simultaneously a justification of the fact of economic inequality—since inequality is an inescapable consequence of a system of property—and a limitation on its justified extent. For this reason, it is misleading, if not exactly false, to conclude, as does Thomas Horne, that 'his property theory is both an explicit defence of inequality and an effort to educate those in polite society to the moral, political and economic virtues that would justify their eminence'.[110] It would be more accurate to say that his theory defends the existence of inequality in a society, but on grounds that may not cause comfort to all those who enjoy the benefits of such inequalities. He does not say, although he might have, that large estates are justified in the hands of the industrious and rational, but not in those of the slothful and self-indulgent. He holds, following Locke, that the pre-eminence of some is justified because, and in so far as, it is a pre-condition for the betterment of all.

Hutcheson's views are, however, significantly different from Locke's on the question of the place of property in civil society. The difference should not be overrated, since Locke's doctrine that the

[108] *System*, i. 326.
[109] Ibid. 326–7. Adam Smith employs the same reasoning to limit extensions to the powers implied by property. His specific concern is to reject entails, which he describes as 'the greatest of all extensions to property'. He adds, 'upon the whole nothing can be more absurd than perpetual entails', precisely because entail is a system which frustrates industry (*Lectures on Jurisprudence*, LJ(B) 166–8).
[110] Horne, 'Moral and Economic Improvement: Francis Hutcheson on Property', 118.

protection of property is the end of government does not imply that the protection of our property in things (estate) is the end of government. Nevertheless Locke does exhibit a marked concern for the protection of the individual's estate from the will of the sovereign power, whereas Hutcheson's concern, here as elsewhere, is for the promotion of the general good. So he accepts that rights of property in things, like other rights, are not necessarily a bar on the actions of governments, but may be judged according to their contribution to the general good. Of course, in any circumstances this contribution will be considerable, so these and comparable rights cannot ever be lightly set aside; but, even if not lightly, they *can* be overridden in pressing cases, where the general good requires. However, the circumstances where the general good does impose such requirements cannot be fully specified in advance, since in the last resort the good can only be determined by the workings of the moral sense in the good man's heart. So it is impossible to avoid the conclusion that 'our *moral Sense*, by a little reflection upon the Tendencys of actions, may adjust the *Rights* of *Mankind*'.[111] This means that the rights of mankind, including property, bind only in the general course of events. Where necessity or emergency requires, they can, indeed must, be set aside.[112] In addition, what is to count as necessity is itself determined by the moral sense, and thus by those agents in the relevant situation. Hutcheson's account of necessity suggests that he envisages such modifications of rights to be comparatively infrequent, or not very extensive, because it exhibits a marked debt to Pufendorf. This may suggest, of course, that he fails fully to appreciate the subversive germ in his doctrine, and so hopes simply to graft his account of the foundations of moral judgement on to Pufendorf's widely respected conclusion; but it also reflects a genuine underlying similarity. The implied rational consensus of beings who recognize a 'debt to the sociable attitude' which underlies Pufendorf's account of the nature and extent of the right of necessity is not uncongenial to the moral sense approach, since both build in a concern for the general good as well as a capacity for flexible adjustment of means to ends.

Hutcheson's view on the possibility of adjusting the rights of mankind has significant implications that go beyond questions of the extent of the right of property in things. Most importantly, it has

---

[111] *Inquiry*, 288.   [112] Ibid. 298.

a profound impact on the justification and extent of political power, and is nowhere shown more clearly than in the twist he gives to the meaning of the Lockian notion of government as a trust. In order properly to understand this twist—and thereby to show the subversive potential of the moral sense foundation for the established doctrines of natural jurisprudence—it will be helpful to begin at the beginning, and determine how the civil polity first arises.

Hutcheson accepts that the civil polity has to be created by human beings from a pre-civil condition. In this respect he diverges sharply from Shaftesbury's interpretation of the implications of the moral sense for political theory. Shaftesbury held that the naturally sociable affections of human nature made political society itself an instinctively natural phenomenon, not the result of artifice. As a result, he was quite dismissive towards those theories which included the notion of an original pre-civil state.[113] Hutcheson, in contrast, offers a much restricted interpretation of the scope of the benevolent affections of the moral sense: although it is indeed the foundation of sociability, it cannot provide an instinctive basis for civil polity. The existence of civil government depends on rational artifice, and therefore it must arise in time from an original state of nature.[114] Recognition of the reality of the moral sense does, however, have a profound impact on our conception of that original state. Since human beings possess the naturally sociable affections of the moral sense, the original state was a peaceful one. Without it, our natural state would indeed be the state of '*universal* War, according to Mr. HOBBS'.[115]

How then is civil government constituted? Hutcheson's account is Lockian in structure, but with significant modifications. It comes into being by men transferring 'their *alienable Rights* to the Disposal of their Governours, under such *Limitations* as their Prudence suggests'.[116] Such alienable rights must include the right to punish and the right to war: the foundation of government depends, among other things, on establishing the magistrate's right to punish.[117] The

---

[113] In the *Characteristics*, he remarks at one point that 'the learned have such a fancy for this notion, and love to talk of this imaginary state of nature' (quoted in I. Kramnick, *Bolingbroke and his Circle* (Cambridge, Mass.: Harvard University Press, 1968), 89).

[114] The reality of the state of nature is made explicit in the *System*, i. 280 ff. Although, in the *Inquiry*, it is not directly connected to a discussion of the first formation of government, it is referred to twice (pp. 278, 303).

[115] *Inquiry*, 303.   [116] Ibid. 287.   [117] Ibid. 278.

limitations of prudence to which Hutcheson refers are the limitations the people choose to place on their government, the alienable rights they choose not to transfer. Where they do not specifically limit the rights transferred, the legitimate powers of the government are still limited by the inalienable rights of the people (the broad outlines of which are readily discerned by the moral sense). For this reason, 'there can be no Government so absolute, as to have even an *external Right* to do or command every thing'.[118] On those occasions when the government does invade inalienable rights, the people can exercise their right of resistance. However, since the effect of exercising the right will vary dramatically according to the circumstances—in some cases producing a net benefit, in others a net harm—the right itself may be either perfect or external. Since external rights are rights which ought not to be exercised, the right of resistance will not always serve to justify actual acts of resistance. Although '*Unalienable Rights* are *essential Limitations* in all Governments',[119] and these rights include the people's right of resistance, actual resistance to government requires a more extensive justification than the mere identification of, or insistence upon, that right. The exercise of the right of resistance is itself constrained by considerations of the general good. So Hutcheson's position differs from Locke's in that the 'appeal to God' must always be tempered by an appeal to our moral (good) sense.

The advantages of civil government are clear, so the motives for entering into it are unexceptionable. The people establish it with an eye to 'promoting the *publick Good*, and of defending themselves against mutual or foreign *Injurys*'.[120] This is therefore the end of government; and Hutcheson follows the Lockian notion that government is a trust designed to achieve this end. However, he gives this idea a twist that Locke did not intend: he conceives of government not merely *as* a trust, an institution designed to achieve a particular worthwhile end, but as necessarily an object of trust by the people. He puts it as follows: 'in all states this *tacit Trust* is presuppos'd . . . that the Power conferr'd shall be employ'd according to the best Judgment of the Rulers for the publick good.'[121] It would not be necessary to speak, as Hutcheson does here, of a tacit trust unless by a trust he has in mind some act of mind

---

[118] *Inquiry*, 294.
[119] Ibid. 295.   [120] Ibid. 287.   [121] Ibid. 295.

by the people, specifically an act of trusting the rulers. But this turns Locke's notion upside down. Instead of the idea of government as a trust being a constraint on the legitimate activities of the government, Hutcheson transforms it into a means of securing the people's compliance—even in those cases where the government oversteps the bounds of its authority as constituted by the transfer of the people's alienable rights. In fact, putting it in these terms helps to identify what, in Hutcheson's own terms, has gone wrong: to presuppose a tacit trust in the established government is to suppose the alienation of an *inalienable* right, the right of private judgement.[122]

Admittedly, Hutcheson is anxious to restrict governmental violations of the Constitution to situations of the direst necessity. He does this by drawing a parallel with the people's right of resistance:

In Cases of *extreme Necessity*, when the State cannot otherwise be preserv'd from Ruin, it must certainly be *Just* and *Good* in limited Governours, or in any other Persons who can do it; to use the Force of the State for its own preservation, beyond the Limits fix'd by the *Constitution*, in some *transitory Acts*, which are not to be made *Precedents*. And on the other hand, when an *equal Necessity* to avoid Ruin requires it, the Subjects may justly resume the Powers ordinarily lodg'd in their Governours, or may counteract them . . . These Necessitys must be very grievous and flagrant, otherwise they can never over-ballance the *Evils* of violating a tolerable Constitution, by *an arbitrary act of Power*, on the one hand; or by an Insurrection, or Civil War, on the other. No Person, or State can be happy, where they do not think their *Important Rights* are secur'd from the *Cruelty*, *Avarice*, *Ambition*, or *Caprice* of their Governours. Nor can any *Magistracy* be safe, or effectual for the ends of its Institution, where there are frequent Terrors of *Insurrections*.[123]

Hutcheson's concerns in this passage are reasonable enough, but the crucial question is whether he has provided the right means to their solution. It has been argued above that he has not; that, by his interpretation of the notion of a trust, he has effectively transferred the right of private judgement, and has thereby provided governments with a power more extensive than the rights of necessity require. He has thus substantially loosened the limits on the just exercise of political power implied by his Lockian point of

---

[122] Ibid. 282–3.   [123] Ibid. 298–9.

departure. He has legitimized the exercise of political virtues beyond the limits set by the constitutional foundations of the state.

The question then arises, Why cannot these virtues, if legitimate, actually ground political power? Hutcheson's answer is that the political virtues on which the legitimacy of extensions to the originally constituted political order depend—'*superior Wisdom*, or *Goodness*'—can give 'no *right* to Men to govern others'.[124] His reason is that 'no *Assumer* of Government, can so demonstrate his superior Wisdom or Goodness to the satisfaction and security of the Governed, as is necessary to their Happiness'.[125] If this is granted, it is not clear why the same reasoning should not also rule out extensions of power. For in both cases the same problem will arise: where the magistrate exercises power which does not promote (or, in the case of emergency, no longer promotes) the general happiness, what powers of redress are in the people's hands? Since both cases can be understood in terms of the alienation of the inalienable, how are they to be distinguished?

Hutcheson's tangles here can once again be traced to the conflicting tendencies of the moral sense viewpoint and the framework of Lockian political concepts. On the one hand, the doctrine of the benevolent moral sense provides a firm foundation of human sociability on which the law of nature can rest; on the other hand it champions the private judgement of benevolent individuals to such an extent that social rules become too readily defeasible. His successors did not fail to discern these instabilities, and so sought to modify his theory accordingly. The main alternatives were twofold: either reinterpret the nature and bearing of the moral sense itself, or limit its scope while at the same time enlarging the scope of reason, and thus of rational artifice.

Hume's response was to take the latter course. His account preserves the role of the moral sense in founding sociability, but stresses its limitations. He argues that human benevolent affections have only a very limited extent,[126] and that therefore justice

---

[124] *Inquiry*, 299–300.

[125] Ibid. 299. (Since, for Hutcheson, the same is not true of God's wisdom and goodness—which cannot be doubted—these virtues do suffice to justify the divine power.)

[126] His aim to shift the emphasis away from benevolence may help to explain some of his very emphatic remarks about the power of self-interest, or of the strict limitations on our benevolence. He says, for example, that the 'avidity . . . of acquiring goods and possessions for ourselves and our nearest friends is insatiable, perpetual,

depends on 'the steady prosecution of the rule',[127] not on the contextual judgements of the moral sense. Since steady rule-following depends on the sense of duty, Hume's task is to find a firm foundation for that sense, a foundation which cannot but be distinct from the moral sense. Reason must step in to augment and to order the limited and unsteady natural affections.

However, the reason on which Hume calls differs significantly from Hutchesonian rationality in an important respect. He abandons the teleology that is so evident a feature of Hutcheson's theory—of the *System* in particular.[128] So, for Hume, the question of what is natural to human beings, and therefore also of what is properly regarded as the law of nature, must be reviewed. He acknowledges this divide between his and Hutcheson's approaches in a letter to Hutcheson himself, written before the publication of Book III of the *Treatise*. He says there:

I cannot agree to your sense of *natural*. It is founded on final causes; which is a consideration, that appears to me pretty uncertain and unphilosophical. For pray, what is the end of man? Is he created for happiness or for virtue? For this life or for the next? For himself or for his Maker? Your definition of *natural* depends on solving these questions, which are endless, and quite wide of my purpose.[129]

This difference has, of course, substantial implications for the proper understanding of human nature and the law natural to it. The next chapter will examine Hume's attempt to establish the sense of duty independently of an 'unphilosophical' conception of nature, and of the law of nature.

universal, and directly destructive of society' (*Treatise*, 491–2). (In Adam Smith's hands, in the doctrine of the 'invisible hand', this avidity would come to be transformed into a force for social good.)

[127] *Treatise*, 497.

[128] The teleology is explicit in the very structure of the *System*. Bk. 1, pt. 2, is an enquiry into the supreme good of human nature, and the result of this enquiry is crucial to the whole direction of the moral argument.

[129] *The Letters of David Hume*, ed. Greig, letter no. 13 (17 Sept. 1739); also in Raphael (ed.), *British Moralists 1650–1800*, ii. 108–9.

5
David Hume

1. THE PROBLEM OF RECONCILIATION

The preceding chapter provides a sketch of how the concern for a psychology of action adequate to the requirements of natural law—that is, a theory of action which is both firmly founded in human nature, and which shows sociability as an essential expression of that nature—leads to the rejection of the 'selfish' aspect of Locke's psychology of action, while retaining its hedonism. By broadening the sources of pleasure to include the perception of beauty, and by providing an account of virtue in terms of the beauty of actions or characters, the theory of the moral sense attempts to provide a foundation for human sociability, as an adequate natural law theory must. But sociability is more than the mere desire for, or enjoyment of, human society. It also requires a social order which reflects the measure of human intelligence; and, of the elements of this order, it is justice—which most essentially means the rules of property—that is of most importance. But justice requires the following of a rule regardless of its consequences in particular cases (in Hutcheson's language, it requires the recognition of external rights), and where these consequences are contrary to benevolence the Hutchesonian moral sense theory cannot account for our obligation to be just. It cannot explain our sense of justice, of duty.

The burden of this chapter is that one central aim of Hume's moral and political theory is to solve this internal problem of natural jurisprudence, and that he can therefore be understood to be a contributor to natural law social theory. Before turning to the problems this view raises, it will be instructive to consider briefly the views of one of Hume's more sympathetic contemporary critics.

In the second of his *Essays on the Principles of Morality and Natural Religion* (1751), entitled 'Of the Foundation and Principles of the Law of Nature', Hume's friend and relative Henry Home, Lord Kames, argues, in typical natural law vein, that the law of nature is founded in human nature, and concludes that, for a complete account of natural law, 'it will be necessary to trace out human nature with all the accuracy possible'.[1] This leads him to give an account of the principles of human action, and, in order to account for our recognition of the beauty of the actions and characters of free agents, a recognition which leads us to praise and, in appropriate circumstances, to emulate them, he defends the reality of the moral sense. However, he criticizes all previous accounts of this sense, including Hutcheson's, for the reason already given. He then goes on to give an account of justice, and of our obligation to justice, which attempts to overcome the shortcomings of the previous theories. (One important insight of this account—the *negativity* of the virtue of justice—is later taken up, in considerably more detail, by Adam Smith.)[2]

Kames's principal target in his *Essays* is Hume's *Treatise*, published just over ten years earlier. But he does not attack Hume for abandoning natural law, nor does he consider the *Treatise* to be outside the context of the natural law debate. In fact, he sees 'the author of the treatise upon human nature'[3] as a contributor to the same debate. And, in the light of Hume's constructive programme—in the second and third books of the *Treatise*—it is easy to see why he should have thought so. For Hume's positive programme there is the same as Kames's in the *Essays*: to provide an account of the principles of action (as part of a more complete account of the constitution of the human passions, which are themselves the mainsprings of all human action), together with an account of the nature and origins of justice, with special attention to the nature of our obligation to obey its rules—the latter following a short section which both defends the moral sense and accepts that alone it cannot provide a complete account of our moral obligations. It is not surprising, then, that Kames should have considered Hume to be a contributor to the development of an adequate account of natural law. This chapter will argue that he was correct to think so.

---

[1] Lord Kames, *Essays on the Principles of Morality and Natural Religion* (1751) (New York: Garland Publishing, 1976), 42.

[2] Ibid. 59–61. Cf. A. Smith, *The Theory of Moral Sentiments*, ed. D. D. Raphael and A. L. Macfie (Oxford: Clarendon Press, 1976), ii. ii. 1. 9 ('justice is, upon most occasions, but a negative virtue') and ii. ii. 1. 5. Justice is a negative virtue in the sense that the moral sense (for Kames), or propriety (for Smith), recognizes the evil of injustice rather than the good of justice.

[3] Kames, *Essays*, 57.

To claim Hume as a contributor to natural law, however, seems to fly in the face of some well-established conceptions of Hume the philosopher. Of these, the conceptions of Hume as the Newtonian philosopher who introduced experimental reasoning into moral subjects,[4] or as the sceptical destroyer of all established philosophy, are here the most pertinent. So, before defending the natural law interpretation of Hume—mainly by showing why he should have described his theory of justice as akin to that of Grotius, and by showing in what way justice is artificial rather than natural—it will first be necessary to show how, or to what extent, a natural law interpretation is compatible with these established conceptions.

At this point it is appropriate to acknowledge that, in defending a natural law interpretation of Hume, I am following a lead established by Duncan Forbes in *Hume's Philosophical Politics*.[5] Further, more specific, debts will become clear along the way. The task itself, of reconciling, as far as possible, the various conceptions of Hume's philosophy, can now be turned to. The picture of Hume as the Newtonian philosopher presents the fewer problems, so it is best considered first.

2. THE NEWTONIAN

Hume owes his reputation as the Newtonian philosopher to his intention, expressed on the title-page of the *Treatise*, 'to introduce the experimental method of reasoning into moral subjects'. At a rather superficial level, this intention leads Hume to engage in the 'thought experiments' of the *Treatise*; more importantly, it is reflected in a self-conscious methodology, involving in particular commitments to the principle of parsimony, and to grounding all conclusions firmly in experience. To illustrate the latter first. In the *Abstract* of the *Treatise* he (indirectly) describes his overall aim in these terms: ''tis at least worth while to try if the science of man will not admit of the same accuracy which several parts of natural philosophy are found susceptible of.'[6] To secure this end, the

---

[4] As the title-page of the *Treatise* announces, *Treatise*, p. xi.

[5] D. Forbes, *Hume's Philosophical Politics* (Cambridge: Cambridge University Press, 1975).

[6] *An Abstract of a Book lately Published; entituled, A Treatise of Human Nature, &c.*, in *Treatise*, 645.

author of the *Treatise* 'proposes to anatomize human nature in a regular manner, and promises to draw no conclusions but where he is authorized by experience. He talks with contempt of hypotheses . . .'[7] The final remark here echoes Newton's statement in the *Opticks* that 'hypotheses are not to be regarded in experimental philosophy'.[8] However, reconciling it with what Hume actually does say about 'hypotheses' in the *Treatise* (where, particularly in Book II, he uses it in much the way we would use a term like 'theory'),[9] requires a good deal of constructive interpretation.

His principal intention is, apparently, to reject a priori principles.[10] An example can be found at the end of the *Enquiry concerning Human Understanding*, where the ancient maxim, *ex nihilo, nihil fit*, is dealt a summary execution: it 'ceases to be a maxim, according to this philosophy'.[11] The same requirement, that all knowledge be grounded firmly in experience, is not to be restricted to natural enquiries, but must occur in morals as well. This is succinctly expressed in the *Enquiry concerning the Principles of Morals*:

Men are now cured of their passion for hypotheses and systems in natural philosophy, and will hearken to no arguments but those which are derived from experience. It is full time they should attempt a like reformulation in all moral disquisitions; and reject every system of ethics, however subtle or ingenious, which is not founded on fact and observation.[12]

The method to be followed requires, according to the *Treatise*, 'a cautious observation of human life . . . in the common course of the world'.[13] The fruit of such labour will be a new science: 'Where experiments of this kind are judiciously collected and compared, we may hope to establish on them a science, which will not be inferior in certainty, and will be much superior in utility to any other of human comprehension.'[14]

These statements can serve to indicate, in broad outline, the nature and aims of Hume's first Newtonian feature, his 'experimentalism'. His second significantly Newtonian principle is parsimony, or as he usually describes it, simplicity. This is illustrated in the opening

---

[7] Ibid. 646.
[8] Quoted in J. Passmore, *Hume's Intentions* (London: Duckworth, 3rd edn., 1980), 45.
[9] Ibid.
[10] For a more detailed discussion, see ch. 3 of Passmore, *Hume's Intentions*.
[11] *Enquiries*, 164.   [12] Ibid. 174–5.
[13] *Treatise*, p. xix.   [14] Ibid.

sections of Book II of the *Treatise*, where he observes that 'we find in the course of nature, that tho' the effects be many, the principles, from which they arise, are commonly but few and simple, and that 'tis the sign of an unskilful naturalist to have recourse to a different quality, in order to explain every different operation'.[15] He adds that, because this principle is so rarely observed, 'moral philosophy is in the same condition as natural, with regard to astronomy before the time of *Copernicus*'.[16] He also invokes this principle in Book III to defend the account given of the role of sympathy in moral judgements.[17] In the *Abstract*, the task of natural philosophy is described as finding 'those few simple principles, on which all the rest depend'.[18] The *Abstract* goes on to place the *Treatise*'s contribution to natural philosophy in its demonstration that 'all the operations of the mind must, in a great measure, depend' on the three principles of the association of ideas; adding that ''tis the use he makes of the principle of the association of ideas', showing it to be one of those few simple principles, that can 'intitle the author to so glorious a name as that of an *inventor*'.[19] Once again, however, the clearest statement is in the *2nd Enquiry*—a work which, unlike the *Treatise*, also attempts to display a simplicity of intellectual structure. The account of the role of utility in the social virtues is there justified on the ground that 'It is entirely agreeable to the rules of philosophy, and even common reason; where any principle has been found to have a great force and energy in one instance, to ascribe to it a like energy in all similar instances. This indeed is Newton's chief rule of philosophizing.'[20]

Despite these remarks, Hume displays a measure of agreement with critics of the Newtonian passion for simple principles. For example, Berkeley criticized the tendency of Newtonian science to encourage 'that eagerness of the mind, whereby it is carried to extend its knowledge to general theorems',[21] and in the *1st Enquiry* Hume allows that moralists, in their 'search for some common principle' on which moral sentiments might depend, 'have sometimes carried the matter too far, by their passion for some one general

---

[15] *Treatise*, 282; and cf. also p. 473, for example.
[16] Ibid.   [17] Ibid. 578, 580, 588.
[18] *Abstract*, in *Treatise*, 646.
[19] Ibid. 661–2.
[20] *Enquiries*, 204. The reference is to Newton's *Principia*, Bk. III. Cf. Passmore, *Hume's Intentions*, esp. 43–4.
[21] G. Berkeley, *Principles of Human Knowledge*, para. 106 (quoted in Passmore, *Hume's Intentions*, 44).

principle'.[22] In this case, he probably has in mind the type of objection raised by Hutcheson against the determination of some moral theorists—particularly Mandeville—to ground all moral distinctions in self-love. In the Preface to *An Essay on the Nature and Conduct of the Passions and Affections*, Hutcheson claims that the drive for simplicity commonly causes a blindness to the relevant facts: 'Some strange love of simplicity in the structure of human nature . . . has engaged many writers to pass over a great many simple Perceptions which we may find in ourselves.'[23] It is most likely that Hume has some such caveat in mind when, in the *2nd Enquiry*'s appendix on self-love he remarks that the 'selfish hypothesis' in morals arises from a determination to reduce all appearances to a single cause. The passage in question is this: 'All attempts of this kind have hitherto proved fruitless, and seem to have proceeded entirely from that love of *simplicity* which has been the source of much false reasoning in philosophy.'[24] To restrict the scope of this remark to the limited context suggested, rather than allowing it to imply a wider methodological commitment—in contrast to the case of Berkeley—is necessary if Hume is not to be caught in self-contradiction. For, only a few pages later in the same appendix, Hume says that 'if we consider rightly of the matter', we would prefer his view to the 'selfish hypothesis' because it 'has really more *simplicity* in it, and is more conformable to the analogy of nature'.[25] So, despite the above remark, Hume does not back away from the search for parsimonious explanation. He does adhere to 'Newton's chief rule of philosophizing', even though, following Hutcheson, he sometimes cautions against pressing it too hard.

Hume's Newtonianism, then, consists chiefly in his adherence to two principal elements of the experimental method—the search for simple general causes, and the determination to found all doctrines on fact and observation. He aims, through the practice of this method, to develop a moral science with the same levels of accuracy as, but with much greater utility than, the philosophy of nature. This moral science would be founded on the science of human nature, because human nature is 'the capital or centre of these sciences'. In fact, he says,

---

[22] *Enquiries*, 15.

[23] F. Hutcheson, *Essay on the Nature and Conduct of the Passions and Affections* (3rd edn., 1742), p. ix (quoted by Selby-Bigge, *Enquiries*, p. xxiv).

[24] *Enquiries*, 298.   [25] Ibid. 301.

There is no question of importance, whose decision is not compriz'd in the science of man; and there is none, which can be decided with any certainty, before we become acquainted with that science. In pretending therefore to explain the principles of human nature, we in effect propose a compleat system of the sciences, built on a foundation almost entirely new, and the only one upon which they can stand with any security.[26]

Hume's Newtonianism can be summed up as a commitment to some central features of Newton's method, in order to produce a new moral science grounded firmly in human nature.

In practice, Hume may not always have conformed with these explicit ideals, but that need not concern us here. The important question is whether these ideals are in any way inconsistent, or even incongruous, with the central principles of natural law. The first clue that they are not is provided by Hume himself in the paragraph immediately following the passage quoted above. For, although his talk of building on a new foundation may suggest he is attempting to tread a course hitherto untrodden, he acknowledges that his aim is to advance an enterprise already underway; an enterprise initiated by 'some late philosophers in *England*, who have begun to put the science of man on a new footing'.[27] The 'late philosophers' in question (not then all dead, incidentally) are indicated in a footnote: 'Mr. *Locke*, my Lord *Shaftsbury*, Dr. *Mandeville*, Mr. *Hutchinson*, Dr. *Butler*, &c.'[28] As Forbes notes, this list is something of a mixed bag, with some surprising omissions.[29] However, the surprising absences are not (*pace* Forbes) Berkeley, Descartes, and Malebranche. Not being English—and hence exceptions to Hume's claim, much developed in his later *Essays*,[30] that 'the improvements in reason and philosophy can only be owing to a land of toleration and of liberty'[31]—the omission of the latter pair is the least surprising; but all three fail to conform to the requirements of the experimental method, at least as Hume understands it. Descartes's search for 'clear and distinct ideas' rather than for empirical evidence, Malebranche's occasionalism about causes, Berkeley's rejection of simple general explanations— all these are doctrines which fail the 'experimental' standard. However, Forbes correctly stresses the omission of Hobbes: although his conclusions hardly commend his inclusion in a list

[26] *Treatise*, p. xvi.   [27] Ibid. p. xvii.   [28] Ibid.
[29] Forbes, *Hume's Philosophical Politics*, 8–9.
[30] Cf., in particular, 'Of Refinement in the Arts'.   [31] *Treatise*, p. xvii.

intended to show the virtues of a land of liberty, his approach is adequately experimental. In all probability, there is a simple reason for the omission: Hobbes is rather too early a figure to illustrate Hume's view that moral philosophy, in the modern as in the ancient world, comes to flourish 'at the distance of above a whole century' after the establishment of a new natural philosophy.[32] Hobbes can thus be classed as a notable precursor of the important recent philosophers, a solution which has the happy implication that his less palatable doctrines can be attributed to the merely partial view possible at his too-early stage in the revolution in philosophical method.

For the purposes of this study, the important thing about Hume's list is that, with the exception of Mandeville, these are not philosophers antipathetic to the natural law tradition. So Hume's support for philosophers who have embraced the experimental method in morals cannot be spelt out in terms of shared opposition to natural law. There is a good reason for this: typically, seventeenth- and eighteenth-century philosophers saw no tension between the aims of natural law and experimental philosophy. In fact, a number of philosophers deeply embedded in the natural law tradition explicitly avow the advantages, even the necessity, of the new experimental science. The 'late philosopher' Hutcheson is an instructive example. He sees no barrier between natural law and experimental philosophy, and identifies the task appropriate to natural law theory as the development of a science of human nature through the adoption of the experimental method. This is shown in the *Short Introduction*, where he describes the task of natural law as follows:

All such as believe that this universe, and human nature in particular, was formed by the wisdom and counsel of a Deity, must expect to find in our structure and frame some clear evidences, showing the proper business of mankind, for what course of life, what offices we are furnished by the providence and wisdom of our Creator, and what are the proper means of happiness. We must therefore search accurately into the constitution of our nature, to see what sort of creatures we are . . . [33]

How should we conduct this search? Hutcheson clearly has in mind an empirical investigation:

[32] Ibid., p. xvi.
[33] F. Hutcheson, *Short Introduction* (1747), 2.

Now the intention of nature with respect to us, is best known by examining what these things are which our natural senses or perceptive powers recommend to us, and what the most excellent among them? . . . In this art, as in all others, we must proceed from the subjects most easily known, to those that are more obscure; . . . and therefore don't deduce our first notions of duty from the divine Will; but from the constitution of our nature, which is more immediately known . . . [34]

Hutcheson shows the same commitment to empirical enquiry, as a necessary feature of natural law theory, in the *System*. In the opening paragraph of that work, he says: 'The intention of moral philosophy is to direct men to that course of action which tends most effectually to promote their greatest happiness and perfection.'[35] The proper method to be followed is 'as far as it can be done by observations and conclusions discoverable from the constitution of nature, without any aids of supernatural revelation: these maxims, or rules of conduct are therefore reputed as laws of nature, and the system or collection of them is called the LAW OF NATURE'.[36] Of course, it may be thought that, since these works by Hutcheson were published *after* the *Treatise*, they may express views designed to defend natural law against the inroads of Newtonian philosophy. However, although it is not impossible that Hutcheson's position in these passages shows Hume's influence, there is no good reason to think he is engaged in a rearguard action against experimental philosophy, rather than simply taking advantage of the resources it provides for better philosophical understanding. The important fact is that Hutcheson's position in these passages is not atypical of contemporary natural law philosophers. This is clearly illustrated by the case of George Turnbull.

The year 1740 saw the publication of Book III of the *Treatise*. In the same year, George Turnbull published his *Principles of Moral Philosophy*. This work announced its aim to be to 'vindicate' human nature. It would do so 'by reducing the more remarkable appearances in the human system' to 'general laws', and by avoiding any hypotheses not grounded firmly in experience. It further held that moral philosophy is not simply a system of facts discovered by observation; like natural philosophy, it is a matter of experiments and reasonings from experiments. If this method is not followed, the result is 'mere' hypotheses. Given this much, it then comes as no

---

[34] F. Hutcheson, *Short Introduction* (1747), 2.
[35] *System*, i. 1.   [36] Ibid.

surprise to be referred to Newton's *Principia*.[37] Turnbull amplifies
these methodological remarks in another work, published the
following year: an edition of one of the well-known natural law texts
of the period,[38] Heineccius's *Methodical System of Universal Law*.
Turnbull not only translated Heineccius, but provided also
extensive annotations, and appended a discourse on the nature and
origin of moral and civil laws. In the Preface, he describes the
appended discourse as 'an attempt to introduce the experimental
way of reasoning into morals, or to deduce human duties from
internal principles and dispositions in the human mind'. The duties
in question are those universal laws which underlie all civil laws:
they are the natural law.[39]

Hume's enthusiasm for the experimental method, since it is
shared with philosophers firmly in the natural law tradition, thus
cannot be taken to be a step away from natural law. The natural
jurists seem to have had much the same reaction to the new
experimental method as the philosophers of nature (the physical
scientists). They enthusiastically adopted the new method, because
its refinements promised more accurate results, and therefore
greater possibility of success in achieving their end: an accurate
specification of the rules of conduct appropriate to human life.
Hume's ambitions are thus, in this respect, unremarkable. The
common picture of Hume the Newtonian philosopher does not rule
out or even discourage the view that he was, and understood himself
to be, a contributor to a more complete and accurate natural law
account of human society.

A shared enthusiasm for the experimental method should not,
however, blind us to an important difference between Hutcheson
and Turnbull on the one hand, and Hume on the other. This
difference cuts very deeply, since it concerns the actual requirements
of the experimental method. Both Hutcheson and Turnbull speak
of an enquiry into the constitution of our nature, and by this mean
the task of discerning the extent and limits of characteristic human
powers and excellences, so that the specific requirements for human

[37] G. Turnbull, *Principles of Moral Philosophy* (1740), pp. ii, iv, 19, 20, 22. My own source is Forbes, *Hume's Philosophical Politics*, 1, on whose account I have relied heavidly in this paragraph.
[38] Cf. K. Haakonssen, 'Natural Law and the Scottish Enlightenment', in D. H. Jory and C. Stewart-Robinson (eds.), *Man and Nature* (Edmonton: Academic Printing and Publishing, 1985), 52–3.
[39] Forbes, *Hume's Philosophical Politics*, 1–2.

happiness can be determined. What is envisaged can perhaps be described, rather broadly, as a biological enquiry which aims to determine the *telos* of human beings. Their experimental method is thus a method for determining a final cause. Hume's objection to the role of final causes in Hutcheson's scheme has already been mentioned, and so his conception of the experimental method deliberately avoids any such element. To conduct the 'science of man' properly, he holds, we must eschew all concern with ultimate principles. Instead, 'We must . . . glean up our experiments in this science from a cautious observation of human life, and take them as they appear in the common course of the world, by men's behaviour in company, in affairs, and in their pleasures.'[40] Although he does not spell the issue out in just these terms, Hume's view amounts to a commitment to uncover the efficient causes of human behaviour, including moral and political behaviour. It will be argued below that his contributions to moral and political theory should be understood in this light.

Nevertheless, he is not always consistently anti-teleological. To take just one example: his famous remark that 'reason is, and *ought only to be* the slave of the passions'[41] shows him to remain under the influence of a conception of human nature which goes beyond the merely observable to the idea of a harmoniously functioning system with its own distinctive *telos*. Such teleological elements may of course be mere fragments or relics, and as such could be discarded to the profit of the whole. If so, the difference between Hume's contemporaries' and his own experimental method would be precisely the presence or otherwise of teleology. However, this still would not be sufficient to distinguish Hume's theory from natural law, since not even the main natural law theories are all uniformly teleological. Grotius's is a case in point; and this may go some way to explaining Hume's willingness to acknowledge a pronounced Grotian debt. But it also shows that Hume's explicit experimentalism, even when conceived more narrowly to exclude teleology, fails to separate his theory from natural law.[42]

---

[40] *Treatise*, p. xix.

[41] Ibid. 415 (emphasis added).

[42] Peter Jones has argued that Hume's Newtonianism has been considerably overrated. He argues that, despite the appeal to Newtonian principles, 'Hume's own philosophical reflections led away from Newton'. See P. Jones, *Hume's Sentiments: Their Ciceronian and French Context* (Edinburgh: Edinburgh University Press, 1982), 19.

3. THE SCEPTIC

The question of Hume's scepticism is much more difficult to resolve. This is principally because scepticism of some form is very close to the heart of Hume's philosophy, so that no attempt to explain it can avoid conclusions about the nature or extent of his scepticism. The problem is, however, that there is room for disagreement over both the nature and the significance of his scepticism. Different interpretations of Hume's philosophy usually differ on precisely this point, not least because the stance taken on this question typically shapes the whole picture of Hume's intellectual activity. Nevertheless, recent work on Hume has shown a discernible tendency to reduce the emphasis placed on his scepticism, at least as it has tended to be understood. One important reason for this tendency has been the attempt to recover the historical Hume from his latter-day ideological career. For much of this century, the interpretation of Hume has been conducted in the context of explaining and justifying positivism. Beatified as a precursor of positivism, Hume has been studied, in the main, by positivists and for positivists. As a result, attention has principally been focused on those parts of Hume's philosophy which most easily lend themselves to positivist concerns. Hume scholarship has thus been excessively influenced by a preconceived idea of its object, and, by selective attention, the philosopher has been found to fit the preconception. So the first important step towards an adequate understanding of Hume is to free him from his posthumous role of positivist saint.

The second, no less important, step is to remove the spectacles ground out by post-Kantian philosophy: the conception that philosophy consists of a core—composed of logic, metaphysics, and epistemology—which is then applied to other, more practical, areas of endeavour. This second preconception has two important consequences for the interpretation of Hume. Firstly, it picks out Book I of the *Treatise*—and, if one is prepared to slum it a little, the *1st Enquiry* as well—as the core of his philosophy. In this way the monument to the positivist saint is fenced off from other, uninteresting, images of the philosopher. Secondly, because Hume's sceptical metaphysics is conjoined with a decidedly non-sceptical philosophy of morals, politics, and 'criticism'[43]—which shows that Hume's own view of his larger philosophy was not the application of a sceptical core to practical affairs—the view has been encouraged that, where he is not being a sceptical metaphysician, Hume is either confused or disingenuous, a charlatan who has sacrificed his principles to his self-confessed 'ruling passion', his 'love of literary fame'.[44] In either case, his corpus cannot be considered a great philosophy; and Hume himself may be regarded as a great philosopher only if attention is charitably restricted to *Treatise*, Book I, the core of his work.

By remembering that Hume was neither a precocious positivist nor a pupil of the modern philosophical curriculum, recent Hume scholarship has been able to loosen the grip of these distorting preconceptions. Most importantly, it has recognized the need to approach Hume's work as a whole, thereby returning attention to previously neglected works, or parts of works. The result of this clearing operation has not been a consensus, but it is true to say that there has been a distinct tendency either to shift the emphasis away from scepticism, or to reinterpret its meaning or extent. Once this has been done, Hume's particular brand of scepticism is shown to be more limited than may have been expected, and therefore also less damaging to the natural jurists' point of view.[45]

The important difference between the Humean and more recent employments of the notion of scepticism is well brought out by John Wright. In his book *The Sceptical Realism of David Hume*, he says:

the present-day notion of scepticism leaves no room for an understanding of the sense in which Hume himself *is* a sceptic. Hume is a sceptic because he thinks that our fundamental beliefs about reality and our inferring procedures cannot be derived solely from scientific investigation; rather, he thinks that they derive from man as a natural organism.[46]

This could appear to be beside the point, but this is because it is easy to overlook the important difference that

[43] That is, aesthetic judgement (see *Treatise*, pp. xv–xvi). The principal vehicle of these concerns is the *Essays*, where Hume also includes some more purely literary essays, e.g. 'The Platonist', 'The Epicurean', 'Of the Delicacy of Taste and Passion'.

[44] 'My Own Life', in *Essays*, i. 8.

[45] See esp. D. F. Norton, *David Hume: Common-Sense Moralist, Sceptical Metaphysician* (Princeton: Princeton University Press, 1982).

[46] J. P. Wright, *The Sceptical Realism of David Hume* (Manchester: Manchester University Press, 1983), 32.

Philosophical scepticism as it appears in the writings of David Hume is not primarily a philosophy of knowledge (a philosophy of science) nor a philosophy of nature (a general metaphysic): it is a philosophy of man. Hume was mainly interested in the philosophy of knowing in so far as it tells us about the knowing being himself.[47]

In the same spirit, it is possible to add that he was also interested in the philosophy of action (that is, in the eighteenth-century sense, in moral philosophy) in so far as it tells us about the active being himself. Thus, Wright concludes,

Instead of being primarily interested in justified or true belief he is interested in the source of belief as such. Instead of being primarily interested in right action he is interested in the source of action as such.[48]

This last remark is something of an oversimplification, because Hume is very interested in virtuous action. Even so, it correctly serves to pick out that Hume's concern with virtuous actions is as a species of *actions*, and is not simply an enquiry into the nature of the good. The central concern of his moral philosophy is with the source of virtuous action. Hume's philosophy of man, and thus also his philosophy of knowing, is sceptical because it affirms both that we hold mutually contradictory beliefs, and that we employ opposed principles in arriving at different, but equally indispensable, beliefs.[49]

Thus understood, Hume's scepticism is not at odds with another recently emphasised feature of his larger philosophy—his Ciceronian humanism.[50] The Ciceronian connection is signalled, most prominently, in the letter to Francis Hutcheson quoted above (at the end of Chapter 4). He says there, referring to Cicero's *De Officiis*, 'I had, indeed, the former book in my eye in all my reasonings.'[51] Although this remark should be treated very carefully—the reasonings referred to are not his complete works, but at most the *Treatise*, and perhaps only Book III—other Ciceronian themes are visible in his stress on the social dimensions of human life, the unacceptability of a destructive 'total' scepticism, and on the consequent need for a

---

[47] Ibid. 30.   [48] Ibid. 32.   [49] Ibid. 31.

[50] This feature of his thought has been particularly emphasized in Jones, *Hume's Sentiments*.

[51] Letter of 17 Sept. 1739, *The Letters of David Hume*, ed. J. Y. T. Greig (Oxford: Oxford University Press, 1932). Ramsay's portrait of Hutcheson nicely catches the difference stressed by Hume in the letter: in the portrait, Hutcheson holds a copy of Cicero's *De Finibus*.

more limited form of scepticism which would encourage moderation in the conduct of one's life.[52] This last feature, the necessity of a mitigated scepticism, is obviously very important, but alone it will not explain Hume's philosophy. This can be shown by examining a recent interpretation which follows just this strategy. It will then be possible to show that, by filling out the distinctive early eighteenth-century content of his notion of moderation, a better account of Hume's overall aims can be provided.

Hume often commends forms of limited scepticism. For example, at one point he distinguishes 'true philosophers' by their 'moderate scepticism',[53] and at several places in the *1st Enquiry* he recommends the perspective provided by a 'mitigated' scepticism.[54] Passages such as these have encouraged David Miller to discern a thread of mitigated scepticism running through Hume's corpus.[55] However, if we restrict ourselves to considering Hume's explicit remarks on mitigated scepticism, this turns out to be a rather unenlightening hypothesis.

In the *1st Enquiry*, Hume distinguishes two kinds of mitigated scepticism. The second is the less important: he describes it as 'the limitation of our enquiries to such subjects as are best adapted to the narrow capacity of human understanding'.[56] This variety provides a clue to the sometimes forgotten question of the purpose of Hume's metaphysical scepticism—*inter alia*, to demonstrate the inevitable absurdities that arise when the narrow limits of human understanding are not observed. However, it achieves little more than this. It fails to distinguish Hume's position from others not normally classed as sceptical—Locke's, for example. In fact, scepticism of this form is so limited it scarcely seems to deserve the name: a practising sceptic of this kind, who faithfully keeps within the necessary bounds of human understanding, can happily espouse the most non-sceptical of views on all topics that fall within those bounds. Even the most unimaginative of souls, who spend their lives without expressing anything more than commonplace views on commonplace subjects, appear to qualify as mitigated sceptics in this sense. To take the case of Hume himself, this form of mitigated scepticism would be

---

[52] All these features are stressed by Jones, *Hume's Sentiments*, 29–43.
[53] See *Treatise*, 224.
[54] See e.g. *Enquiries*, 161–2.
[55] D. Miller, *Philosophy and Ideology in Hume's Political Thought* (Oxford: Clarendon Press, 1981).
[56] *Enquiries*, 162.

exhibited by his essays on morals, politics, and aesthetics irrespective of their content. The subject-matter alone guarantees his sceptical credentials. So, while this type of mitigated scepticism helps to explain why Hume wrote essays on morals, politics, and aesthetics, it is of no help whatever in explaining why those essays express the views they do.

The other form of mitigated scepticism has more interpretative value, but equally cannot stand alone as an explanatory device. It is the maintenance of an undogmatic spirit. Hume describes it as the recognition that 'there is a degree of doubt, and caution, and modesty, which, in all kinds of scrutiny and decision, ought for ever to accompany a just reasoner'.[57] His practice of the principle appears less than perfect: the concluding section of the *2nd Enquiry* both avows and manifests it,[58] but it appears to be forgotten in the concluding paragraph of the *1st Enquiry*, where Hume's main epistemological principles lead him to recommend a biblioclastic orgy which, as John Passmore observes, ought not to exclude the *1st Enquiry* itself![59]

Outside these cases, scepticism of this form provides little help in interpreting Hume's work. Although some insights can be gained, they are not of any great power or detail. For example, it is able to provide reasons for Hume's preference for the polite essay over the traditional styles of academic treatise. As Phillipson observes, Hume's attachment to the essay form is more than mere convenience. He deliberately exploits its virtues to create 'a sophisticated and flexible mode of moral discourse, capable of attracting an intelligent salon and coffee-house readership as well as philosophers and men of letters'.[60] It also helps to explain a good deal of his practice in the specifically political essays (at least), where he undermines the more pretentious claims of Whig and Tory alike, typically coming to settle on a 'middling' position of some sort. In a letter to Kames, referring to his essay 'Of the Protestant Succession', he says that 'the conclusion shows me a Whig, but a very sceptical one'.[61] Nevertheless, these essays can be explained at

---

[57] Ibid.

[58] Ibid. 278.

[59] *Enquiries*, 165. Cf. J. Passmore, *Philosophical Reasoning* (London: Duckworth, 1961), ch. 1.

[60] N. Phillipson, 'Adam Smith as Civic Moralist', in I. Hont and M. Ignatieff (eds.), *Wealth and Virtue* (Cambridge: Cambridge University Press, 1983), 180.

[61] Quoted in Grose's introd., 'History of the Editions', to Hume's *Essays*, i. 48.

least as well by stressing, as Forbes does, Hume's commitment to
the doctrine of moderation made famous by the third Earl of
Shaftesbury.

It will be remembered that Shaftesbury is one of the 'late
philosophers in *England*, who have begun to put the science of man
on a new footing' listed in the Introduction to the *Treatise*.[62] His
fame came to rest principally on the *Characteristics of Men,
Manners, Opinions, Times* (1711), a collection of works on virtue
and related subjects. In the *Characteristics*, Shaftesbury champions
the notion of moderation, and also sets out a political outlook he
takes to be characteristic of 'men of moderation'. The qualities of
such men are well caught by Forbes's summary: 'men who were too
secure of their temper and who possessed themselves too well "to be
in danger of entering warmly into any cause, or engaging deeply
with any side or faction" .'[63] The politics of such men he describes as
being 'the science of men united in society and dependent on each
other. This science was modern in style, suited to the circumstances
and interests of a modern, commercial society, informed by the new
scientific method and the predominantly secular outlook.'[64]

It is evident that Hume would be temperamentally suited to this
view.[65] It is also clear that he has the concept frequently in mind in
the *Essays*—for example, when he speaks of the necessity of
moderating the zeal of party-men,[66] observing along the way that
'moderation is not to be expected in party-men of any kind',[67] and so
on. More importantly, the idea of the moderate man, as expounded by
Shaftesbury, can explain some of Hume's most spectacularly non-
sceptical views, such as his great optimism about the benefits to be
secured by the development of commerce, and by the refinement of
the arts in general. On these subjects, Hume is so removed from a
sceptical view of the consequences of promoting commerce and
refinement in the arts it is tempting to charge him with 'enthusiasm'—
a quality which, in another context, he attributes principally to hope, a

---

[62] *Treatise*, p. xvii.
[63] Forbes, *Hume's Philosophical Politics*, 91.
[64] Ibid.; cf. *Treatise*, p. xv.
[65] Cf. Adam Smith's eulogistic remarks, in a letter to William Strahan
immediately after Hume's death, that Hume's 'constant pleasantry was the genuine
effusion of good-nature and good-humour, tempered with delicacy and modesty,
and without even the slightest tincture of malignity', etc.; in *Essays*, i. 13.
[66] *Essays*, i. 107–8. Cf. also *Treatise*, 559 n.
[67] Ibid. 121. See also 126, 162, 184 n, 300, 464, 469, 475, 478.

warm imagination, and ignorance![68] Admittedly, this would be more than a little unfair, since 'enthusiasm' also involves the quite un-Humean characteristic of blindness to argument. Nevertheless he is anything but a sceptic on this question. In the economic writings his great optimism renders any sceptical tag, even the most mitigated, thoroughly inappropriate: his main thesis is 'that the ages of refinement are both the happiest and the most virtuous'.[69] Even comparatively he is quite the optimist, lacking many of the misgivings of other leading figures of the Scottish Enlightenment. To take the obvious example: Adam Smith, frequently perceived as an enthusiastic advocate of commercial development, is considerably more cautious than Hume (even, at times, pessimistic) about the consequences likely to flow from refinement in the arts of production and exchange.[70]

Hume's optimistic appraisal of the benefits to be achieved through the further development of commerce and the productive arts is clearly at odds with mitigated scepticism in the second (tighter) sense, showing nothing of the 'degree of doubt, and caution' that constitutes such scepticism. So, even the figure of Hume the mitigated sceptic is inadequate to explain this conspicuous feature of his outlook. An adequate explanation would need to invoke the more complex figure of Hume the man of moderation, a man who incorporates many of the characteristics of mitigated scepticism, but more besides. It is also evident that the modern, secular style of such a man accords well with the figure of the Newtonian. So it is worth considering how Hume's Newtonianism and scepticism both contribute towards a philosophy of human life, that is, towards a philosophical defence of human practice.

In so far as Hume is a Newtonian, he is not sceptical. The commitment to retain only principles firmly grounded in experience or reasonings from experience is not *per se* sceptical, even if a strict adherence to such principles would inevitably produce conclusions which, to the intellectual world of the eighteenth century, displayed a decidedly sceptical countenance. The Newtonian position is

[68] 'Of Superstition and Enthusiasm', ibid. 145.
[69] 'Of Refinement in the Arts', ibid. 300.
[70] Cf. Forbes, *Hume's Philosophical Politics* 87–8. For a specific ex., compare Hume's untroubled optimism on the effect of the arts on martial spirit (*Essays*, i. 304), with Smith's views on martial spirit and standing armies after 'refinement', discussed in D. Winch, *Adam Smith's Politics* (Cambridge: Cambridge University Press, 1978), 103–20.

sceptical only in the sense that it holds the truth to be hard to come by, and certainly beyond the reach of mere speculative reasoning. It therefore involves a commitment to a rigorous methodology, so that error may be filtered out. However, it is more than this, as the stress on experience shows. The methodology is not without its own epistemological commitments, since there is no point to restricting methods of enquiry to experience and its fruits unless there is genuine benefit to be gained thereby. Hume's own explicit intention, of establishing a science of human nature which will provide the only secure foundation for 'a compleat system of the sciences',[71] makes little if any sense if the methods appropriate to establishing such a science do not themselves admit of *some* security.

Nevertheless the security Hume offers is rather thin. We trust to experience, he says, not because we have any sound arguments for doing so—in fact, we cannot have any such arguments, since our reasonings are themselves uncertain—but because we have no room for choice. We are simply compelled by nature—by *our* nature—to believe in the reality of our experience. Some of the most famous passages in Book I of the *Treatise* assert just this. For example, when discussing 'the sceptical philosophy', he points out that

the sceptic still continues to reason and believe, even tho' he asserts, that he cannot defend his reason by reason; and by the same rule he must assent to the principle concerning the existence of body, tho' he cannot pretend by any arguments of philosophy to maintain its veracity. Nature has not left this to his choice, and has doubtless esteem'd it an affair of too great importance to be trusted to our uncertain reasonings and speculations. We may well ask, *What causes induce us to believe in the existence of body?* but 'tis in vain to ask, *Whether there be body or not?* That is a point, which we must take for granted in all our reasonings.[72]

Perhaps more importantly for Hume's philosophy as a whole, it is also a point which we must take for granted in all our practice. He makes this point in the famous, but sometimes underestimated, passage in the conclusion to Book I, where the sceptical problem is taken up as his own problem. The melancholy condition to which scepticism reduces him is described as follows: 'to fancy myself in the most deplorable condition imaginable, environ'd with the

---

[71] *Treatise*, p. xvi.   [72] Ibid. 187; cf. *Enquiries*, 55.

deepest darkness, and utterly depriv'd of the use of every member and faculty.'[73] It is not, however, a permanent condition. Nature, particularly in the guise of ordinary life, provides the solution:

Most fortunately it happens, that since reason is incapable of dispelling these clouds, nature herself suffices to that purpose, and cures me of this philosophical melancholy and delirium, either by relaxing this bent of mind, or by some avocation, and lively impression of my senses, which obliterate all these chimeras. I dine, I play a game of back-gammon, I converse, and am merry with my friends; . . . Here then I find myself absolutely and necessarily determin'd to live, and talk, and act like other people in the common affairs of life.[74]

Nature, through the common affairs of human life, provides the effective foundation for all our thought and practice.

This is a theme to which Hume frequently returns throughout his writings, whether explicitly or implicitly. To help show just how persistent a theme it is, some examples are in order. Of the explicit examples, perhaps the best known is the observation in the *1st Enquiry* that 'custom . . . is the great guide of human life',[75] but in many places he appeals to the superior rationality of practice.[76] The theme is implicit, however, in both a great number and a great variety of locations in his writings. In the first place, it underlies his various accounts of the 'artificial' virtues—of justice, promises and contracts, and allegiance to government. It is shown in the concern with economic issues in Part 2 of the *Essays*, and in the use made of history in writing *The History of England*. Similarly, we may note the summary dismissal of 'any fine imaginary republic, of which a man may form a plan in his closet',[77] and the insistence that justice is

---

[73] *Treatise*, 269.

[74] Ibid. It is important to recognize here that by 'determin'd' Hume does not mean an act of will, but quite the opposite: he is *compelled by his (human) nature* to live, and talk, etc.

[75] *Enquiries*, 44.

[76] See esp. *Treatise*, 569: 'The practice of the world goes farther in teaching us the degrees of our duty, than the most subtile philosophy, which was ever yet invented.' Cf. also *Treatise*, 547, 552, 558; *Enquiries*, 201 n., 230, 236, 269; *Essays*, i. 126, 185, 292, 295, 374, 447–51, 460; and cf. also Adam Smith's *Lectures on Jurisprudence*, which further develop this line of thought.

[77] 'Whether the British Government inclines more to Absolute Monarchy, or to a Republic', *Essays*, i. 126; and cf. also 'Idea of a Perfect Commonwealth', ibid., esp. 480–1.

a slow growth,[78] which reflects the particular 'convenience and necessities of mankind',[79] and which 'acquires force . . . by our repeated experience of the inconveniences of transgressing it'.[80] These can all stand as examples of his commitment to ordinary life as the foundation on which human life, including reliable human knowing, depends. This practical foundation must also be kept in mind when interpreting the *2nd Enquiry's* frequent insistence on the role of utility. Hume does not invoke utility, as does the modern utilitarian, as an abstract principle by which any existing social institution or practice is to be judged. Rather, his view is that social institutions (at least, all those not corrupted by obscure metaphysics) necessarily reflect utility: to some degree at least, they must be founded in useful or practical considerations, because only such considerations are efficacious in ordinary life. On this point, he offers the supporting observation that even system-builders, when confronted with the task of providing rules for human life, have to resort to utility as their ultimate justification, whatever the requirements of their systems.[81]

This very compressed summary of some characteristic Humean doctrines provides a rough picture of Hume's philosophy of common life.[82] As a motto for this philosophy, none is better than his claim in the *Abstract*'s preface, that in matters of common life our knowledge is securely based, because we can there make '*an appeal to the people*, who in all matters of common reason and eloquence are found so infallible a tribunal'.[83] Further, by its stress on the superior rationality of human practice, Hume's philosophy of human nature is neatly conformable with the implicit commitment to rational practices, and thus to historical development, implicit in natural law accounts of human social institutions. The practical spirit of the *Treatise* thus provides one, if not the most important,

---

[78] *Treatise*, 490; cf. *Enquiries*, 192; and cf. also K. Haakonssen, *The Science of a Legislator: The Natural Jurisprudence of David Hume and Adam Smith* (Cambridge: Cambridge University Press, 1981), 17.

[79] *Enquiries*, 195.   [80] *Treatise*, 490.   [81] *Enquiries*, 195.

[82] See D. Livingston, *Hume's Philosophy of Common Life* (Chicago: University of Chicago Press, 1985).

[83] *Abstract*, in *Treatise*, 644. The happy situation in common life is contrasted with the very unhappy situation in metaphysics and theology, where we must depend on the judgement of the few, 'whose verdict is more apt to be corrupted by partiality and prejudice'. Also, as he says in a letter to Gilbert Elliot of Minto in 1751, in such abstract endeavours, 'nothing there can correct bad Reasoning but good Reasoning: and Sophistry must be oppos'd by Syllogism' (quoted in Norton, *David Hume*, 192).

reason for Kames's untroubled belief that Hume was to be understood as a contributor to the tradition of natural jurisprudence.

Others among Hume's contemporaries, however, understood him to be essentially sceptical, and therefore antipathetic to natural law. The alleged artificiality of the virtue of justice (in the broad sense, including rules of property, promise-keeping, and allegiance to government), and the greater importance attributed to the artificial, rather than the natural, virtues,[84] were the principal causes of this particular charge. This is well illustrated by a pamphlet circulated against him in Edinburgh in 1745, as part of a successful campaign to prevent his appointment to Edinburgh's Chair of Moral Philosophy. According to Hume's account, the pamphlet, *inter alia*, charged the author of the *Treatise* 'With sapping the Foundations of Morality, by denying the natural and essential Difference betwixt Right and Wrong, Good and Evil, Justice and Injustice; making the Difference only artificial, and to arise from human Conventions and Compacts.'[85] The fairness of this charge will be determined in the following two sections. It will be argued there that Hume's notion of an artificial virtue is not evidence of moral scepticism, but the simple adaptation of Pufendorf's distinction between natural and adventitious states in order to solve the twin problems of the origin of justice and of our obligation to observe the rules of justice. He is therefore best understood to be responding to a problem within the natural law tradition, a problem brought into sharp relief by the attempt to provide a psychology of action adequate to the requirements of natural law doctrines, and which he seeks to resolve by deploying conceptual resources provided by the tradition itself. The next two sections will seek to establish this broad claim. Section 4 will consider whether Hume's works show any evidence of destructive intentions, particularly addressing some aspects of his relationship to Grotius. Section 5 will show the artificiality of the virtue of justice to be derived from Hume's Newtonian project to establish the efficient causes of moral entities, by determining what, if any, are the 'original instincts' which give rise to the rules of property, and to the other elements of justice.

[84] *Treatise*, 590.
[85] Quoted by Hume in *A Letter from a Gentleman to his friend in Edinburgh* (1745), ed. E. C. Mossner and J. V. Price (Edinburgh: Edinburgh University Press, 1967), 18.

4. THE DIVISION OF THE VIRTUES: HUME'S INTENTIONS

For an adequate understanding of Hume's division of the virtues into the 'natural' and the 'artificial', it is not enough merely to spell out the explicit features of the distinction. Rather, it is necessary to ask why he thought the distinction important, and also what impact he intended (or hoped) his distinction would have on his readers. The two questions are not unrelated, since they focus on different aspects of the same general issue—the nature of Hume's intentions. Explaining these intentions is crucial if the general outlines of his philosophy, and Book III of the *Treatise* in particular, are not to be misunderstood. So this section will address two issues which help to throw light on Hume's intentions in moral philosophy.

The first requires only a brief treatment, because it poses in a general way a problem which will be considered in more detail in the next section. It is the question of the somewhat curious structure of Book III itself. The issue is best indicated by summarizing the subdivisions of the text and the topics covered there. It is also best explained by clarifying the reasons for the structure being as it is.

In part 1, entitled 'Of Virtue and Vice in General', it is argued that moral distinctions derive not from reason, but from a moral sense. The first of the two sections rehearses a set of arguments against the ethical rationalists—including, for example, Samuel Clarke and William Wollaston—all of whom explained moral goodness in terms of conformity with some abstract rational relation.[86] The section concludes with an 'observation' which Hume admits he 'cannot forbear adding'[87]—the famous (and, as I shall endeavour to show, in some respects undeservedly famous) 'is–ought' passage. The second section is quite surprising. It quickly reaches its main conclusion, that because moral distinctions are perceptions, they are impressions rather than ideas, and that morality is therefore 'more properly felt than judg'd of'.[88] Immediately it stresses how little is gained by this result. The 'in a manner, infinite' number and variety of our moral duties is itself sufficient to show this, since ''tis absurd to imagine, that in every particular instance, these sentiments are produc'd by an *original*

---

[86] Cf. Francis Hutcheson's arguments against the same views in *Illustrations on the Moral Sense* (1728), *Collected Works*, ii.

[87] *Treatise*, 469.   [88] Ibid. 470.

quality and *primary* constitution'.[89] The supposition is absurd
because it would render all moral education unnecessary by
reducing moral behaviour to the purely instinctive, and the
absurdity is evidenced by the implication that we are pre-
programmed to respond appropriately to the greatly diverse and
variable situations which call for moral assessment and action. As
Hume notes, this view also runs directly counter to the principles of
simplicity championed by the experimental method: 'Such a
method of proceeding is not conformable to the usual maxims, by
which nature is conducted, where a few principles produce all that
variety we observe in the universe, and everything is carry'd on in
the easiest and most simple manner.'[90] Consequently, the conclusion
reached above, that morality derives from a 'moral sense'—a
primary impulse or constitution—is of rather little value. Rather, to
explain moral notions successfully, ''Tis necessary . . . to abridge
these primary impulses, and find some more general principles,
upon which all our notions of morals are founded'.[91] Hume
proposes that these more general principles may be found in 'the
designs, and projects, and views of men', since these 'are principles
as necessary in their operation as heat and cold, moist and dry'.
However, since it is usual for us to set our own activities 'in
opposition to the other principles of nature' simply because they are
our own, the fruit of our choices and actions, it follows that to locate
general principles of morals in human activity is, in one sense at
least, to deny them a natural foundation. Moral distinctions
founded in human social practices can therefore be called artificial
virtues.[92]

In part 2, entitled 'Of Justice and Injustice', Hume's aim is to
establish that many of our most established virtues *are* artificial in
the sense outlined. These include justice (which, first and foremost,
means abstaining from the property of others), promise-keeping,
allegiance to government, laws of nations (international justice),
and the characteristically female virtues of chastity and modesty.
These virtues, because grounded in human social practices, have
two important features. The first is that it is not individual acts but
the whole system of such acts that has value. The second is the
central role of reason in the determination of these virtues, because
the 'designs, and projects, and views of men' all essentially involve

[89] Ibid. 473.   [90] Ibid.   [91] Ibid.   [92] Ibid. 474-5.

the employment of reason. This intimate connection between reason and practical affairs leads Hume to stress the importance of reason, even though it cannot found human practice. For this reason, when Hume returns, in part 3, to give an account of the natural virtues, the virtues founded purely and directly on a 'primary impulse', he devotes much of the opening section to stressing the greater practical importance of reason and the artificial virtues founded on it: it is by reason that we 'determine all the great lines of our duty'.[93] The insistence on the greater importance of reason in a work which begins by denying a rational foundation to its subject matter is unexpected, and is best explained by attributing a complex purpose to its author. The full complexity of this purpose will emerge below, but we can begin by attributing to Hume two aims: first of all, to show his colours on an issue that had generated much debate among his older contemporaries, by plumping for the 'moral sense' position against the rationalists; and secondly, to show that, whatever the original foundation of morals, reason plays a central role in settling many of the most important of the moral issues. He offers a compromise solution to the dispute between the moral sense school and the rationalists.

Part 3, on the natural virtues, seeks to achieve more limited goals. It is over-simplifying, however, to say, as Mackie does, that in part 3 'Hume turns to the natural virtues, having rather oddly dealt first with those aspects of morality which are the more puzzling from his general point of view, and only later coming to more straightforward matters'.[94] The procedure is not puzzling if part 2 is the heart of Hume's account of morals, with part 3 being more necessary for the sake of completeness, for rounding off the final part of a major treatise of human nature, than for any vital didactic purpose. Hume's overall plan for the *Treatise* requires his contribution to moral philosophy to have the character of a complete system. His main purpose there is, in fact, to underline the argument of parts 1 and 2: to show that the virtues most necessary to society are not those virtues grounded in some primary impulse, however important those impulses are, but those generated by human beings through the non-metaphysical reasonings of everyday life. The

[93] *Treatise*, 590.
[94] J. L. Mackie, *Hume's Moral Theory* (London: Routledge & Kegan Paul, 1980), 5.

most important virtues are those generated by (rational) artifice:
the artificial virtues.

Having sketched in the main outlines of the argument of Book III
of the *Treatise*, we can now address the second question concerning
Hume's intentions: What impact (if any) did he seek to have on his
readers by stressing that justice, fidelity, allegiance, and chastity
and modesty are all artificial? In the opinion of the 1745 pamphlet
referred to above, he had sapped the foundations of morality, and
had denied the 'natural and essential Difference betwixt Right and
Wrong'. Was this reaction in any sense sought? Selby-Bigge, in his
introduction to the *Enquiries*, has no doubts. He says there that 'In
the Treatise he insisted vigorously, though not very intelligibly, that
justice was not a natural but only an artificial virtue, *and it is pretty
plain that he meant to be offensive in doing so*'.[95] Only a casual
observation is offered in support of this claim, but some further
reasons can be given in its support, especially when it is
remembered that the allegedly female virtues of chastity and
modesty are among the artificial virtues. To show why the
classification of these virtues should be a particular cause for
concern, especially for the contemporary reader, one characteristic
feature of the artificial virtues is especially important. It is that the
value of the artificial virtues resides in the whole, not in the individual
parts, a feature Hume explicitly discusses when considering the case of
justice. It is the same basic issue as that addressed by Hutcheson
under the heading of external rights, but the problem is particularly
sharp when couched in characteristic Humean fashion as a problem
of *motivation*.

Hume stresses that, although the whole system of justice is
beneficial to society, 'a single act of justice is frequently contrary to
public interest', and 'may, in itself, be very prejudicial to society'.[96]
The examples he offers—such as that of a beneficent man who
restores a fortune to its rightful owner, a miser or a seditious bigot,
'has acted justly and laudably, but the public is a real sufferer'[97]—
clearly show the Hutchesonian connection. But Hume draws a
disturbing moral: if justice, or any other artificial virtue, depends
for its value not on the effects of each virtuous act, but only on 'the

[95] *Enquiries*, pp. xxvii–xxviii (emphasis added).
[96] *Treatise*, 497.
[97] Ibid.

mutual assistance and combination of its corresponding parts',[98] there seems to be no reason to be more virtuous than the next man or woman. Certainly there is no reason for the conscientious pursuit of such virtues, at least in the strong sense of pursuing virtue whatever the circumstances. The practice of the artificial virtues.is a conditional matter. If this is granted, the consequences for the female virtue of chastity seem particularly dire because, in sharp contrast to the central artificial virtues of justice and allegiance, violations of chastity have both a constant motive in natural pleasure as well as an ease of opportunity.[99] Adding to these attractions a theory of virtue in which no value is located in each particular instance of chastity is to run the risk of misleading the incautious reader, and therefore also to create an environment particularly encouraging to the libertine! This is unlikely to have been lost on Hume's (male) readers, all of whom would have had cause for anxiety about the implications, for their households, of a doctrine that could be taken (even if mistakenly) to excuse individual licentiousness. (Could Hume himself have feared suspicion on this score? He was well known for his enjoyment of female company: could it be significant that in his short autobiography he should mention that it was in the company of *modest* women that he 'took a particular pleasure'?)[100]

These observations show how Hume could have offended some of his readers, but not that any offence taken was reasonable. Whether he actively *sought* to offend is yet a further question. It seems likely that the youthful author of the *Treatise*, in labelling the relevant virtues 'artificial', sought to be provocative, but quite unlikely that he sought to offend. His subsequent treatments of the issue suggest a man anxious to allay public suspicions. The implication is that, in the *Treatise*, he failed fully to appreciate the strength of the public reactions, and, his fingers having been once

[98] *Enquiries*, 305. Hume's analogies of the vault and the wall in this passage show the Stoic influence on his treatment of justice. See Ch. 2 above.

[99] Cf. *Enquiries*, 238–9; *Treatise*, 570–3.

[100] 'My Own Life', in *Essays*, 8. He may, of course, have been commending himself for his manners. The positive role of virtuous women is spelt out in such terms in another passage: 'What better school for manners, than the company of virtuous women; where the mutual endeavour to please must insensibly polish the mind, where the example of the female softness and modesty must communicate itself to their admirers, and where the delicacy of that sex puts every one on his guard, lest he give offence by any breach of decency' ('Of the Rise and Progress of the Arts and Sciences', *Essays*, i. 194).

burnt, he subsequently took great care to avoid repeating the offence.

Before turning to consider the various formulations of the distinction, it is necessary to clear away one possible source of misunderstanding: Hume's attempt to account for the origins of justice without appealing to divine purposes, etc., cannot itself be judged a source of offence. Hutcheson had already argued that by appealing only to the constitution of our nature, more particularly to our moral sense, the law of nature could be determined without reference to any law, whether human or divine. And this view is itself new only in its details: in general outline it is simply the rationalist version of natural law as developed by Grotius, Suárez, and others, and encapsulated in Grotius's *etiamsi daremus* passage. Although it was not a position that enjoyed widespread support, it seems quite fanciful to imagine that advocating such a familiar position could be considered offensive.

It may be thought that, in one crucial respect, the positions of Grotius and Hutcheson are quite different from Hume's, since they both accord at least some recognition to the divine will: neither denies God's existence, nor his concern for human affairs. However, Hume's position on these issues is a good deal more difficult to determine than is often supposed. Developing a system of morals in which God plays no part need not be seen as a problem, even from a theistic point of view: it may rather be taken as evidence of a more complete theory. For appeals to divine activity may principally be occasioned by the need to paper over cracks in the moral edifice. God will therefore be absent, but not denied, in any account of the natural moral order if the constitution of nature is indeed a fully interlocking system capable of harmonious functioning without relying on the cosmic repair man. So, as long as divine existence is not denied, a theory of natural morals will imply no irreligious conclusions by failing to allocate a special divine role. In fact, the extent to which it avoids a role for special divine action will be directly proportionate to its conception of the efficacy of the original divine creative act.

How does this bear on Hume? Interestingly, although it is difficult to interpret his views on these questions, there is evidence that he held to the sort of view outlined above. Although his moral theory very largely avoids any references to a divine being, and especially to any divine role in morals, this is not because the existence of a deity is denied outright. In fact, in one place he clearly acknowledges the existence of a divine being, allocating to him an overarching (constituting) role. This is towards the end of the first of the appendices to the *2nd Enquiry*: the standard of morals, he says, 'arising from the internal frame and constitution of animals, is ultimately derived from that Supreme Will, which bestowed on each being its peculiar nature, and arranged the several classes and orders of existence'.[101] This is exactly Grotius's view. So the conclusion seems irresistible that, whether or not Hume's views offended his contemporaries, there is no sound basis for regarding them, as does Selby-Bigge, as deliberately offensive. Hume's position is, at bottom, a commonplace of natural law: that justice arises from, or reflects the requirements of, human sociability. The rules of justice are necessary for the establishment of a social order which, as Grotius puts it, is 'consonant with human intelligence'.[102]

So far, we have examined the substance of Hume's views. Is there reason for classing his *terminology* offensive? There are two distinct reasons for concluding the opposite: his initial apprehensions about the distinction, and, once offence had clearly occurred, his efforts to remove the perceived cause without changing the distinction itself. A third, more general, factor should also be acknowledged, although it will not be pursued further here: Hume's frequently repeated ambition 'of being esteemed a friend to virtue'.[103] If this claim can be taken at face value, it reveals a most unexpected ambition in a man intending to offend his readers! It is also worth noting that Hutcheson, in the *Short Introduction*, allows that the notion of a moral law can be called artificial because it is not innate,[104] but 'formed upon observation';[105] and he also refers, in the *Essay*, to moral distinctions which are the 'Effect of Art'.[106]

[101] *Enquiries*, 294 (the conclusion of app. I, 'Concerning Moral Sentiment').

[102] *DJBP*, Prol. 8.

[103] Letter to Hutcheson, 17 Sept. 1739, *Letters of David Hume*, ed. Greig. For other indications of Hume's aim to be a friend of virtue, cf. *Essays*, 151–2 and 219 n.; the conclusion of the *Treatise*, where he includes himself among 'lovers of virtue', seeks to show the *nobility* of his theory, and concludes with the analogy of the anatomist and his service to the painter (pp. 619–21); and also his defence, in *A Letter from a Gentlemen*, that, like Hutcheson, he 'concurs with all the antient moralists' against the modern (p. 30), but does not, either in fact or intention, undermine morality.

[104] Cf. *Inquiry concerning Beauty and Virtue* (2nd edn.), 135.

[105] *Short Introduction*, 110.

[106] *Essay on the Nature and Conduct of the Passions* (quoted by D. F. Norton, 'Hutcheson's Moral Realism', *Journal of the History of Philosophy*, 23 (1985), 399.

To turn now to the first indicator of Hume's innocence: his obvious apprehensions about the terminology when introducing it. The apprehension is visible in the *Treatise* itself, where, on first introducing the distinction, Hume stresses the difficulty of defining the word 'nature': 'than which there is none more ambiguous and equivocal'.[107] He immediately goes on to distinguish three senses of the term, arguing that in one of these senses, virtue is not clearly natural, whereas in the other two senses it is. Shortly afterwards, at the end of the next section, he again stresses how the distinction is to be understood: when the naturalness of justice is denied, it is only in the third sense of 'natural', in which something is natural in so far as it is not a human construction. He reiterates the point because of his desire '*to avoid giving offence*',[108] adding that 'tho' the rules of justice be *artificial*, they are not *arbitrary*'. He then concludes with the following crucial remark: 'Nor is the expression improper to call them *Laws of Nature*; if by natural we understand what is common to any species, or even if we confine it to mean what is inseparable from the species.'[109] Since, for Hume's predecessors, the law of nature is constituted by those necessary laws of human conduct, necessary because they are grounded firmly in human nature, this quotation provides a perfectly adequate non-voluntarist account of natural law—as in Grotius, for example. The cautious form of expression is most readily interpreted in terms of a desire not to be misunderstood. It does not appear to be hesitation over the use of the term, nor does this particular use indicate that the notion of natural law is being seriously thinned-out.

Further evidence that, from a very early stage, Hume entertained doubts about his terminology can be found in the letter to Francis Hutcheson referred to previously. In that letter, one of his aims, apparently, is to overcome Hutcheson's misinterpretation of just the point at issue: 'I have never called justice unnatural,' he insists, 'but only artificial.'[110] He then proceeds to a brief explanation and defence of his real position, beginning by quoting a line from 'one of the best moralists of antiquity', the poet and satirist Horace: 'atque ipsa utilitas justi prope mater et aequi.'[111] The passage can be roughly translated as 'usefulness can be said to be the mother of

---

[107] *Treatise*, 474.
[108] Ibid. 484 (emphasis added).   [109] Ibid.
[110] Letter to Hutcheson, 17 Sept. 1739, *Letters of David Hume*, ed. Greig.
[111] Ibid.

---

justice and right', and may thus be thought to imply a a sceptical principle: that justice is, after all, mere expediency. A closer examination of the relevant passage from the *Satires* suggests, however, that this is not Hume's intention.

The passage shows that Horace's point is not sceptical. He aims rather to demonstrate that an awareness of the relevant facts of human existence is the key to a more sensitive moral and legal code than that implied by the Stoic paradox that all offences are equal.[112] He may even be understood to be providing an empirically minded protest against the plausible foolishness of a priori reasoning—a protest of a characteristically Humean spirit. In fact, Horace can be taken as making two distinct points, both of which are Humean in flavour. The first is that the Stoic view is too crude because repugnant to common sense: 'Those whose creed is that all sins are much on a par are at a loss when they come to face facts. Feelings and customs rebel, and so does Expedience herself, the mother, we may say, of justice and right.'[113] This we can call the negative thesis. The second is a positive thesis, in that it shows how social institutions develop in response to changes in human circumstances, or, in more familiar language, how moral and legal codes reflect human social evolution. In making this second point Horace relies on the speculative account of social evolution advanced by Lucretius in *De Rerum Natura*.[114] Horace's version is worth quoting at some length, because it helps to bring out features that Hume wanted to emphasize in his own account of justice. It runs as follows:

When living creatures crawled forth upon primeval earth, dumb, shapeless beasts, they fought for their acorns and lairs with nails and fists, then with clubs, and so on step by step with the weapons need had later forged, until they found words and names wherewith to give meaning to their cries and feelings. Thenceforth they began to cease from war, to build towns, and to frame laws that none should thieve or rob or commit adultery . . . If you will but turn over the annals and records of the world, you must needs confess that justice was born of the fear of injustice.[115]

In other words, the primitive history of human life is a history of violence, until the increasing sophistication of human life led to the

---

[112] Horace, *Satires, Epistles, and Ars Poetica*, trans. and ed. H. Rushton Fairclough (London: Heinemann, 1942), introd. to *Satires* I. iii. 30–1. Cf. Cicero, *De Finibus*, IV. 19.

[113] Horace, *Satires, Epistles, and Ars Poetica*, ed. Fairclough, 41.

[114] Ibid. 41 n; cf. *De Rerum Natura*, v, 780 ff.

[115] Ibid.

recognition that rules of justice were necessary in order to safeguard social advances, and to make further developments possible. Accounts of this sort are a commonplace of the main natural law theories, as has been shown in earlier chapters. Most simply put, natural law theories account for the development of rules of property within a larger history of the development of societies from primitive simplicity to more complex forms of social interdependence.

Although Hume does not himself tell such a story in the *Treatise*, he takes it for granted that there is some such story to tell. This is perhaps most clearly implied by his insistence that justice is a gradual development. The *2nd Enquiry*, for example, gives the following instructive example:

suppose, that several distinct societies maintain a kind of intercourse for mutual convenience and advantage, the boundaries of justice still grow larger, in proportion to the largeness of men's views, and the force of their mutual connexions. History, experience, reason sufficiently instruct us in this natural progress of human sentiments, and in the gradual enlargement of our regards to justice, in proportion as we become acquainted with the extensive utility of that virtue.[116]

It is in this sense that Hume agrees with Horace's claim that utility is the mother of justice. Justice is a historical development, made necessary by changes in society. Its utility is shown most emphatically by the negative case, that without justice society would simply collapse. Hume extends the point by building in the characteristic motivational point: the historical growth of justice shows the absence of a pre-rational impulse to be just; and we learn its value over time as its utility becomes evident. In this sense, utility is indeed the mother of justice, a sense which enables him to conclude, in the letter to Hutcheson, with the observation that 'Grotius and Pufendorf, to be consistent, must say the same'.[117] They must say the same because their own accounts show the historicity of justice, and therefore also the crucial role played by utility.

This is a provocative claim, because Grotius explicitly resists Horace's view that usefulness (or expediency) is the mother of justice. However, part of the problem here is the very ambiguity of the word

---

[116] *Enquiries*, 192.
[117] Letter to Hutcheson, 17 Sept. 1739, *Letters of David Hume*, ed. Greig.

'nature', of which Hume complains in the *Treatise*. For Grotius, after stressing that justice is founded in nature, albeit remotely, being three degrees removed ('nature may be considered . . . the great-grandmother of municipal law'), nevertheless concedes that there is no opposition between nature and expediency. Rather, 'the law of nature . . . has the reinforcement of expediency', and so 'those who prescribe laws for others in so doing are accustomed to have, or ought to have, some advantage in view'.[118] So Grotius's opposition to utility is limited to the extent that utility is opposed to nature. For Horace, opposition of this kind is inevitable—and his reason for so thinking provides a clue to why Hume should have agreed. What he says is this: 'Between right and wrong Nature can draw no such distinction as between things gainful and harmful, what is to be sought and what is to be shunned.'[119] Although a little unclear, the point of this remark seems to be that we are not directly led by nature to seek justice, but to seek what is clearly gainful and avoid what is harmful. Or, to put it another way, we have no natural motive, no original instinct, to pursue justice. This is exactly Hume's point when, in the *Treatise*, he argues that justice is artificial; and which, despite terminological changes, remains essential to the account of justice in both the *Essays* and the *2nd Enquiry*.[120] The important conclusion to be drawn here is that, by describing justice as artificial, Hume is not propounding a new, more sceptical, theory of this virtue. He grounds justice in sociability in just the way his natural law predecessors do: by insisting that it is dependent on utility, he does not deny sociability, but affirms it.

This explanation accords well with Hume's own account of the matter in the *Letter from a Gentleman*. He there stresses the long and respectable pedigree of his opinions: like Hutcheson, 'he concurs with all the antient Moralists'[121] in his moral theory. He

---

[118] *DJBP*, Prol. 16.

[119] Horace, *Satires, Epistles, and Ars Poetica*, ed. Fairclough, 41.

[120] *Treatise*, 477–84; 'Of the Original Contract', *Essays*, 454–5; *Enquiries*, 202, 307, 307 n. 2.

[121] *A Letter from a Gentleman*, ed. Mossner and Price, 30. Cf. *Enquiries*, 170–1, where this issue is also discussed, and where 'the elegant Lord Shaftesbury' is mentioned as one 'who, in general, adhered to the principles of the ancients'. Also, in 'Of the Rise and Progress of the Arts and Sciences', *Essays*, i. 191, Shaftesbury is classed among 'some of the more zealous partizans of the ancients'. This passage is particularly important, because it clearly shows the *status* of ancient opinions:

adds that, in the *Treatise*, the author (i.e. himself) 'seems sensible that he employed Words that admit of an invidious construction; and therefore makes use of all proper Expedients, by *Definitions* and *Explanations*, to prevent it'.[122] The truth of this claim has already been illustrated. What reason remains, then, for doubting Hume's insistence that his is an inoffensive doctrine? He asks just this question in the *Letter* (again speaking of himself in the third person):

by the *artificial Virtues* he means *Justice*, *Loyalty*, and such as require, along with a *natural Instinct*, a certain Reflection on the general Interests of Human Society, and a Combination with others. In the same Sense, Sucking is an Action natural to Man, and Speech is artificial. But what is there in this Doctrine that can be supposed in the least pernicious?[123]

In subsequent statements of his position, Hume took a more 'moderate' course, in that, without altering the distinction, he sought to remove the offence by removing its source in the troublesome terminology. So, for example, in the essay 'Of the Original Contract' (1752) he makes the same distinction between two kinds of moral duties, but the offending terminology has disappeared:

All *moral* duties may be divided into two kinds. The *first* are those, to which men are impelled by a natural instinct or immediate propensity, which operates on them, independent of all ideas of obligation, and of all views, either to public or private utility . . . The *second* kind of moral duties are such as are not supported by any original instinct of nature, but are performed entirely from a sense of obligation, when we consider the necessities of human society, and the impossibility of supporting it, if these duties were neglected.[124]

Since our primary instincts are too unruly to conform to the stringent requirements of justice, loyalty, and allegiance, these virtues must be of the second kind: founded on an established recognition of 'the general interests or necessities of society'.[125] This is precisely the reasoning underlying the *Treatise*'s classification of

---

Shaftesbury and others criticized some modern manners by adopting the standpoint of the ancients.

[122] *A Letter from a Gentleman*, ed. Mossner and Price, 30–1.
[123] Ibid. 31.
[124] *Essays*, i. 454–5.
[125] Ibid. 456.

justice, fidelity, etc., as artificial; but in this essay justice and fidelity are described only as 'natural duties'.[126]

The tactic of the *2nd Enquiry*, published a year earlier than 'Of the Original Contract', is similar, except that it does not so completely break with the language of the *Treatise*. Justice is explicitly grounded entirely in utility, but, at least in the body of the work, the language of artificiality is absent. Hume's method is, in part, to replace a troublesome dichotomy with the emphatic mode. For example, 'public utility is the *sole* origin of justice, and . . . reflections on the beneficial consequences of this virtue are the *sole* foundation of its merit'.[127]

The artificiality of justice, although implied by this doctrine, makes only a timid appearance in a footnote to the appendix on justice. In the text to this footnote, justice is classed as natural because it arises necessarily—a point made in the *Treatise*, but there treated as of less importance than its foundation in rational artifice. In the *2nd Enquiry* the roles have been reversed. Firstly we are told that justice arises necessarily in human life, and that 'In so sagacious an animal, what necessarily arises from the exertion of his intellectual faculties may justly be esteemed natural.'[128] The footnote then adds a toned-down version of the distinctions made in the *Treatise*:

Natural may be opposed, either to what is *unusual*, *miraculous*, or *artificial*. In the two former senses, justice and property are undoubtedly natural. But as they suppose reason, forethought, design, and a social union and confederacy among men, perhaps that epithet cannot strictly, in the last sense, be applied to them . . . *But all these disputes are merely verbal.*[129]

The final disclaimer here shows how far we have moved from the mood of the *Treatise*. The author of the earlier work, despite some caveats in the text, could boldly ask, in one of his section titles, 'Justice, whether a natural or artificial virtue?' The important substantive question in 1740, however, has become, by 1751, a merely verbal dispute worth only a footnote.

So it is clear that, in later attempts to restate his views on justice and fidelity, Hume sought, as far as possible, to avoid the troublesome terminology of the *Treatise*, terminology which had

---

[126] *Essays*, i. 455.
[127] *Enquiries*, 183.   [128] Ibid. 307.
[129] Ibid. 307–8 n. (emphasis added to last sentence).

caused both confusion and offence. In so doing, he acts very oddly for
a man seeking to offend. The oddity disappears if we conclude the
opposite: that, anxious to be esteemed a friend of virtue, he was upset
to be thought one of its enemies. He therefore did his best to remove
the unfortunate terminology responsible for the misunderstanding,
and sought to emphasize the respectable character of his work.
Thus he stresses, in the *2nd Enquiry*, that, by basing justice entirely
on utility, he is not introducing a new doctrine, but making more
visible the foundations put in place, if not always clearly, by 'the
writers on the law of nature'. These authors 'assign, as the ultimate
reason for every rule which they establish, the convenience and
necessities of mankind'.[130] Here we see very clearly one important
reason why Hume could judge his theory of justice to be 'in the
main, the same with that hinted at and adopted by Grotius'.[131] To
emphasize the point, he includes the longish quotation from
Grotius which shows the historical, and thus (in his terms) utility-
dependent character of the explanation of property in *De Jure Belli
ac Pacis*.[132]

There remains no good reason for believing Hume to have had
sceptical or offensive intentions in describing the important virtues
of justice, fidelity, and allegiance as artificial. Nevertheless, Grotius
and his immediate successors saw no need for such a description.
We need to understand why Hume *did*, so that question will be
addressed in the next section.

Before turning to that task, one final point should be made. It has
been argued that, by dividing the virtues into the natural and the
artificial, Hume cannot be understood to be dividing the genuine
from the purely imaginary, or false, virtues. He does not seek
thereby to separate the real virtues from the mere pretenders.
However, this does not mean that he is uninterested in making such
a distinction. In fact, the reverse is true. He does seek to separate
the genuine from the false virtues, but by quite different means. The
test for the genuineness of a putative virtue lies not in its source, but
in whether it is individually or socially beneficial. Qualities widely
thought to be virtues, but which fail this test, are the mere
pretenders, as the discussion of the 'monkish virtues' in the *2nd
Enquiry* clearly shows. Precisely (and wholly) because these
qualities fail the test of usefulness, and despite their widespread

[130] Ibid. 195.   [131] Ibid. 307 n.   [132] Ibid.; *DJBP* II. 2. ii. 4–5.

acceptance, Hume judges it appropriate to 'transfer them to the opposite column, and place them in the catalogue of vices'.[133] In this operation, the natural–artificial distinction is not invoked, and for good reason: it is neither intended for, nor capable of doing, critical assessment of this sort. The 'monkish virtues' are, on Hume's view, *neither* natural *nor* artificial virtues, and therefore are not virtues at all.[134]

5. MORAL BEAUTY, MOTIVES, AND OBLIGATIONS

The distinction between natural and artificial virtues can safely be taken as Hume presents it—as a distinction between those virtues which are always morally good, independently of any particular circumstances, and those which, because they are a rational response to the exigencies of particular circumstances, only have value *given* those circumstances, and only achieve their end when part of an interdependent system of like actions. However, this leaves the problem of explaining why he saw the distinction in terms of the *natural* and the *artificial*. Why not, more simply, put the matter in terms of the simple and the complex, or of the individual and the social? After all, he allows, in both the *Treatise* and the *2nd Enquiry*, that justice, because it is necessary to (or inseparable from) human life, can be correctly described as natural.[135] Why then does he *not* esteem it natural? What is it about a virtue founded in reason and reflection that makes him unwilling to call it natural?

Answering this question successfully requires an understanding of Hume's view of virtue in general. This is, in some respects at least, a difficult task, since in the *Treatise* he says little of direct

---

[133] *Enquiries*, 270.

[134] Thus David Miller's claim that Hume's attack on the monkish virtues does not 'derive from philosophical reflection,' but mirrors 'a social outlook which Hume has absorbed from his environment' (*Philosophy and Ideology in Hume's Political Thought*, 120), fails to recognize the philosophical impetus behind Hume's critique. In fact, Miller's distinction between philosophy and ideology—better described as a distinction between epistemology and unexamined assumptions (see pp. 12–13)—tends to be an unhelpful instrument. It encourages questions shaped by concerns and assumptions quite different from those which occupied 18th-cent. Scottish philosophers, a procedure which, although sometimes very enlightening, runs the risk of forcing its objects into an unsuitable mould. Since Miller's distinction is itself not free of dubitable assumptions, the risk is all the greater.

[135] *Enquiries*, 307; cf. *Treatise*, 484.

relevance to the topic, and what he does say can prove more of an obstacle than an aid to interpretation. However, the problems can be significantly reduced if we return to the question of the structure of *Treatise*, Book III. That issue is particularly pertinent here because Hume's general remarks on morality are very largely contained in the brief first part. To understand the place of part 1 in Book III as a whole is thus to become capable of conducting further enquiries more successfully by knowing where to look for their solution.

As suggested above, one of Hume's main aims in Book III, part 1 is to show his colours on a dispute familiar to his readers, the controversy over the apparently competing claims of reason and the moral sense as the foundation of morals. His further aim is to show that, despite being manifestly the correct viewpoint, the moral sense theory is not a sufficient foundation for our moral convictions. In fact, it shows some of our convictions to be quite paradoxical— most obviously, those concerning justice. The task of part 2, Hume's principal contribution in the area of moral theory, is to remove these paradoxes. If this picture is substantially correct, part 1 is very brief not because it is unimportant for his overall position, but because of its relation to Book III's main purpose. This purpose, to resolve a problem generated by moral sense theory, requires no more than a brief introduction, a sketch of the main outlines of that theory (including its most apparent strengths and weaknesses), in order to pose the problem to be discussed in the body of the work. In other words, moral sense theory slips from view in the later parts of the Book in part *because* the work is a contribution to, or refinement of, moral sense moral theory. This is only apparently paradoxical: intellectual enquiries conducted within a particular framework or paradigm do not typically refer to the paradigm. If a work is directed at an educated audience, it is directed at an audience who can be presumed to know the point of the enquiry, and thus not to need more than minimal reminders. In any intellectual dispute, the key to understanding lies in recognizing what is *not* being discussed. This is a requirement often easily satisfied, but it is always more problematic when investigating the meanings of historical texts.

If the purpose of *Treatise*, Book III, part 1, is principally to situate the discussion, any opaque or obscure Humean remarks can be clarified by an appeal to the unstated background—which in this case means by consulting other moral sense writers, or by considering central features of the moral sense viewpoint. Of course, this needs to be done with care, since the moral sense theorists are not all of a piece. This applies especially to Hume, since part 3 of *Treatise*, Book III, clearly shows him to be aiming to sophisticate the moral sense position, not merely to repeat it, by explaining the notion of moral sense itself in terms of the operation of the more general psychological principle of sympathy.[136] As long as this constraint is not forgotten, Hume's less transparent remarks can be examined in the light of other moral sense theories. And, no less importantly, the same insights can be employed to educate our approach to the *2nd Enquiry*: in that work, the term 'moral sense' does not appear at all, but it retains the commitment to found morals in 'sentiment' or feeling, rather than reason[137]—and this, as *Treatise*, Book III, part 1, shows, is the distinguishing mark of the moral sense position. Furthermore, if Hume attributed misinterpretations to a failure to recognize his commitment to a broad moral sense perspective, he could be expected to make this and other non-sceptical commitments more visible in his later work. This he does, as will be shown more fully below.

Hume's central argument against the possibility of founding morals in reason is that moral considerations move us to action. This reason alone cannot do, because it allows only 'the discovery of truth or falsehood'.[138] It is essentially passive, and so can neither move us to action nor determine ends: all it can do is help us to select the best means to any given end. Ends themselves are ends only in so far as they are desired states, so all ends are founded in passions, with reason the instrument to their effective achievement: 'reason is, and ought only to be the slave of the passions.'[139] The same point, put less colourfully, is 'that reason alone can never be a motive to any action of the will'.[140] So, if unaided reason cannot

---

[136] This is esp. clear in the concl., 618–21, and 611–12. The final sentences of the *Treatise*, where the importance of the anatomist is stressed, also imply the necessity of an accurate moral psychology. As Bk. II shows, the principle of sympathy is intended to fill just this requirement.

[137] At one point, Hume employs very Hutchesonian terminology: he speaks of a 'finer internal sense' (*Enquiries*, 170).

[138] *Treatise*, 458.   [139] Ibid. 415.

[140] Ibid. 413. The reference to 'motive' here should not be misunderstood. Hume does not mean a reason for action, but *motive force*, what pushes or pulls us into action. It will be argued below that remembering this is the key to understanding a famous Humean remark.

influence the will, it cannot provide the foundation of morals, since moral considerations do influence the will:

as reason can never immediately prevent or produce any action by contradicting or approving of it, it cannot be the source of the distinction betwixt moral good and evil, which are found to have that influence . . . Moral distinctions, therefore, are not the offspring of reason. Reason is wholly inactive, and can never be the source of so active a principle as conscience, or a sense of morals.[141]

It deserves to be emphasized that for Hume moral awareness 'is an active principle', that there is an essential connection between morality and action,[142] not least because, in some places, he appears to undermine the connection. The distinction between the anatomist and the painter at the close of the *Treatise* is a case in point. Persuaded himself of the activating role of sentiment in morals, Hutcheson complained of the *Treatise*'s want of 'a certain warmth in the cause of virtue'.[143] Hume's defence is to appeal to the different roles of the anatomist and the painter, but he apparently came to accept the criticism, since the *2nd Enquiry* not only manifests a good deal of warmth in the cause of virtue, it also implicitly undermines the value of the anatomist–painter distinction. His concern there, he says, is 'more the speculative, than the practical part of morals',[144] but he also adds that 'the end of all moral speculations is to teach us our duty'.[145] If this is so, then the moral sentiments have a place to play in the study of morals itself, since reason alone cannot reveal to us our duty: it can only reveal means to ends, and thus *possible* duties. But it cannot select between different achievable ends. So, to teach us our duty, the study of morals must call on both reason *and* sentiment; and, since to call on sentiment is to excite it, warmth is a necessary part of the study of virtue. If it is further added that there is little point to teaching virtue unless it is tied to the promotion of virtuous action, the conclusion is strengthened. This appears to be Hume's own assessment. At least, he becomes very conscious of the importance of promoting the appropriate sentiments: 'Extinguish all the warm feelings and prepossessions in favour of virtue, and all disgust or

[141] Ibid. 458.   [142] Cf. *Essays*, i. 244.
[143] Hume, letter to Hutcheson, 17th Sept. 1739, *Letters of David Hume*, ed. Greig.
[144] *Enquiries*, 177–8.
[145] Ibid. 172.

aversion to vice: render men totally indifferent towards these distinctions; and morality is no longer a practical study, nor has any tendency to regulate our lives and actions.'[146] It should be said that the context of this passage shows Hume to be presenting a possible view; a view that he does not identify as his own. However, it seems most likely that it *is* his own, or at least the sort of view he would defend.[147] If so, he accepts that the writer on morals cannot properly extinguish all warm feelings on the matter.

Moreover, on this view warm feelings naturally arise in connection with morals because of the active nature of morals itself. Hume hints at the connection when he speaks of 'that which renders morality an active principle and constitutes virtue our happiness, and vice our misery'.[148] This connection, between activity on the one hand, and happiness or misery on the other, exists because we are moved to action by sensations (or conscious prospects) of pleasure or pain. As he puts it, 'the chief spring or actuating principle of the human mind is pleasure or pain'.[149] Desires and aversions, happiness and misery, are real or imagined pleasures or pains which we see to be connected either to ourselves or others. Since passions move us to action, and since pains and pleasures are the source of passions,[150] then we are moved to act by pains and pleasures. In Hume's language, pains and pleasures are motives to action.

Moral motives, in turn, are pleasures or pains of a particular sort, and for this reason Hume insists that morality 'is more properly felt than judg'd of'.[151] And, since the subject-matter of morals is the actions or characters of human beings,[152] moral approbation is precisely the feeling of pleasure generated by the contemplation of a certain sort of character or action. By the 'contemplation' of a character or action Hume means the recognition of the 'principles in the mind and temper', the 'qualities or durable principles', that the character or action exhibits.[153] It is feeling that moves or activates us, but what we approve of in any act of moral approbation is not

---

[146] *Enquiries*, 172.
[147] He describes it as a 'specious' view, and puts aside its resolution to app. 1. The account there suggests that its speciousness is not *mere* speciousness.
[148] *Enquiries*, 173.
[149] *Treatise*, 574.
[150] Cf. ibid. 276.
[151] Ibid. 470.
[152] Cf. Hume to Hutcheson, letter no. 16, in D. D. Raphael, *British Moralists 1650–1800* (Oxford: Clarendon Press, 1969), ii. 111.
[153] *Treatise*, 477; letter no. 13, in Raphael, *British Moralists*.

feelings but the durable motives displayed by others in their actions or characters.[154] Hume's aim is not to reduce morality to 'mere' feeling, but to explain the psychological mechanisms of moral reality. It is in this spirit that observations like the following are best understood:

We do not infer a character to be virtuous, because it pleases: But in feeling that it pleases after such a particular manner, we in effect feel that it is virtuous. The case is the same as in our judgements concerning all kinds of beauty, and tastes, and sensations. Our approbation is imply'd in the immediate pleasure they convey to us.[155]

It remains to explain what it is that makes approbation, in any particular case, *moral* approbation. Given the foregoing account, it must be a pleasurable feeling generated by contemplation of a character or action. However, since the contemplation of manifestly non-moral, even immoral, characters or actions can generate pleasure, the question is how moral contemplation, or moral pleasure, is to be distinguished. Hume does not answer the question directly, but it is not difficult to determine his position. The clue lies in another of his short summaries of the basic facts of moral psychology. He says there that 'virtue is distinguished by the pleasure, and vice by the pain, that any action, sentiment or character gives us by the mere view and contemplation'.[156] In the immediately following sentence, he speaks of the reaction produced in us by an action viewed from 'the general view or survey'. It is most likely that the expressions 'the general view or survey', and 'the mere view and contemplation', have the same meaning, and that that meaning is disinterested contemplation. Moral pleasure is thus distinguished by the fact that it is caused by an action or character, when perceived without regard for any advantages or disadvantages that the action or character has for the observer; it can be described as the pleasure caused by the action or character considered for its own sake. Our sense of self-interest or advantage causes us to be pleased by actions or characters that benefit us; moral approbation is the pleasure caused by actions or characters considered independently of our interest or advantage.

At this point, interpreting Hume is substantially assisted by calling on the moral sense context. While his remarks do suggest the type of interpretation offered, it is Hutcheson who frequently stresses that considerations of interest and advantage can contaminate or

---

[154] *Treatise*, 477.   [155] Ibid. 471.   [156] Ibid. 475.

overrule moral perceptions, and that moral perceptions themselves are entirely disinterested. For example, he describes moral good as 'our Idea of some Quality apprehended in Actions, which procures Approbation, and Love toward the actor, from those who receive no Advantage by the Action'.[157] For this to be possible—for disinterested contemplation to produce pleasure—moral qualities must exhibit a kind of beauty, because beauty is the quality possessed by objects that can cause disinterested approbation. The distinctive beauty of the action or character motivates our actions: 'The AUTHOR of Nature has much better furnished us for a virtuous conduct, than our Moralists seem to imagine . . . He has made *Virtue* a *lovely Form*, to excite our pursuit of it; and has given us strong *Affections* to be the Springs of each virtuous action.'[158] Hume's view is similar in essentials. He differs from Hutcheson in his assessment of the strength of the disinterested affections, as shown by the stress he lays on the *limited* benevolence of human beings. He thus backs away from Hutchesonian strong benevolence, but without defecting to the camp of 'self-love' moral theorists.[159] His position is, in other words, a medium between extremes—just what should be expected from a man of 'moderation'.

It is now possible to sketch in the general outlines of the moral sense view of the nature and practice of morality. A characteristic concern of this outlook is the close connection between moral judgement and action. The task of moral philosophy is thus understood to include not only an account of the nature of moral goodness, etc., but also of the sources of moral action—of what makes moral thought and action a practice characteristic of human beings. And, because of his particular concern with the efficient causes of action, this latter issue features prominently in Hume's moral theory. So a central purpose of the following sketch is to show the nature and causes of a characteristic form of human behaviour.

In the first place, as the above quotation from Hutcheson shows, the moral sense perceives (or, human beings sympathetically respond to) the beauty of certain kinds of characters or actions. Moral goodness is a species of beauty. It is thus no accident that

---

[157] *Inquiry*, 111.   [158] Ibid. pp. xiv–xv.

[159] For Hume, the latter camp includes not only Mandeville, but also Hobbes and Locke, both of whom, he says, 'maintained the selfish system of morals' (*Enquiries*, 296). In this view he is certainly at one with Shaftesbury (cf. Norton, *David Hume*, 34–5). Hutcheson appears to be committed to much the same conclusions, although he appears somewhat hesitant about where to place Locke (see *Inquiry*, 81).

Hutcheson should write an *Inquiry concerning Beauty and Virtue*, or that Hume occasionally speaks of beauty as a genus, divided into the two species of moral and natural: for example, 'beauty whether moral or natural',[160] and 'if we compare moral beauty with natural'.[161] These are not examples of a theoretically innocent eighteenth-century idiom, but part and parcel of the moral sense perspective. (The rationalists, in contrast, speak not of moral beauty, but simply of moral good and evil.)[162] Moral actions are founded on the apprehension of a species of beauty. The apprehension of beauty is capable of moving us to action because pleasure is the mainspring of human action, and, as Hume puts it in *A Dissertation on the Passions*, 'the very essence of beauty consists in its power of producing pleasure'.[163]

Following Hutcheson, Hume explains moral and aesthetic perception in terms heavily indebted to the Lockian account of the secondary qualities. As noted in the previous chapter, however, his account differs from Hutcheson's in its pronounced focus on the mind of the observer. The difference is preserved in his account of beauty: the beauty of a circle, he says, 'is only the effect which that figure produces upon the mind, whose peculiar fabric or structure renders it susceptible of such sentiments'.[164] This does not necessarily mean that beauty has no real existence, but the issue need not be pursued further here, since, from the point of view of moral philosophy, the precise location of perceptions of moral beauty is not of great importance. What matters is that beauty is perceived, and reliably so. Thus Hume can happily agree with Hutcheson's confident assertion that we know an object is beautiful because, whenever we perceive that object, we perceive the beauty. Beauty, Hutcheson says, 'will as necessarily strike the Mind, as any Perceptions of the external Senses'.[165]

To explain the perception of beauty, including moral beauty, as akin to the secondary qualities—differing only in that it is perceived by a 'finer internal sense'[166] rather than by another external sense-organ—has a significant implication. All ideas of secondary

---

[160] *Enquiries*, 165.   [161] Ibid. 291.
[162] See the writings of Samuel Clarke and William Wollaston included in Raphael, *British Moralists*, i.
[163] *Essays*, ii. 148.
[164] *Enquiries*, 291–2. The same passage occurs in 'The Sceptic', *Essays*, i. 219.
[165] Hutcheson, *Passions and Affections*, 101.
[166] *Enquiries*, 170; cf. also 294; and cf. *Inquiry*, 8.

qualities require for their realization perception by an appropriate perceiver, so the same must be true of moral goodness. Thus the moral sense theorists occasionally speak of the role of a spectator in moral determinations. Since the moral viewpoint is the disinterested viewpoint, it becomes possible to think of settling moral disputes by appealing to the impartial spectator.[167] Both Hume and Hutcheson occasionally appeal to this figure, but the idea is worked out in great detail by Adam Smith, who, in *The Theory of Moral Sentiments*, provides an account of moral good, and of our motivations to pursue moral courses of action, in terms of the complex constitution of the impartial spectator of human affairs.

Of more immediate importance, however, is the fact that any theory of moral goodness which assigns a central role to the perceptions of appropriately placed minds must insist on the uniformity of the disinterested perceptions of the relevant minds if the public, or social, character of the moral world is to be retained. If this seems an impossibly stringent requirement, it needs only to be remembered that, with respect to the classical secondary qualities, the requirement enjoys widespread acceptance. There is no ordinary resistance to saying that sugar is sweet, or that fire engines are red. So, if Hume thinks of moral beauty in ways that parallel the secondary qualities, he should acknowledge the existence of the relevant kind of uniformity in human minds, or human nature. He should also accept that moral beauty and deformity can therefore be recognized as real features of characters and actions, and of the motives revealed by them. And, in fact, he does, in a 'philosophical' footnote to his essay 'The Sceptic':

Were I not afraid of appearing too philosophical, I should remind my reader of that famous doctrine, supposed to be fully proved in modern times, 'That tastes and colours, and all other sensible qualities, lie not in the bodies, but merely in the senses'. The case is the same with beauty and deformity, virtue and vice. This doctrine, however, takes off no more from the reality of the latter qualities, than from that of the former; nor need it give any umbrage either to critics or moralists. Tho' colours were allowed to lie only in the eye, would dyers or painters ever be less regarded or esteemed? There is a sufficient uniformity in the senses and feelings of mankind, to make all these qualities the objects of art and reasoning, and to have the greatest influence on life and manners. And as 'tis certain, that the

---

[167] Both Hume and Hutcheson speak of the spectator. For Hume, see *Enquiries*, 292, and also *Treatise*, 472, 581–2, 589, 591.

discovery above-mentioned in natural philosophy, makes no alteration on action and conduct; why should a like discovery in moral philosophy make any alteration?[168]

Hume here adopts the secondary quality model, complete with its two important consequences—the uniformity of the relevant perceptions, and their undiminished reality. The parallelism between natural beauty and virtue is also evident. He thus accepts the extended implication of the moral sense–secondary qualities model: that moral approbation is founded in the perception of moral beauty, which is the perception, by any disinterested observer, of the beauty of particular actions or characters.

This is the foundation of the moral sense outlook. The claim that moral distinctions are founded on a moral sense is the claim that morality begins with the perception of moral beauty. Beauty itself, whether moral or natural, is simply a pleasing perception—but it is not therefore arbitrary. There is considerable uniformity in human nature, and what is pleasing to any sense is, in like manner, not arbitrary. This can be illustrated by considering perceptions which are predictably pleasurable or painful. Kames provides some instructive examples: 'a spreading oak, a verdant plain, a large river, are objects which afford great delight. A rotten carcase, a distorted figure, create aversion, which in some instances, goes the length of horror.'[169] For Hutcheson, natural beauty requires uniformity amidst variety; Hume is more circumspect, but agrees, in one of his best-known essays, that there is a standard of taste. Both show a firm belief in the uniformity of the basic principles of human nature, including the principles of moral action, and demonstrate this conviction by agreeing that acts of benevolence, in particular, are pleasing to any disinterested observer.

---

[168] 'The Sceptic', *Essays*, 219 n. It is important to point out here that, although this essay and its 3 immediate companions—'The Epicurean', 'The Stoic', and 'The Platonist'—are literary or imaginative constructions of the four different positions, rather than Hume's own view, there is good reason for taking this particular essay as a literary device precisely for airing his own views. There is particular reason for taking this part of the essay to represent his views, because the text that this footnote is commenting on includes a passage—6 sentences long—identical to a paragraph of the *2nd Enquiry* (pp. 291–2). This passage is quoted above (in part) as the text to n. 164. It should also be noted that Hume errs in his footnote, suggesting that, according to the 'famous doctrine', *all* sensible qualities lie in the senses. This is not true. Shape and size, for example, are primary sensible qualities, and hence remain firmly in the object.

[169] Kames, *Essays*, 43.

The second crucial feature of the moral sense outlook, the feature the theorists themselves consciously recognized as the distinctive advantage of their position, is its insistence that a theory of morals must explain the fact of human moral activity. Morals influences the will, and no theory is complete if it cannot explain why this is so. The moral sense view meets this requirement by incorporating a hedonistic and deterministic account of human motivation. Moral considerations can move the will because moral perception is the perception of a particular kind of pleasure, and as such is intrinsically motivating. The finer details of this view, and its implications for Hume's theory of justice, can now be spelt out.

As Hume puts it, 'the chief spring or actuating principle of the human mind is pleasure or pain'.[170] Pleasure moves us to action because what pleases is attractive—i.e. we are attracted to it. Our nature is such that, by being pleased by particular objects or events, we are attracted to them, and thus seek to secure or preserve or repeat them. We pursue what pleases us, and thereby are moved to action. In like manner we seek to avoid what is painful or disturbing, or, more generally, causes us unease. A principal reason for our finding an event pleasing or painful is its bearing on our private interests. These pleasures or pains, and hence these interests, are not moral in character, because morality is essentially disinterested. All and only our disinterested perceptions, and the pleasures or pains that arise from them, give no pre-eminence to our private ambitions, and thus display the public character of the moral viewpoint. So all and only disinterested perceptions are moral perceptions, and the pleasures, and thus also motivations, that arise from such perceptions are moral pleasures and motivations. And, since moral actions are actions which spring from moral motives, they are actions where the motive force is an attraction to a moral pleasure, a pleasing disinterested perception. Benevolent acts, for example, are moral acts because benevolence is a moral motive: it is the motive force generated by the disinterested, pleasing perception of the happiness of others. Only because human nature is as it is, only because we are pleased by the disinterested perception of the happiness of others, do we have a motive to perform benevolent acts. Without such pleasures there can be no moral motivation.

This is an important conclusion, but its importance is not visible

---

[170] *Treatise*, 574.

until the relationship between motivation and obligation in the moral sense outlook is explained. The best approach to understanding this relationship is to consider Hutcheson's account of obligation. He defines obligation as follows: it is 'a Determination, without regard to our own Interest, to approve Actions, and to perform them; which Determination shall also make us displeas'd with our selves, and uneasy upon having acted contrary to it.'[171] The first part of this definition is a definition of moral motivation—the disinterested motive to approve and perform certain actions. The second part is simply a consequence of the former. Where we act contrary to our disinterested motive, it is because this has been outweighed by a stronger, (self-) interested one. But the stronger motive, despite outweighing the weaker, does not destroy it; and, once the stronger motive has been successful in moving us to a self-interested action, it typically dissipates. We are then left with the disinterested motive alone, and, where the self-interested act has cut off the possibility of performing the disinterested act, the disinterested motive remains, but without means of its satisfaction. Consequently, we remain 'uneasy', or 'displeas'd with our selves'.

If this account is substantially correct, then, for Hutcheson, obligation and moral motivation are identical. Obligation is the push or pull exerted on the will by the disinterested pleasing perception of a particular action or character, and moral motivation is the same. The identity of these two moral elements in Hutcheson's theory can be confirmed by the example of benevolence—for Hutcheson the moral motivation *par excellence*. If moral motivations are obligations, he must accept that there is an obligation to be benevolent. Since benevolence is a mental state, it may sound odd to suggest—even impossible to require—that it could be the object of an obligation. Hutcheson, however, sees no such difficulty: 'there is,' he says, '*naturally* an *Obligation* upon all Men to *Benevolence*.'[172] He sees no difficulty because he believes all men to have a natural inclination, a natural moral motive, to benevolence: where self-interest does not interfere, we enjoy and so seek to support the well-being of others. The identity of obligation and moral motivation thus implies that there is a natural obligation to benevolence.

If moral motivation and obligation are identical, then the absence of one implies the absence of the other. Where there is no moral

[171] *Inquiry*, 266 (but cf. Kames, *Essays*, 56–7).
[172] Ibid. 267.

motivation, there is no obligation.[173] For the interpretation of a famous Humean passage, this is a significant implication, although its significance may not be immediately obvious. It can be brought out better by some rephrasing. First of all, the pleasing perception of moral beauty, moral perception, is the task carried out by the moral sense. The pleasing perception is necessary for there to be a motive, so without reference to a moral sense there can be no explanation of obligation: that is, no meaning can be given to the word 'ought'. All the rationalist moral theories, with their attempts to found morals entirely in reason, or abstract rational relations, implicitly deny the reality or significance of moral sense. So, when these theories introduce the word 'ought', they have introduced a new relation which they cannot explain. This is a decisive failing. A moral theory without obligation is no moral theory at all, since morality is a practical matter, and the obligation is precisely the action-making element—the motive force—in moral practice. Through 'this small attention', then, it is possible to show 'that the distinction of vice and virtue is not founded merely on the relations of objects, nor is perceiv'd by reason'.[174]

This should sound familiar, since it is a brief summary of the famous 'is–ought' passage at the end of *Treatise*, III. I. i. Placing that passage in the light of the general moral sense perspective shows that Hume is not there attempting to draw a distinction between facts and values, nor between facts and interpretations; nor is he claiming that there is an unbridgeable gap between 'is' statements and 'ought' statements.[175] And, since these various misinterpretations have all at some time or other gone under the name, neither is he asserting 'Hume's Law'. The point of the passage is, more simply,

---

[173] For Hume, obligation is motivation *simpliciter*: thus he talks of natural obligation and moral obligation. However, this does not affect things here, and so can safely be set aside. For a further discussion, see E. Sapadin, 'Hume's Law, Hume's Way', in G. P. Morice (ed.), *David Hume: Bicentenary Papers* (Edinburgh: Edinburgh University Press, 1977); and M. Baron, 'Hume's Noble Lie: An Account of his Artificial Virtues', *Canadian Journal of Philosophy*, 12 (1982), 540–1.

[174] *Treatise*, 470.

[175] Nevertheless, there is a sense in which he *is* saying that every 'ought' conclusion must have an 'ought' premiss, but not if this claim is taken in its customary 20th-cent. sense. His point is that any conclusion about moral actions or motivations can only derive from premisses that include reference to moral motivations. So, to put it in terms of his general belief–desire account of action, his position can be summed up as the claim that any valid moral argument must have the following form: 'is' premiss plus impartial desire (moral motivation) premiss implies 'ought' conclusion.

that an adequate explanation of morality must include an account of why it moves people to action, and that the common moral theories, by ignoring the moral sense, fail this test. The gap between 'ought' statements and 'is' statements is a gap between obligations or motivations (and therefore actions) on the one hand, and facts *and* values on the other.[176] The essential passivity, the instrumentality, of reason, guarantees the failure of the rationalist theories. Reason is a tool we use in order to achieve our ends. Our use of this tool depends on our purposes and so cannot explain them. The rationalist theories fail because they cannot explain why there are moral—that is, morally active—beings. The central point here could also be put by the insistence that an adequate moral philosophy must include a moral psychology, a psychology of moral action.[177]

It was claimed above that Hume's 'is–ought' passage is undeservedly famous. The reason can now be given: in that passage he does little more than repeat Hutcheson. In the *Inquiry concerning Beauty and Virtue*, and again in the *Illustrations upon the Moral Sense*, Hutcheson charges the rationalists with being unable to explain some important words in the moral vocabulary: principally, 'ought', 'must', and 'should'.[178] Hume follows suit, rehearsing Hutcheson's argument against the rationalists before concentrating on his main concerns—justice, government, etc. His account adds only a memorable final paragraph, a paragraph which brought him fame by coming to the attention of philosophers who read him for their own purposes, and misunderstood him accordingly. Hutcheson, spared the later fame, was also spared this fate.

---

[176] Cf. Sapadin, 'Hume's Law, *Hume's* Way', 214–17. Sapadin rightly emphasizes that when Hume contrasts 'is' statements and 'ought' statements he means just that. Thus statements which say of something that it 'is conducive to happiness', or 'is good', or 'is the right thing to do', are all, as they appear to be, 'is' statements— and so to be distinguished from 'ought' statements and the new relation the latter introduce.

[177] The larger commitments of moral sense moral philosophy are thus in sharp opposition to one prominent strand in recent moral philosophy, which separates moral philosophy from questions of the psychology of moral action. See, in particular, R. M. Hare, *The Language of Morals* (Oxford: Oxford University Press, 1952), pp. iii–iv.

[178] See *Inquiry*, 266–75; *Illustrations*, 229–30, 244, 246, 252, 262, 269, in particular. The same general issue is also considered in the *System*, i. 264.

The issue did not end with these two, however. Kames, who also held to a moral sense viewpoint, criticizes both Hutcheson and Hume in his *Essays* on this very point. In his view, both failed to provide an adequate account of these terms. Acknowledging this serves, in the first place, to underline the fact that a concern for the proper explanation of 'ought' and comparable words is typical of the moral sense philosophers, and is so because the question of how morality moves us to action is taken by them to be a crucial question, and one which decisively favours their position over that of the rationalists. Hume's 'is–ought' passage is no more than a neat encapsulation of a commonplace of moral sense moral philosophy. In the second place, examining Kames's criticisms of Hume and, particularly, Hutcheson, helps to provide a useful foothold on the problem posed for moral sense theory by the virtue of justice, the problem that Hume's doctrine of artificial virtue is designed to solve.

6. JUSTICE AS AN ARTIFICIAL VIRTUE

Kames criticizes both Hume and Hutcheson on the nature of obligation, but his objection to the former need only be mentioned in passing. It is simply that sympathy is insufficient to the task: it is 'far too faint a principle to control our irregular appetites and passions'.[179] His criticism of Hutcheson, however, is very instructive, in that it clarifies the nature of the problem that justice (in particular) poses for moral sense theory. The problem with Hutcheson's account of obligation, he says, is its failure to measure up to the facts: 'this account falls far short of the whole idea of obligation, and leaves no distinction betwixt it and a simple approbation or disapprobation of the moral sense; feelings that attend many actions, which by no means come under the notion of *obligation* or *duty*'.[180] In particular, Hutcheson's problem is that he

founds the morality of actions on a certain quality of actions, which procures approbation and love to the agent. But this account of morality is imperfect, because it excludes justice, and everything which may be strictly called Duty. The man who, confining himself to strict duty, is true to his word, and avoids harming others, is a just and moral man; is intitled to

---

[179] Kames, *Essays*, 58.   [180] Ibid. 57.

some share of esteem, but he will never be the object of love or friendship.[181]

Kames's point is that justice (principally 'avoiding harm to others') is an essential part of morals, but the moral sense theory cannot explain our obligation to justice, since justice is without moral beauty. For this reason the just man 'will never be the object of love or friendship'. Objects of love or friendship are pleasing perceptions, but the perception of justice is not pleasing—even though the perception of injustice is very displeasing—because justice is action solely from duty, not from any benevolent motive.

The problem, then, is this: if justice does not procure the approbation of the moral sense, what is the foundation of its approval? What is our motive to just actions? This is the same problem faced by Hutcheson, when addressing the question of the 'external' rights. External rights imply moral duties unaccompanied by moral beauty—so what is the source of our approval of them? Kames's question about justice is thus Hutcheson's external rights problem generalized.

Hume recognizes the problem, and clearly understands it in just these terms, because he addresses it by considering Hutcheson's examples of external rights:

when I relieve persons in distress, my natural humanity is my motive; . . . But if we examine all the questions, that come before any tribunal of justice, we shall find, that considering each case apart, it wou'd as often be an instance of humanity to decide contrary to the laws of justice as conformable to them. Judges take from a poor man to give to a rich; they bestow on the dissolute the labour of the industrious; and they put into the hands of the vicious the means of harming both themselves and others. The whole scheme, however, of law and justice is advantageous to the society [and to every Individual]; and 'twas with a view to this advantage, that men, by their voluntary conventions, establish'd it.[182]

Hume does not dispute the advantage, and thus the virtue, of justice. The problem is that, because many individual acts of justice lack moral beauty, the moral sense theory finds itself unable to

---

[181] Ibid. 55–6.
[182] *Treatise*, 579. The addition in square brackets is Hume's manuscript amendment to the 1st edn. See Nidditch's textual notes, *Treatise*, 672. Also note in the first sentence of this passage the use of 'motive' where it can only mean motive (or driving) force, as argued for above.

explain the motivation, and thus the obligation, to be just. It thus suffers from a special case of the general problem afflicting rationalist moral theories. And, since individual men and women do perform just acts, including those which are entirely lacking in moral beauty, there *is* a motivation to be just, and which therefore must be explained. The human will is moved to perform just actions, despite the fact that there is no 'original instinct' available to do the job. So the problem of justice can be set out as follows. Justice cannot be a natural virtue because there is no natural inclination—and thus no natural obligation—to be just. It is, however, a genuine virtue because it is founded on a real obligation. The reality of the obligation is demonstrated simply by the existence of just actions themselves. So Hume's task is to explain how this real obligation arises.

The immediate obligation to perform acts of justice is evident: it is the *sense* of justice, the sense of duty. However, this sense cannot found justice, since it arises only where justice already exists. It can no more found justice than a sense of morals can found morality itself. The founding principle or obligation which establishes a virtue must be '*some motive to produce it, distinct from the sense of its morality*'.[183] The problem of the motivation to be just is that there is no such distinct motive to just acts. Hutcheson's remedy was to appeal to a more extensive benevolence, the good of mankind as a system. To Hume, however, this is not enough, since 'that is a motive too remote and too sublime to affect the generality of mankind'. He adds: 'In general, it may be affirm'd, that there is no such passion in human minds, as the love of mankind, merely as such, independent of personal qualities, of services, or of relation to ourself.'[184] In fact, the partiality of our affections restricts even our benevolence to a fairly limited sphere. But the natural insecurity of external goods, in particular, makes a system of justice absolutely necessary to the security of society. How then is this obstacle to justice overcome? Not by any natural, i.e. original, means: 'In vain should we expect to find in *uncultivated nature*, a remedy to this inconvenience; or hope for any inartificial principle of the human mind, which might control those partial affections, and make us overcome the temptations arising from our circumstances.'[185] If no natural means can effect the establishment of justice, but social

---

[183] *Treatise*, 479.   [184] Ibid. 481.   [185] Ibid. 488.

harmony requires that justice be established—which is shown by the fact of the existence of a system of justice—some sort of non-natural, or artificial, means must be employed. The obvious candidate is reason, so Hume concludes that the artificial virtues are established by rational reflection on the advantages they provide for securing peaceful social life.

In the case of the artificial virtue of justice, Hume offers the following explanation. Rational reflection on the natural instability of the possession of external goods, and on the great advantages that flow from overcoming this instability and securing to individuals the fruits of their industry—a necessary task if the 'additional *force*, *ability*, and *security*' made possible by social life is to be preserved[186]—shows the necessity of establishing rules of property. In this way, justice becomes established despite the absence of a natural motive to perform just acts: 'The remedy, then, is not deriv'd from nature, but from *artifice*; or more properly speaking, nature provides a remedy in the judgment and understanding, for what is irregular and incommodious in the affections.'[187] So the system of justice is generated by, and founded in, rational reflection concerning the necessary supports for the social life, a life which is itself necessary because of the great advantages it procures for human life. The product of rational artifice, justice is an artificial virtue.

Hume's account of justice is thus thoroughly in tune with the natural jurists. In the older vocabulary, his position is simply that justice is a dictate of right reason, because necessary for sociability and self-preservation. The advantages that the establishment of property procures for social life are so considerable that it cannot be resisted, and in this sense is a necessary development. Among these advantages, 'the encouragement given to industry and labour'[188] looms large, especially in the political essays, and shows Hume to have adopted and extended the political economy that is an increasingly prominent feature in the theories of his predecessors. The advantages, taken as a whole, are so overwhelming that, he concludes in the *Treatise*, it is not improper to call property a law of nature. Although not the fruit of an original instinct in human nature, human society cannot prosper without it, so in this sense it is inseparable from the species. The same is also true of the other

---

[186] Ibid. 485.   [187] Ibid. 489.   [188] *Enquiries*, 309 n.

artificial virtues, fidelity and allegiance to government, and so the artificial virtues can all be truly described as dictates of right reason. In this respect they all satisfy the central requirement of a law of nature, and it is only Hume's preoccupation with the sources of moral action, inherited from Locke and Hutcheson, that obscures the fact. In the same manner as Pufendorf, he binds natural law to the *rational* utility of laws necessary for human social life. Once this is recognized, there remains no serious bar to taking Hume at his word, and accepting his account of justice as an account of the development of a natural law founded in rational reflection. The rules of justice are the nucleus of *adventitious* natural law.

If this view is to be taken seriously, one question remains outstanding: What has happened to the *suum*? Hume's theory makes no explicit appeal to the necessity of protecting a realm which is 'one's own', to which end the edifices of justice and political society naturally (justly) tend. The short answer is that the *suum* has been naturalized in just the same fashion as have the virtues. The inviolable realm of 'one's own' is spelt out in terms of a natural, i.e. original, motive; a motive which, but for the corrupting influence of the 'monkish virtues', would need no defence. This motive is self-love: a natural disposition to which Hume frequently returns in his account of justice and political order in both the *Treatise* and the *2nd Enquiry*. Thus he maintains, for example, that '*self-interest is the original motive to the* establishment *of justice*'.[189] And, far from apologising for the fact, he defends the importance of a healthy self-love, or well-founded *pride*, for social intercourse, being both useful to ourselves and agreeable to others: 'there is no quality of the mind, which is more indispensibly requisite to procure the esteem and approbation of mankind.'[190] So, although the social virtues play a vital role in the formation of social existence by extending our originally limited affections, a measure of self-love is also important in firming up social relations by establishing mutual respect between persons. And it is self-love, the restricted concern for what is our own, that founds the jealous virtue of justice.

If this suggestion is accepted, it is also possible to provide a tentative explanation for the absence of any overt appeal in Hume's

---

[189] *Treatise*, 499.
[190] Ibid. 598. Note that Hume distinguishes this well-founded pride from 'over-weaning conceit' (p. 596). The former, not the latter, provides the foundation for his account of the passions in *Treatise*, Bk. II.

account to other characteristic concepts of modern natural jurisprudence, such as individual rights and negative community. The rights of an individual are powers to act with a moral effect, natural powers which are legitimately exercised, and concern the legitimacy of self-preservation, and thereafter those actions which tend to the improvement of human life. Hume can thus be understood to have bypassed the language of rights while preserving its essential content, in that his account of the origin of justice implicitly accepts the legitimacy of the natural desire for self-preservation, and, through the generous sentiments of the moral sense, similarly identifies a natural motive to promote utility.[191] In the earliest stages of human life, the first of these desires is the more salient, since in that condition there is no social bounty of those goods necessary for survival. So the legitimate natural desire of the earliest human beings will be to take and directly make use of those goods which support life. In so doing they will be treating the natural world as belonging to no one, and open for their use. To treat the natural desire for self-preservation as sufficient legitimation for original appropriation is thus to treat the original condition of the earth as a negative community.[192] So Hume's psychological theses can be cashed out in terms of the secular theory of natural social order hinted at by Grotius.

They also, however, reopen a question that Grotius had failed to deal with adequately, and which preoccupied his successors. For Hume's approach implicitly rejects the Lockian argument against the compatibility of slavery with a just social order. Slavery once

[191] See, in particular, *Enquiry concerning the Principles of Morals*, sect. 5, 'Why Utility pleases'. (Some other possible explanations for Hume's abandonment of the notion of rights are mentioned in the App.)

[192] Thus interpreted, Hume's position should not be confused with Nozick's in *Anarchy, State, and Utopia* (New York: Basic Books, 1974). If Nozick's account of individual rights began with an insistence that one of the fundamental rights we possess is a right to preserve ourselves, and that this right in turn implied that claims of necessity could outweigh property rights, then the differences would be largely overcome. But Nozick backs away from such possibilities. He insists that rights are based purely on 'the fact of our separate existences' (p. 33). There are ways of taking this claim which would not be so problematic: if he had offered a 'thick' account of what these existences imply, he could have made the legitimacy of self-preservation an integral part of the theory of rights. He does not do so, as is shown by his own formulation of, and response to, the problem of necessity: 'the question of whether these side constraints are absolute, or whether they may be violated in order to avoid catastrophic moral horror . . . is one I hope largely to avoid' (p. 30 n.). By removing claims of necessity to the margins of the theory of justice, Nozick has decisively separated his position from all forms of natural law.

more appears to be a possible, if undesirable, aspect of natural society. Although he nowhere gives the issue a systematic treatment, Hume's response can be understood in the same terms as above. He attempts to demonstrate the *degree* of its undesirability, and thereby show that, once its effect is rightly understood, neither of the natural desires of self-love and utility encourage its implementation or protection. In the essay 'Of the Populousness of Ancient Nations', he demonstrates the inhumanity of the ancient system of slavery, and thus its offensiveness to all generous sentiments. The major part of his criticism, however, is concerned to point up the hidden practical problems of a system of slavery, and thereby to show its disutility. By showing how unfavourably slave economies fared when compared with modern commercial society, Hume introduces an argument which was to receive a thorough treatment at the hands of Adam Smith.[193] The argument cannot show that slavery violates an inalienable right, but it can show the absence of any reasons for promoting or allowing such a system. So, given his enthusiastic support for the virtues of commercial society, Hume's response to the problem of slavery is that commercial society renders it obsolete.

Two further features of Hume's account remain to be addressed. The first is that the utility of a system of justice is distinct from its visible utility: its advantages may at times be obscured, whether by short-sightedness, partiality, or other factors. For this reason the development of a system of justice will typically be a slow growth over time, and therefore a historical construction. This is an important feature of Hume's account, and shows up in two ways. The first is the importance of convention in the development of a stable system of property. For present purposes, the significant feature of Hume's account of convention is not merely that it illustrates how tacit, rather than express, agreements arise, but that it is clearly a process which occurs over time, becoming established by habit or custom. As such, it has local beginnings, steadily spreading outwards to other parts of human society as its advantages become more readily apparent.[194] Secondly, justice is also a slow growth in that the rules of justice do not develop all at

---

[193] 'Of the Populousness of Ancient Nations', *Essays*, i. 385 ff. Smith stresses the economic inefficiencies of slave economies throughout the *Lectures on Jurisprudence*. See, in particular, LJ(A) iii. 105–47; LJ(B) 290–301.

[194] *Treatise*, 489–91.

once, but steadily, through the natural workings of the human mind—through either the natural association of ideas, or rational reflection on the utility of particular innovations. Thus Hume accounts for the origins of the four main rules of property: occupation, prescription, accession, and succession.[195]

Of these rules, the case of prescription is the most interesting, because it requires not merely the passage of time before it can arise at all (it is not a rule established before the fact, which is then applied as it comes to bear on particular cases), but is effected by the influence of time on the human imagination itself. So, even though there is no original instinct to observe rules of property, time and the natural workings of the human mind combine to generate distinct inclinations to respect what is connected with others. He puts it in this way:

Possession during a long tract of time conveys a title to any object. But as 'tis certain, that, however every thing be produc'd in time, there is nothing real, that is produc'd by time; it follows, that property being produc'd by time, is not any thing real in the objects, but is the offspring of the sentiments, on which alone time is found to have any influence.[196]

The particular rules of property, arising as they do from the natural workings of the human mind, arise necessarily and therefore naturally. They are not invented in advance of the specific circumstances which come to manifest them, and, because they come to be manifest by convention, through the (in this respect) unaimed practices of ordinary individuals going about their everyday business, they also arise peacefully. This whole process occurs in time, steadily, as the exigencies of human life come to bear: so Hume's theory also implies that property has a natural history, as the seventeenth-century natural jurists assumed.

The second important feature of Hume's account is its only limited success in resolving the very problem he set out to solve—the problem of the motivation to be just, especially in hard cases like Hutcheson's problem of external rights. In Hume's theory, the problem has the following form. What is our motive for observing the rules of justice? It is the sense of justice, the sense of duty. This sense is not the original foundation of justice, because justice arises from the rational apprehension of the utility of the rules of justice. Rational insight, being merely instrumental to the achievement of

[195] Ibid. 501–14.   [196] Ibid. 509.

our goals, cannot motivate the will to perform just acts; and the sentiment which would be most useful in prompting us towards just acts—love of humanity as a whole—does not exist.[197] So, although in specific cases (such as those involving prescription), there may be natural associations of ideas which prompt the observance of the rule, in the main the performance of just acts depends on the sense of duty. Again, however, as Hutcheson and Hume are aware, and Kames in particular emphasizes, the sense of duty has no durable motivational base. Duty has not the appearance of beauty. In many ordinary cases, where there is no contrary moral beauty to contend against, or where self-interest does not intervene, this shortcoming in the motive to be just may not matter much. But in the not infrequent cases where these limits do not obtain, the motivation to perform the just action is notoriously weak; and the frequency of acts of injustice are a visible reminder that this is so. What, then, can prop up the sense of duty, and protect the fragile edifice of justice from erosion?

Hume recognizes the problem, and at the very end of the *2nd Enquiry* attempts to meet it. He notes that, if we treat vice 'with the greatest candour', then, 'in the case of justice . . . a man, taking things in a certain light, may often seem to be a loser by his integrity'.[198] A man may therefore decide to observe the rules of justice when it suits him, but not otherwise: 'That *honesty is the best policy*, may be a good general rule, but is liable to many exceptions; and he, it may perhaps be thought, conducts himself with most wisdom, who observes the general rule, and takes advantage of all the exceptions.'[199] The man who decides this has a difficult task confronting him, since, as Glaucon describes such a man in the *Republic*, he must maintain the appearance of acting justly, if he is to maintain control of his situation. The completely unjust man must be 'perfect in his wickedness'.[200]

With his eye on views like Glaucon's, Hume remarks that one stimulus to acting justly is therefore 'the frequent pleasure of seeing knaves, with all their pretended cunning and abilities, betrayed by their own maxims'. He offers this only as an incidental support. His principal objection to opportunism is that it is incompatible with

[197] *Treatise*, 481.
[198] *Enquiries*, 282.   [199] Ibid. 282–3.
[200] Plato, *The Republic*, trans. H. D. P. Lee (Harmondsworth: Penguin Books, 1955), 361a.

personal integrity. Before extolling the pleasures of integrity, however, he has to admit that it does not always cut a lot of ice:

I must confess that, if a man think that this reasoning much requires an answer, it will be a little difficult to find any which will to him appear satisfactory and convincing. If his heart rebel not against such pernicious maxims, if he feel no reluctance to the thoughts of villainy or baseness, he has indeed lost a considerable motive to virtue; and we may expect that his practice will be answerable to his speculation. But in all ingenuous natures, the antipathy to treachery and roguery is too strong to be counterbalanced by any views of profit or pecuniary advantage. Inward peace of mind, consciousness of integrity, a satisfactory review of our own conduct; these are circumstances, very requisite to happiness, and will be cherished and cultivated by every honest man, who feels the importance of them.[201]

Indeed they will. But as an answer to the problem of the motivation to justice, this is in fact a counsel of despair. It amounts to saying only that those who feel the importance of justice, who feel strongly the sense of duty, will continue to observe it, even when not to their advantage, and gain pleasure from doing so—but that those who do not, will not. And, since the problem of the motivation to be just most concerns those who are not strongly moved by the sense of duty, then the problem has not been resolved, merely restated.

If we may read between the lines a little, it seems that Hume may be aware that the problem remains. For he ends the discussion, and the work itself, with a further recommendation of the pleasures of a good character. This time, however, there is a significant twist. Instead of appealing to the pleasures of a good character as a reason simply for observing the rules of justice, and thus for eschewing opportunism, the goods of character are invoked as an alternative, indeed an antidote, to the preoccupation with material goods which makes the system of justice such a vital feature of the social order, even after the basic necessities of survival have been satisfied. The pleasures of personal integrity are transformed from a support for the system to a form of insulation against its shallow pleasures. So he concludes that the opportunists are the real losers:

were they ever so secret and successful, the honest man, if he has any tincture of philosophy, or even common observation and reflection, will discover that they themselves are, in the end, the greatest dupes, and have sacrificed the invaluable enjoyment of a character, with themselves at least,

[201] *Enquiries*, 283.

for the acquisition of worthless toys and geegaws. How little is requisite to supply the *necessities* of nature? And in a view to *pleasure*, what comparison between the unbought satisfaction of conversation, society, study, even health and the common beauties of nature, but above all the peaceful reflection on one's own conduct; what comparison, I say, between these and the feverish, empty amusements of luxury and expense? These natural pleasures, indeed, are really without price; both because they are below all price in their attainment, and above it in their enjoyment.[202]

In all probability, those with a tincture of philosophy will agree. Even so, the practical problem remains, because many lack entirely this tincture, and, even more commonly, many come to possess it only after the fact, having experienced at first hand the deceptions and insecurities of toys and gewgaws. For the unphilosophical and the inexperienced, no mean proportion of mankind, the problem of the allurements of injustice is a pressing one, and ironically Hume himself, in another passage, emphasizes that it is so. Unlike other passions, which are quite inconstant, material interests, he says, are constant and difficult to restrain: 'this avidity alone, of acquiring goods and possessions for ourselves and our nearest friends, is insatiable, perpetual, universal, and directly destructive of society.'[203] So the problem of the weakness of the motive to respect what is another's cannot, for a society at large, be settled by an appeal to the superior pleasures of conversation, society, study, etc.

In any case, it is very surprising that Hume should have taken this particular tack. For, in his political essays, the avaricious pursuit of material wealth plays a different role. In the essay 'Of Commerce', for example, he rejects, because 'too difficult to support,' the possibility of founding social advantage on a disinterested regard for the public good, and concludes instead that 'it is requisite to govern men by other passions, and animate them with a spirit of avarice and industry, art and luxury'.[204] And, in 'Of Refinement in the Arts', he argues that 'the ages of refinement are both the happiest and the most virtuous'. His reasons include the not implausible claim that happiness depends on purposeful activity:

In times when industry and the arts flourish, men are kept in perpetual occupation, and enjoy, as their reward, the occupation itself, as well as those pleasures which are the fruit of their labour. The mind acquires new

---

[202] *Enquiries*, 283–4.
[203] *Treatise*, 491–2.   [204] 'Of Commerce', *Essays*, i. 295.

vigour; enlarges its powers and faculties; and by an asiduity in honest industry, both satisfies its natural appetites, and prevents the growth of unnatural ones, which commonly spring up, when nourished by ease and idleness.[205]

If all this is so, then there is a closer connection—even if indirect—between the pursuit of material prosperity and happiness than the closing remarks of the *2nd Enquiry* suggest. So the problem of containing the motive to acquire material goods within just bounds cannot be easily overcome, even though, as Hume goes on to argue in 'Of Refinement in the Arts', the pleasures of the industrious society depend partly on the fact that people 'flock into cities' and develop a more sociable way of life, where they come 'to receive and communicate knowledge; to show their wit or their breeding; their taste in conversation or living . . . Both sexes meet in an easy and sociable manner: and the tempers of men, as well as their behaviour, refine apace.'[206] The connections between industry, happiness, and the cultivation of the virtues are too close to allow the problem of the motive to respect what is another's to be solved by abandoning the desire for material goods. In Hume's moral and political thought, the relationship between the motives to material advancement and to respecting what is another's remains awkward and complex.

7. HUME'S FOOTNOTE

It is time to sum up. Hume observes that his theory of property is much the same as Grotius's. In this chapter it has been argued that there is no bar, and substantial support, for accepting his claim, and therefore for recognizing his theory as a contribution to the modern theory of natural law. This conclusion is not debarred by the familiar figures of Hume the Newtonian or Hume the sceptic; and the doctrine of the artificiality of justice, which may also be thought an implicit rejection of natural law, is in fact an attempt to solve a problem created by grafting the moral sense account of the psychology of action on to the natural law account of the origins of justice and social order. In other respects his account of justice conforms with the main aims of the seventeenth-century natural law

[205] 'Of Refinement in the Arts', ibid. 301.   [206] Ibid. 301–2.

theories, stressing that the system of justice is both adventitious and necessary—arising steadily over time as circumstances require, and arising necessarily because it is the only secure foundation for the successful regulation of human social life.

Hume explicitly acknowledges Grotius, but it was pointed out at the beginning that he may have meant Grotius in particular, or the tradition of modern natural law, or both. It is now possible to offer a brief resolution of that issue. The theory of justice as an account of the necessary development over time of an adventitious rule for the regulation of human society, the theory that justice is a dictate of right reason, is common to the tradition of modern natural law as a whole, and is so because it is a defining characteristic even of ancient natural law. The other determining factor identified above, the influence of theories of the psychology of action, including moral action, is, in sharp contrast, a late development. It is best understood as part of the new 'experimental' philosophy of nature, being an attempt to explain human action in terms of efficient causes. It is not considered by Grotius, and neither does Pufendorf devote much attention to it—his strong concern with developing a moral science is with the attempt to provide a systematic account of morals, not with its efficient causes. It is towards the end of the seventeenth century that 'experimental' or 'Newtonian' ambitions are grafted on to natural jurisprudence, and the theory of moral sense is then developed in order to overcome an important tension in the alliance. In these two respects, then, Hume's debts are, firstly, to an essential feature of any natural law theory, established long before Grotius or Pufendorf; and, secondly, to subsequent extensions of the traditional doctrines, extensions which owed much to Locke and Hutcheson. His other debts, however, can be spelt out in terms of Pufendorfian or Grotian features.

The debts to Pufendorf are the less substantial. In the first place, Hume takes up Pufendorf's distinction between the different senses of 'natural' in order to include virtues produced by human artifice within a general theory of natural law. Secondly, following Hutcheson, he restricts the realm of natural law to intrinsic or material obligations, and, by combining this with an insistence on explanation in terms of efficient causes, makes the problem of motivation central to his theory in the *Treatise*. Thirdly, his view reflects Pufendorf's reformulation of the foundation of natural law, in which the contrast between human nature and utility is overcome. Hume's appeals to utility are always to rational or genuine utility, never to mere expediency, and so the practical part of his treatise on human nature is simultaneously a theory of utility.

Hume's debts to Grotius are not more numerous, but run more deeply. Firstly, his frequent insistence on the limitations on our natural benevolence—for example, that it is far too weak to serve as a foundation for the system of justice—is a return to a more limited conception of the nature of human sociability, and thus to a position not unlike Grotius's. He clearly believes that more refined tempers come to possess more extensive social affections than the vulgar, but accepts that sociability requires only a very limited benevolence. He therefore accepts a baseline of social affections and corresponding interdependence considerably more narrow than Pufendorf's stipulation that sociability requires the performance of beneficial actions, such that each of us are glad that there are others of our kind.

Secondly, and most importantly, Hume accepts Grotius's *etiamsi daremus* passage, with all its implications for a fully secular social theory. In coming to appreciate these implications to the fullest, he may have been influenced by Pierre Bayle, whose defence of the possibility of a society of (speculative) atheists owed much to Grotius.[207] It should not be forgotten that a secular social theory is not implicit atheism—not even 'practical atheism'.[208] The pivotal issue is whether a complete account of moral obligation is possible without reference to a divine legislator, and Hume's answer is unequivocally in the affirmative. He sees no need for a formal element in moral obligation, instead founding human society entirely on the social affections and the common reasonings of ordinary life. He describes his theory as the same as that *hinted at* by Grotius, and it is reasonable to take this to indicate a background feature of Grotius's work, rather than any detailed discussion of more specific issues of law and justice in the body of *De Jure Belli ac Pacis*. If this seems reasonable, the *etiamsi daremus* passage, with the accompanying introductory discussion of the foundations of natural law in the Prolegomenon to that massive work, appears to fit

---

[207] On Bayle, and his connections with Grotius and Hume, see E. Labrousse, *Bayle* (Oxford: Oxford University Press, 1983), ch. 4; and M. Ignatieff, *The Needs of Strangers* (London: Chatto & Windus, 1984), 90 ff.

[208] For an account of the different senses of 'atheism' in 18th-cent. Britain, see Norton, *David Hume: Common-Sense Moralist, Sceptical Metaphysician*, ch. 6.

the bill. Perhaps it is also noteworthy that the remark occurs in the *2nd Enquiry*, a work in which the earlier preoccupation with the sources of moral motivations has been considerably trimmed, thereby bringing into clearer focus the theory's broadly secular and utilitarian character.

In the *Abstract*, Hume claims that, 'if any thing can intitle the author to so glorious a name as that of an *inventor*, 'tis the use he makes of the principle of the association of ideas, which enters into most of his philosophy'.[209] This is an appropriate note on which to conclude, since it illustrates the centrality of Hume's psychological concerns. In both the *Treatise*, where he describes his account of property as an account of the development of a law of nature, and in the *2nd Enquiry*, where he acknowledges the debt to Grotius from which this study began, Hume clearly signals a debt to the main strands of modern natural law. If these claims have proven hard to accept, one principal reason is the extent to which his account of the psychological mechanisms at the very centre of the citadel of human nature has shaped his work, and obscured some of its affinities. Hume's aim is not to replace natural law, but to complete it, by calling on the powerful resources of the new experimental philosophy. He aims to ground moral obligations firmly in the soil of human nature itself, in the natural workings of the human mind, and thereby fulfil the bold ambitions of the theory of natural law.

[209] *Abstract*, in *Treatise*, 661–2.

Appendix

The Psychology of Moral Action
From Locke's *Essay* to Hutcheson's *Inquiry*

For Locke, happiness and misery are the two great springs of human action.[1] Happiness, he says in the *Essay*, 'every one constantly pursues, and *desires* what makes any part of it'.[2] Happiness is then defined as a simple relation between pleasure and pain: '*Happiness* . . . in its full extent is the utmost Pleasure we are capable of, and *Misery* the utmost Pain: and the lowest degree of what can be called *Happiness*, is so much ease from all Pain, and so much present pleasure, as without which any one cannot be content.'[3] Furthermore, pleasure and pain are the source of our valuations:

> Now because Pleasure and Pain are produced in us, by the operation of certain Objects, either on our Minds or our Bodies; and in different degrees: therefore what has an aptness to produce Pleasure in us, is that we call *Good*, and what is apt to produce Pain in us, we call *Evil*, for no other reason, but for its aptness to produce Pleasure and Pain in us, wherein consists our *Happiness* and *Misery*.[4]

Since we always pursue our happiness, this means that we also pursue what is good. Human action naturally is directed at achieving pleasure, a reasonable predominance of which is happiness, and this amounts to the pursuit of natural goodness. Moral goodness is a distinctive species of natural goodness. It introduces further features which will be described below.

What is it that prompts us to pursue happiness? After all, it is one thing to show that happiness is, of all possible ends, the most desirable, but quite

---

[1] This is most explicit in 'Of Ethick in General'—see J. Colman, *John Locke's Moral Philosophy* (Edinburgh: Edinburgh University Press, 1983), 179. Colman goes on to argue that Locke shifts 'from a quasi-mechanistic theory of the "springs" of action to a hedonistic theory of reasons for action' (pp. 179–80). This is, I think, mistaken. Locke's account of the springs of action *is* an account of the causes of action, but it is not thereby a denial of reasons. Colman appears to require a sharp distinction between reasons and causes, and in doing so tends to misrepresent Locke, who allows reason a role in a causal story. (Locke does separate rational from 'mechanistic' accounts, but because the latter are defined as non-rational, not because they are causal, see *Essay*, I. 3. 14.)

[2] *Essay*, II. 21. 43.   [3] Ibid. 42.   [4] Ibid.

another to show that we therefore (or even *in fact*) pursue it. The question first of all requires an answer to the more general question, What is it that moves us to action? By what means do human beings act? As a psychological (rather than physiological) question, it is to ask: What determines the will? Locke's original answer to this question was, simply, that the will is determined by its apprehension of the greatest good in view. However, in the second edition of the *Essay* he offers a different solution:

> *what is it that determines the Will in regard to our Actions?* And that upon second thoughts I am apt to imagine is not, as is generally supposed, the greater good in view: But some (and for the most part the most pressing) *uneasiness* a Man is at present under. This is that which successively determines the *Will*, and sets us upon those Actions, we perform.[5]

This uneasiness of the will is the psychological state called desire: 'This *Uneasiness* we may call, as it is, *Desire*; which is an *uneasiness* of the Mind for want of some absent good.'[6]

This introduces a problem: if desire is the want of an absent good, is not the account of action in terms of the uneasiness of the will equivalent to the account it replaces, that the will is determined by the apprehension of the greatest good in view? The difference, Locke holds, is this:

> I am forced to conclude, that *good*, the *greater good*, though apprehended and acknowledged to be so, does not determine the *will*, until our desire, raised proportionably to it, makes us *uneasy* in the want of it. Convince a Man never so much, that plenty has its advantages over poverty; make him see and own, that the handsome conveniences of life are better than nasty penury: yet as long as he is content with the latter, and finds no *uneasiness* in it, he moves not; his *will* never is determin'd to any action, that shall bring him out of it.[7]

The revised account thus differs in two respects. It shows that human action is not always directed to the greatest good (although it is always directed to *some* good), and it provides an efficient cause for human action. The efficient cause identified is, in fact, the flight from pain, since uneasiness is a kind of pain. Locke comes close to explicitly asserting this when he says that 'all pain of the body of what sort soever, and disquiet of the mind, is *uneasiness*'.[8] In another passage the identity is implicit:

> whilst we are under any *uneasiness*, we cannot apprehend ourselves happy, or in the way to it. Pain and *uneasiness* being . . . inconsistent with happiness; spoiling the relish, even of those good things which we have . . . And therefore that, which of course determines the choice of our *will* to

[5] *Essay*, II. 21. 31.
[6] Ibid.   [7] Ibid. 35.   [8] Ibid. 31.

the next action, will always be the removing of pain . . . as the first and necessary step towards happiness.[9]

Locke's psychology of action thus hinges not so much on the pursuit of pleasure as on the flight from pain. It is of course a flight towards pleasure, but the actual motivating force, what 'determines the will', is the attempt to escape present pain. The pursuit of happiness, or of the greatest good, is thus rather haphazard, or zigzagging. The zigzagging is partly a function of our limited knowledge—a theme of great importance in the *Essay*—since our perception of our good will not always be accurate; but it is the perception, rather than the genuine good, which plays a role in our behaviour. The account of action in terms of uneasiness, however, provides a further reason for allowing misperceptions to be efficacious, since the greater the unease, the more pressing is the need to act—and hence the greater possibility of acting on insufficient reflection. The proverbial inadequacies of hasty action are to the point here. The account of action in terms of unease implicitly recognizes the problems of hasty, misdirected actions.

Locke's account of the efficient cause of human action therefore weakens the case for allotting a major role to the final cause which, he tells us, 'when I first published my thoughts on this Subject, I took . . . for granted'.[10] If motivated by unease, human actions aim only haphazardly at the greatest good. Locke's revised psychology of action thus weakens the supports of the 'workmanship' model, with its strong teleology. This is not to say, of course, that it fatally or irreparably weakens them—especially since Locke was almost certainly aware of ways of reconciling mechanistic and teleological types of explanation. Given his close association with Robert Boyle, it is unlikely that he was unaware of the latter's views on efficient causes and teleology. According to Boyle, ends can be either *sought* by purposive actions, or *served* by non-purposive causes. An explanation in terms of efficient causes is compatible with a teleological explanation as long as the end in question is served. It does not have to be sought. Locke's shift from an account couched in terms of the pursuit of the greatest good to one couched in terms of unease is thus a shift from a teleological explanation in which the end (human happiness) is sought to an explanation in which that end may still be served. The problem, of course, is that there is no guarantee that unease will reliably serve the end of human happiness.

However, Locke is not without a response to this problem. His view is that, by reflecting on the nature and order of the world, we are able to recognize that the world has a designer, and that this designer has not only power, but legitimate power over his creatures. Once we recognize that we are subject to 'the Will and Law of a God, who sees Men in the dark, has in

[9] Ibid. 36.   [10] Ibid. 35.

his Hand Rewards and Punishments, and Power enough to call to account the Proudest Offender',[11] we also recognize that there is one class of pleasures and pains which, although distant, are unavoidable, and that these therefore have an overriding significance. These are the moral pleasures and pains, which comprise moral good and evil. So moral goodness has an overriding significance not because moral goods are intrinsic goods, nor because they are qualitatively different from other natural goods. Moral goodness is just the pleasure afforded by the rewards attached to conforming to the laws which express the divine will.[12] The overriding significance of moral good or evil is identical to the unparalleled uneasiness excited by the contemplation of the pleasures or pains to be dispensed by the 'God, who sees Men in the Dark'.

Locke also recognizes that even the contemplation, or at least awareness, of such ultimate happiness or misery is not always sufficient to determine the will, and that moral practices therefore do not always measure up to moral professions.[13] However, the gap can be narrowed (if not bridged) because, although men have no natural veneration for moral rules,[14] they can learn to take pleasure in virtue: even though 'the Mind has a different relish, as well as the Palate', and therefore 'the Philosophers of old did in vain enquire, whether *Summum bonum* consisted in Riches, or bodily Delights, or Virtue, or Contemplation',[15] nevertheless through education men can be 'made alive to virtue and can taste it'.[16] The task of education is thus clearly an important one, and Locke devotes a number of works to the topic.

As several passages in the writings on education suggest, the (admittedly rocky) path to a state in which virtue is enjoyed depends on the natural sociability of human beings, especially their desire to be esteemed by others. Children are, from a very early age, 'sensible of Praise and Commendation', and 'find a Pleasure in being esteemed, and valued'. As a result they come to care about those things which will win them approval, at first for the sake of approval, but later simply for the things themselves. At first, 'the Objects of their own Desires are made assisting to Virtue', and from being 'in Love with Pleasure of being well thought on' they can come to be 'in Love with all the ways of Virtue'.[17] In this way a self-centred

---

[11] *Essay*, I. 3. 6.
[12] Locke distinguishes between natural and moral good along these lines in 'Of Ethick in General'. Moral good 'draws pleasure or paine after it . . . by the intervention of divine power' (quoted in Colman, *John Locke's Moral Philosophy*, 168).
[13] *Essay*, I. 3. 7. [14] Ibid. [15] Ibid. II. 21. 55.
[16] Commonplace Book entry 'Ethica' (1693), quoted in Colman, *John Locke's Moral Philosophy*, 206.
[17] *Some Thoughts concerning Education* (sects. 57–8), in J. Axtell (ed.), *The Educational Writings of John Locke* (Cambridge: Cambridge University Press, 1986).

psyche—concerned only with its own pleasures—can come to care for wider social goods for their own sakes. The necessity of society for human survival as well as for the peculiar pleasures it affords a nature which has a strong inclination to sociability and the social life makes adaptation of this kind a rational development which supports human ends.[18] So Locke is able to conclude that the preoccupation with self-interest has 'always been opposed by the more rational part of men, in whom there was some sense of a common humanity, some concern for fellowship'.[19] The concern for virtue for its own sake arises steadily and in parallel with the development of this sense of common humanity.

This feature of Locke's view—the construction of the disinterested love of virtue from an originally self-regarding psychology—implies an important further conclusion. In the *Essay*, he holds that there are three '*Laws* that Men generally refer their Actions to, to judge of their Rectitude, or Obliquity'.[20] They are the Divine Law, the Civil Law, and the 'Law of *Opinion* or *Reputation*'. The Divine Law includes both special divine positive laws, and also natural laws; it specifies strict moral rectitude—duties and sins. The Civil Law determines which actions are criminal. Unlike the former, it measures actions by rewards or punishments imposed by the force of the Commonwealth, not by God.[21] The third law concerns virtue and vice. It therefore may have the same content as the Divine Law, as Locke observes: 'Vertue and Vice are names pretended, and supposed every where to stand for actions in their own nature right and wrong: And so far as they really are so applied, they so far are co-incident with the *divine Law* abovementioned.'[22] The Law of Opinion is not, therefore, a law whose content is inferior to, or necessarily distinct from, the provisions of natural law. It is distinguished from natural and other Divine Law in that it reflects what men happen to believe, whether or not those beliefs are grounded in right reason. It is constituted by the established beliefs of particular societies, and so varies from society to society. Virtue and vice, in this sense, are constituted by the actual judgements of men concerning praiseworthiness or blameworthiness:

> this is visible, that these Names, *Vertue* and *Vice*, in the particular instances of their application, through the several Nations and Societies of Men in the World, are constantly attributed only to such actions, as in each Country and Society are in reputation or discredit. Nor is it to be

---

[18] Locke's account of the necessity and pleasures of the social life is clearly indebted to the natural lawyers. God, he says, put Man 'under strong Obligations of Necessity, Convenience, and Inclination to drive him into *Society*, as well as fitted him with Understanding and Language to continue and enjoy it' (*Two Treatises*, ii. 77).

[19] Essay viii, *ELN* 205.

[20] *Essay*, ii. 28. 7.

[21] Ibid. 8–9.

[22] Ibid. 10.

thought strange, that Men every where should give the name of *Vertue* to those actions, which amongst them are judged praise worthy; and call that *Vice*, which they account blamable: Since otherwise they would condemn themselves, if they should think any thing *Right*, to which they allow'd not Commendation; any thing *Wrong*, which they let pass without Blame. Thus the measure of what is every where called and esteemed *Vertue* and *Vice* is this approbation or dislike, praise or blame, which by a secret and tacit consent establishes itself in the several Societies, Tribes, and Clubs of Men in the World: whereby several actions come to find Credit or Disgrace amongst them, according to the Judgment, Maxims, or Fashions of that place . . .

That this is the common *measure of Vertue and Vice* will appear to any one, who considers, that though that passes for Vice in one Country, which is counted a *Vertue*, or at least not *Vice* in another; yet every-where *Vertue* and Praise, *Vice* and Blame, go together.[23]

So, unlike Divine Law and Civil Law, the Law of Opinion is distinguished not by a different kind of formal obligation—a difference in the power which enforces it—but by the manner of its generation, and in fact by an absence of formal obligation. It comes about because certain practices are considered praiseworthy, and it is maintained by the efficacy of praise and blame.[24]

As the passages on the education of children show, the 'Law of Opinion' is the pre-eminent motivation of human action. Human practice, even if it properly should conform to the provisions of the Divine Law (or to a lesser degree, of the Civil Law), is in fact principally shaped by the forces of opinion. It is therefore very important for human society that there exist a general agreement between the Law of Opinion and the other two laws. In particular, the Law of Opinion is necessary to support, to encourage adherence to, the Divine Law, since the remoteness of the latter's rewards and punishments (in the future life), leaves it most vulnerable to abuse. In fact, Locke's account of the development of virtuous conduct through the child's simple desire to please shows that the Law of Opinion is a crucial support for the law of nature, where their provisions coincide, and, where they do not, is a powerful obstacle to the pursuit of natural justice.

[23] *Essay*, II. 28. 10–11.

[24] Since the Law of Opinion is not dependent on any legitimate authority, it is doubtful whether Locke can appropriately describe it as a *law*. On his account, a law is the decree of a rightful authority; laws depend on both a material and a formal obligation. He argues that the Law of Opinion is truly a law because it effectively motivates compliant behaviour, but this is beside the point. It simply affirms the effectiveness of the material element; the *rightfulness* of the effect—which must be established if there is to be a valid law—is not addressed. So the Law of Opinion cannot be properly described as a law. Although it controls, it does not *govern*, human actions. See *Essay*, II. 28. 12; and Colman, *John Locke's Moral Philosophy*, 170.

When, if ever, can we expect the provisions of the two laws to coincide? There is room for confidence in those cases where a particular rule is necessary for human social life itself. But such necessity is precisely the distinguishing mark of natural law itself. As Pufendorf puts it, natural law is distinguished by the fact that 'the reason for [it] is sought from the condition of mankind as a whole', it 'so harmonizes with the natural and social nature of man that the human race can have no wholesome peaceful social organization without it'.[25] In similar vein, Hume describes the law of nature as 'what is common to any species, or even . . . what is inseparable from the species'.[26] So the very necessity of natural law will serve to secure a rough harmony between it and the Law of Opinion, even though the latter implies a great variety of views concerning the farther reaches of virtue and vice amongst the 'Clubs of Men in the World'. For this reason, the law of nature's dependence on the Law of Opinion in order to secure general compliance is not so much a weakness as a strength: the Law of Opinion will generally support the rational dictates of the natural law, and, since it is the 'law' which most effectively motivates human beings, it will therefore help to ensure that the law of nature is not merely recognized, but practised.

Recognizing this broad harmony between opinion and nature allows us also to see a significant further implication. If, in the spirit of Grotius's *etiamsi daremus*, the theory of natural law were to be revised by denying the necessity of the formal element of obligation, and affirming instead the sufficiency of the material element (so that the obligatory force of the natural law could be derived entirely from the constitution of human nature itself), then, because the operations of the Law of Opinion are sufficient to generate rules of behaviour which conform to the rational dictates of the natural law, this would open up the possibility that the kind of pre-reflective, or semi-reflective, practices presupposed by the Law of Opinion are themselves sufficient to generate the content of the natural law. The rationality of the natural law could then be shown not by affirming the rationality of the processes that produce it, but by rational reflection on the results of non-reflective (non-rational) processes. In other words, by distinguishing between the context of discovery and the context of justification (a distinction which becomes necessary in order to maintain such a view), it would then be possible to account for the development of dictates of right reason, natural laws, entirely by means of non-reflective practices, or conventions. This is just what Hume does. His account of the origins of justice is an account of the establishment, through conventions, of rules necessary for human social life. Rational reflection on the rules thus established affirms their real utility for human life, so the rules can then be recognized to be dictates of right reason—laws natural to human beings.

[25] *DJNG* II. 3. 24; I. 6. 18.
[26] Hume, *Treatise*, 484.

The first task of political authority is then to establish civil laws to protect these rational underpinnings of the social order.

This speculation about the origins of Hume's theory can be pressed to two further conclusions. In the first place, it may be possible to explain why Hume ignores the jurisprudential language of rights and duties in his account of natural law, preferring instead to speak entirely in terms of virtues and vices. If the system of justice arises as the result of processes whose tendency and ultimate justification are sensed only dimly, if at all, by the actors who serve to bring it about, it is inappropriate to describe their behaviour in terms which draw on the features of that final outcome. Law is the end of the process, not the beginning, so juristic notions like right and duty would, if applied to the behaviour of the participants in its formation, substantially misrepresent that behaviour. It would be far preferable to rely on concepts which reflect the important roles played by habit and character in that process, and the language of virtues and vices therefore fits the bill.[27]

Secondly, it may help to explain the meaning of the concept of opinion which plays such an important role in his account of the foundations of the social and political order.[28] If Locke's 'Law of Opinion' is in the back of his mind in these passages, then to ground the social order in opinion is to ground it in the beliefs specific to each actual society. It is, first and foremost, to deny the existence of a general (universal) justification of any form of political order. As beliefs in any given society change, so too will the considerations which serve to justify (or not) its political system. This conclusion is clearly implicit in his account of the foundations of the English political order in *The History of England*, and it also underlies his apparent tendency to argue from right to fact in some of the political essays—in particular, in 'Of the Original Contract'. So, on this interpretation, by founding political society on opinion Hume clearly opposes those who sought to find a timeless or even 'ancient' foundation for the political order. He does not, however, advance a sceptical thesis—at least, no more than Locke does by advancing the idea of a 'Law of Opinion'. His aim is not to reduce politics to *mere* (fickle) opinion, rather than to secure beliefs. It is to argue, firstly, that it is precisely beliefs that are fundamental in this sphere, and, secondly, that therefore the justification of political order varies across

[27] This is a suggestion only. It is certainly not meant as a definitive account, nor is it intended to rule out other (perhaps other complementary) possibilities. To take just 2 exs.: his avoidance of the notion of rights could be attributed simply to the desire to avoid associations with Hutcheson's doctrine. Alternatively, it may reflect his enthusiasm for the ancient moralists, with their greater emphasis on the virtues of character.

[28] Hume stresses the importance of opinion in the essays 'Of the First Principles of Government' and 'Of the Original Contract', in *Essays Moral, Political, and Literary*, i, esp. 110, 460.

Appendix

307

time and space. It could perhaps be described as a thesis in the sociology of knowledge.[29]

To return to Locke. It has been shown that his account of the psychology of action, despite holding that all human beings aim only at their own pleasure (albeit indirectly, by fleeing painful uneasiness), is nevertheless able to show how the desire for praise presupposed by the Law of Opinion can lead to a disinterested pursuit of the sociable maxims of natural law. This aspect of his thought was not always recognized by his contemporary critics, and, given also his very limited account of the content of the *suum*,[30] he thus came to be charged with failing to understand the full ramifications of the sociable nature of human beings. In particular, he was charged with failing to recognize that the story of the origins of political society, property, etc., is, even at its most atomic, the story of the interactions of human families.[31]

This is argued most forcefully by Bolingbroke, who attacks Locke for overlooking the intimate interconnection of natural law and sociability. However, Bolingbroke accepts the standard natural law view of the centrality of self-love. Sociability is not thought to be incompatible with self-love, but to be implied by it. Thus in an important passage in his collected 'fragments' of essays, he argues that:

> There is a sort of genealogy of law, in which nature begets natural law, natural law sociability, sociability union of societies by consent, and this union by consent the obligation of civil laws. When I make sociability the daughter of natural law, and the granddaughter of nature, I mean plainly this. Self-love, the original spring of human actions, directs us necessarily to sociability. [32]

---

[29] The sociological interpretation of 'opinion' proposed here is also indicated by the title of Shaftesbury's *Characteristicks of Men, Manners, Opinions, Times* (1711), a work which enjoyed great popularity amongst early 18th-cent. moralists, Hume included. So Nicholas Phillipson's interpretation of the meaning of 'opinion'—see his *Hume* (London: Weidenfeld Nicolson, 1989), ch. 4 (esp. p. 62)—seems unnecessarily sceptical.

[30] Even Hobbes's account of the *suum* gives more recognition of the importance of the social. In *Leviathan*, his account of 'things held in propriety' includes not only life and limbs, but also those relations 'that concern conjugall affection' (ch. 30). Locke, in contrast, explicitly identifies only life, liberty, and estate. Admittedly, he does not discuss the possibility of different levels of propriety, and perhaps if he had a more generous conclusion would be possible, since he does insist that men are 'under strong Obligations of Necessity, Convenience, and Inclination' to enter into society, and are adapted for the sociable life (*Two Treatises*, ii. 77).

[31] This is not to defend such criticisms. Locke frequently is more individualistic than his contemporaries, but he nevertheless did understand the natural state to be an association of natural families. See e.g. R. Ashcraft, *Locke's Two Treatises of Government* (London: Unwin Hyman, 1987), ch. 5.

[32] Viscount Bolingbroke, *Works* (Farnborough: Gregg International, 1969), iv. 164.

In Bolingbroke's view, Locke's errors all come down to the failure properly to understand sociability, and in particular the intimacy of its connection with the self-love which founds natural law. He goes on to argue that, by representing mankind 'like a number of savage individuals out of all society', Locke, one of 'our best writers', has reasoned 'both inconsistently, and on a false foundation'.[33]

A more radical critique than Bolingbroke's, however, comes from Locke's own former pupil, the third Earl of Shaftesbury. In the *Characteristics of Men, Manners, Opinions, Times* (1711), and even more forcefully in his letters, Shaftesbury denounces the very attempt to derive moral practices from self-love. It is, he believes, to abolish sociableness and morality, and to replace it with mere self-interest.[34] Against the self-love account he both stresses the strength of the social passions, and also argues against their reducibility to any hidden principles of self-love. He suggests that even social disorder can be traced to the strength of the social passions: 'For my own part, methinks, this herding principle, and associating inclinations, is seen so natural and strong in most men, that one might readily affirm 'twas even from the violence of this passion that so much disorder arose in the general society of mankind.'[35] The irreducibility of the social passions is affirmed by the crucial doctrine of the moral sense, the importance of which for the later Scottish natural law theorists is difficult to overstress. It provides the cornerstone of a psychology of action in which irreducibly social passions are at the heart. Sociability comes to be constructed directly from the social passions.

This is best shown by Hutcheson's defence of Shaftesbury's doctrine of the reality of a moral sense, a fundamental benevolent principle in human nature. In Hutcheson's terms, we are so constituted to perceive 'an *immediate natural Good* in the Actions call'd *Virtuous*; that is, That we are

---

[33] Viscount Bolingbroke, *Works* (Farnborough: Gregg International, 1969), IV. 194–5.

[34] Lord Shaftesbury, *Characteristics of Men, Manners, Opinions, Times* (New York: Bobbs-Merrill, 1969), 2 vols. in 1, i. 63–5, 280–2, in particular. Shaftesbury's position is neatly summed up in D. F. Norton, *David Hume: Common-Sense Moralist, Sceptical Metaphysician* (Princeton: Princeton University Press, 1982): 'Such words as *courage, friendship, love,* and *public interest,* words which seem to denote altruistic acts or tendencies, are found to mean [on the self-love view] nothing different from their apparent opposites, for all acts and tendencies are similarly motivated and hence all are at bottom alike' (pp. 34–5).

[35] Shaftesbury, *Characteristics*, i. 75. Hume acknowledges his indebtedness to Shaftesbury on just this point. In the earlier versions of the essay 'Of the Dignity or Meanness of Human Nature', he says: 'I shall observe, what has been prov'd beyond Question by several great Moralists of the present Age, that the social Passions are by far the most powerful of any, and that even all the other Passions receive from them their chief Force and Influence. Whoever desires to see this Question treated at large, with the greatest Force of Argument and Eloquence, may consult my Lord SHAFTSBURY's Enquiry concerning Virtue' (*Essays*, i. 154 n.).

determin'd to perceive some *Beauty* in the Actions of others, and to love
the Agent, even without reflecting upon any *Advantage* which can in any
way rebound to us from the Action'.[36] Of course, if, as Bolingbroke and
others believed, self-love itself suffices to generate social affections, and
generally drive us to the social life, then there will be no special incentive to
abandon the self-love account in favour of a moral sense theory. This will be
so even if the latter is able to capture some of our intuitions about how we
see ourselves to be affected by the actions, or the fortunes or misfortunes,
of others. A well-worked-out theory of the springs of action will survive
apparent weaknesses if it is thought to offer a unifying account of human
action. If the alternative theory is itself seen to embody seriously
implausible assumptions, then the established theory will win by default.
This is Bolingbroke's view. He holds that the moral sense alternative
requires committing oneself to discredited or absurd views. In his *Essays on
Human Knowledge* he rejects any appeal to a moral sense, 'for to assume
any such natural instinct is as absurd as to assume innate ideas, or any other
of the Platonic whimsies'.[37]

Bolingbroke is mistaken, but the mistake is understandable. Shaftesbury's
view is Platonic in this sense, apparently because he believes that the
objects of moral sensing, if they are not to be dangerously changeable, must
be innate. In his view, innate ideas are an integral part of true morality, the
only sure defence against morality's enemies, the self-love theorists. This
explains the hostility of his reaction to Locke's critique of innate ideas: it is,
for him, an attack on the very foundation of moral virtue. Shaftesbury's
conclusion is that Locke is therefore an even greater enemy of morals than
Hobbes: although the latter's reduction of all virtue to self-interest
manifests an opposition to morals, Locke's account of morals in terms of
experience and custom makes him a more dangerous, because more
insidious, enemy of virtue:

> It was Mr. Locke that struck the home blow: for Mr Hobbes' character
> and base slavish principles in government took off the poison of his
> philosophy. 'Twas Mr Locke that struck at all fundamentals, threw all
> order and virtue out of the world and made the very ideas of these . . .
> unnatural and without foundation in our minds.

---

[36] *Inquiry*, (2nd edn.), 115. Hutcheson shows himself to be offering a defence of
Shaftesbury in the subtitle to the 1st edn., where he says that in this work 'the
Principles of the late Earl of Shaftesbury are explained and defended'. The subtitle
was dropped from later edns., but not because of any change of heart by the author.
Shaftesbury remains 'that ingenious Nobleman', his works a model of humane
learning: 'To recommend the *Lord SHAFTESBURY's* Writings to the World, is a very
needless Attempt. They will be esteemed while any *Reflection* remains among Men'
(2nd edn., p. xxi).
[37] *Works*, iii. 399.

This is so because

> virtue, according to Mr. Locke, has no other measure, law, or rule, than fashion and custom; morality, justice, equity, depend only on law and will . . . And thus neither right nor wrong, virtue nor vice, are anything in themselves; nor is there any trace or idea of them naturally imprinted on human minds. Experience and our catechism teach us all.[38]

Hutcheson, however, does not go along with this. Although he presents himself as a defender of Shaftesbury's doctrine, and identifies the self-love theory of morals as his target—represented by Hobbes,[39] and also by 'the Author of the Fable of the Bees'[40]—he explicitly detaches moral sense theory from the doctrine of innate ideas: 'We are not to imagine that this moral Sense, more than the other Senses, supposes any innate ideas, Knowledge, or practical Proposition.'[41] As a result, Hutcheson shows none of Shaftesbury's antipathy to Locke. Although the latter founds morality on self-love, this does not make him (or even Hobbes, for that matter) an enemy of morality. The self-love theory fails not because it undermines morality, but because it does not measure up to the facts. It is thereby forced to provide tortuous stories for the most simple and familiar of unselfish acts. Hutcheson sums up its deficiencies as follows: in treating of 'our *Desires* or *Affections*', the self-love theorists have been forced to make 'the most generous, kind, and disinterested of them, to proceed from *Self-Love*, by some subtle Trains of Reasoning, to which honest Hearts are often wholly Strangers'.[42] Moral sense theory thus embarks on the plausible and attractive programme of deriving our beneficent behaviours directly from an original benevolent impulse. The problem it encounters, as Chapters 4 and 5 show, is that sociability depends on benevolence or fellow-feeling only to a limited degree. The fundamental virtue of justice, respect for what is another's, is founded in a rational utility which inevitably comes into conflict with benevolent impulses. The central problem for moral sense theory, as a putative science of moral behaviour, is to explain how this virtue comes into being, without threatening its stability or restricting its scope.

[38] *Letters of the Earl of Shaftesbury to a Student at the University* (1716), 45; quoted in J. Aronson, 'Shaftesbury on Locke', *American Political Science Review*, 53 (1959), 1103. Cf. also Norton, *David Hume*, 35.

[39] The doctrine that 'all the desires of the *human Mind*, nay of all *thinking Natures*, are reducible to *Self-Love*, or *Desire of private Happiness*' is the doctrine of 'the old *Epicureans*', now 'revived by Mr *Hobbes*, and followed by many better Writers' (introd. to *Illustrations on the Moral Sense*, *Collected Works*, ii. 207–8).

[40] *Inquiry* (1st edn., 1725), subtitle.

[41] *Inquiry*, 135. See also the revised and expanded discussion of the nature of moral perception in the 4th edn. (1738), 129–31.

[42] Preface to *Passions and Affections* (and see also introd. to *Illustrations*), *Collected Works*, ii, p. vi (and p. 209).

Select Bibliography

AQUINAS, THOMAS, *The Political Ideas of St. Thomas Aquinas*, trans. English Dominican Fathers, ed. Dino Bigongiari (New York: Hafner Press, 1953).

ARDAL, PALL S., *Passion and Value in Hume's Treatise* (Edinburgh: Edinburgh University Press, 1966).

ARISTOTLE, *Nicomachean Ethics*, trans. W. D. Ross, revised J. L. Ackrill and J. O. Urmson (Oxford: Oxford University Press, 1980).

ARONSON, JASON, 'Shaftesbury on Locke', *American Political Science Review*, 53 (1959), 1101–4.

ASHCRAFT, RICHARD, *Revolutionary Politics and Locke's 'Two Treatises of Government'* (Princeton: Princeton University Press, 1986).

—— *Locke's Two Treatises of Government* (London: Unwin Hyman, 1987).

BALDWIN, THOMAS, 'Tully, Locke, and Land', *Locke Newsletter*, 13 (1982), 21–33.

BARON, MARCIA, 'Hume's Noble Lie: An Account of his Artificial Virtues', *Canadian Journal of Philosophy*, 12 (1982), 539–53.

BECKER, LAWRENCE, *Property Rights: Philosophic Foundations* (London: Routledge & Kegan Paul, 1977).

BOLINGBROKE, HENRY ST. JOHN, Viscount, *The Works*, 4 vols. (Philadelphia: Carey and Hart, 1841; repr. Farnborough: Gregg International 1969).

CAMPBELL, R.H., and SKINNER, A. S., (eds.), *The Origins and Nature of the Scottish Enlightenment* (Edinburgh: John Donald, 1982).

CAMPBELL, THOMAS D., *Adam Smith's Science of Morals* (London: George Allen & Unwin, 1971).

CICERO, MARCUS TULLIUS, *De Officiis*, trans. W. Miller (London: Heinemann, 1913).

—— *De Finibus Bonorum et Malorum*, trans. H. Rackham (London: Heinemann, 1914).

COLMAN, JOHN, *John Locke's Moral Philosophy* (Edinburgh: Edinburgh University Press, 1983).

DALY, JAMES, *Sir Robert Filmer and English Political Thought* (Toronto: University of Toronto Press, 1979).

DAY, J. P., 'Locke on Property', *Philosophical Quarterly*, 16 (1966), 207–21.

DEFOE, DANIEL, *The Life and Adventures of Robinson Crusoe* (1719), ed. Angus Ross (Harmondsworth: Penguin Books, 1965).

DRURY, S. B., 'Locke and Nozick on Property', *Political Studies*, 30 (1982), 28–41.

DUNN, JOHN, 'Justice and the Interpretation of Locke's Political Theory', *Political Studies*, 16 (1968), 68–87.

—— *The Political Thought of John Locke* (Cambridge: Cambridge University Press, 1969).

—— *Locke* (Oxford: Oxford University Press, 1984).

FERGUSON, ADAM, *An Essay on the History of Civil Society*, ed. Duncan Forbes (Edinburgh: Edinburgh University Press, 1966).

FILMER, Sir ROBERT, *Patriarcha and other Political Works of Sir Robert Filmer*, ed. with an introd. by Peter Laslett (Oxford: Basil Blackwell, 1949).

FORBES, DUNCAN, *Hume's Philosophical Politics* (Cambridge: Cambridge University Press, 1975).

—— 'Sceptical Whiggism, Commerce, and Liberty', in A. S. Skinner and T. Wilson (eds.), *Essays on Adam Smith* (Oxford: Clarendon Press, 1975).

—— 'Hume's Science of Politics', in G. P. Morice (ed.), *David Hume: Bicentenary Papers* (Edinburgh: Edinburgh University Press, 1977).

FORSYTH, MURRAY, 'The Place of Richard Cumberland in the History of Natural Law Doctrine', *Journal of the History of Philosophy*, 20 (1982), 23–42.

GIERKE, OTTO VON, *Natural Law and the Theory of Society 1500–1800*, 2 vols., trans. Ernest Barker (Cambridge: Cambridge University Press, 1934).

GRANT, RUTH W., *John Locke's Liberalism* (Chicago: University of Chicago Press, 1987).

GROTIUS, HUGO, *Grotius on the Freedom of the Seas*, trans. R. V. D. Magoffin (New York: Oxford University Press, 1916).

—— *De Jure Praedae Commentarius* (1604), trans. G. L. Williams, with W. H. Zeydel (Oxford: Clarendon Press, 1950).

—— *De Jure Belli ac Pacis Libri Tres* (1625), trans. F. W. Kelsey (New York: Oceana Publications, 1964).

HAAKONSSEN, KNUD, *The Science of a Legislator: The Natural Jurisprudence of David Hume and Adam Smith* (Cambridge: Cambridge University Press, 1981).

—— 'Natural Law and the Scottish Enlightenment', in D. H. Jory and C. Stewart-Robinson (eds.), *Man and Nature*, Proceedings of the Canadian Society for Eighteenth Century Studies, 4 (Edmonton: Academic Printing and Publishing, 1985).

—— 'Hugo Grotius and the History of Political Thought', *Political Theory*, 13 (1985), 239–65.

HELD, VIRGINIA, 'John Locke on Robert Nozick', *Social Research*, 43 (1976), 16–95.

HINTON, R. W. K., 'HUSBANDS, FATHERS AND CONQUERORS', 2 PARTS, *Political Studies*, 15 (1967), 291–300, and 16 (1968), 53–67.

Hirschman, Albert 0., *The Passions and the Interests* (Princeton: Princeton University Press, 1977).

Hobbes, Thomas, *Leviathan*, ed. C. B. Macpherson (Harmondsworth: Penguin Books, 1968).

—— *Man and Citizen*, ed. Bernard Gert (Brighton: Harvester, 1972).

Honoré, A. M., 'Ownership', in A. G. Guest (ed.), *Oxford Essays in Jurisprudence* (Oxford: Oxford University Press, 1961).

Hont, Istvan and Ignatieff, Michael, 'Needs and Justice in the *Wealth of Nations*: An Introductory Essay', in Istvan Hont and Michael Ignatieff (eds.), *Wealth and Virtue: The Shaping of Political Economy in the Scottish Enlightenment* (Cambridge: Cambridge University Press, 1983).

Hope, Vincent, *Virtue by Consensus: The Moral Philosophy of Hutcheson, Hume, and Smith* (Oxford: Clarendon Press, 1989).

Horace [Quintus Horatius Flaccus], *Satires, Epistles and Ars Poetica*, trans. H. Rushton Fairclough (London: Heinemann, 1926).

Horne, Thomas A., 'Moral and Economic Improvement: Francis Hutcheson on Property', *History of Political Thought* 7 (1986), 115–30.

Hume, David, *The Letters of David Hume*, ed. J. Y. T. Greig, 2 vols. (Oxford: Oxford University Press, 1932).

—— *Dialogues concerning Natural Religion*, ed. H. D. Aiken (New York: Hafner Press, 1948).

—— *Essays Moral, Political, and Literary*, ed. T. H. Green and T. H. Grose, 2 vols. (London, 1882); repr. Aalen: Scientia Verlag, 1964).

—— *A Letter from a Gentleman to his Friend in Edinburgh* (1745), ed. E. C. Mossner and J. V. Price (Edinburgh: Edinburgh University Press, 1967).

—— *Enquiries concerning Human Understanding and concerning the Principles of Morals*, 3rd edn., ed. L. A. Selby-Bigge, rev. P. H. Nidditch (Oxford: Clarendon Press, 1975).

—— *A Treatise of Human Nature* (1739–40), 2nd edn., ed. L. A. Selby-Bigge, rev. P. H. Nidditch (Oxford: Clarendon Press, 1978).

—— *The History of England*, 6 vols. (Indianapolis: Liberty Classics, 1983).

Hutcheson, Francis, *Collected Works*, facsimile edn., 7 vols. (Hildesheim: Olms, 1969).

—— *An Inquiry concerning Beauty and Virtue* (2nd edn., 1726), facsimile edn. (New York: Garland Publishing, 1971).

—— *An Inquiry concerning Beauty and Virtue* (4th edn., 1738), facsimile edn. (Farnborough: Gregg International, 1969).

Ignatieff, Michael, *The Needs of Strangers* (London: Chatto & Windus, 1984).

Jones, Peter, *Hume's Sentiments: Their Ciceronian and French Context* (Edinburgh: Edinburgh University Press, 1982).

—— (ed.), *The 'Science of Man' in the Scottish Enlightenment* (Edinburgh: Edinburgh University Press, 1989).

KAMES, HENRY HOME, Lord, *Essays on the Principles of Morality and Natural Religion* (1751), facsimile edn. (New York: Garland Publishing, 1976).

KEMP SMITH, NORMAN, *The Philosophy of David Hume* (London: Macmillan, 1949).

KRAMNICK, ISAAC, *Bolingbroke and his Circle* (Cambridge, Mass.: Harvard University Press, 1968).

KRIEGER, LEONARD, *The Politics of Discretion* (Chicago: University of Chicago Press, 1965).

LABROUSSE, ELIZABETH, *Bayle*, trans. Denys Potts (Oxford: Oxford University Press, 1983).

LEIBNIZ, GOTTFRIED WILHELM VON, *The Political Writings of Leibniz*, trans. and ed. Patrick Riley (Cambridge: Cambridge University Press, 1972).

LEITES, EDMUND, (ed.), *Conscience and Casuistry in Early Modern Europe* (Cambridge: Cambridge University Press, 1988).

LEYDEN, WOLFGANG VON, 'John Locke and Natural Law', *Philosophy*, 31 (1956), 23–35.

LIVINGSTON, DONALD, *Hume's Philosophy of Common Life* (Chicago: University of Chicago Press, 1985).

LOCKE, JOHN, *Essays on the Law of Nature*, ed. Wolfgang von Leyden (Oxford: Clarendon Press, 1954).

—— *Two Treatises of Government* (1690), critical edn. with introd. and notes by Peter Laslett (Cambridge: Cambridge University Press, 2nd edn., 1967).

—— *An Essay concerning Human Understanding* (1690), ed. P. H. Nidditch (Oxford: Clarendon Press, 1975).

LUCRETIUS [Titus Lucretius Carus], *De Rerum Natura*, trans. W. H. D. Rouse, rev. M. F. Smith (London: Heineman, 1924).

MACINTYRE, ALASDAIR, *Whose Justice? Which Rationality?* (London: Duckworth, 1988).

MACKIE, J. L., *Hume's Moral Theory* (London: Routledge & Kegan Paul, 1980).

MACPHERSON, C. B., *The Political Theory of Possessive Individualism: Hobbes to Locke* (Oxford: Clarendon Press, 1962).

—— *Democratic Theory: Essays in Retrieval* (Oxford: Clarendon Press, 1973).

—— (ed.), *Property: Mainstream and Critical Positions* (Toronto: University of Toronto Press, 1978).

—— *The Rise and Fall of Economic Justice and Other Essays* (Oxford: Oxford University Press, 1985).

MAUTNER, THOMAS, 'Locke on Original Appropriation', *American Philosophical Quarterly*, 19 (1982), 259–70.

—— 'Natural Rights in Locke', *Philosophical Topics*, 12 (1982), 73–7.

—— 'Pufendorf and 18th-century Scottish Philosophy', in id., *Samuel von*

Pufendorf 1632–1982: Ett rättshistoriskt i Lund (Lund: Bloms Boktryckeri, 1986).

MICHAEL, EMILY, 'Francis Hutcheson on Aesthetic Perception and Aesthetic Pleasure', *British Journal of Aesthetics*, 24 (1984), 241–53.

MILLER, DAVID. *Philosophy and Ideology in Hume's Political Thought* (Oxford: Clarendon Press, 1981).

—— 'The Macpherson Version', *Political Studies* 30 (1982), 120–7.

MOORE, JAMES, 'Hume's Theory of Justice and Property', *Political Studies*, 24 (1976), 103–19.

—— 'The Social Background of Hume's Science of Human Nature', in D. F. Norton, N. Capaldi, and W. L. Robison (eds.), *McGill Hume Studies* (San Diego: Austin Hill Press, 1976).

—— 'Locke and the Scottish Jurists', unpublished paper delivered to the Conference for the Study of Political Thought (1980).

—— and SILVERTHORNE, MICHAEL, 'Gershom Carmichael and the Natural Jurisprudence Tradition in Eighteenth-century Scotland', in Istvan Hont and Michael Ignatieff (eds.), *Wealth and Virtue: The Shaping of Political Economy in the Scottish Enlightenment* (Cambridge: Cambridge University Press, 1983).

—— and —— 'Natural Sociability and Natural Rights in the Moral Philosophy of Gerschom Carmichael', in Vincent Hope (ed.), *Philosophers of the Scottish Enlightenment* (Edinburgh: Edinburgh University Press, 1984).

NORTON, DAVID FATE, 'History and Philosophy in Hume's Thought', in D. F. Norton and R. H. Popkin (eds.) *David Hume: Philosophical Historian* (Indianapolis: Bobbs-Merrill, 1965).

—— 'Hutcheson on Perception and Moral Perception', *Archiv für Geschichte der Philosophie*, 59 (1977), 181–97.

—— *David Hume: Common-Sense Moralist, Sceptical Metaphysician* (Princeton: Princeton University Press, 1982).

—— 'Hutcheson's Moral Realism', *Journal of the History of Philosophy*, 23 (1985), 397–418.

NOZICK, ROBERT, *Anarchy, State, and Utopia* (New York: Basic Books, 1974).

NUTKIEWICZ, MICHAEL, 'Samuel Pufendorf: Obligation as the Basis of the State', *Journal of the History of Philosophy*, 21 (1983), 15–29.

OLIVECRONA, KARL, *Law as Fact* (London: Stevens & Sons, 2nd edn., 1971).

—— 'Appropriation in the State of Nature: Locke on the Origin of Property', *Journal of the History of Ideas*, 35 (1974), 221–30.

—— 'Locke's Theory of Appropriation', *Philosophical Quarterly*, 24 (1974), 220–34.

O'NEILL, ONORA, 'Nozick's Entitlements', *Inquiry*, 19 (1976), 468–81.

PAGDEN, ANTHONY, (ed.), *The Languages of Political Theory in Early-Modern Europe* (Cambridge: Cambridge University Press, 1987).

PAREL, ANTHONY, and FLANAGAN, THOMAS (eds.), *Theories of Property: Aristotle to the Present* (Calgary: Wilfrid Laurier University Press, 1979).

PARRY, GERAINT, *John Locke* (London: George Allen & Unwin, 1978).

PASSMORE, JOHN, *Hume's Intentions* (London: Duckworth, 3rd edn., 1980).

PHILLIPSON, NICHOLAS, *Hume* (London: Weidenfeld & Nicolson, 1989).

PUFENDORF, SAMUEL, *De Officio Hominis et Civis Juxta Legem Naturalem Libri Duo* (1673), trans. F. G. Moore (New York: Oxford University Press, 1927).

—— *De Jure Naturae et Gentium Libri Octo* (1672), trans. C. H. and W. A. Oldfather (New York: Oceana Publications, 1964).

RAPHAEL, DAVID DAICHES, (ed.), *British Moralists 1650–1800*, 2 vols. (Oxford: Clarendon Press, 1969).

REEVE, ANDREW, *Property* (London: Macmillan, 1986).

ROUSSEAU, JEAN-JACQUES, *On the Social Contract*, ed. R. D. Masters, trans. J. R. Masters (New York: St Martin's Press, 1978).

RYAN, ALAN, 'Locke and the Dictatorship of the Bourgeoisie', *Political Studies*, 13 (1965), 210–30.

—— *Property and Political Theory* (Oxford: Basil Blackwell, 1984).

—— *Property* (Milton Keynes: Open University Press, 1987).

SAPADIN, EUGENE, 'Hume's Law, Hume's Way', in G. P. Morice (ed.), *David Hume: Bicentenary Papers* (Edinburgh: Edinburgh University Press, 1977).

SCHLATTER, RICHARD, *Private Property: The History of an Idea* (London: George Allen & Unwin, 1951).

SCHOCHET, GORDON J., *The Authoritarian Family and Political Attitudes in 17th-Century England: Patriarchalism in Political Thought* (New Brunswick, NJ: Transaction Books, 1988).

—— 'Radical Politics and Ashcraft's Treatise on Locke', *Journal of the History of Ideas*, 50 (1989), 491–510.

SCOTT, WILLIAM ROBERT, *Francis Hutcheson* (1900) (New York: Augustus M. Kelley, 1966).

SHAFTESBURY, ANTHONY ASHLEY COOPER, 3rd Earl of, *Characteristics of Men, Manners, Opinions, Times* (1711), 2 vols. in 1, ed. J. M. Robertson (New York: Bobbs-Merrill, 1969).

SKINNER, QUENTIN, *The Foundations of Modern Political Thought*, 2 vols. (Cambridge: Cambridge University Press, 1978).

SMITH, ADAM, *An Inquiry into the Nature and Causes of the Wealth of Nations* (1776), ed. R. H. Campbell, A. S. Skinner, and W. B. Todd (Oxford: Clarendon Press, 1976).

—— *The Theory of Moral Sentiments* (1759), ed. D. D. Raphael and A. L. Macfie (Oxford: Clarendon Press, 1976).

—— *Lectures on Jurisprudence*, ed. R. L. Meek, D. D. Raphael, and P. G. Stein (Oxford: Clarendon Press, 1978).

—— *Essays on Philosophical Subjects*, ed. W. P. D. Wightman, J. C. Bryce, and I. S. Ross (Oxford: Clarendon Press, 1980).

STROUD, BARRY, *Hume* (London: Routledge & Kegan Paul, 1977).

SUAREZ, FRANCISCO, *Selections from Three Works*, trans. G. L. Williams, A. Brown, and J. Waldron (Oxford: Oxford University Press, 1944).

TEICHGRAEBER, RICHARD F., III, *'Free Trade' and Moral Philosophy* (Durham, NC: Duke University Press, 1986).

TUCK, RICHARD, *Natural Rights Theories: Their Origin and Development* (Cambridge: Cambridge University Press, 1979).

—— 'Grotius, Carneades and Hobbes', *Grotiana*, NS 4 (1983), 43–62.

—— *Hobbes* (Oxford: Oxford University Press, 1989).

TULLY, JAMES, *A Discourse on Property: John Locke and his Adversaries* (Cambridge: Cambridge University Press, 1980).

—— 'A Reply to Waldron and Baldwin', *Locke Newsletter*, 13 (1982), 35–46.

WALDRON, JEREMY, 'Enough and As Good Left for Others', *Philosophical Quarterly*, 29 (1979), 319–28.

—— 'The Turfs My Servant Has Cut', *Locke Newsletter*, 13 (1982), 9–20.

—— 'Locke, Tully, and the Regulation of Property', *Political Studies*, 32 (1984), 98–106.

—— *The Right to Private Property* (Oxford: Clarendon Press, 1988).

WATT, IAN, *The Rise of the Novel* (Harmondsworth: Penguin Books, 1957).

WINCH, DONALD, *Adam Smith's Politics* (Cambridge: Cambridge University Press, 1978).

WOOD, NEAL, *John Locke and Agrarian Capitalism* (Berkeley: University of California Press, 1984).

WRIGHT, JOHN P., *The Sceptical Realism of David Hume* (Manchester: Manchester University Press, 1983).

YOLTON, J. W., (ed.), *John Locke: Problems and Perspectives* (Cambridge: Cambridge University Press, 1969).

—— *Locke and the Compass of Human Understanding* (Cambridge: Cambridge University Press, 1970).

Index

Abram and Lot 40–1, 43
Aesop 116 n.
agreements:
  explicit 1–2, 41–4, 93, 102–5, 107,
    183–5
  implicit (tacit) 2, 42, 102–4, 107, 111,
    164, 184–5, 190, 290
  in Pufendorf's moral theory 106–7,
    116–17, 163
Aquinas, Thomas 11–12, 13 n., 24, 46,
  138 n.
Arcesilaus 17
Aristotle 54 n., 56, 57 n., 60, 63, 69 n.,
  70 n., 76, 82, 111 n., 132 n., 137
Ashcraft, Richard 307 n.
avidity, *see* luxury

Babel, Tower of 39, 43
Barbeyrac, Jean 54 n.
Baron, Marcia 282 n.
Baxter, Richard 173
Bayle, Pierre 297
beauty (sense of beauty) 202, 204–5,
  207, 234, 275–9, 285, 292
Becker, Lawrence 171 n., 180 n., 181–2
Bentham, Jeremy 22
Berkeley, George 196 n., 238–40
Berlin, Isaiah 177
Bolingbroke, Henry St John,
  Viscount 307–9
Bowles, Paul 4 n., 35 n.
Boyle, Robert 301
Butler, Joseph 240

Cain and Abel 39, 41, 43
Campbell, Tom 198
Carmichael, Gershom 193–5, 212 n.,
  223 n.
Carneades 17–18, 68, 139, 146
Cato 25 n., 145
charity 46, 124, 159–61, 217
Cicero 25, 26 n., 27, 36, 54 n., 69, 73,
  75, 145, 247, 264 n.

Clarke, Samuel 202 n., 256, 277 n.
Colman, John 129–31, 139 n., 196 n.,
  229 n., 302 n., 304 n.
Copernicus, Nicholas 238
Cudworth, Ralph 132, 202 n.
Cumberland, Richard 51 n.

Daly, James 162 n.
Descartes, René 23, 55, 58, 60, 240
Dunn, John 123–4 n., 128, 130, 139 n.,
  151 n., 153 n., 192 n.
Dworkin, Ronald 214 n.

efficient causes 58, 196, 276, 296, 300–1
Epicurean 20 n.
experimental philosophy 237, 239–44,
  296, 298

Filmer, Sir Robert 4, 83 n., 150 n.,
  162–8, 184–5, 187, 224 n.
Foot, Philippa 218 n.
Forbes, Duncan 4–5, 6 n., 236, 240,
  243 n., 250, 251 n.
Foriers, Paul 4, 6

Glaucon 292
government:
  origins of 229
  as a trust 191, 229–31
Grant, Ruth W. 168 n.
Grass, Gunter 22 n.
Grotius, Hugo:
  and a posteriori method 5–6, 12,
    57 n., 69, 146
  and a priori method 5–6
  and absolutism 3–4
  etiamsi daremus clause 23, 59, 128,
    147, 200, 261, 297, 305
  and Filmer 162–9
  history, idealization of 15
  as irenicist 22–3
  natural law, early theory 7–10, 16–17
  natural law, mature theory 17–32